Simple

LANDSCAPE PAINTING

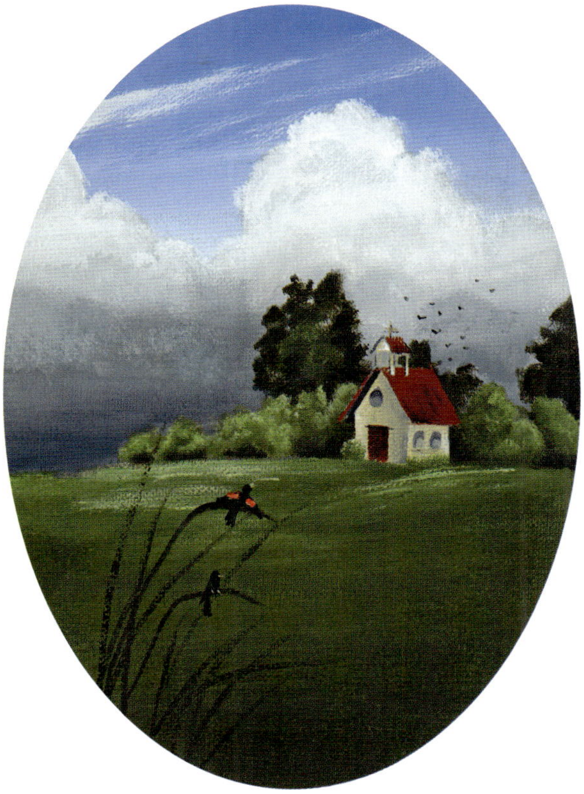

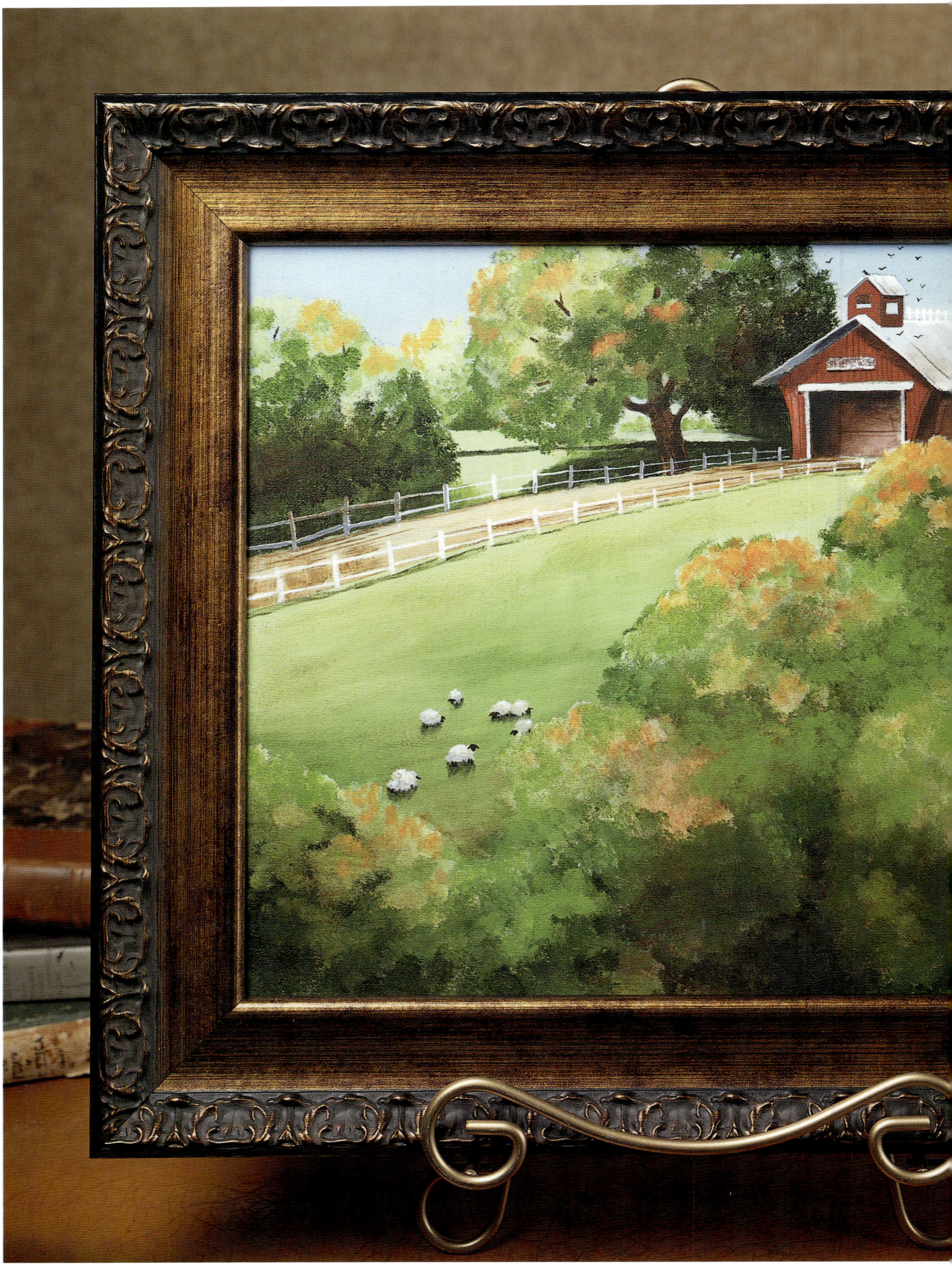

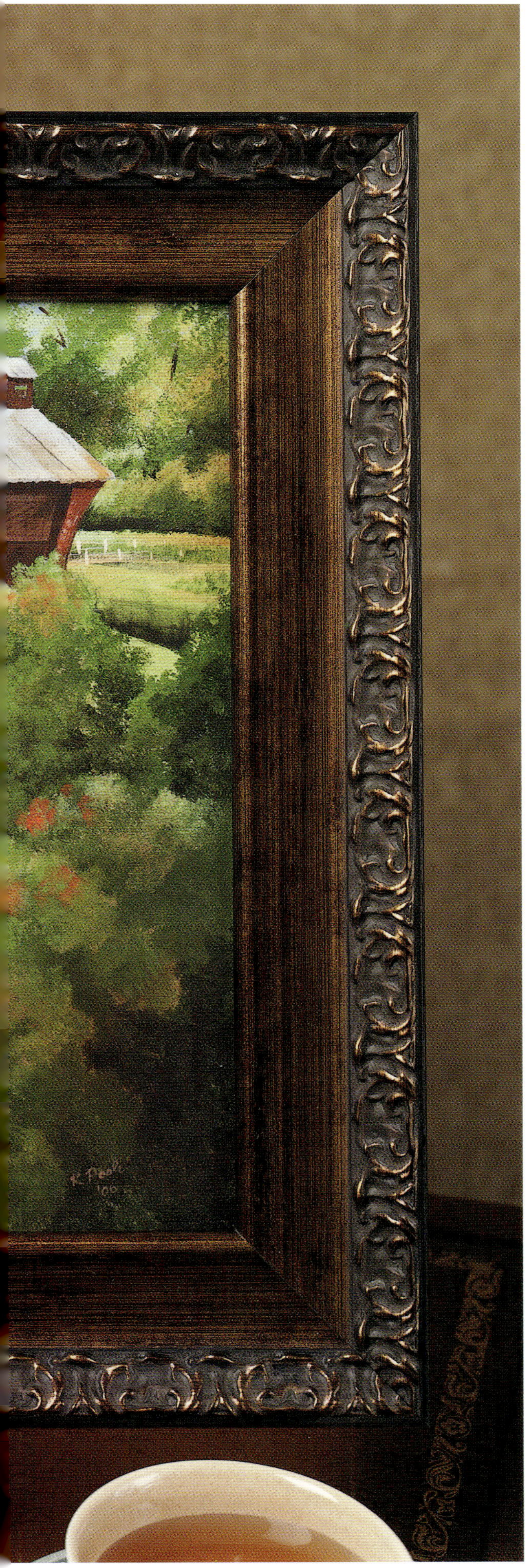

Simple LANDSCAPE PAINTING

Kaaren Poole

Sterling Publishing Co., Inc.
New York

Prolific Impressions Production Staff:
Editor in Chief: Mickey Baskett
Copy Editor: Ellen Glass
Graphics: Dianne Miller, Karen Turpin
Styling: Lenos Key
Photography: Jerry Mucklow
Administration: Jim Baskett

Every effort has been made to insure that the information presented is accurate. Since we have no control over physical conditions, individual skills, or chosen tools and products, the publisher disclaims any liability for injuries, losses, untoward results, or any other damages which may result from the use of the information in this book. Thoroughly read the instructions for all products used to complete the projects in this book, paying particular attention to all cautions and warnings shown for that product to ensure their proper and safe use.

Library of Congress Cataloging-in-Publication Data

Poole, Kaaren.
Simple landscape painting / Kaaren Poole.
p. cm.
Includes index.
ISBN-13: 978-1-4027-3516-5
ISBN-10: 1-4027-3516-2
1. Landscape painting--Technique. 2. Acrylic painting--Technique. I. Title.

ND1342.P66 2007
751.42'6 22

2006100797

2 4 6 8 10 9 7 5 3 1

Published by Sterling Publishing Co., Inc.
387 Park Avenue South, New York, NY 10016

Distributed in Canada by Sterling Publishing
c/o Canadian Manda Group, 165 Dufferin Street,
Toronto, Ontario, Canada M6K 3H6
Distributed in the United Kingdom by GMC Distribution Services,
Castle Place, 166 High Street, Lewes, East Sussex, England BN7 1XU
Distributed in Australia by Capricorn Link (Australia) Pty. Ltd.
P.O. Box 704, Windsor, NSW 2756, Australia

Printed in China

ISBN-13: 978-1-4027-3516-5
ISBN-10: 1-4027-3516-2

For information about custom editions, special sales, premium and corporate purchases, please contact Sterling Special Sales Department at 800-805-5489 or specialsales@sterlingpub.com.

ABOUT THE AUTHOR

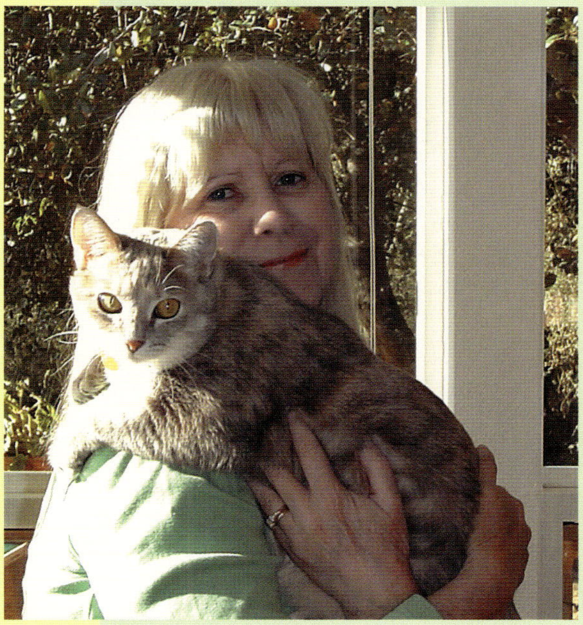

Kaaren Poole

Kaaren lives on ten beautiful acres in the rural foothills of Northern California with her three dogs, twelve cats, and four ducks. She has published two previous books, the first on decorative painting and the second on drawing animals. Retired from the computer industry, she now devotes her time to her first love, painting and drawing.

You may reach her through her website, *kaarenpoole.com.*

Special Thanks

Thank you to my painting friends, Carol, Nancy, Sue, and Mollie, who have encouraged me every step of the way.

Special thanks to Mickey Baskett, who made this book possible and transformed my material into a beautiful book.

Dedication

For my extended family of friends, family, and pets who make life so joyous, and for my late husband, Doug, who continues to inspire my every effort.

TABLE OF CONTENTS

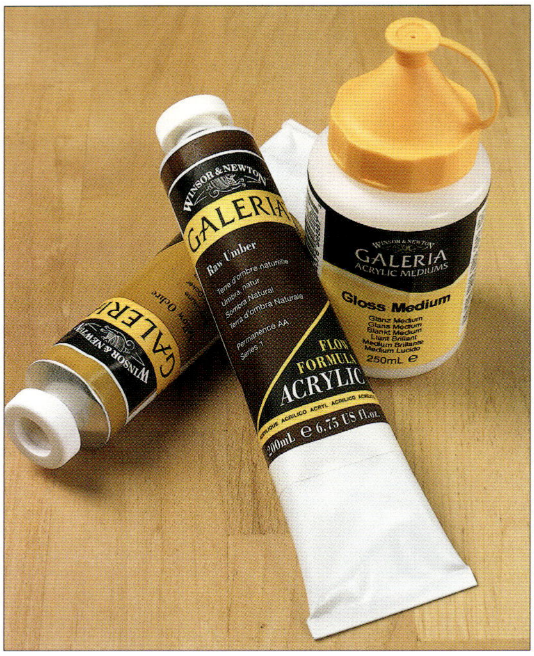

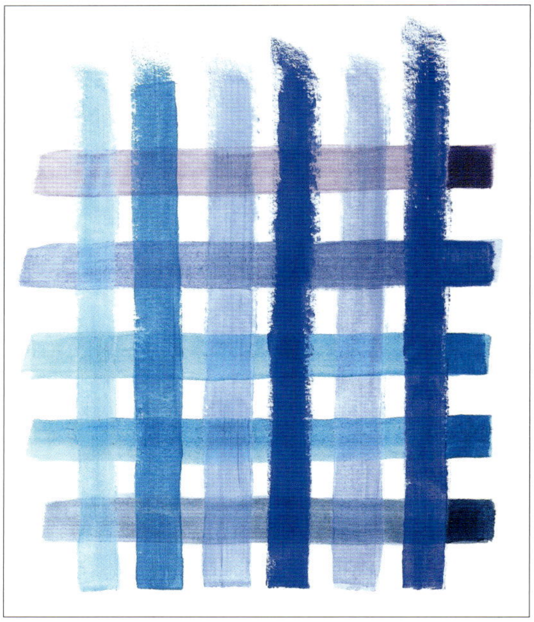

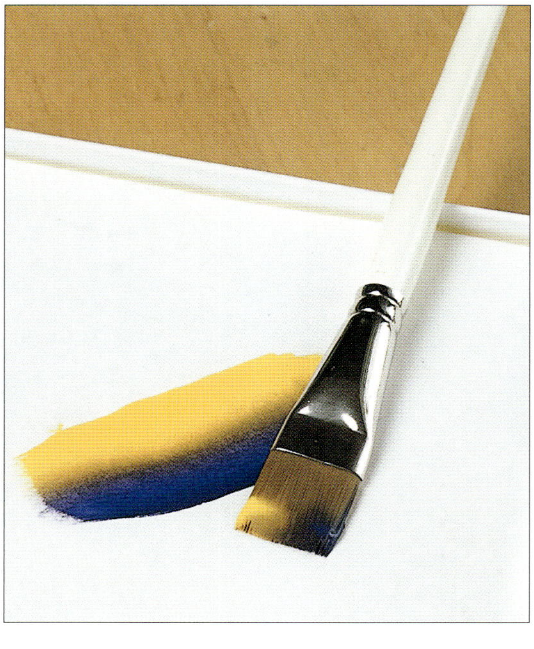

WHY PAINT LANDSCAPES?

Painting landscapes is a wonderful way to give voice to our inner selves by creating places we would love to be. Whenever we look at our work, we can transport ourselves to the place we have created - a place of peace, beauty, mystery, history, or whatever we find especially captivating and renewing. Places carry so much emotional impact: memories, hopes, disappointments, meetings, partings, and the saddest and happiest of times. Painting landscapes is a way to remember and preserve moods. I enjoy creating settings that reflect my happiest memories and greatest hopes. Places of peace, joy, and the exuberance of life, indulging in the blessing of color - the promise of renewal in spring, the celebration of life's fullness in summer, the surprising burst of warm color as the landscape prepares for rest in autumn, and the quiet solitude of sleep in winter, interrupted by the occasional insomniac fox or bird.

My inspiration comes from memories, imagination, and observation. The beauty of unique places captivates me, and I find myself "taking pictures in my mind." This is true not only of big pictures - an entire vista - but also of tiny corners of beauty - the moss and lichen on an old tree trunk. I combine my mental pictures into a composition for painting.

I intend my landscape paintings as reminders of the beauty of God's creation and inspirations for reverie and renewal. "Go to your happy place" has become a cliché, but it works! Every landscape I paint is a place I want to be. My sincere hope is that the information in this book will help you in your artistic journey, wherever it may lead you. Blessings.

HOW TO USE THIS BOOK

I have designed this book as both a landscape painting workbook and a learning resource for basic artistic skills that will serve you in painting landscapes as well as other subjects.

The section on "Color" presents basic color theory, explains the color wheel, introduces standard color schemes, and provides guidelines for mixing color.

Many people are intimidated by the rules of perspective, but drawing in perspective is actually a straightforward process. Mastering perspective will be invaluable to you, no matter what your subjects. This is one of the topics discussed in the section on "Creating the Illusion of Depth."

I hope you will create your own landscapes. You will feel more confident when you understand a little about composition. Applying a few simple guidelines will improve your paintings.

Finally, there is the language of art, which I use throughout the book. Every discipline has its own language, and art is no exception. At times, the terms can seem irrelevant or arcane, but it is helpful to know the language. It helps you focus your thoughts, questions, and observations about your work, and also allows you to communicate with other artists.

So that you may use this as a landscape painting workbook, I have included both entire paintings and details of the individual elements of landscapes. Because each painting is shown in several stages, along with instructions, you can see how colors are added and forms are developed. I have included line drawings of some elements that may be difficult to draw, and step-by-step painting demonstrations of other elements. I hope you will find several images - either elements or paintings - that you will want to paint as exercises.

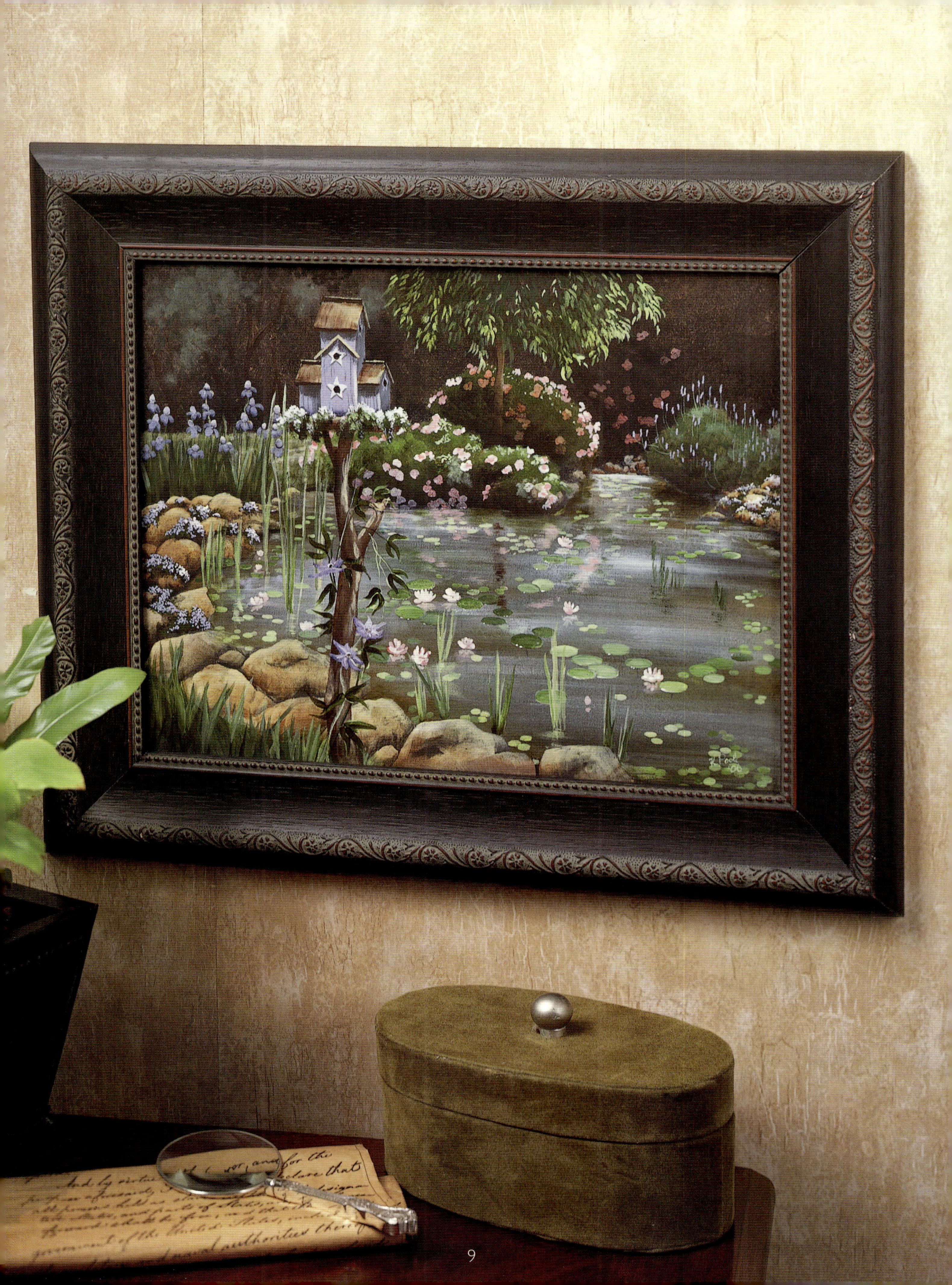

Chapter 1

PAINTING SUPPLIES

Brushes, paint, and canvas - it sounds like a simple list, but you will be surprised by the variety of sizes, brands, and styles available at your art supply store.

This chapter is your guide to choosing the most suitable supplies for beginning your landscape painting. Artist grade acrylic paints in tubes will give you the best colors, and good brushes are necessary for developing your brush technique. Buy the best brushes you can afford, and take care of them. They are an investment in your painting pleasure.

Surfaces

CANVAS

Closely-woven artist's canvas provides a definite surface texture for holding paint. Canvas must be primed and held rigid for painting. The primer, known as gesso, provides the bond between the paint and the canvas. Pre-primed canvas is readily available.

Prepared canvases are available in several standard sizes. For most of the paintings in this book, I chose 11" x 14". It is large enough to allow for several elements, but not so large as to be overwhelming or cumbersome to paint.

After you feel comfortable with painting landscapes, you may want to paint even larger-18" x 24" or even 30" x 40". Of course you will need a good supply of big brushes!

Within the realm of canvas, there are many types available. Your local art and craft shop will be able to help you locate the type that suits your needs. Following is a list of types that are suitable for landscape paintings.

Stretched canvas is rigid and ready to prime, paint, and frame. The canvas fabric is stretched taut and stapled over a wooden frame backing. The staples may be on either the edges or the back of the stretcher frame. If they are on the back, the edges have a finished appearance and may be painted as a continuation of the painting on the front of the canvas; this eliminates the need to frame the finished painting. Stretched canvases come in standard sizes such as 8" x 10", 9" x 12", 14" x 17", 18" x 24", and 30" x 40". These sizes fit ready-made frames.

Canvas board is artist's canvas that is firmly glued to rigid board panels, with edges turned in to prevent fraying. Canvas board comes in the same standard sizes as stretched canvas, and may be purchased pre-primed and ready to paint.

Canvas sheets are pre-cut to standard sizes, but must be stapled to a rigid surface before you paint, and must be attached to a rigid backing for framing. They are economical, and good for practicing techniques and experimenting with color schemes. Wooden stretcher bars may be purchased at the same art and craft supply stores that sell canvas.

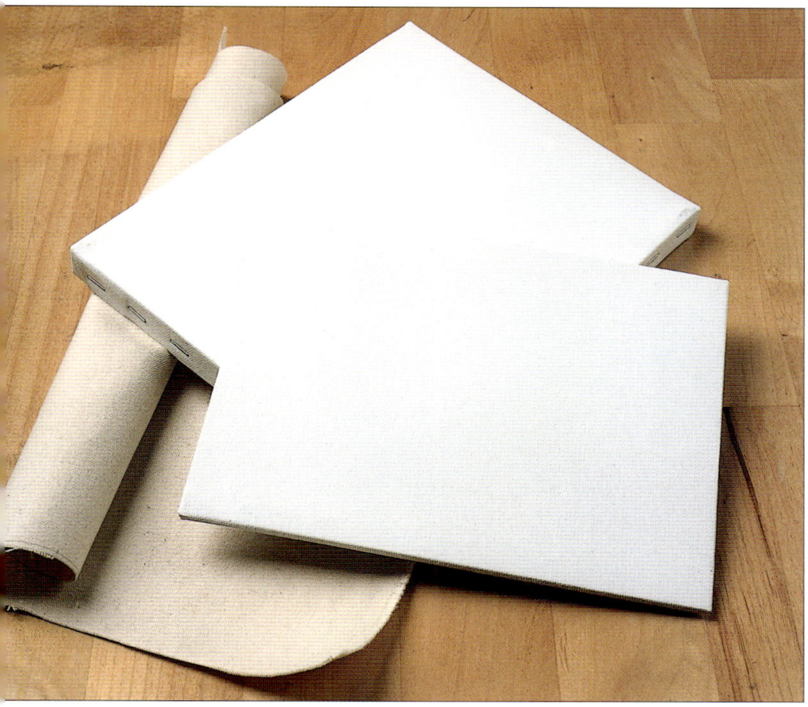

Rolled canvas, stretched canvas, and canvas board.

WOODEN SURFACES

Consider painting your landscapes on wooden surfaces such as flea market finds, welcome signs, or cabinet fronts. To prepare the wood, begin by sanding away any existing finish. Fill holes or cracks with wood filler and sand smooth. Finally, spray the piece with sandable primer (available from home improvement stores) and sand it smooth with fine grit sandpaper. Remove all traces of sanding dust before priming the surface.

EASEL

Painting with your surface flat on the table distorts your view because you are looking at it at an angle. A small tabletop easel will hold your surface at the proper angle. As an alternative, you can simply put a drawing board at a slant by propping up the back edge on a couple of books.

Canvas on rolls can be cut to any size and stretched on stretcher bars.

Watercolor canvas was developed for watercolor but is suitable for all water-based mediums, including acrylic. This canvas has a smoother surface and finer texture than most other canvas. Most of the demonstrations in this book are painted on watercolor canvas.

GESSO

Gesso primes and seals the surface of canvas, paper, or wood. It makes the surface stiffer, provides a slightly rough *tooth,* or texture, and prevents the paint from soaking into the surface.

POSTER BOARD

An alternative, low-cost surface for practicing techniques is poster board, sealed with a spray primer. Spray primer is available from home improvement stores. This surface was used for the illustrations in the "Painting Basics" and "Landscape Elements" sections.

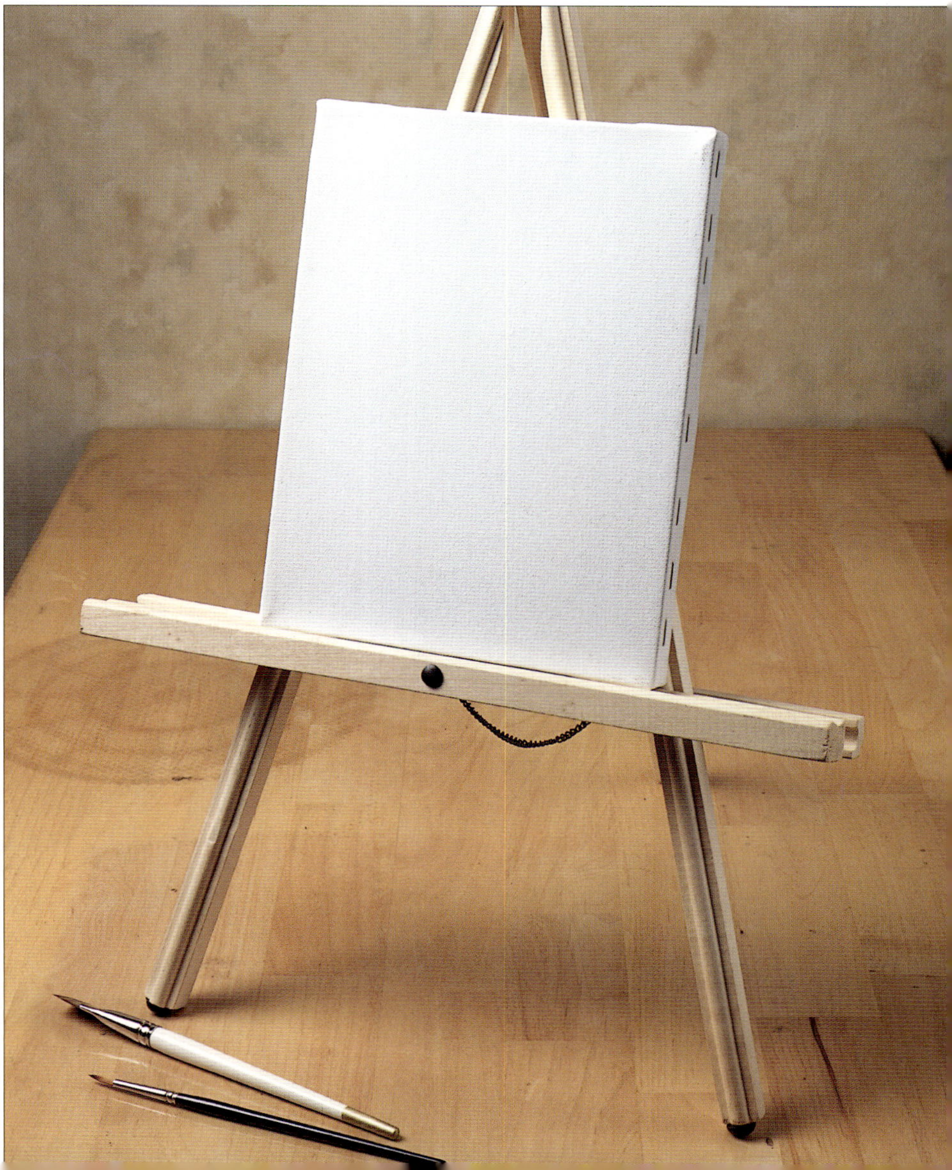

Paints

ARTIST GRADE ACRYLICS

Artist grade acrylic colors, sold in tubes, are excellent for landscape painting. Color names tend to be standardized across brands because they are often named for their pigments. The manufacturers rate each color for permanence and light-fastness. Unlike oils, they clean up with soap and water and have very little odor.

Expect to mix these paints for a full range of color. Sometimes new painters find mixing colors intimidating, but following the simple guidelines in the "Color" section should bring you success.

ACRYLIC PAINTS FOR DECORATIVE PAINTING

The manufacturers of decorative acrylic paints produce hundreds of colors and, if you have room for all the containers, you would never have to mix. There is little standardization of color names in these products. Also, although permanence and light-fastness are pretty good, do not expect the life and durability available from artist grade acrylics.

TIP: If you don't want to mix colors, use the color palette to select decorative acrylics that approximate the mixed colors.

USING ACRYLIC PAINTS

Because they are water-based, acrylic paints dry relatively quickly. This presents both advantages and disadvantages. Since paintings are often completed in layers, they can be finished more quickly than oil paintings. The major drawback is that the paints can dry on the palette or in the brush, and do not have a long open time for blending and shading on the canvas. Using a wet palette, working quickly, and being diligent about cleaning brushes are very important habits.

Acrylic paints darken slightly as they dry. This makes it difficult to mix an exact match for a color that has already dried on your painting. To ease this problem, keep notes on your mixes. Where exact matches are critical (the smooth, even color of the sky, for example), be sure to mix plenty of your color and store the extra in a tightly covered container until the painting is completed.

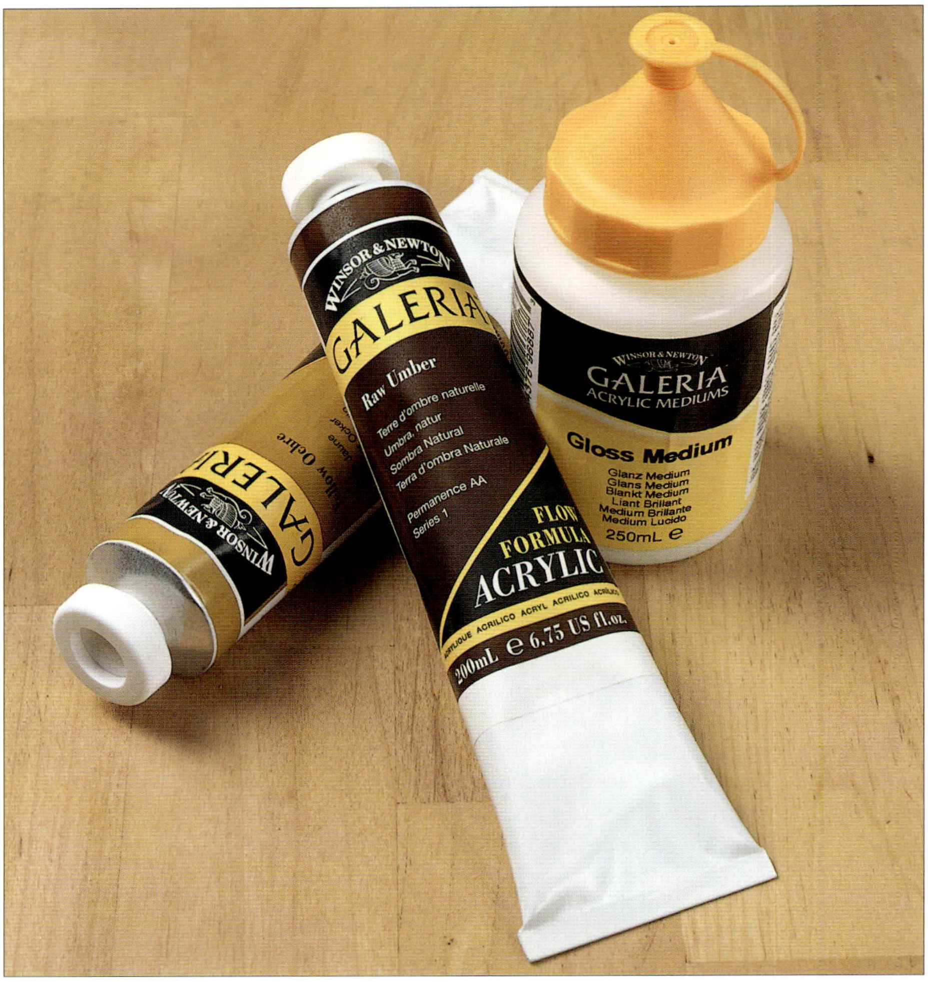

MEDIUMS

Mediums are materials that are mixed with paint to alter the paint's characteristics. A few of the most popular are glazing medium, extender, and gel mediums.

Glazing medium thins the paint for glazing. It is often milky but dries clear. In addition to thinning the paint, it lengthens drying time.

Extender is used to lengthen, or "extend," the working time of the paint. Many artists prefer to have more time to work with the paint before it dries, especially with wet-in-wet blending techniques.

Gel mediums thicken the paint and allow the texture of the brush strokes to show.

I do not use extender or gel mediums because I like the quick-drying time of acrylics and like to work as smooth as I can. Occasionally I use glazing medium for glazes, but I often simply use water. The use of mediums is an individual preference.

Brushes

There is a wide variety of brushes on the market, for different media and different strokes. Be sure to buy brushes designed specifically for use with acrylic paints. Buy the best quality brushes you can afford, and take good care of them. I prefer golden taklon (the fiber used for the brush hairs) but I also use a few types of bristle brushes.

BRUSH SHAPES AND SIZES

Brushes come in different shapes, and each has its purpose. The parts of the brush are the handle, the brush fibers, and the metal ferrule, which attaches the fibers to the handle and holds them in shape. Long-handled brushes are good for very loose work on large surfaces, where you hold the brush far back on the handle. Short-handled brushes are best for small work, where you hold the brush close to the ferrule for tighter control. The paintings in this book were done with short-handled brushes.

Each type of brush comes in a range of sizes. The smaller the number, the smaller the brush. Flats and rounds are the workhorses, used for both detail and large areas, and it seems that each artist prefers one over the other. I prefer flats and use them for most of my painting.

Flats
Flats come in a variety of sizes, from very small to quite large, and with short and long brush heads. One advantage of the long brush heads is that you are less likely to get paint close to the ferrule; getting paint close to the ferrule makes the brush harder to clean.

Rounds
Like flats, rounds come in many sizes. The points are good for painting details, but they are also used for painting large areas.

Wash
Wash brushes are similar to flats, but hold more paint. They are good for painting large areas such as skies.

Liners
Liners are indispensable for detail work. They come to a very fine point, and are used with thinned paint for a flowing line.

Fans and Scumblers
Fans and scumblers are especially useful for painting foliage. If you can't find scumblers, stiff bristle rounds are a good substitute.

A good selection of brushes includes:
Flats: #2, #4, #6, #10, #14, #20
Wash: 3/4"
Rounds: #3, #5, #7, #10
Liners: #00, #1
Fans: #1, #4
Scumblers: #2, #4

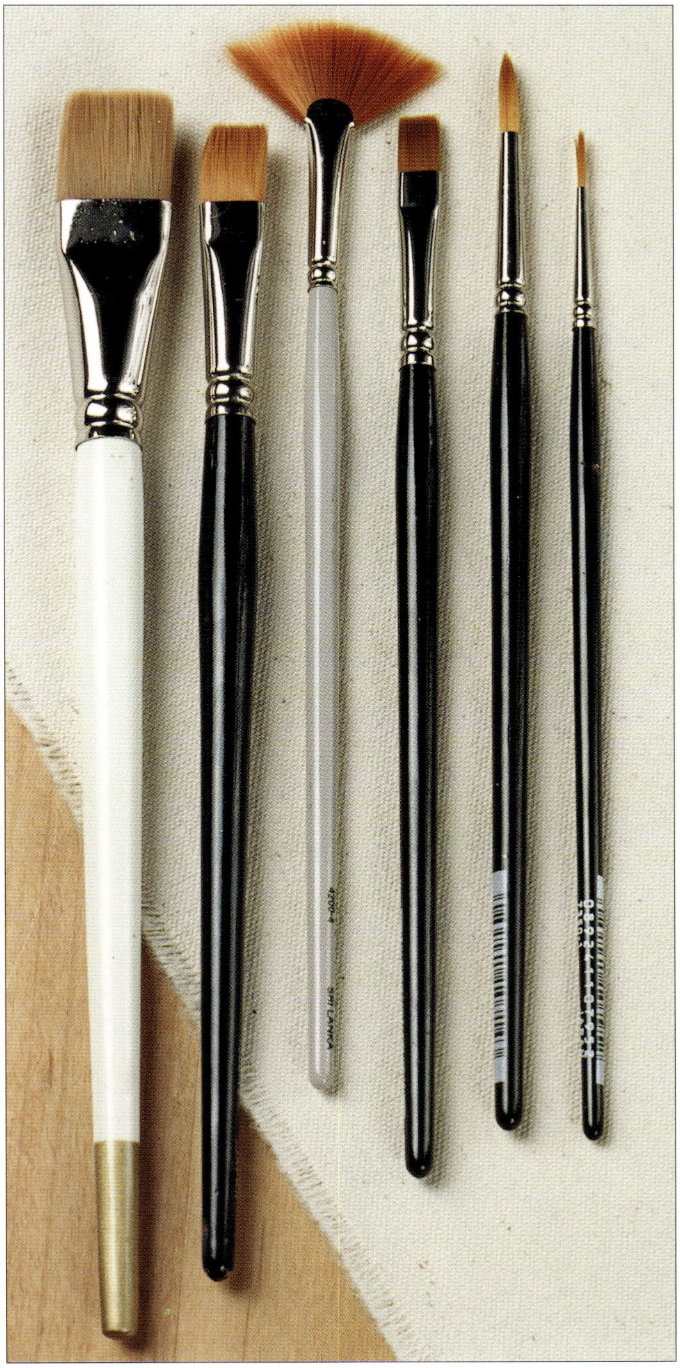

Pictured above, left to right: basecoat, flat, fan, flat, round, liner.
Pictured below: scumblers.

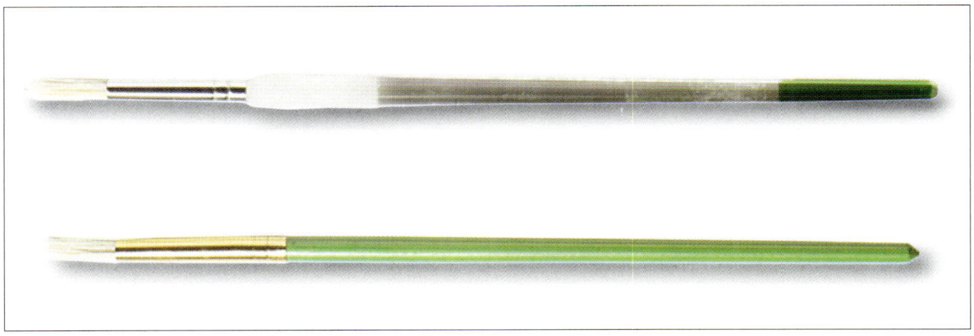

Brushes, continued

Toothbrush
An old toothbrush is useful for spattering and other special effects.

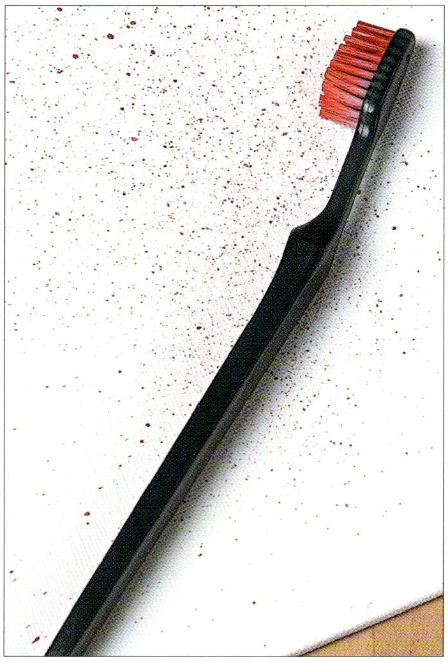

BRUSH CARE

When you are done with a painting session, rinse brushes well with water, then wash them with a cleaner/conditioner made especially for art brushes. Cleaners come in cake, lotion, or liquid form. Work the cleaner thoroughly into the brush hairs, let it sit on the brushes for a few minutes, then rinse brushes thoroughly. Wipe brushes across an absorbent towel to remove excess water, then re-form their tips with your fingers.

Store brushes so their hairs are not pressed against anything and they are not crowded. I keep mine in a flared jar, handles down. Store brushes in a cupboard to protect them from dust or pet hairs.

- Never load a dry brush with paint. Dampen it thoroughly with water first to facilitate cleaning. Do not get paint near the ferrule. It's almost impossible to clean out.
- Treat brush hairs gently. Stroke the brush against the ridges in the water basin rather than scrubbing it. You may also clean brushes in a jar with a plastic "scrubber" in the bottom.
- Change water frequently. Not only does dirty water muddy up your painting, but the paint particles in the water get in your brushes.
- As you paint, keep your brushes clean. Before you set a brush down, rinse it in water and blot on a paper towel, turning the brush to re-form the tip. If paint dries in the brush, it will be ruined. You may be able to remove dried paint by soaking the brush in rubbing alcohol or paint remover, but the brush will never be the same.

Other Supplies

Besides canvas, paint, and brushes, you will need a few other supplies. The main one is the palette, which is the surface you keep your paints on as you paint.

PALETTE

Because acrylic paints are water-based, they dry relatively quickly. Select a palette with a lid - essentially a covered, flat plastic box.

When working with acrylic paints, you will need a "wet" palette to keep acrylic paints from drying so quickly while you are painting. You can purchase a wet palette or you can make your own. To prepare your own *wet palette* Lay several damp paper towels in the bottom of the palette, then cover the towels with a sheet of palette paper. When you are finished painting, simply discard the paper towels and palette paper.

To keep your mixed colors between painting sessions, cover

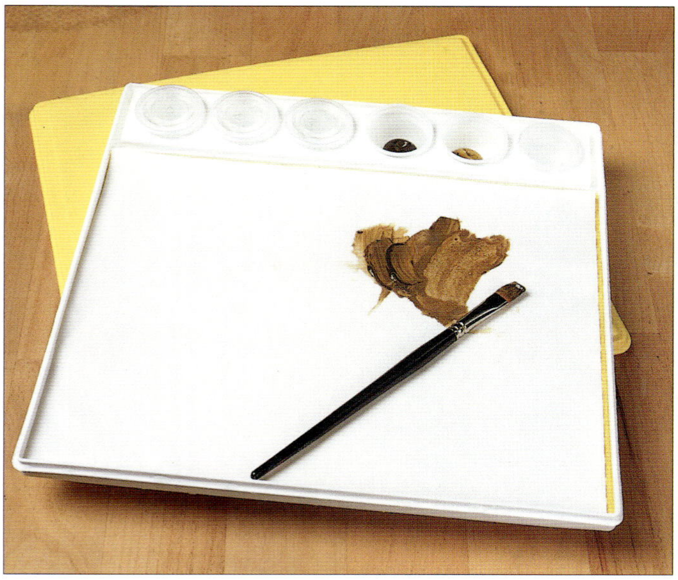

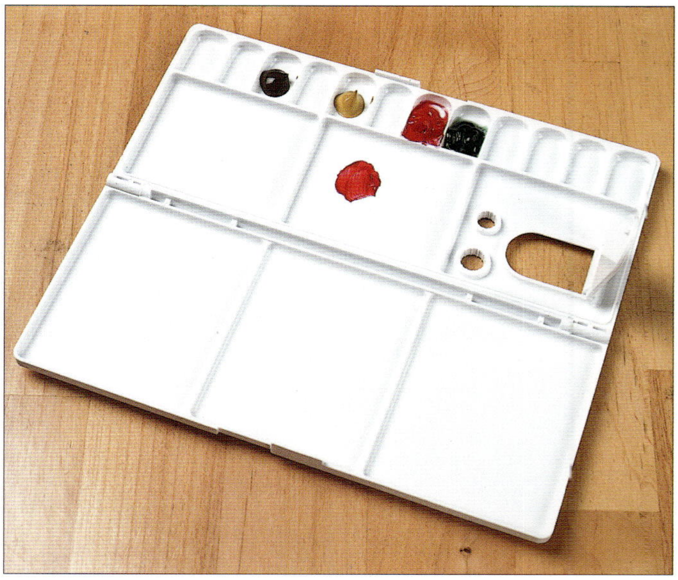

your palette. Even in a covered palette the paints will dry over a few days' time. Store the palette in the refrigerator to slow the drying process.

When I am painting with a small number of colors, I like to use a plastic pencil box with a "snap closed" lid. It is about 5" x 9". It will keep my paint fresh for a few days.

PALETTE PAPER

Available in pads, palette paper is a thick, waxy paper that will not absorb paint. It's a great surface for mixing paints. (Oil painters can use a palette paper pad as their palette because oil paints dry slowly.)

PALETTE KNIFE

You will need a palette knife for mixing paint. (Some artists also use a palette knife to apply paint to the canvas.) I prefer a small, thin, flexible palette knife without an angle in the blade.

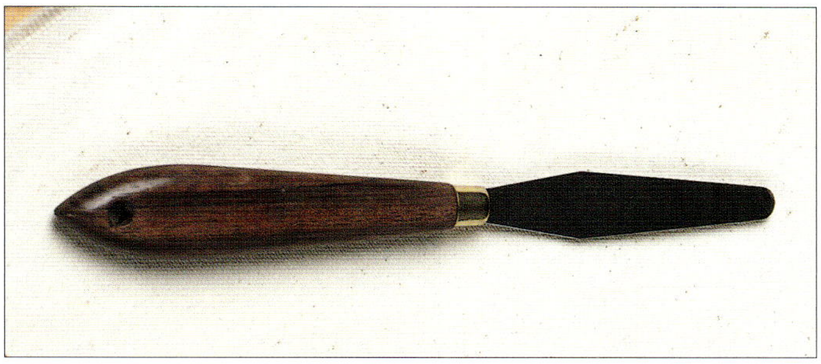

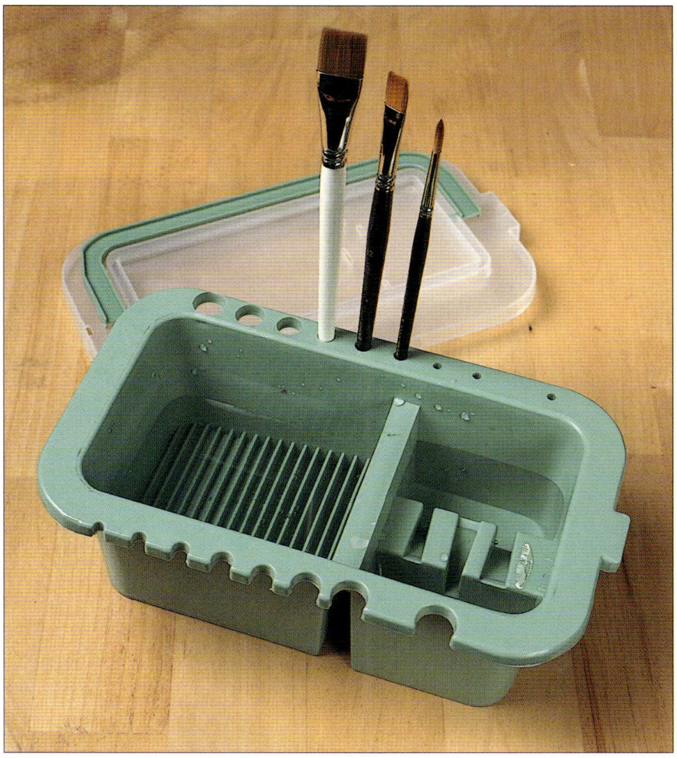

Pictured above: 2 compartment water basin.

WATER BASIN

You will need water for two reasons: to keep your brush damp, and to clean paint from your brushes between colors. Use a single basin with two chambers - a "dirty" one and a "clean" one. The dirty basin has a ribbed bottom. To clean your brush between colors, stroke it back and forth over the ribs. The clean basin holds clean water for loading your brush; it has slots that allow your brushes to sit in the water without resting on their hairs. Keeping your brushes in water during your painting session helps guard against any paint drying in the brush.

An alternative is to use two jars, one for clean water for loading your brush, and the other for washing your brush between colors. Keep a plastic mesh scrubber in the "dirty" jar. Stroking your brush over the scrubber will remove paint when you want to change colors. If you use two jars, DO NOT leave your brushes in the water. The hairs will bend on the bottom of the jar and your brushes will lose their shapes.

PAPER TOWELS

Use thick, absorbent paper towels to remove excess water from your brush as you work.

STORAGE JARS

Small "snap top" paint pots can be used to store your mixed paint colors. They are available in crafts stores. As long as the pots are mostly full, the paint will keep for a week or more. Unless you are storing a lot of paint, empty film cans aren't a good choice; there will be too much air space in the container and the paint will dry.

SKETCHING SUPPLIES

You will need drawing paper, pencils, and an eraser to plan your drawing. You may also sketch guidelines directly onto the canvas.

PATTERN TRANSFERRING SUPPLIES

Whether you sketch your own drawing or use the designs from this book, you will find it much easier to transfer the design to your piece of canvas to use as a guide for painting. You will need **tracing paper, transfer paper, a pencil** and a **stylus.**

WHITE CHALK PENCIL

A white chalk pencil is useful for drawing on dark areas of your painting.

Chapter 2

COLOR BASICS

Color is the heart and soul of a painting. It conveys mood and emotion that enhance the viewer's reaction to the subject. A basic understanding of color theory is helpful, if not essential, to those of us who paint. Fortunately, people have been working to understand the effects and interaction of color for hundreds of years. Perhaps the most useful fruit of their labor is the color wheel.

The Color Wheel

The color wheel is a way of arranging colors that illustrates the relationships between them. It shows the composition of colors from the basic three - red, yellow, and blue - and maps out complementary colors and standard color schemes.

Red, yellow, and blue are the primary colors of pigment. The primary colors of light are red, blue, and green. The color wheel applies to pigment.

Understanding the organization of colors on the color wheel helps the artist combine and mix colors successfully. The ability to mix colors is important for achieving a range of harmonious color in your paintings.

Red, Yellow, and Blue, the three *primary* colors, are placed evenly around the wheel. The *secondary* colors result from mixing two primary colors. Mixing a primary color with an adjacent secondary color yields a *tertiary* color.

WARM AND COOL COLORS

We perceive colors as being either "warm" or "cool." A line drawn across the circle between Red and Green divides the colors on the wheel into a warm half and a cool half. Note that there are both warm and cool reds and greens. While Red is warm, Red-Violet is cool; although Green is cool, Yellow-Green is warm.

A painting will be more unified if the colors in it are either predominantly warm or predominantly cool. "Predominantly" does not mean "all." A little cool in a warm painting or a little warm in a cool painting adds interest.

COMPLEMENTARY COLORS

Complementary colors lie across from each other on the color wheel (for example, Red and Green). They are, in color terms, as far apart from each other as possible! Placing complementary colors next to each other in a painting creates visual excitement and draws the eye. On the other hand, complementary colors, when mixed together, tend to cancel each other out and produce grays or browns.

COLOR SCHEMES

The combination of colors we use in our painting is its *color scheme.* A pleasing color scheme is unified but interesting. An unsuccessful color scheme is confusing and distracting. Successful color schemes often rely on a few basic colors supplemented with mixes among them. Several commonly used color schemes get their names from the relationship between the colors on the color wheel. Basing your color choices on one of these schemes will improve your chances of creating a successful painting. Add colors outside your basic color scheme in moderation, to draw attention to an area of the painting.

The Twelve-Color Color Wheel

Complementary colors are opposite each other.

There are 6 pairs of complements on a 12-color wheel.

The primaries – Red, Yellow, Blue are placed evenly around the wheel.

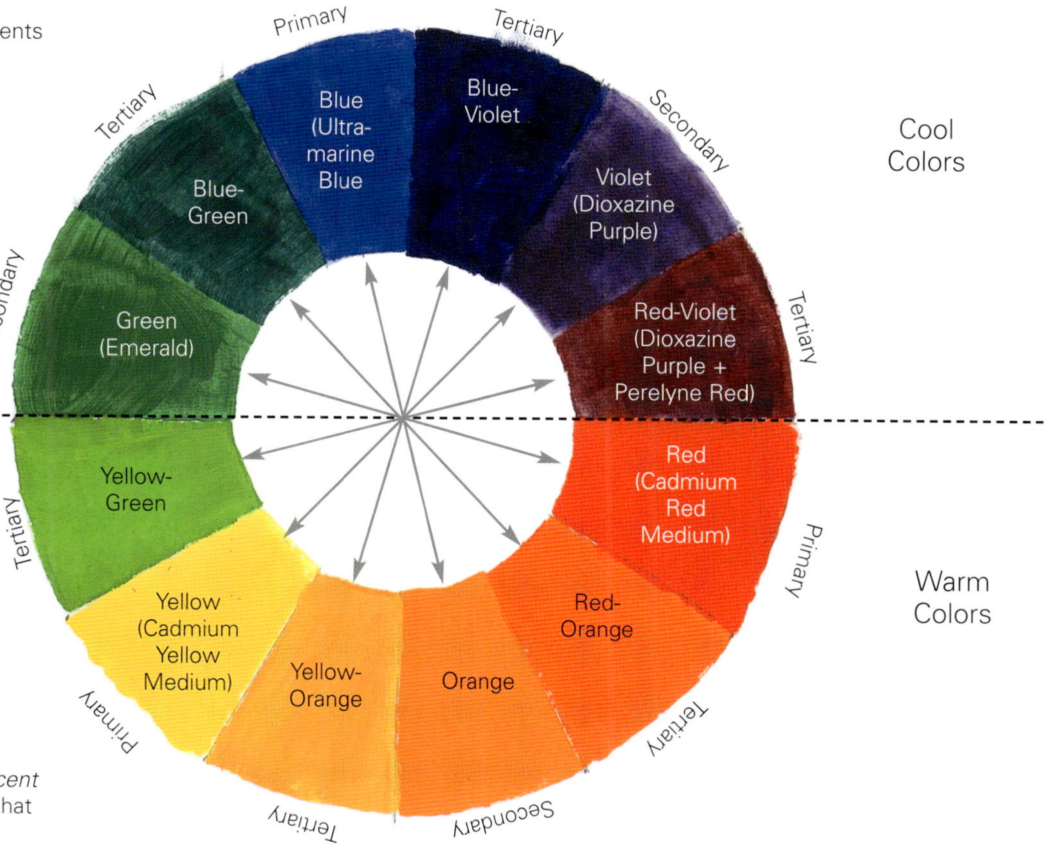

Mixing two primaries yields a secondary.
Yellow + Red = Orange

Mixing a primary with an *adjacent* secondary yields the tertiary that lies between them.
Yellow + Orange = Yellow-Orange

A note on the colors used in the wheel: Although understanding basic color theory is invaluable, its translation to using the paints in front of you is not always straightforward. Painting a color wheel from just the three primary colors requires true yellow, true red, and true blue paints. These "true" primary colors are not always available in all lines of paint. Additional colors were used to mix the clean colors for the color wheel. (Their names appear in parentheses.) For example, Red-Violet is Dioxazine Purple plus Perelyne Red. Perelyne Red is a slightly bluish red. Cadmium Red Medium is slightly yellowish and so produces a muddy color when mixed with purple.

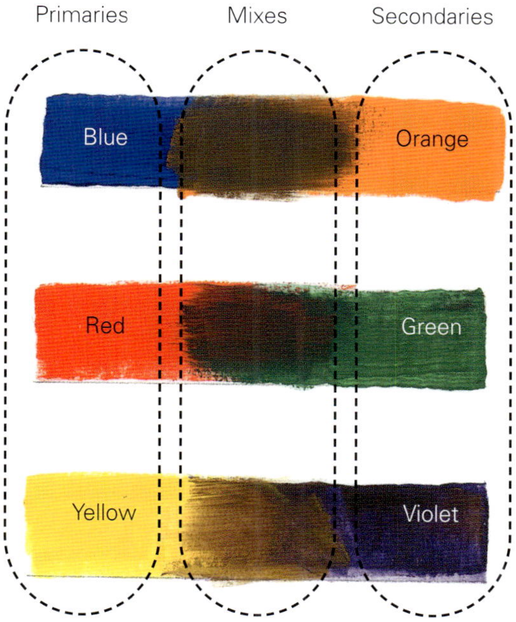

Examples of complementary colors

Common Color Schemes

COMPLEMENTARY

- Based on a pair of complementary colors and mixes between them.
- Mixing complementary colors produces browns and grays.

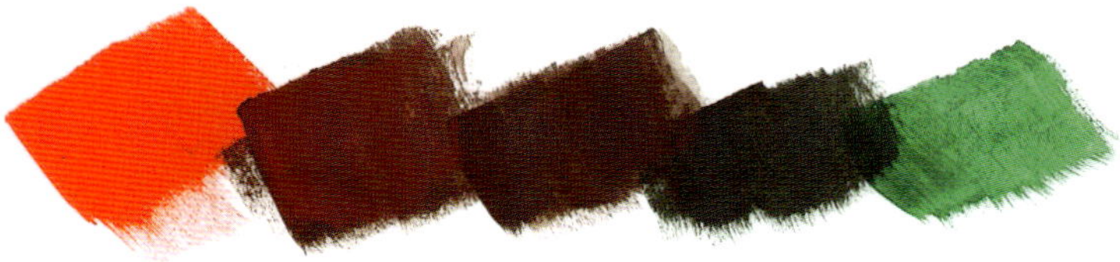

The Red-Green complementary color scheme is useful because of the predominance of greens and browns in landscapes. The red adds "punch."

You are not limited to pure Red and pure Green. Use complimentary colors in the red and green families, and the mixes between them.

TRIADS

Based on three predominant colors, evenly spaced on the 12-color wheel, and the mixes between them.

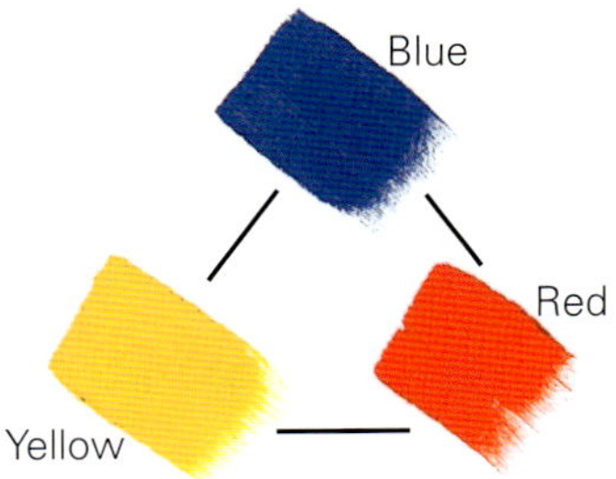

Primary Triad
- Happy, straightforward, and upbeat.
- Useful for autumn landscapes.

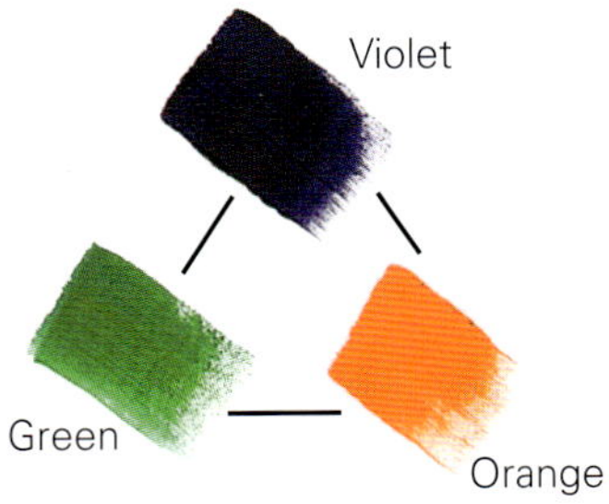

Secondary Triad
- Great for landscapes. Green is a natural landscape color.
- Mixes yield a rich range of greens and earthtones.

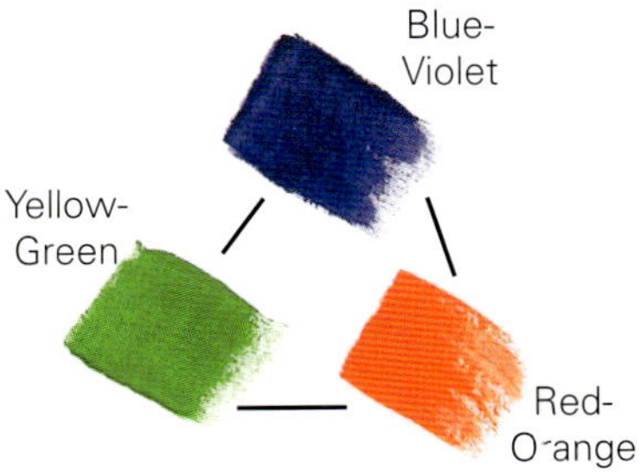

A Tertiary Triad

Analogous Color Schemes

- Based on three colors that lie next to each other on the 12-color wheel.
- Blue-Green/Blue/Blue-Violet is a good color scheme for evening snow scenes.

"Natural" Color Schemes

Simply paint the landscape you see, following the color scheme provided by Nature.

Red, Green, and Blue Color Scheme

- The three primary colors of light. When mixed together, they yield white light. A prism illustrates that white light contains all colors.
- The pink, green, and blue form of this color scheme is good for landscapes.

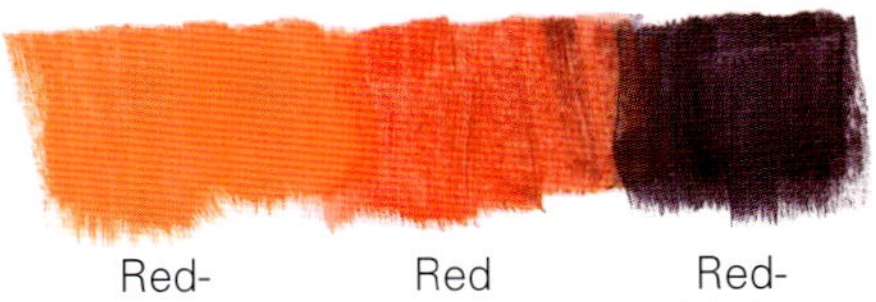

Analogous

Characteristics of Color

VALUE

- Value is the lightness or darkness of a color.
- White is the lightest value. Black is the darkest value.
- Pure hues have an intrinsic value. For example, pure Yellow is light while pure Blue is dark.
- Colors that are light in value tend to "come forward" in a painting. Colors that are dark in value tend to recede.

TINTS AND SHADES

of the Six Primary and Secondary Colors

The amount of white or black in the mix determines the lightness or darkness (value) of the resulting color.

Tints
Mix hue + white

Pure Hue
(Color)

Shades
Mix hue + black

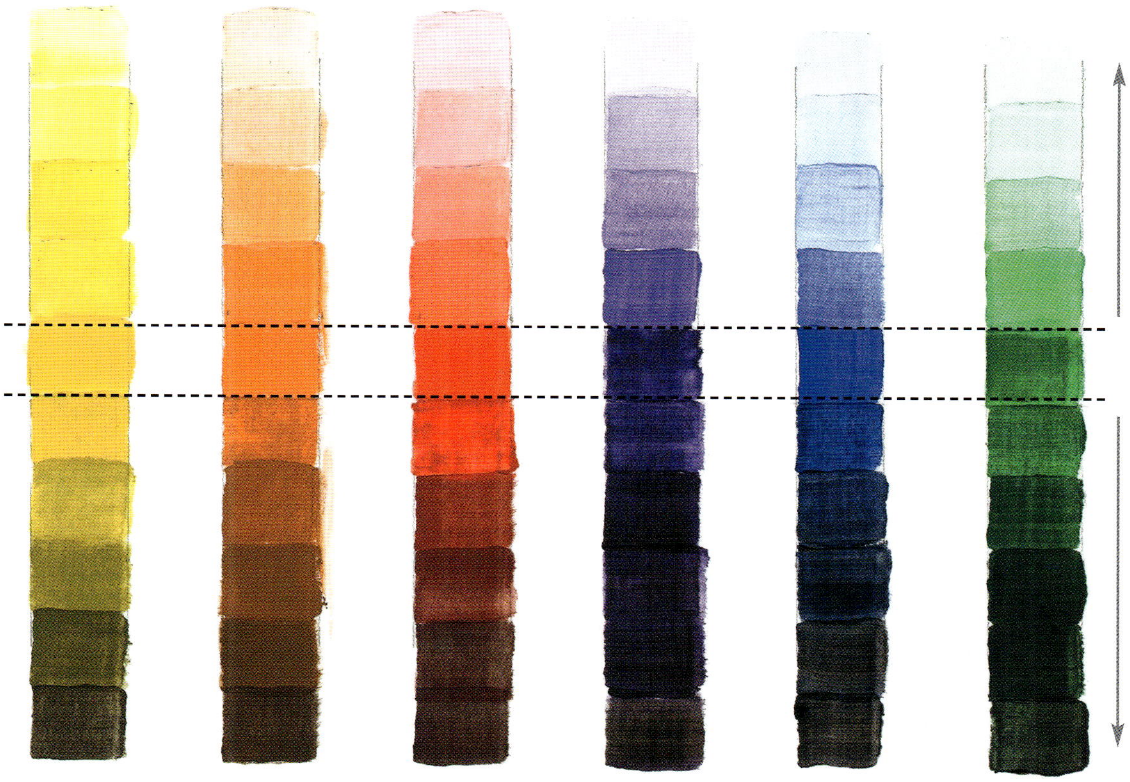

High Key
In a "high key painting," light colors dominate.

Low Key
In a "low key painting," dark colors dominate.

Notice the brownish colors in the shades of orange and red.

TRANSPARENCY AND OPACITY

- Paints are a combination of a *pigment* (the substance that contributes the color) with a *binder* (the substance that holds the pigment together).
- Transparency/opacity is the degree to which you can or can't see through a film of the paint. It is a characteristic of the pigment, not the color. Some pigments are transparent; some are opaque.
- To paint a transparent color over another without the base color showing through, *undercoat* the transparent color with an opaque white.
- Titanium White and Mars Black are opaque. When you mix a tint or shade from this white or black plus a transparent color, the result is more opaque. The lighter the tint (more Titanium White - opaque) or darker the shade (more Mars Black - opaque), the more opaque the mixture.

Transparent Paints

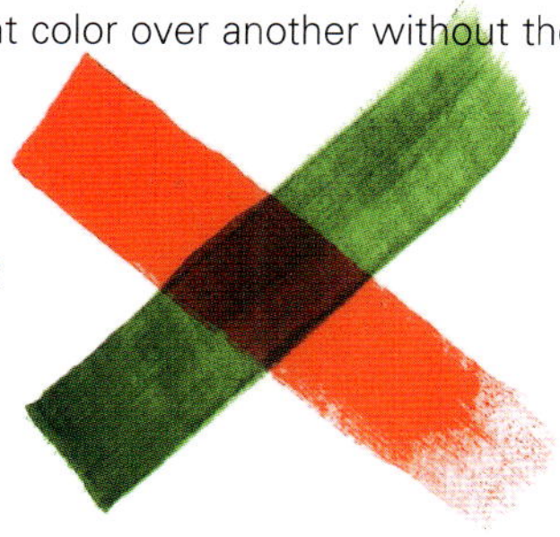

Example: Sap Green is transparent.
- Overlap is similar to the result of mixing the colors.
- Good for glazes.

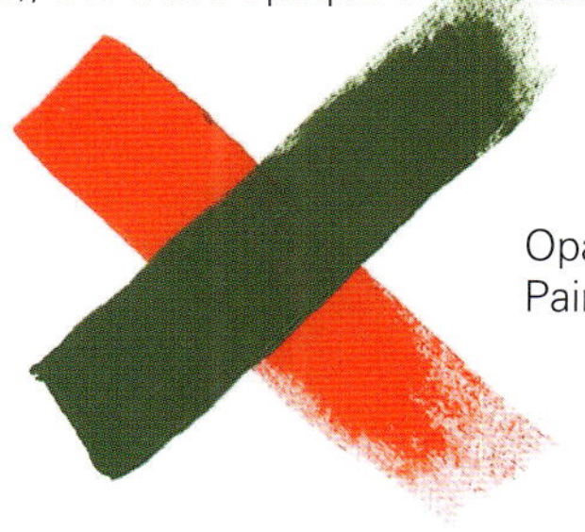

Opaque Paints

Example: Chromium Oxide Green is opaque.
- Good for painting over other colors.
- Opaque paints often look somewhat chalky out of the tube.

Landscape Colors

BLUES AND PURPLES

Several beautiful blues and one beautiful purple are available straight from the tube. The figure shows the opaque and semi-opaque blues in horizontal stripes, with the transparent blues and purple in vertical stripes. The bottom portion of the transparent colors is the color from the tube. The stripes over the opaque colors are glazes of the transparent colors, showing their effect when glazed over the opaques.

Tints of Cerulean Blue and Cobalt Blue are wonderful for skies. The Phthalos are very bright and should be used sparingly.

EARTHTONES

As with blues, a good range of earthtones is available from the tube. The figure shows the opaque and semi-opaque colors in horizontal stripes, and the transparent colors in vertical stripes. Burnt Sienna and Burnt Umber make beautiful glaze colors.

REDS, YELLOWS, AND ORANGES

See Page 22 for illustration.

In landscape painting, reds are used for accent color, and for mixing with greens to dull them. Cadmium Red Medium, Deep, and Light are workhorse reds. They are bright and warm, and the light shade is nearly orange. Napthol Red and Perylene Red are cooler reds. Tints mixed from Permanent Rose are lovely pinks.

Oranges are also used as accent colors, or to mix with greens for autumn foliage. Cadmium Orange, Perinone Orange, and Quinacridone Burnt Orange are a nice progression from light to dark. Most reds and oranges are transparent.

Cadmium Yellow Medium and Deep are warm yellows. Cadmium Yellow Light is lemony. These yellows are transparent and make good glazes to warm things up.

Naples Yellow and Buff Titanium are semi-opaque, rather dull yellows. They are good for mixing with greens.

GREENS

See Pages 24-26 for illustrations.

Greens dominate many landscape paintings. The many variations of greens in nature are duller and more complex than the colors that come straight from the tube. Most of the greens used in landscape painting are mixed colors.

It is important to have several different *sequences* of harmonious greens transitioning from light to dark. Depending on the tree or shrub, nature's greens may be bluish, grayish, brownish, or yellowish.

GUIDELINES FOR MIXING COLORS

- To make a color lighter, add white. For opacity, add Titanium White. For transparency, add Mixing White.
- To make a color darker, add black. For opacity, add Mars Black. For less opacity, add Ivory Black.
- To make a red, green, or blue warmer, add yellow.
- To make a purple warmer, add a cool red, not a warm red.
- To make a green or red cooler, add blue.
- To make a color duller, add the complementary color (red for green, orange for blue, etc.) or Graphite Gray.
- Start with the color that is dominant in the mixture and slowly add the other to it. For example, light pink has more white in it than red; begin with white and gradually add a little red. (If you begin with red, you will need to add a very large amount of white to get a light pink.) To mix a light, bright green, begin with yellow and gradually add a little green.
- When mixing three colors, mix the first two to establish the color, then dull it, lighten it, or darken it by adding the third color. For example, to mix a slightly grayish lavender, begin by mixing Dioxazine Purple into Titanium White, a little at a time. Then add a little Graphite Gray, a little at a time, to dull it.

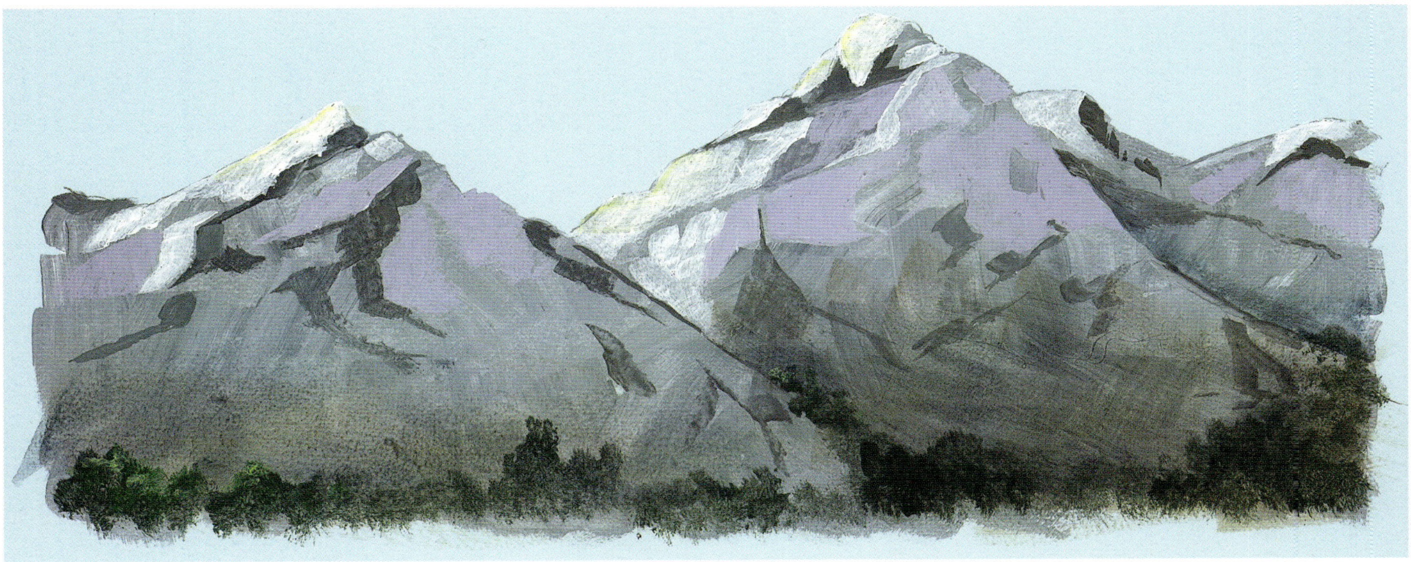

Blues and Purple

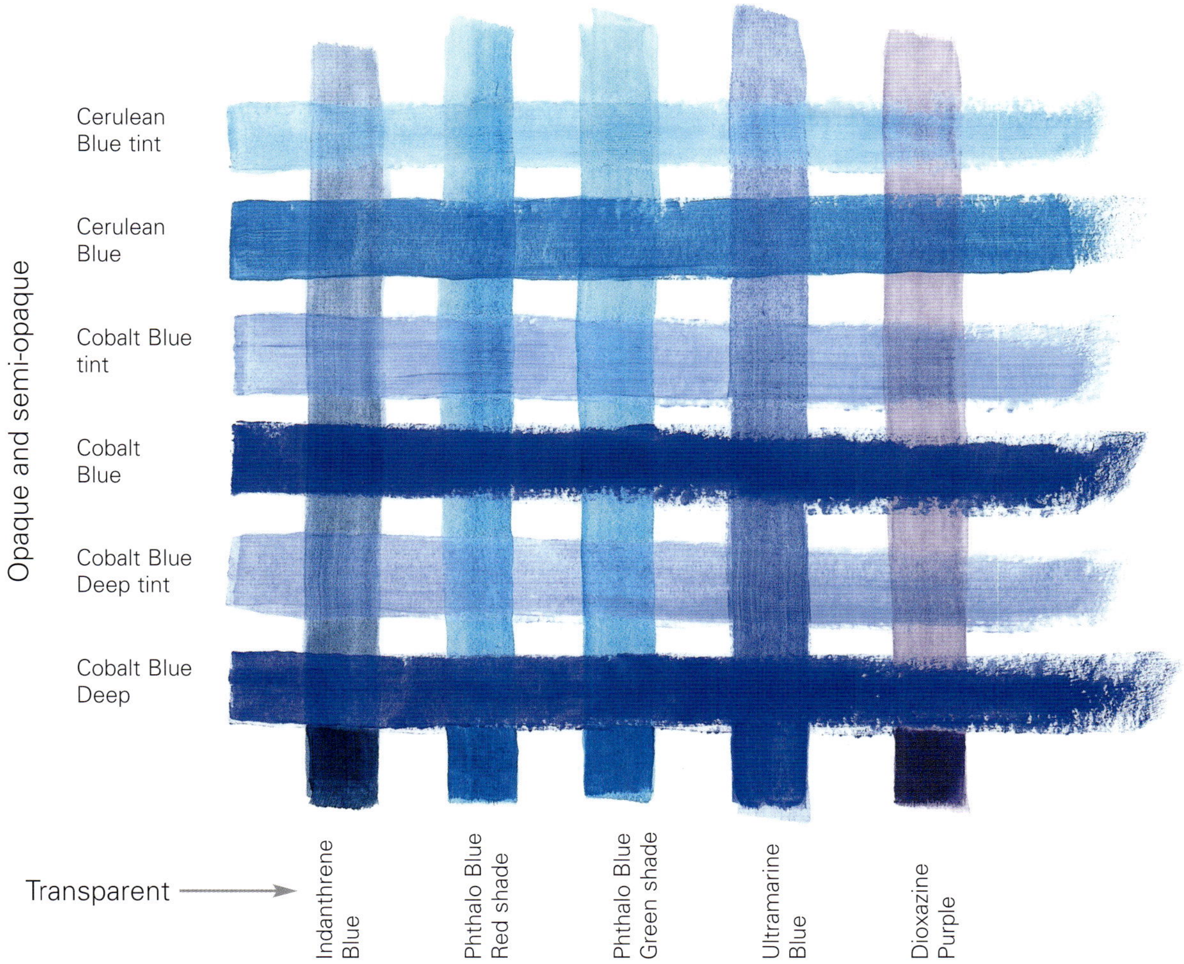

Earthtones

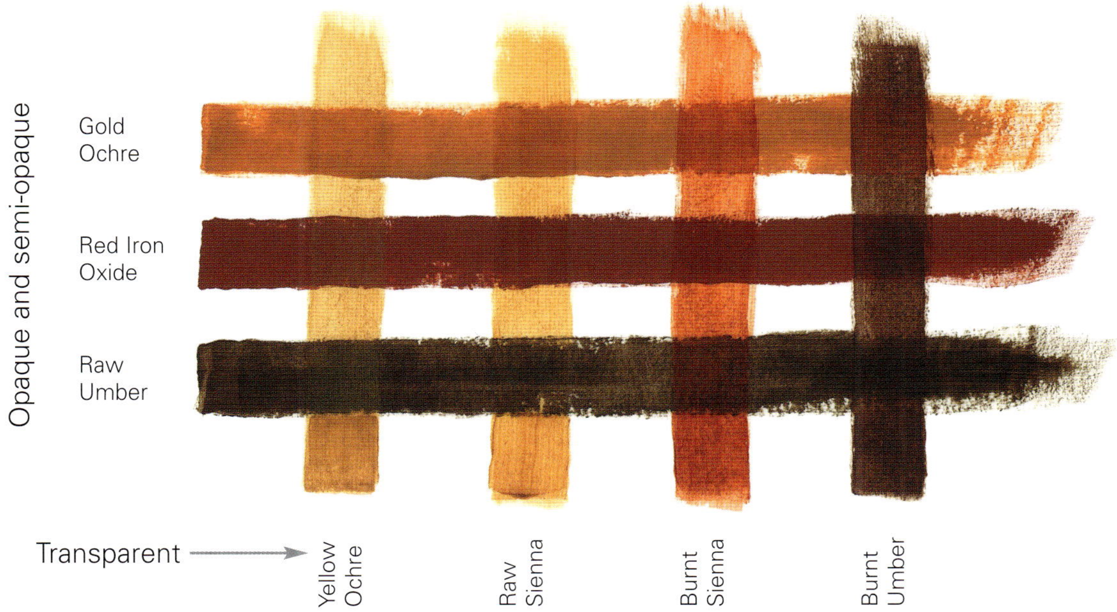

Reds

WARM REDS

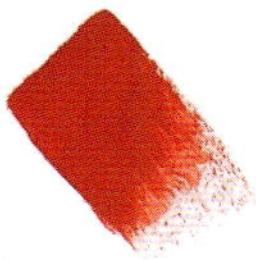

Cadmium Red Deep

Cadmium Red Medium

Cadmium Red Light

COOLER REDS

Napthol Red

Perylene Red

Permanent Rose

ORANGES

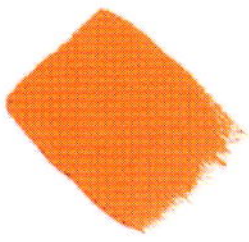

Cadmium Orange

Perinone Orange

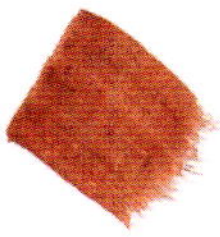

Quinacridone Burnt Orange

YELLOWS

Bright Yellows

Cadmium Yellow Deep

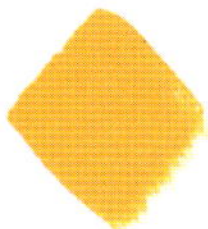

Cadmium Yellow Medium

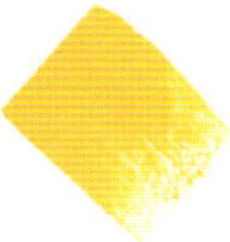

Cadmium Yellow Light

Dull Yellows

Naples Yellow

Buff Titanium

Blacks, Grays and Whites

BLACKS

Ivory Black and Mars Black are made from different pigments.

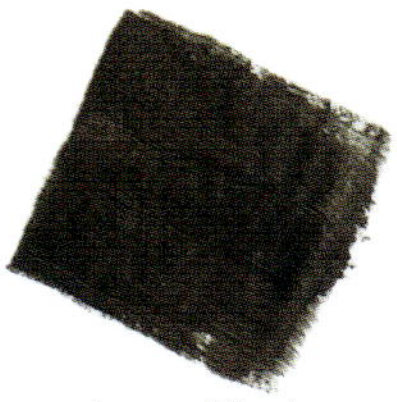

Ivory Black
Semi-transparent

Mars Black
Opaque
Deep, rich black.

GRAYS

Graphite Gray
Opaque
Dark, warm gray.

Davy's Gray
Transparent
Pale tan-gray.

Payne's Gray
Transparent and bluish
Often used for shadows, straight from the tube.

Shadow Mix

Burnt Umber

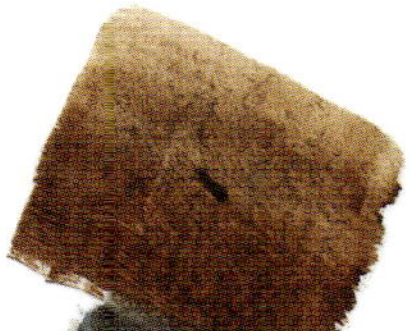

A good mixed gray for shadows.

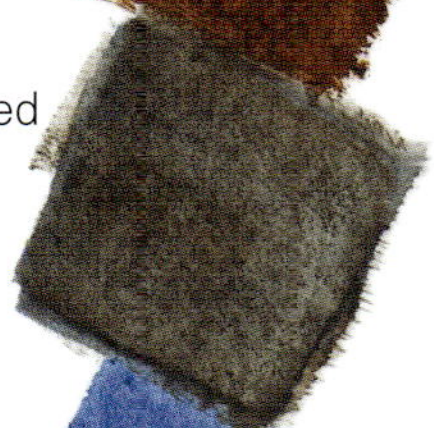

Ultramarine Blue

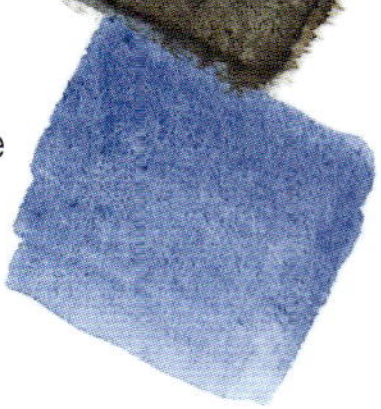

WHITES

Mixing White is semi-transparent and doesn't cover other colors well. Titanium White is opaque.

Greens I

GREENS "FROM THE TUBE"

Transparent Greens

- Use for mixing other greens.
- Use as thin glazes to unify areas of foliage that are painted with a variety of greens.

Hooker's Green

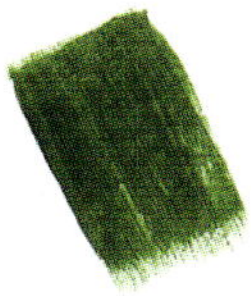

Sap Green

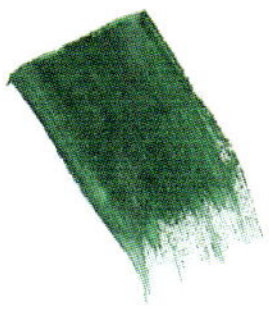

Phthalo Green
(Blue shade)

Phthalo Green
(Yellow shade)

Opaque Greens

- Use for mixing other greens.

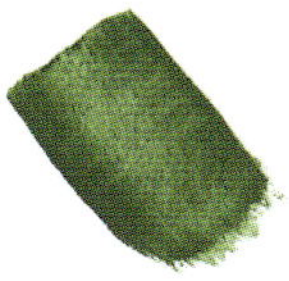

Chromium Oxide Green

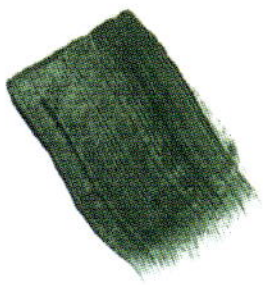

Cobalt Green Deep

Cobalt Green Light

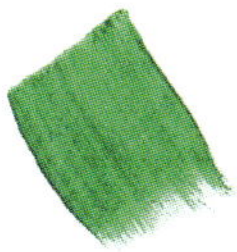

Emerald

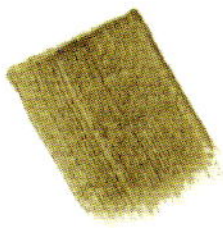

Olive Green

SIMPLE MIXED GREENS

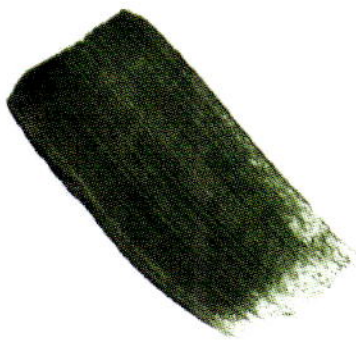

black/green
Hooker's Green
+ Lamp Black

An essential dark green.

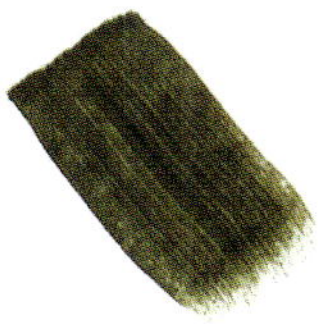

brown/green
Hooker's Green
+ Burnt Umber

An essential dark green.

Olive Green
+ Buff Titanium

Good for dried grasses.

Cobalt Green Light
+ Cadmium Yellow Light
+ Mixing White

Good for sunlit meadows.

Greens II

MIXED GREEN SEQUENCES

As you mix these sequences, consciously work on developing your "eye" - being aware of what the colors do to each other - rather than following recipes. That is how you develop the skills to mix your own colors.

Each sequence is based on an "out of the tube" green. The mixes do not have exact formulas for amounts. Add the second color a little at a time until you reach the desired value. Follow this procedure:

1. Mix the medium value first. Squeeze out green; gradually add second color.
2. Light value-begin with the medium mix, gradually add second color.
3. Very light value-begin with Titanium White, gradually add light mix.
4. Dark value-squeeze out green, gradually add complement.
5. Very dark value-begin with dark mix, gradually add black (or Burnt Umber).

Sap Green Sequence

A warm, bright group of colors. Sap Green is transparent, so these mixes are transparent or semi-opaque. The medium and light colors are good for spring trees, and the full sequence works well for trees in full summer foliage.

very dark

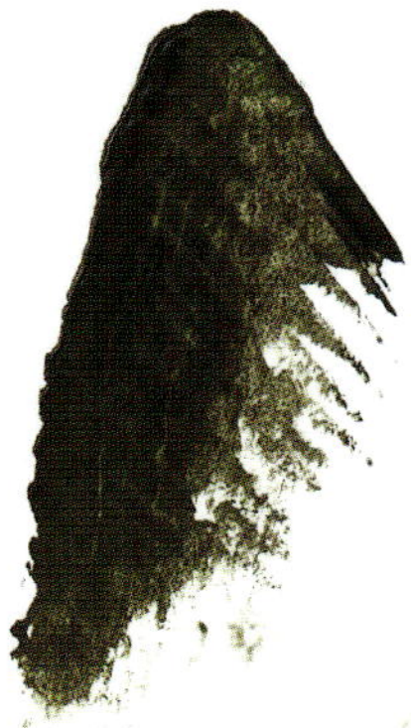

dark mix
+
Mars Black

dark

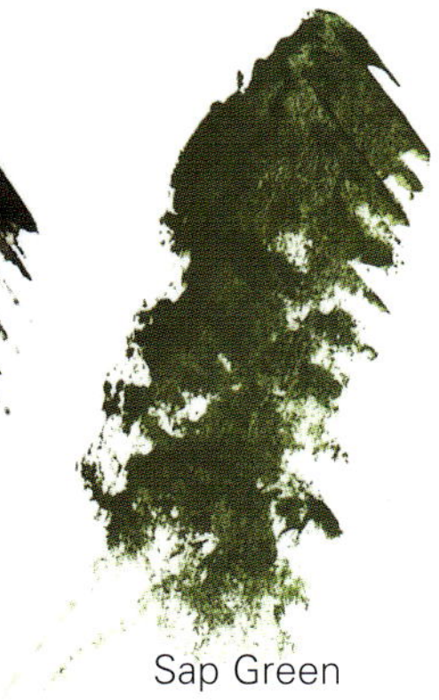

Sap Green
+
Cadmium Red Deep

Adding the complement rather than black gives a warmer color.

medium
Mix first

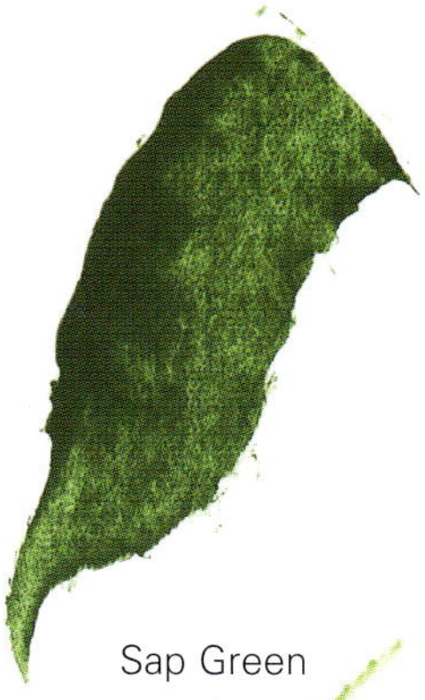

Sap Green
+
Cadmium Yellow Deep

light

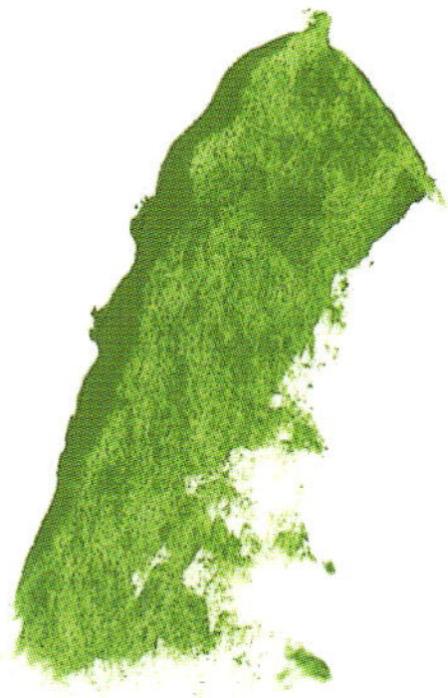

medium mix
+
Cadmium Yellow Light

very light

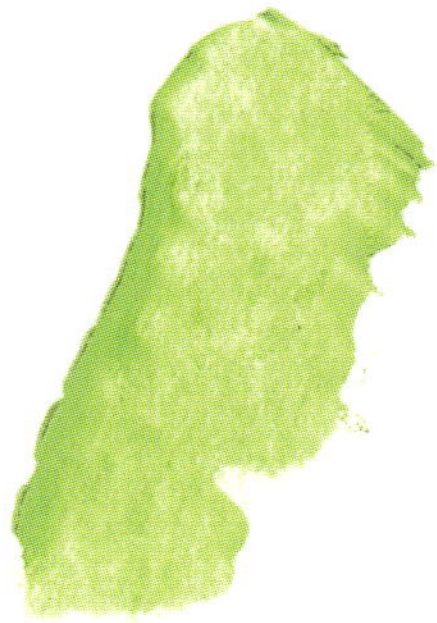

Titanium White
+
light mix

Chromium Oxide Green Sequence

A sequence of somewhat dull colors. Chromium Oxide Green is opaque, as are the other colors in the sequence. This sequence works well for trees, such as live oaks, that have a brownish tint to their foliage.

very dark

dark mix
+
Mars Black

dark

Chromium Oxide Green
+
Cadmium Red Deep

Adding the complement rather than black gives a warmer color.

medium
Mix first

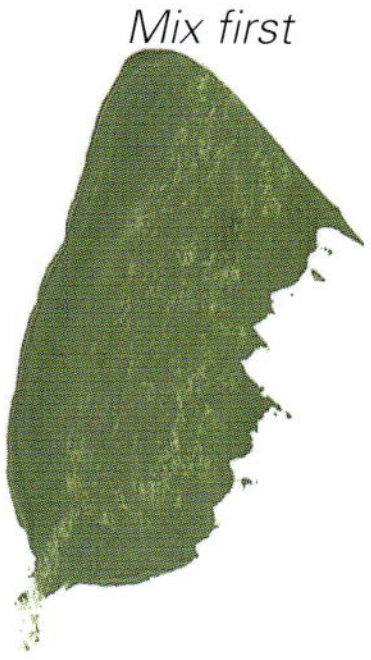

Chromium Oxide Green
+
Naples Yellow

light

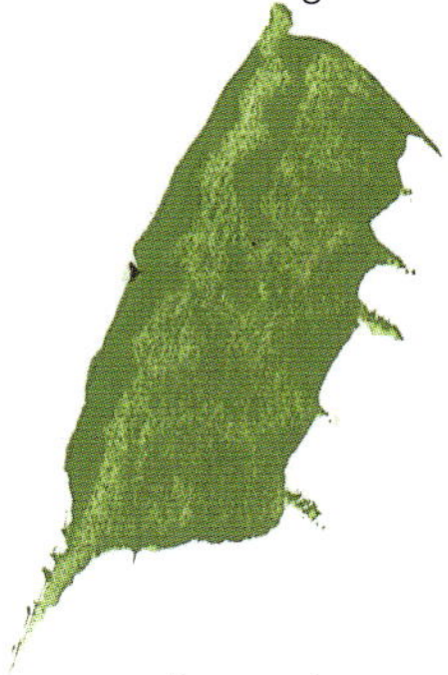

medium mix
+
Cadmium Yellow Light
+
Buff Titanium

The yellow warms the green, and the buff lightens the value.

very light

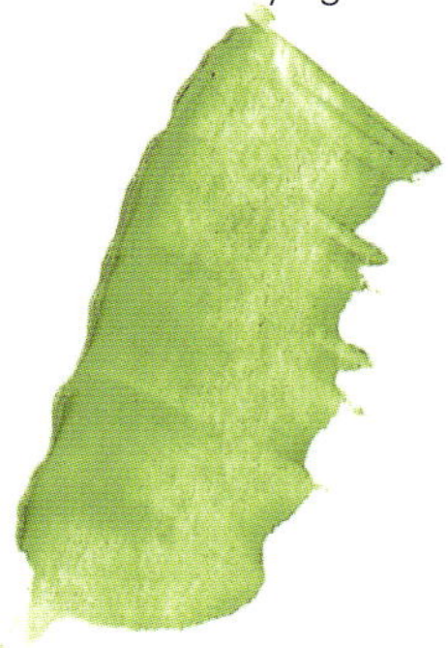

Titanium White
+
light mix

Greens III

MIXED GREEN SEQUENCES

Cool Green Sequence

Based on the cool Cobalt Greens. It is a good sequence for conifers.

very dark

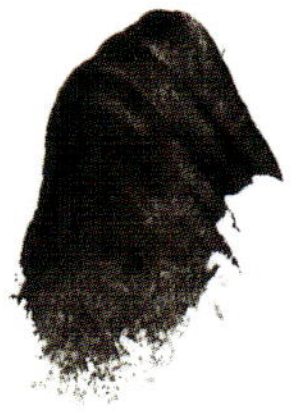

dark mix
+
Mars Black

dark

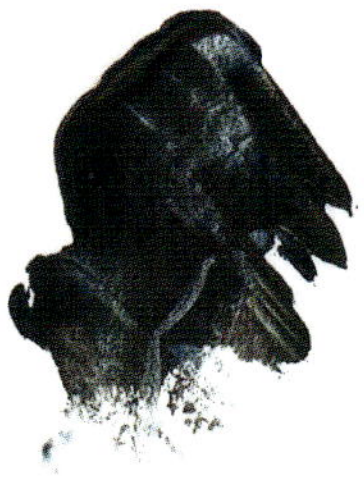

Cobalt Green Deep
+
Ultramarine Blue
+
Cadmium Red Deep

Add blue to preserve the cool feel, then add the complementary red to darken the mix.

medium

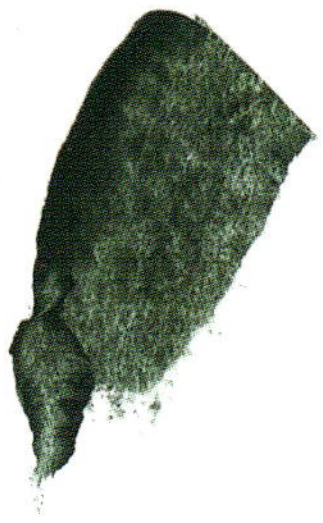

Cobalt Green Deep

light

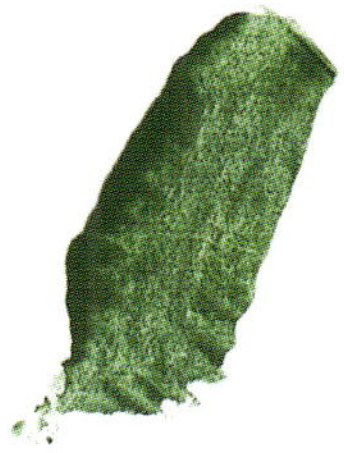

Cobalt Green Light

very light

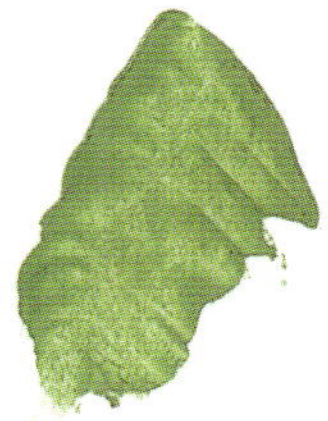

Titanium White
+
Cobalt Green Light
+
Cadmium Yellow Light

The yellow makes the color a little warmer.

Phthalo Green Sequence

Phthalo Green (Yellow Shade) is a very bright, warm color. It needs to be dulled a little to fit into a landscape.

very dark

dark mix
+
Burnt Umber

dark

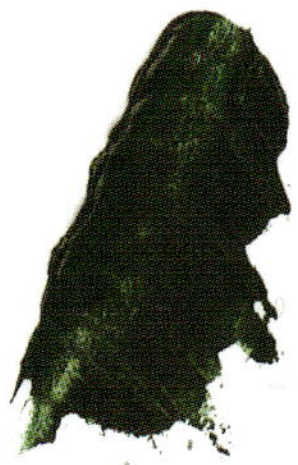

medium mix
+
Cadmium Red Deep

Adding the complementary red darkens the mix.

medium
Mix first

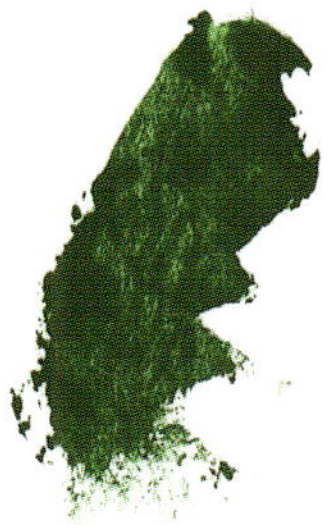

Phthalo Green (Yellow Shade)
+
Cadmium Yellow Light
+
Cadmium Red Medium

The yellow lightens the value, and the red dulls the mix.

light

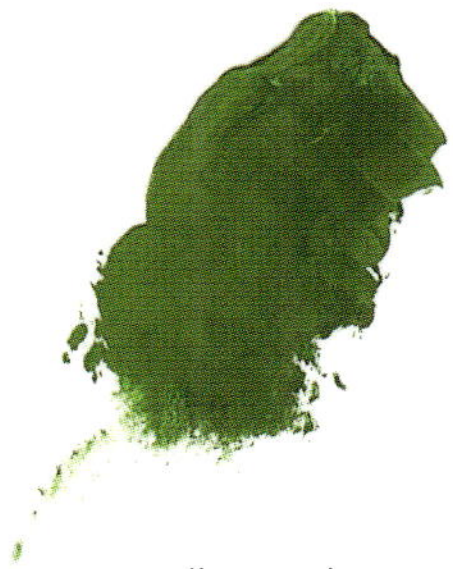

medium mix
+
Cadmium Yellow Light
+
Cadmium Red Light

very light

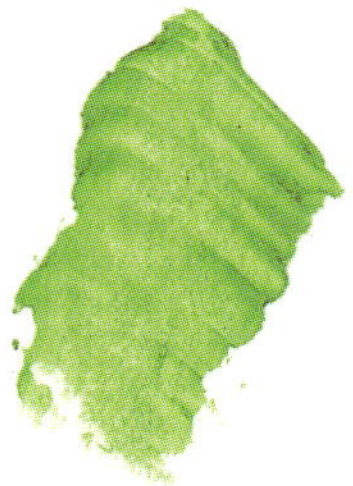

Titanium White
+
light mix

The yellow lightens the value further, and the red dulls the lighter mix.

Color Mixing Examples

Here is a series of lavenders...

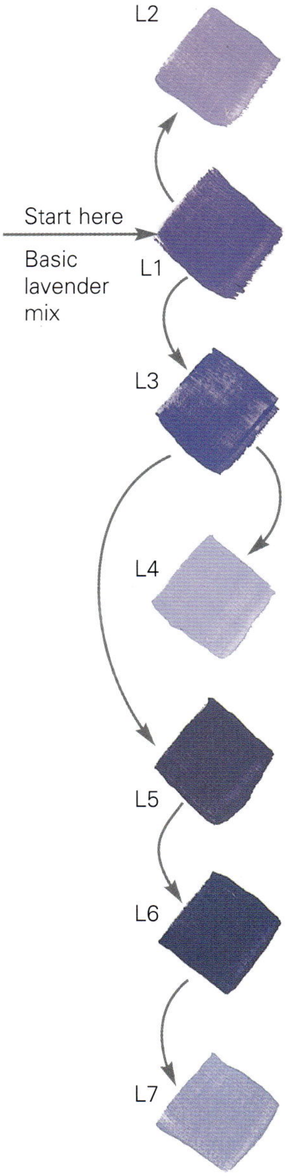

L2: *Add white to make color lighter.*
Titanium White
+ lavender mix 1 (L1)

L1: Dioxazine Purple
+ Titanium White

L3: *Duller and darker*
lavender mix 2 (L2)
+ Graphite Gray

L4: *Lighter and cooler*
Titanium White
+ lavender mix 3 (L3)

L5: *Duller and darker*
lavender mix 3 (L3)
+ Graphite Gray

L6: *Darker and cooler*
lavender mix 5 (L5)
+ Ultramarine Blue

L7: *Lighter and cooler*
Titanium White
+ lavender mix 6 (L6)

...mixed from these tube colors:

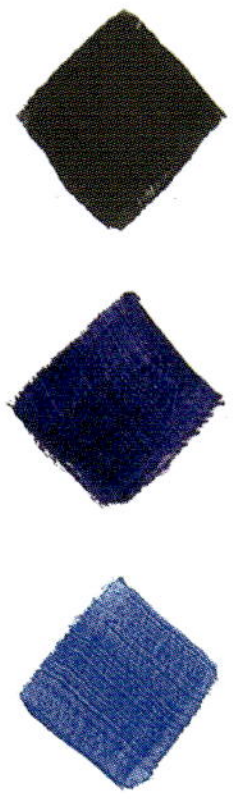

Graphite Gray

Dioxazine Purple

Ultramarine Blue

and Titanium White

Dulled Primary Colors

Here are dulled primary colors...

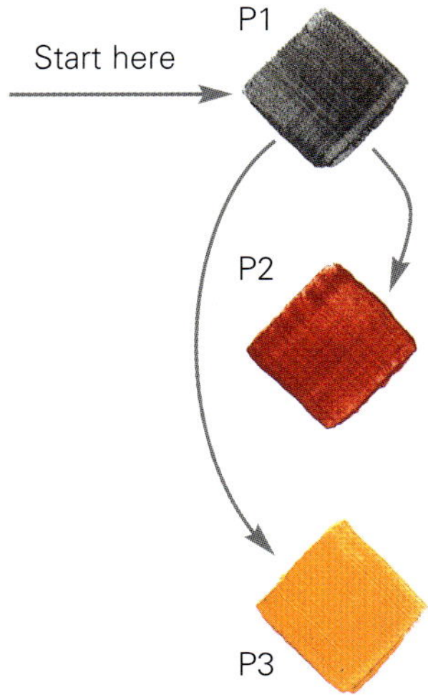

P1: Mix complementary colors to make Dulled Primary 1 (P1).
Ultramarine Blue
+ Cadmium Orange

P2: Cadmium Red Medium
+ P1

P3: Cadmium Yellow Medium
+ P1

...mixed from these tube colors:

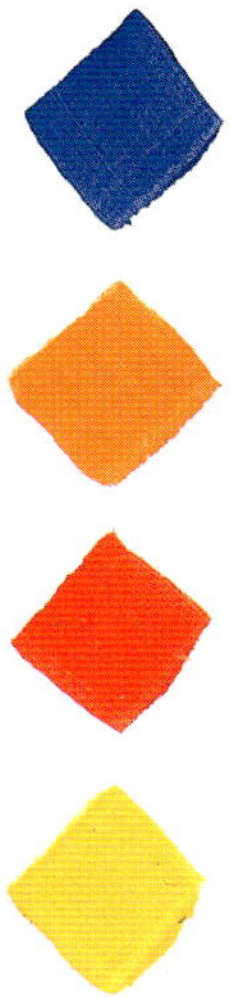

Ultramarine Blue

Cadmium Orange

Cadmium Red Medium

Cadmium Yellow Medium

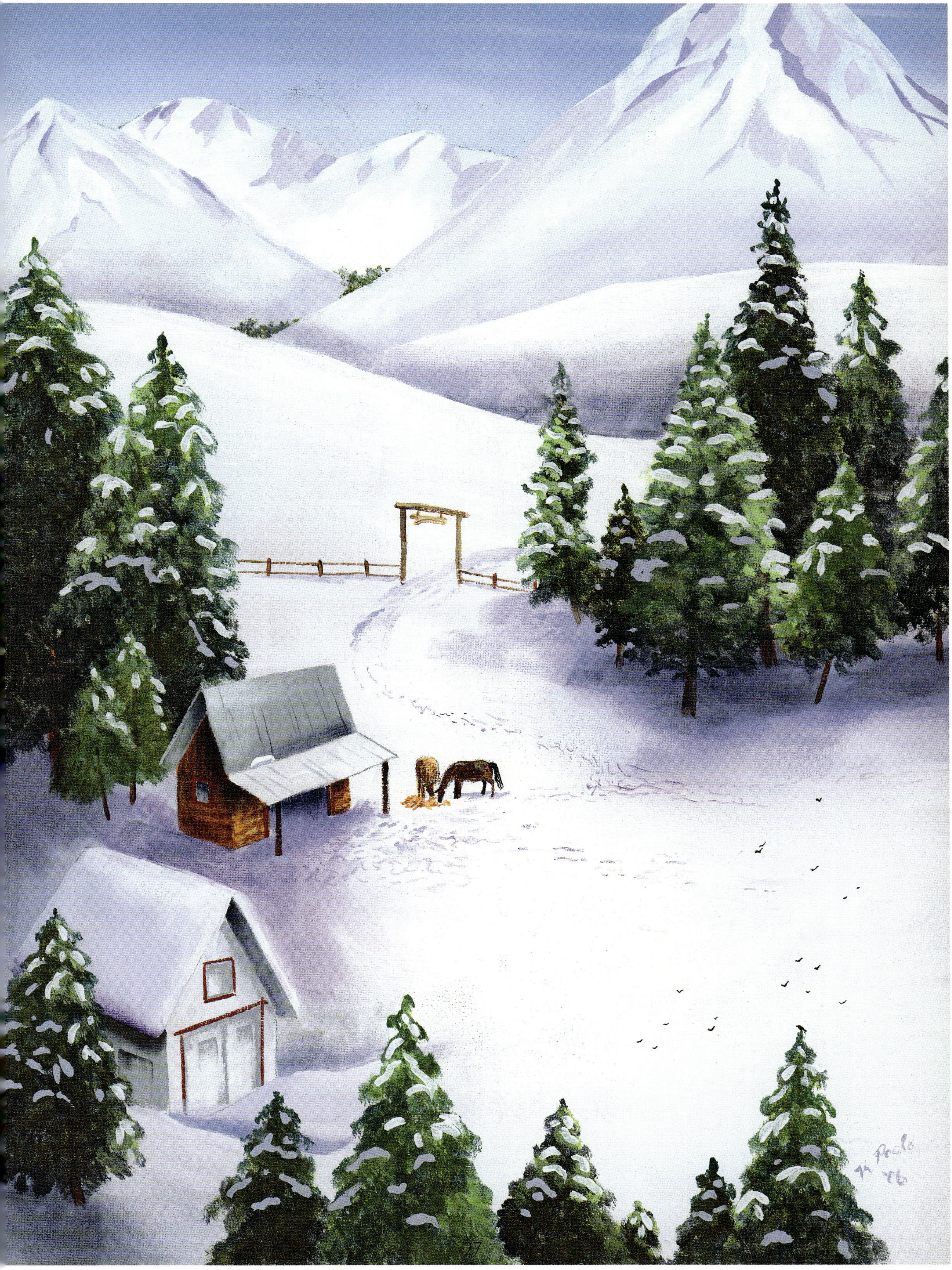

Chapter 3

BRUSH TECHNIQUES

Different areas and elements of a painting require different brushes, different loading techniques, and different ways of applying paint to the canvas. An understanding of basic brush techniques will help you achieve the effects you want in every part of a painting.

Brush Strokes

Understanding the strokes made by different kinds of brushes will help you select the proper brush for each painting task.

- Flats are good for evenly covering large areas or for painting shapes with straight edges.
- Large rounds can also be used for large areas, and the rounds are good for painting shapes with rounded edges.
- Liners are great for line work, such as painting branches.
- Fans and scumblers work well for roughing in foliage.
- Toothbrushes are great for spattering snow.
- Always use the largest brush you can for the task at hand. Not only does it save time, it gives a fresher look.

Loading Brushes

Properly loading the brush is important for accomplishing a good brushstroke. Whatever type of brush you are using, avoid getting paint close to the ferrule. It is difficult to remove paint that is close to the ferrule. The paint will dry there and ruin your ferrule.

Squeeze out dabs of the colors you will be using onto your palette. A quarter-sized dab is usually sufficient, but only experience will teach you to estimate how much paint you will need. Leave plenty of empty space on your palette for mixing colors, or use a separate sheet of palette paper for mixing. Before you load a brush with paint, wet it with clean water and blot it on a paper towel to remove the excess.

LOADING A FLAT BRUSH

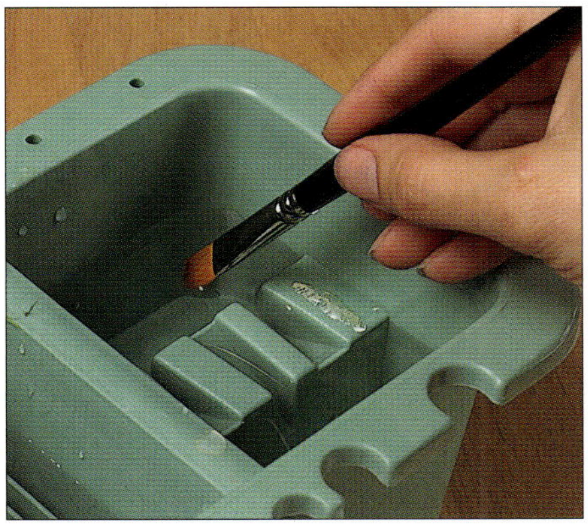

This technique can also be used with a fan brush.

1. Dip the brush in clean water.

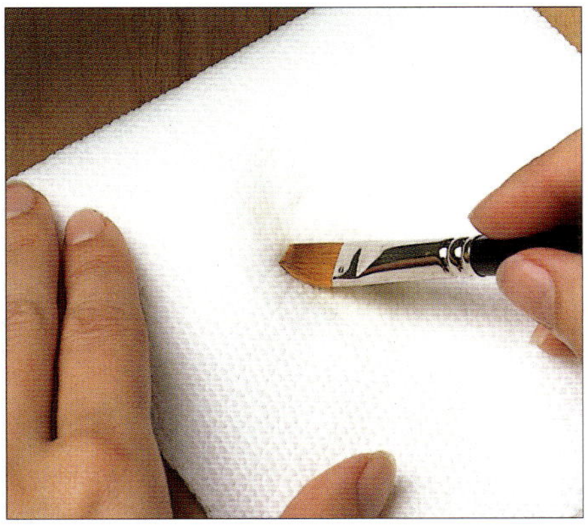

2. Blot it on a paper towel to remove excess water.

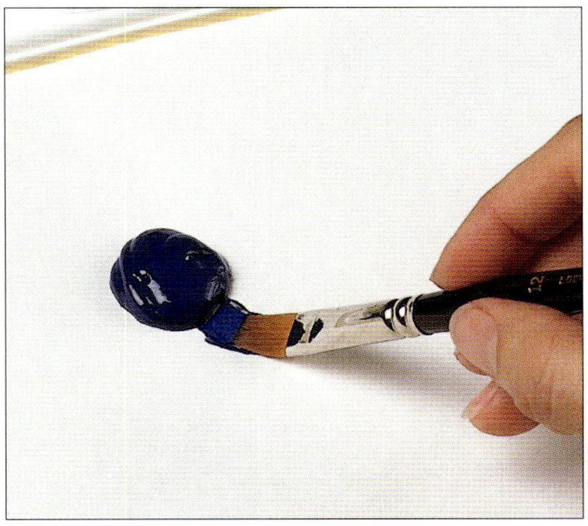

3. Dip the brush tip in the dab of paint near the edge and pull outward, away from the paint.
4. Turn the brush over and repeat to ensure an even load of paint. Too much paint can result in ridges on the sides of your brushstrokes.

LOADING A ROUND BRUSH

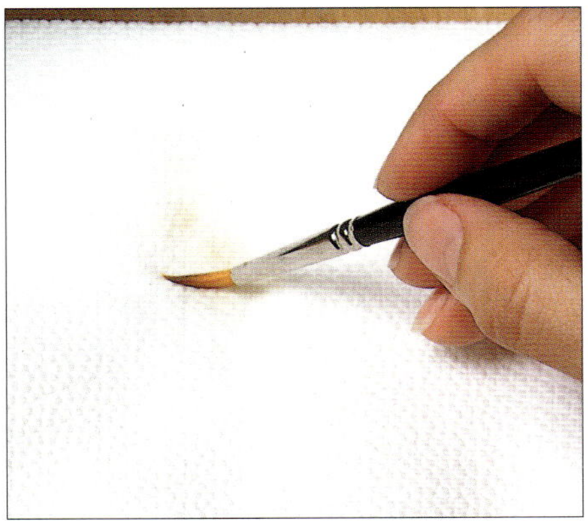

1. Dip the brush in water and blot.

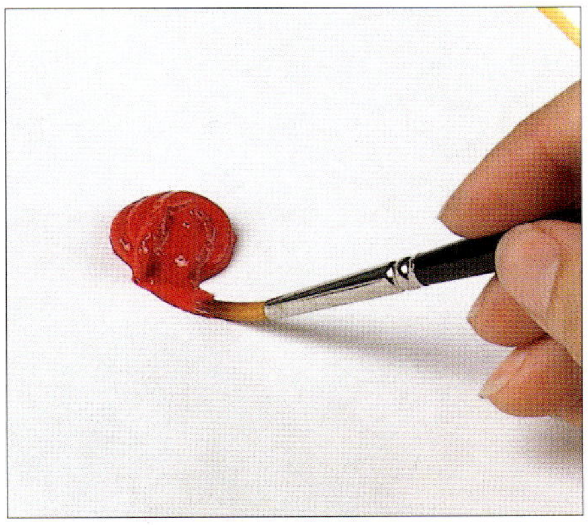

2. Dip the tip in the dab of paint near the edge and pull outward.

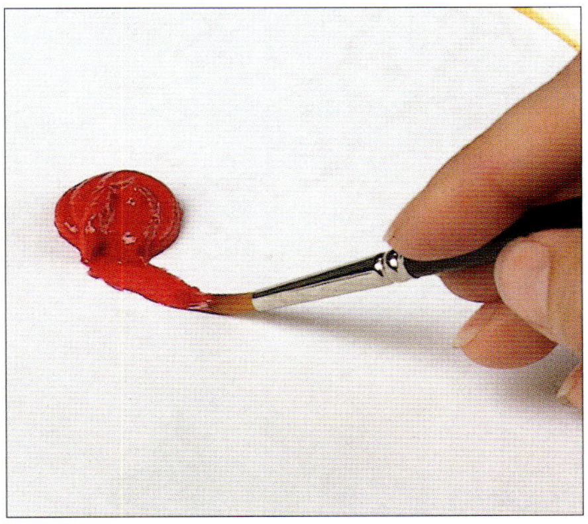

3. Rotate the brush by about a third and repeat. Rotate and repeat once more to ensure an even load all around the brush.

TIP-LOADING A ROUND BRUSH

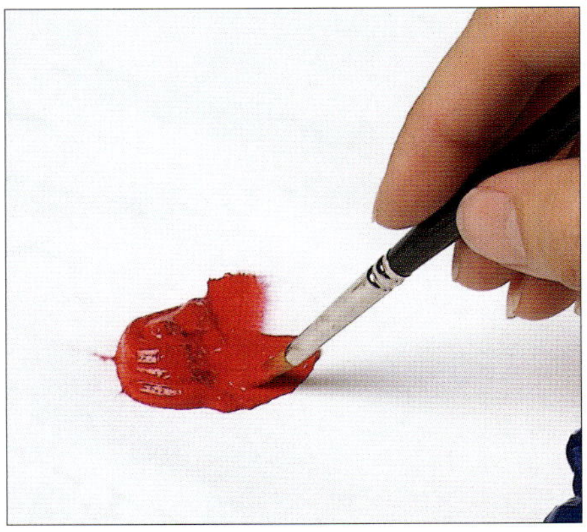

1. Fully load the brush with one color

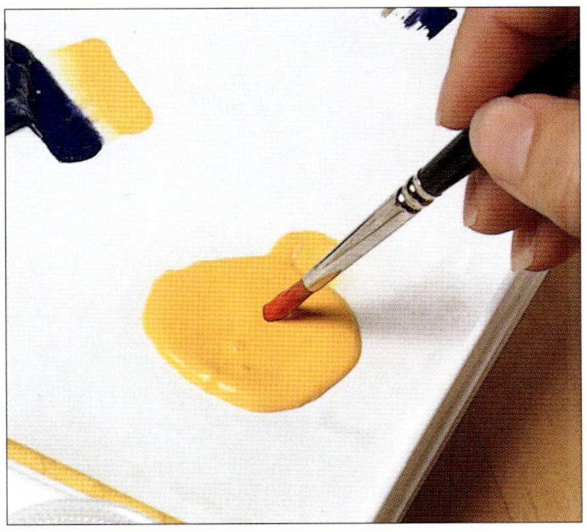

2. Then dip the tip in another color.

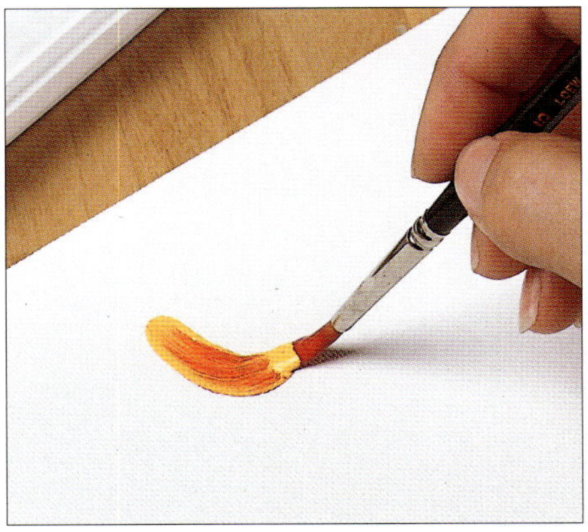

3. As you paint, the two colors will blend unevenly on the canvas.

DOUBLE LOADING A FLAT BRUSH

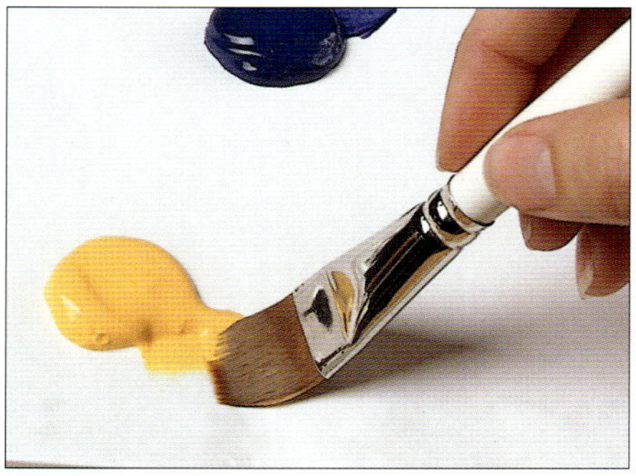

1. Dip one corner in one color paint.

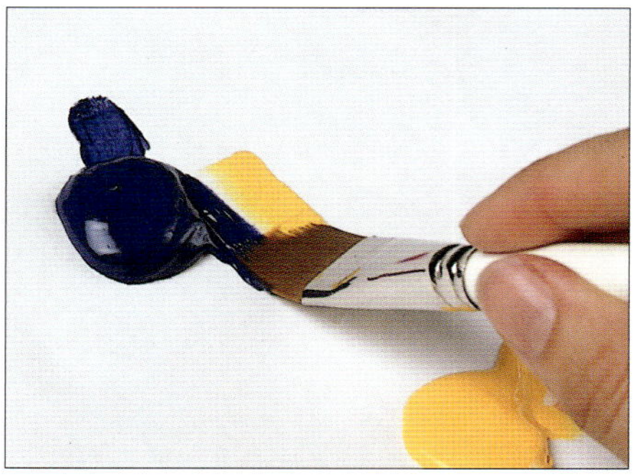

2. Dip the other corner in another color.

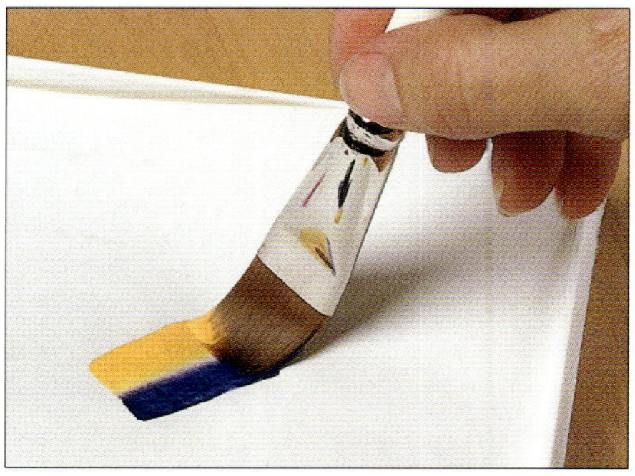

3. Stroke the brush from left to right on a clean piece of palette paper.

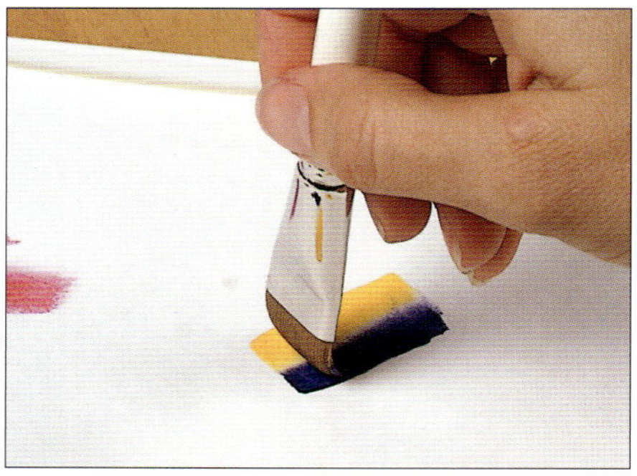

4. Then, without turning the brush, stroke back from right to left.

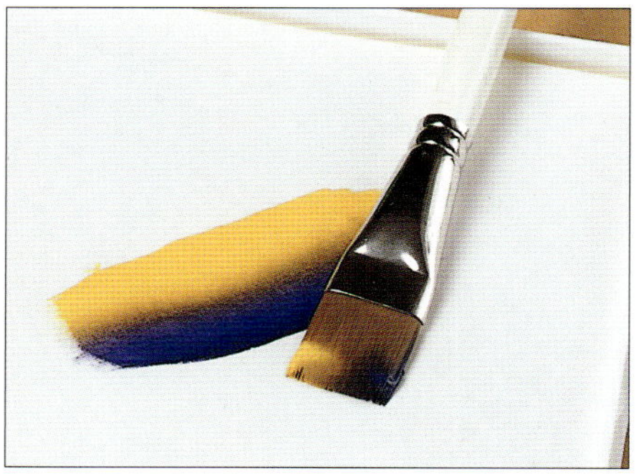

5. The colors mix in the center of the brush.

SIDE LOADING A FLAT BRUSH

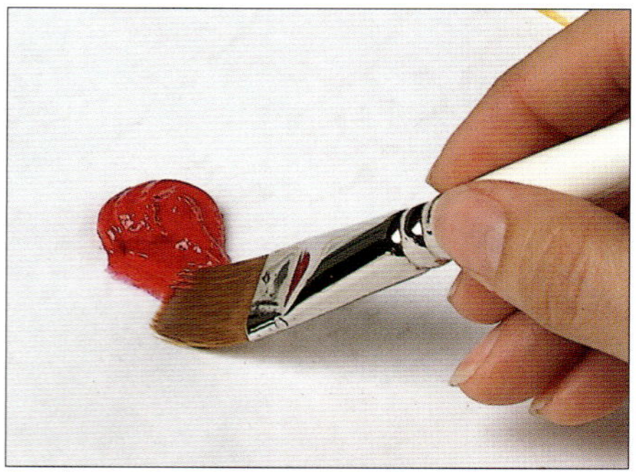

1. Dip one corner of a damp brush in the paint.

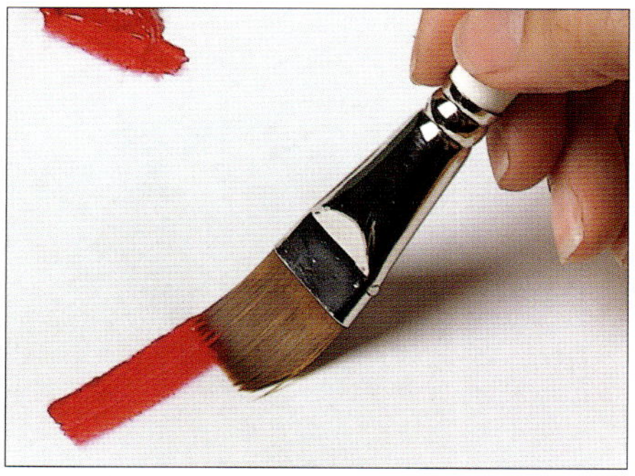

2. Stroke the brush on a clean piece of palette paper, pulling it from left to right.

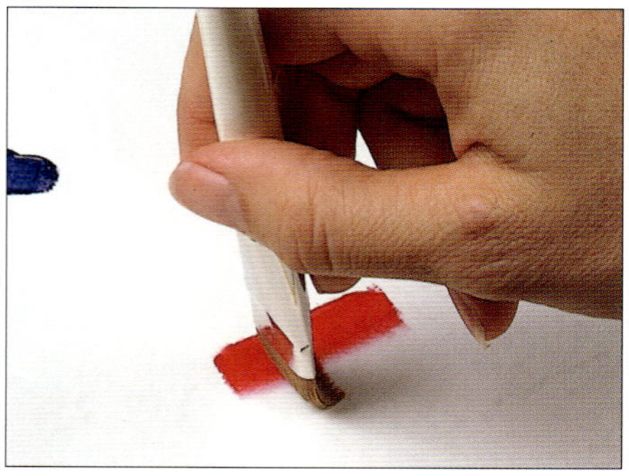

3. Then, without turning the brush, pull back from right to left.

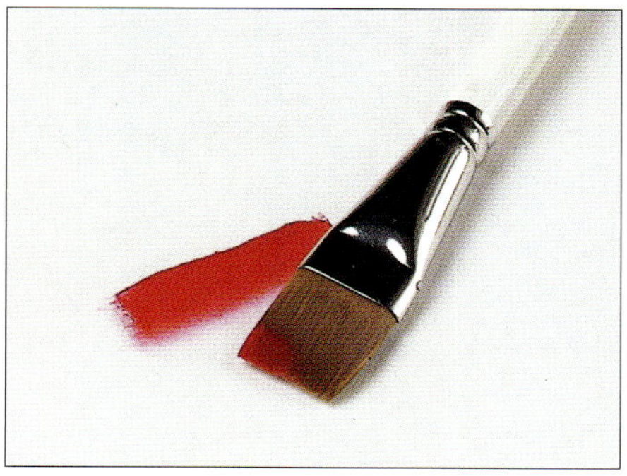

4. Repeat a few times. This distributes the paint smoothly over the hairs on the loaded side of the brush.

LOADING THE LINER

Load a liner brush in the same manner as a round brush. The long hairs on a liner let you load more paint on the brush for painting a long stroke.

LOADING A SCUMBLER

1. Dip brush in water and blot.
2. Hold the brush upright and dip it in the paint.
3. Dab brush on the palette to remove much of the paint.
4. The brush should be lightly loaded so the texture of the stroke will show. Too much paint on the brush will result in a blob.

SPATTERING WITH A TOOTHBRUSH

1. Thin the paint to an inky consistency.
2. Press the bristles flat into the paint, then dab on the palette to remove much of the paint.
3. To spatter, run your thumb across the bristles, directing the spatters towards the surface. Practice first on a piece of scrap paper. If the paint drips off the brush or spatters off in big blobs, it is probably too thin.

Basic Brush Strokes

FLATS

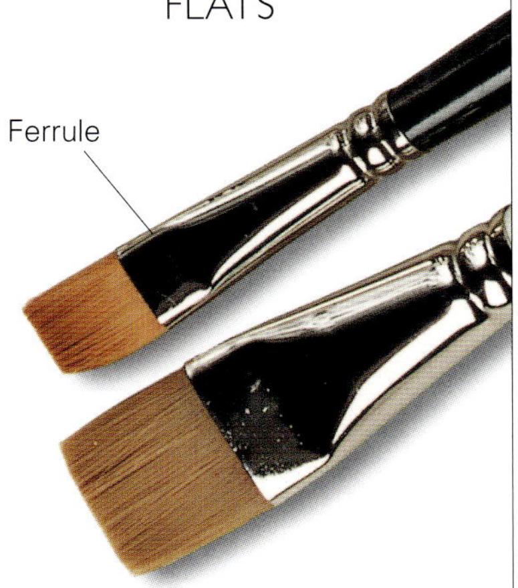

Flats come with long or short hairs. The ones with short hairs are sometimes called "brights."

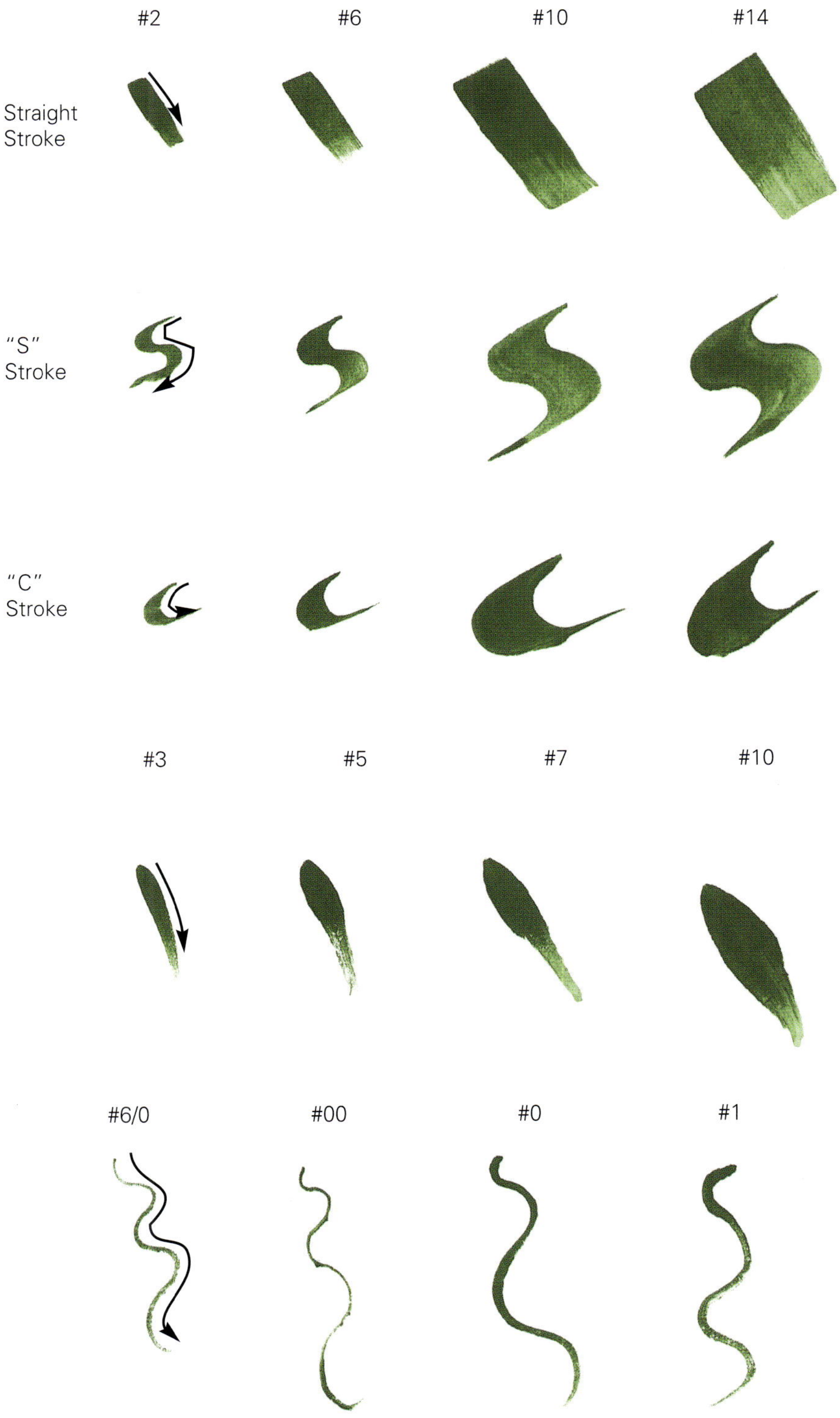

ROUNDS

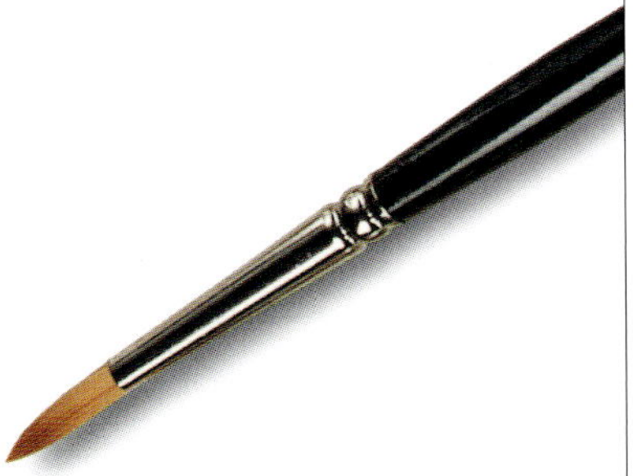

LINERS

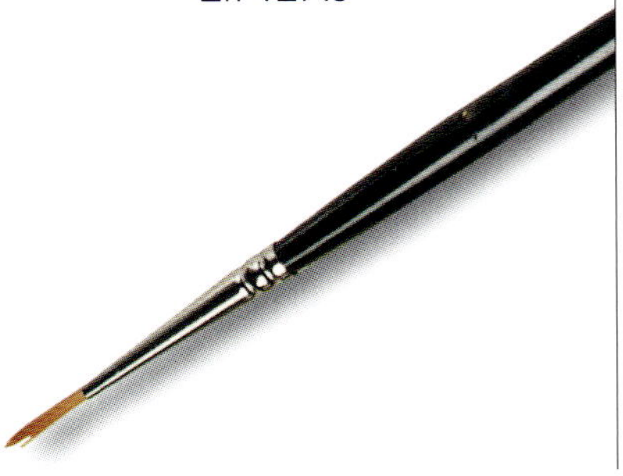

Specialty Brush Strokes

FAN

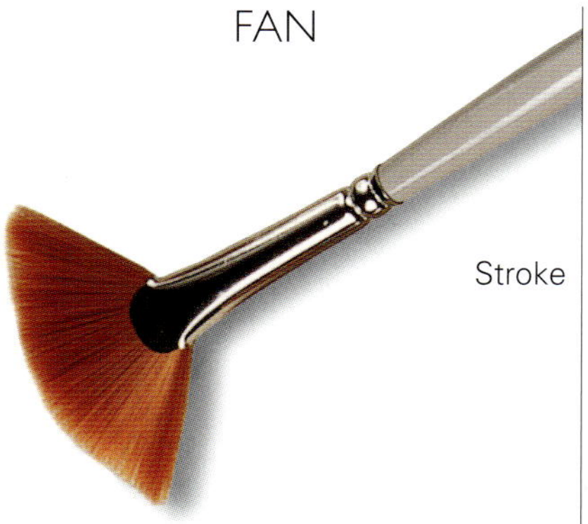

Stroke

#1

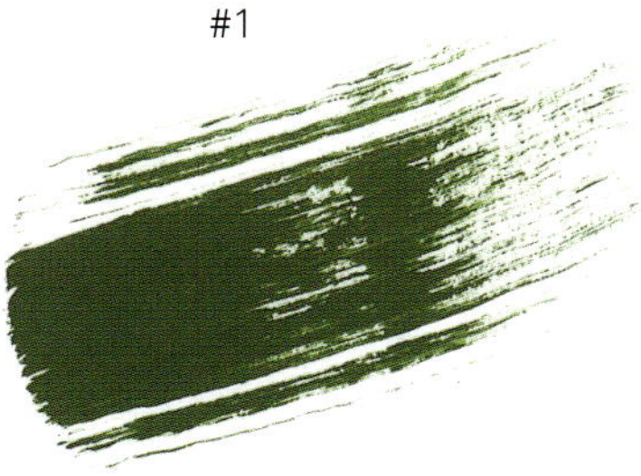

#4

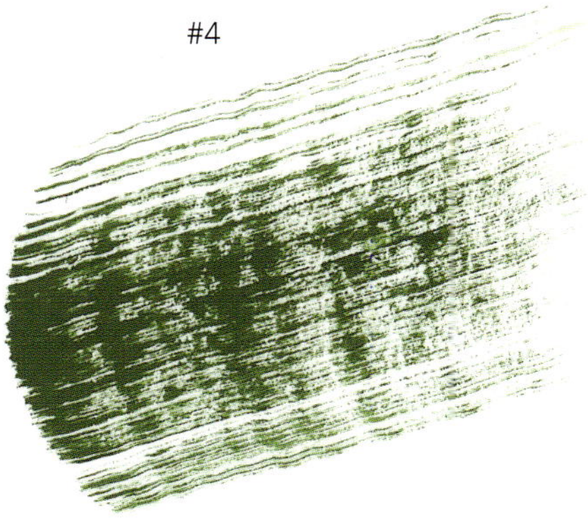

Dab

Cluster

Single

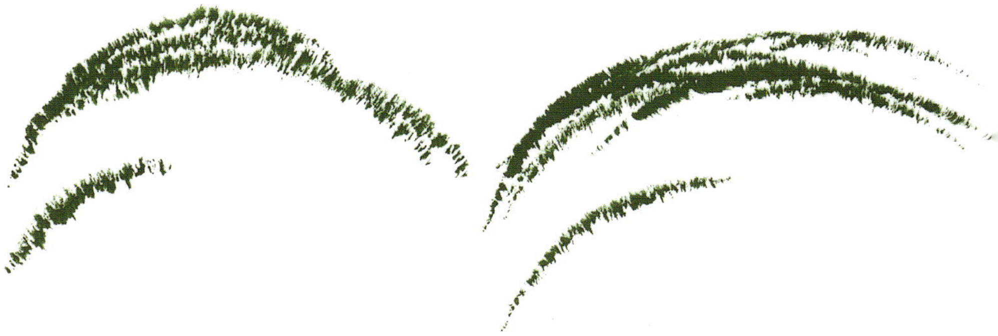

SCUMBLER

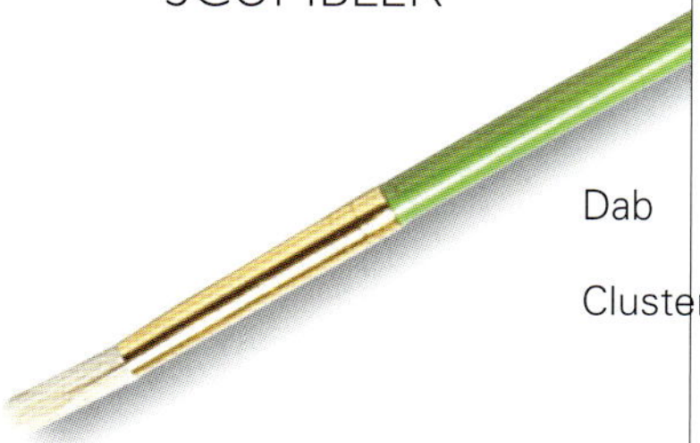

Dab

Cluster

Single

#2

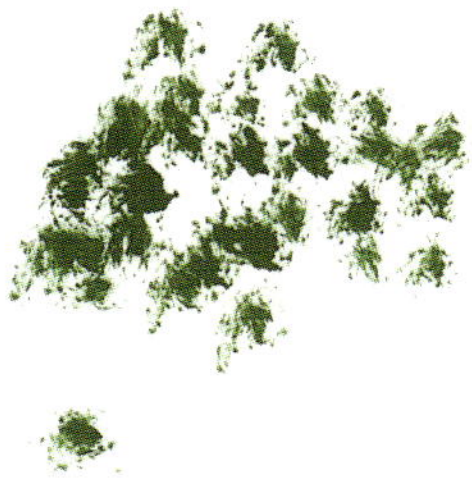

#6

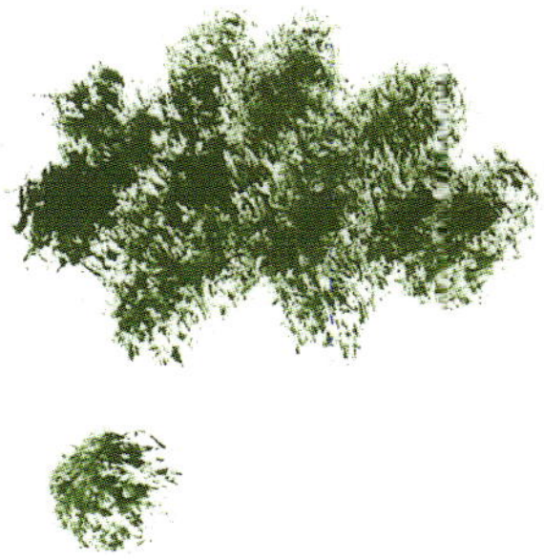

To *scumble* means to dab paint on with a scumbler brush.

TOOTHBRUSH

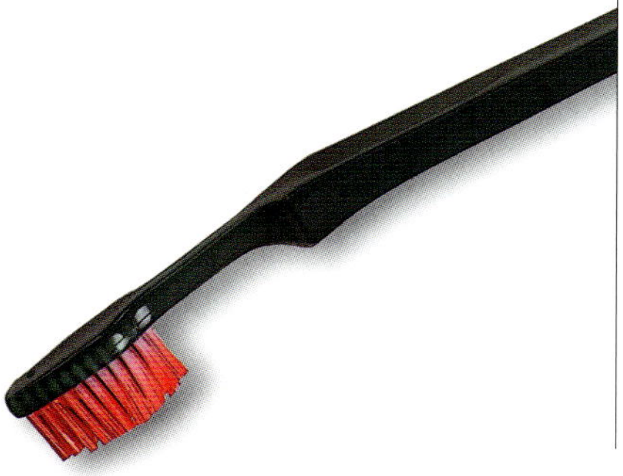

1. Thin paint to inky consistency.
2. Dab brush in thinned paint, then on palette to remove excess.
3. Spatter by flicking thumb across bristles.

Blending

Techniques for transitioning between colors include special brush loads, wet-in-wet blending, and glazing.

SPECIAL BRUSH LOADS

Flat Brush
Sideload

Good for shading/highlighting small areas.

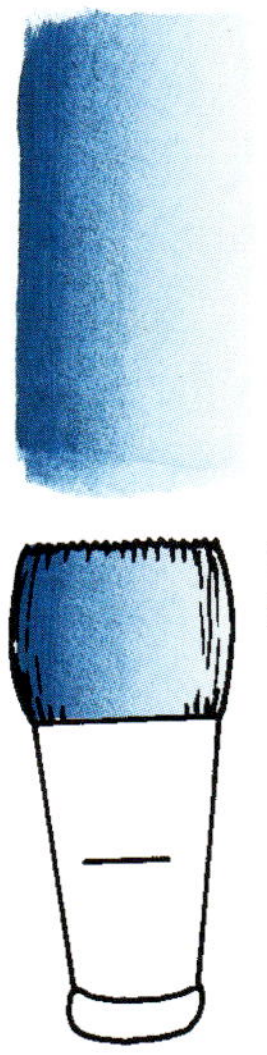

1. Dip one corner in paint.
2. Stroke brush on clean palette paper.
3. Without turning the brush, stroke back over stroke in opposite direction.
4. Repeat to distribute paint in a smooth gradation.

Flat Brush
Double load

Good for tree trunks and large branches.

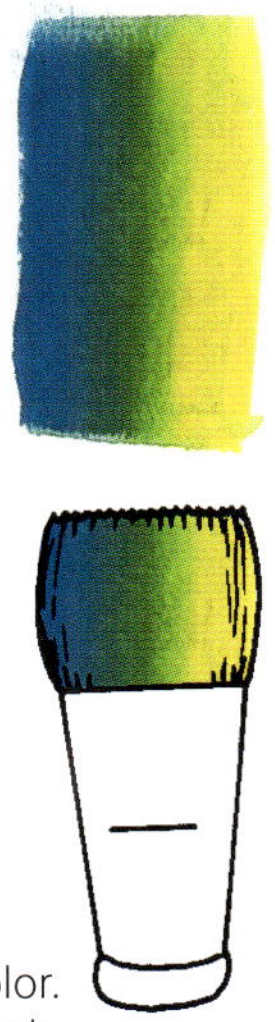

1. Dip one corner in first color.
2. Dip other corner in second color.
3. Stroke brush on clean palette paper.
4. Without turning the brush, stroke back over stroke in opposite direction.
5. Repeat to blend paint smoothly.

Round Brush
Tip load

Gives a nice variety of color for painting foliage.

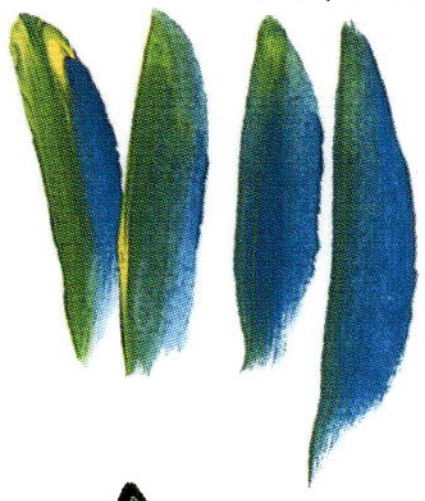

1. Fully load brush with first color.
2. Dip tip in second color.
3. As you paint, the colors blend unevenly on the canvas.

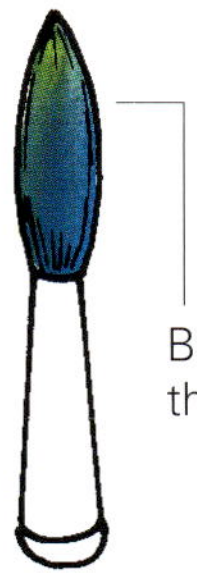

WET-IN-WET BLENDING

Wet-in-Wet Blending: Adjacent Colors

"Wet-in-wet" techniques blend wet paint colors on the canvas. The paints must be wet as you blend, so you must work quickly, with large brushes.

A useful blending technique for skies, meadows, and still water.

A

Lay in first color.

B

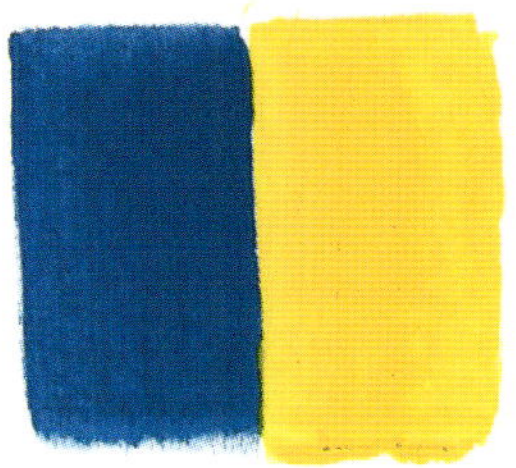

Quickly clean brush. Paint second color next to first.

C

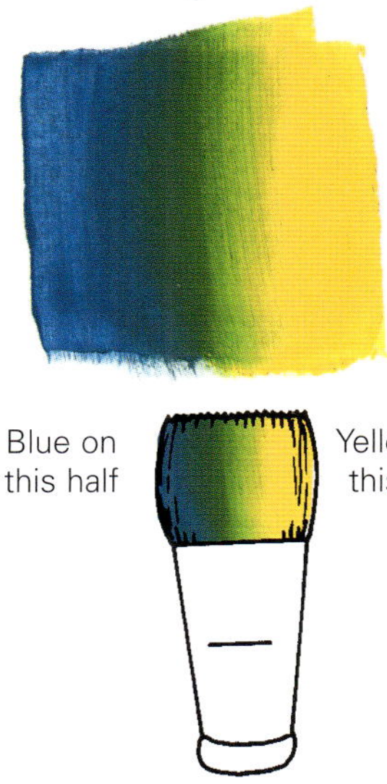

1. Double load a clean brush.
2. Stroke back and forth over seam. Always stroke parallel to seam.
3. Widen blended area by traveling a little to each side.

D

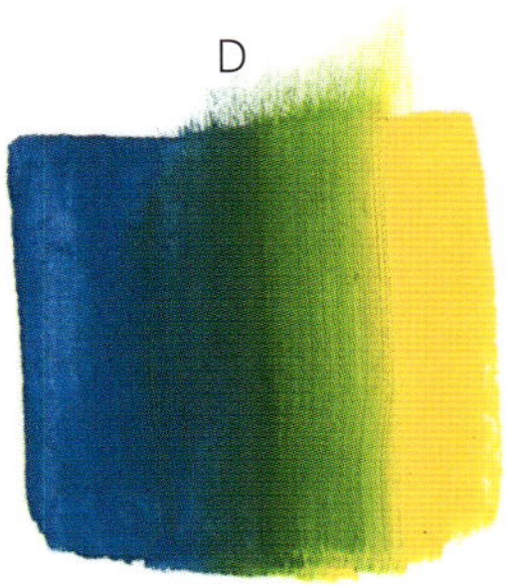

Let dry.
Add second coat if necessary.

Wet-in-Wet Blending

ONE COLOR OVER ANOTHER

A useful technique for painting high clouds or ripples in water.

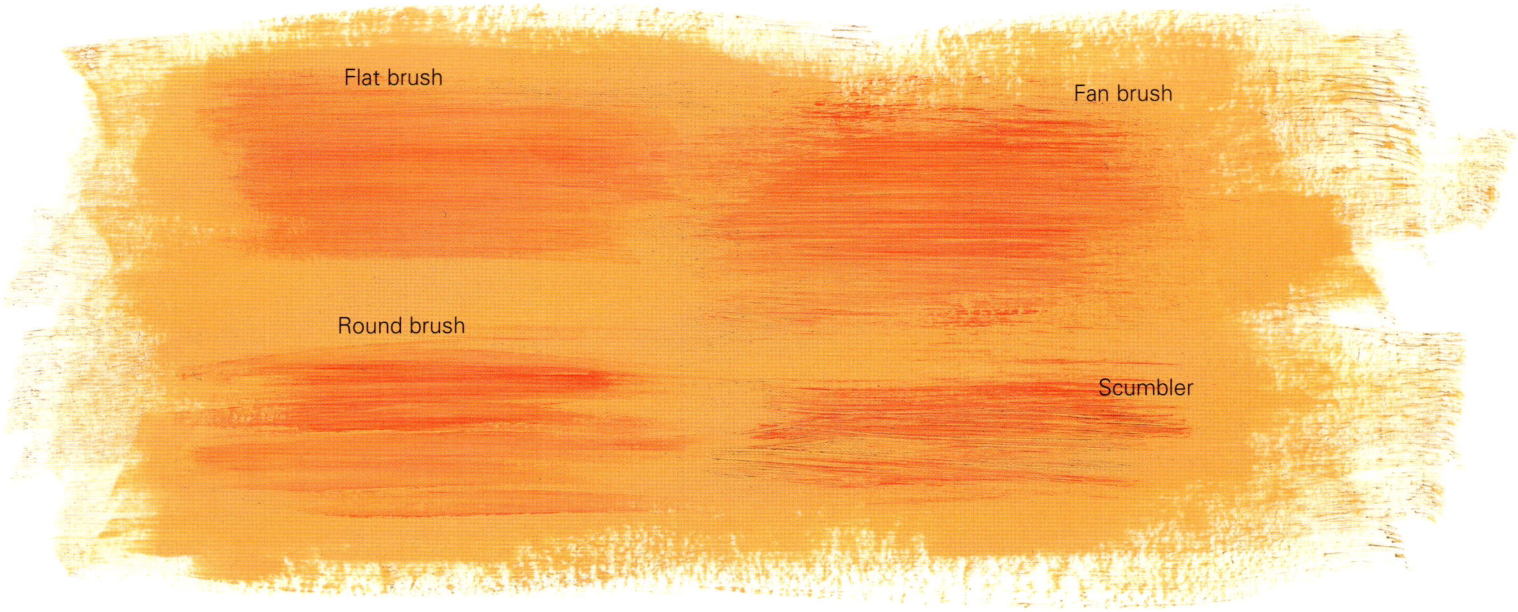

1. Place the first color.
2. While paint is wet, stroke another color (or colors) over the first, blending them on the canvas.

DABBING MULTIPLE OVERLAPPING COLORS

Haphazard blending is good for painting foliage.

Example dabbed with scumbler

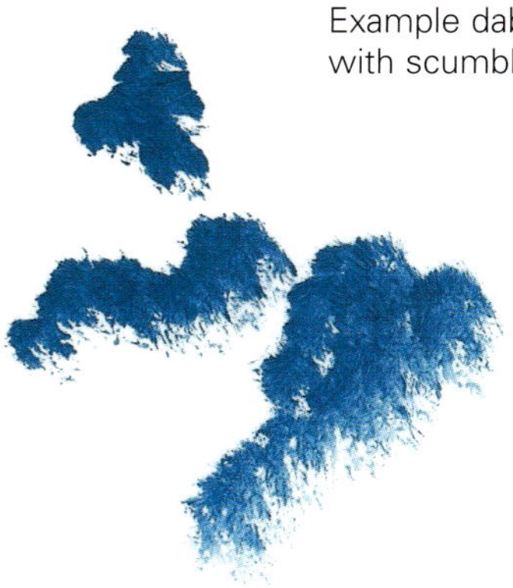

Cerulean Blue

1. Dab first color.

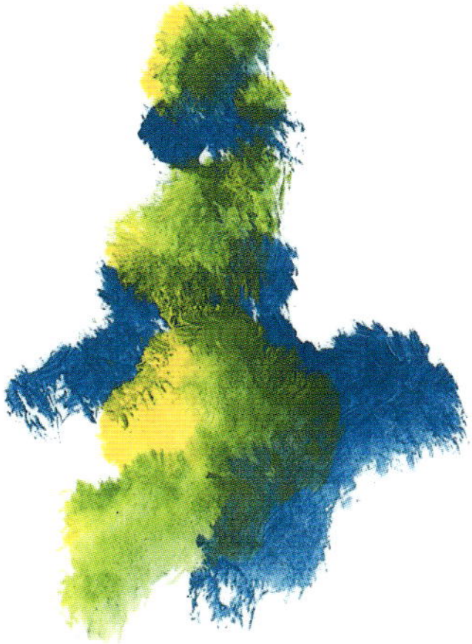

Cadmium Yellow Medium

2. Dab second color.

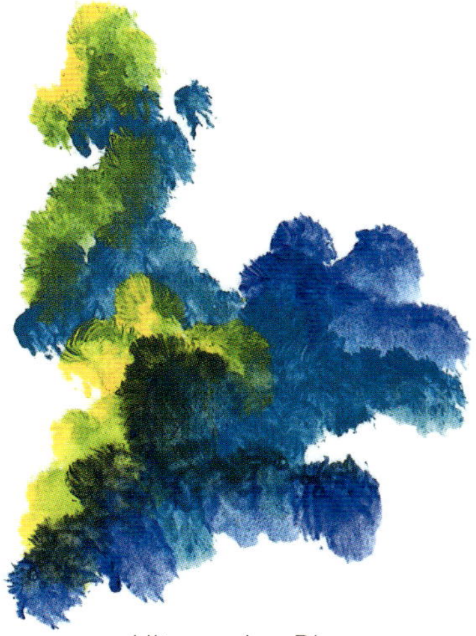

Ultramarine Blue

3. Dab third color.

Dabbing overlapping color areas while they are still wet yields a wide variety of intermediate colors as the colors mix on the canvas.

Glazes

Glazing techniques layer a thinned transparent color over an area of dried paint. The bottom color shows through the top, transparent one, and the eye blends the colors. Glazed color can be built in layers, one glaze over another, giving rich and subtle results.

- Wonderful for shadows, sunbeams, and adding unifying thin films of color to clumps of foliage.
- Generally, transparent or semi-transparent colors are used for glazing.
- Very thin semi-opaque or opaque colors yield an interesting misty or dusty look.
- Glaze will "catch" in any surface texture. If you want very smooth glazes, keep your painting smooth.

APPLYING GLAZES

1. Paint the underlying layer. Allow it to dry thoroughly.
2. Thin the glazing color with water or glazing medium. Mix until glaze is smooth, with no clumps.
3. Apply a coat of the glaze with a large brush. Allow it to dry thoroughly.
4. Add as many layers as you like, drying after each layer.

Even glaze

Graduated glaze with large side-loaded brush

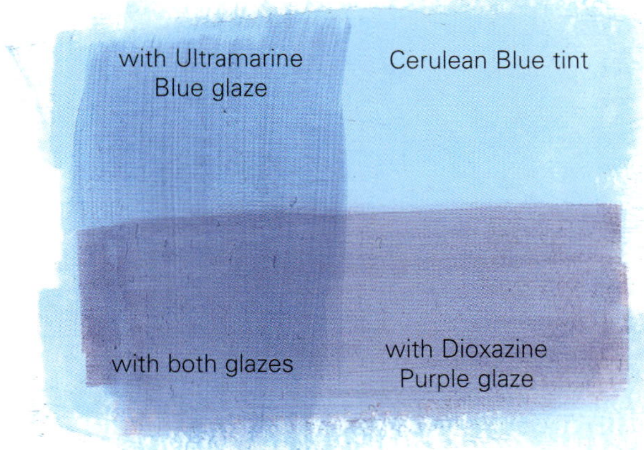

Overlapping glazes

Glaze of opaque color Titanium White

GLAZING TRANSPARENT COLORS

When you make a tint of a transparent color (such as Sap Green, Burnt Sienna, and Burnt Umber) by adding white, the result is often chalky and dull. To maintain luminosity, undercoat with white, then paint over the white with a glaze of the transparent color. This gives the effect of a tint of the transparent color but has a richer look - like a sheet of colored cellophane laid over white.

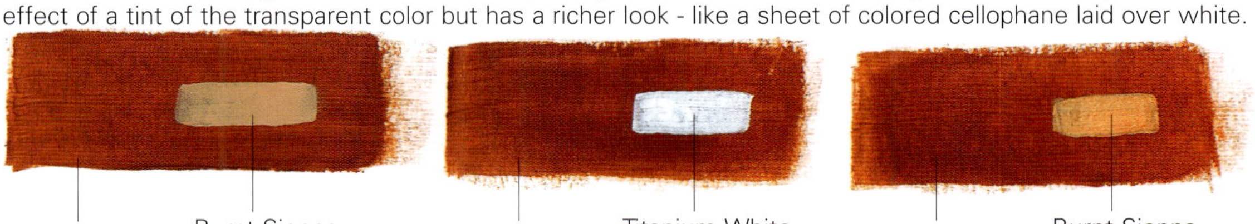

Burnt Sienna — Burnt Sienna mixed with Titanium White

Burnt Sienna — Titanium White

Burnt Sienna — Burnt Sienna glaze over Titanium White

Chapter 4

LANDSCAPE ELEMENTS

Artists compose many beautiful landscapes from water, rock, and plant life, but sometimes a landscape painting benefits from the addition of a few animals or a hint of human civilization.

Not only are trees the mainstay of many landscapes, they're fun to paint. Each seems to have its own personality expressed in the slant of the trunk, the pattern of the branches, and the shape of the foliage. In fact, the form of each tree reflects the conditions - weather, ground, and flora and fauna companions - that it grew up in.

Trees may be the major vegetation in many landscapes, but the lower growth of bushes, brambles, and vines adds texture not only in a planned garden, but also in the wild.

I am constantly amazed at the variety of skies and clouds. The colors are gorgeous, even on a stormy day. The weather determines the quality of light in a landscape, so it determines the warmth or coolness of colors, the value contrasts, and the sharpness of details.

There's no way to avoid the fact that water is complicated, with its reflections, depths, waves, and ripples. But ponds, lakes, and streams (the ocean is beyond the scope of this book) are beautiful additions to the landscape, and I encourage you to plunge in!

For me, nothing enlivens the landscape like animals. Because they are painted so small it is critical to recognize and capture their essence, both in appearance and in gesture. Keep people small and simple, too, so they won't attract all the attention to themselves. As with animals, it is important to capture the proportions and gesture when painting a small figure.

Boats and docks, flower containers, or outdoor furniture such as benches and chairs often find a place in a landscape painting. Use your imagination to add a touch of life to your paintings!

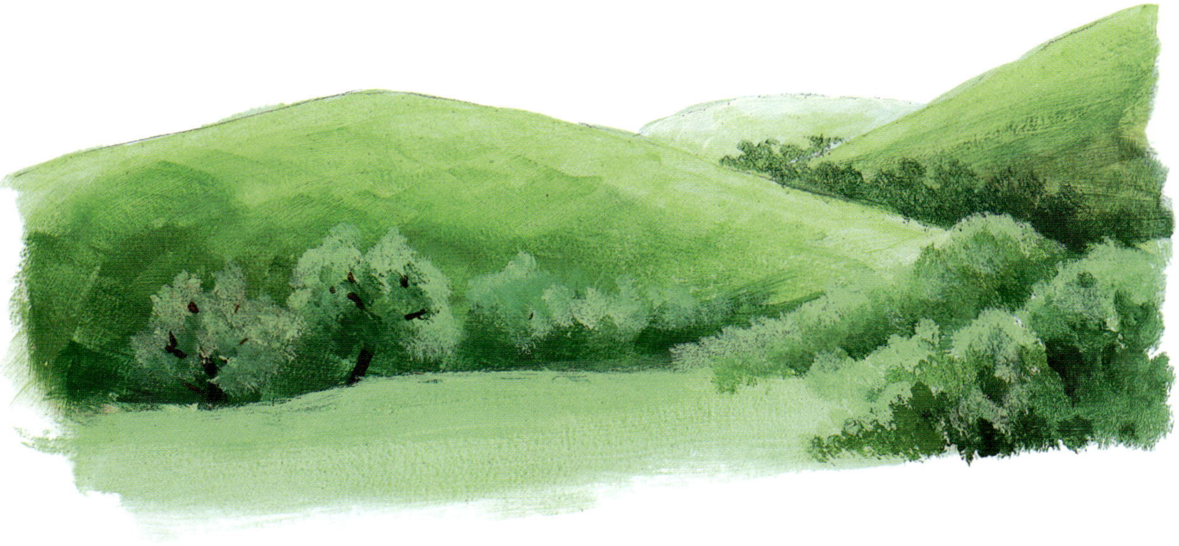

Deciduous Winter Tree

Deciduous trees show their shapes in winter - bare branches against winter sky. Observe the color and texture of the bark; some bare trees have a red cast, and others a green. There may be moss or lichen, or even mistletoe, especially on oaks. Observe the trees around you and paint the ones you know.

Shadow
#3 Round
Glaze mix Ultramarine Blue/Burnt Umber
Deepest color, most defined edges close to trunk.

Shadows consistent with light source.

Straight shadows - smooth ground.

Wavy shadows - undulations in the snow.

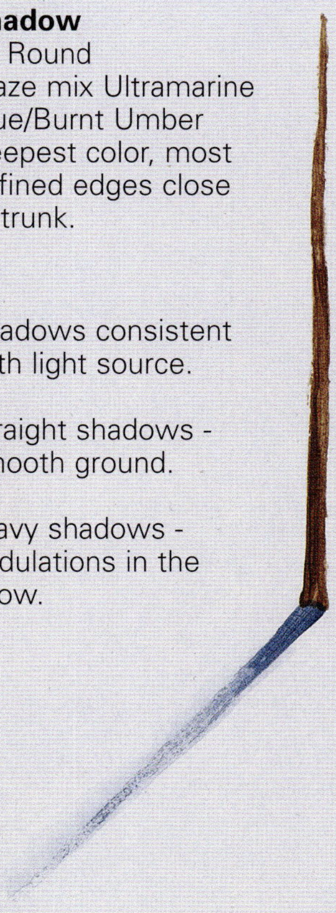

Light source at 2 o'clock

Trunk & branches
Burnt Umber
Raw Umber
Burnt Sienna
Use randomly; variation adds interest.

#1 Liner
Lay strokes side by side for width.
Multiple strokes give texture.

Begin with the trunk. Stroke upward from ground.

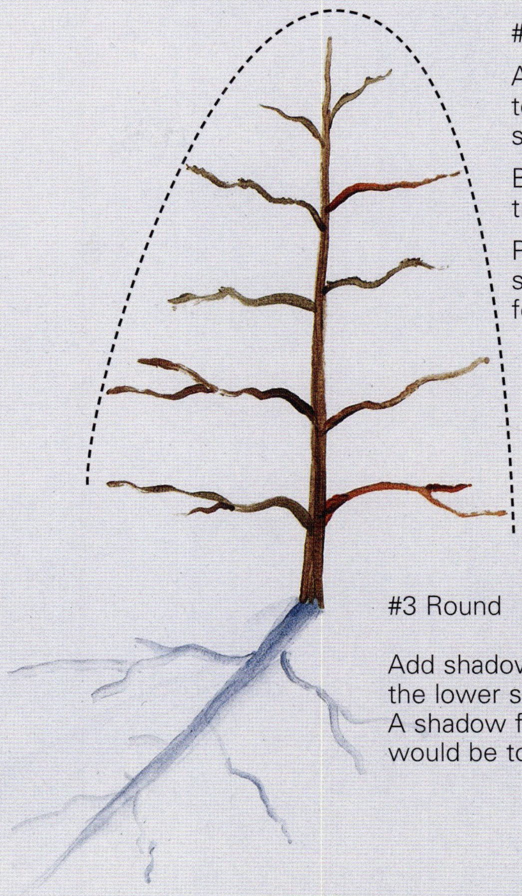

#1 Liner

Add side branches to define silhouette.

Begin strokes at trunk, pull outward.

Place branches slightly unevenly for interest.

#3 Round

Add shadows for a few of the lower side branches. A shadow for each branch would be too much.

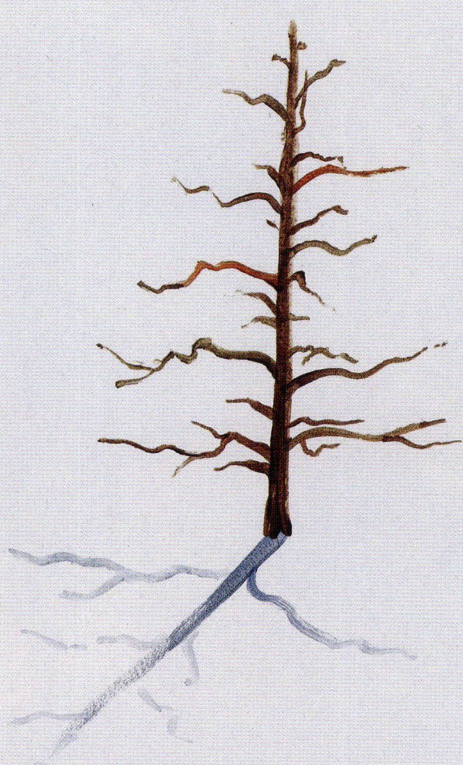

#1 Liner

Paint side branches that are growing toward or away from the viewer. These *foreshortened* branches appear shorter than the side branches that define the silhouette.

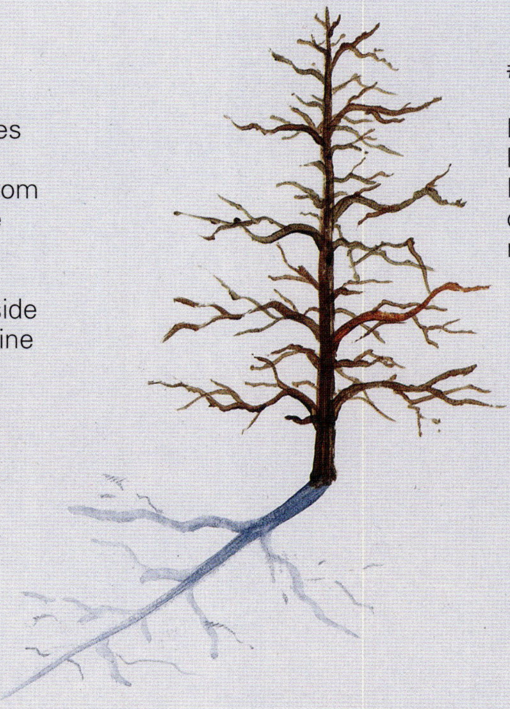

#00 Liner

Finally, add lots of little branches. Many cross each other, giving a more natural look.

A Selection of Deciduous Winter Trees

The trunk and branching structure of trees are as distinctive as their leaves. Trunks may be single, branched, or clustered. Branches may be upright or drooping. The angles of the crotches - where a sice branch connects to a main branch - may be narrow or wide. And the tree's silhouette may be round, conical, teardrop, or boxy. Some trees, like sumac or willow, grow in thick clusters.

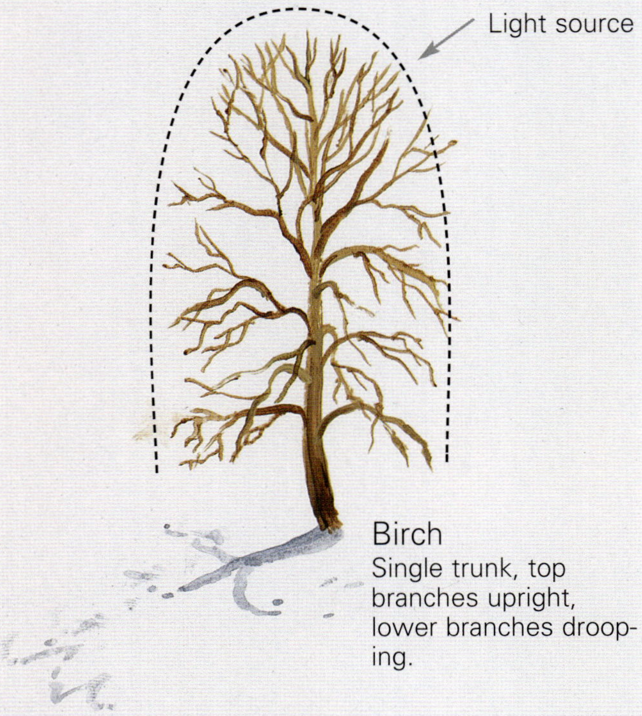

Birch
Single trunk, top branches upright, lower branches drooping.

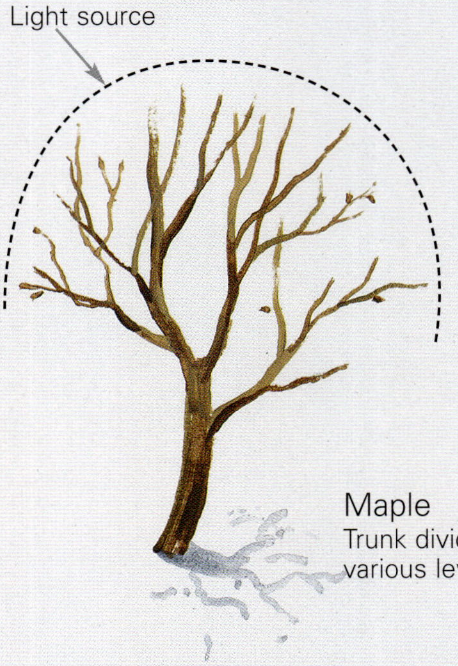

Maple
Trunk divides at various levels.

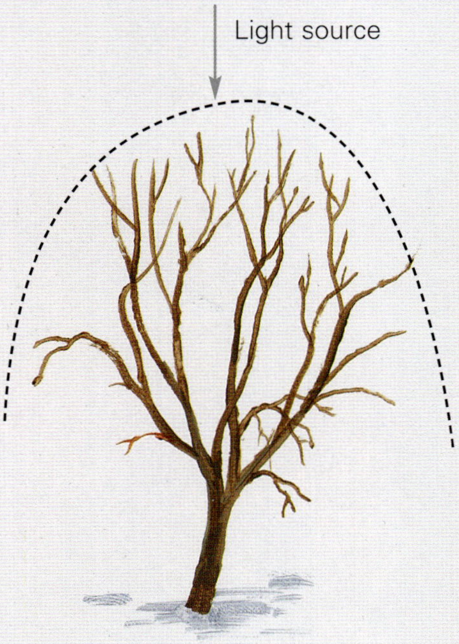

Elm
Trunk divides into many branches at a single height. Branches are strongly upright.

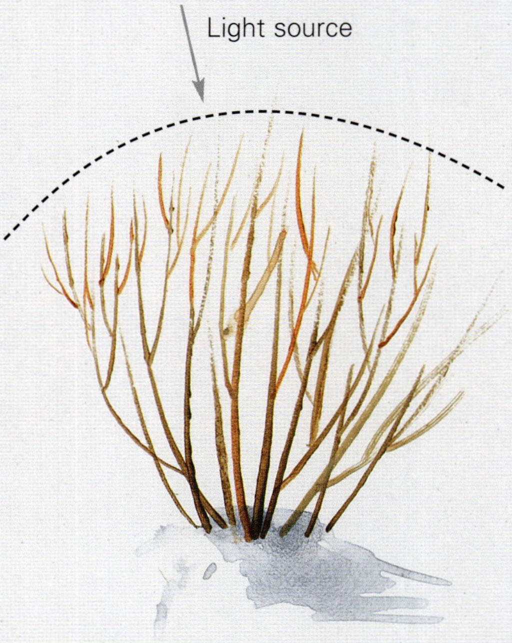

Willow
Grows in clumps of multiple trunks. Side branches attach at narrow angles.

Groups of Winter Deciduous Trees

SAME SPECIES

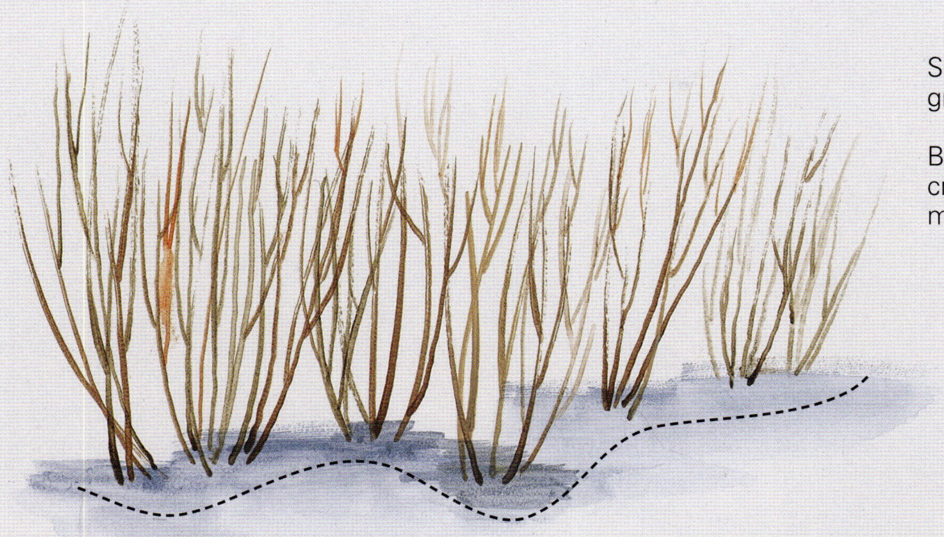

Some shrubby trees grow in thick groups.

Branches overlap, creating an interesting mass.

Their bases can form a line which becomes a composition element in a landscape.

Very light washes can suggest lots of tiny twigs.

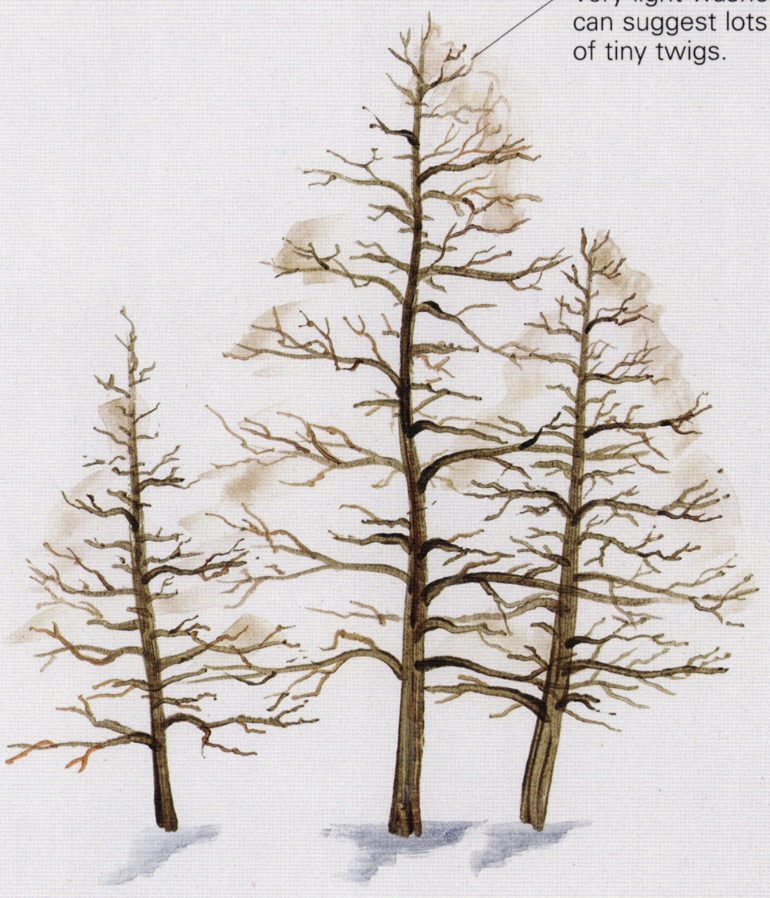

In groups where the individual trees are visible:

- Paint the trunks at different angles, with the outside trees angling away from the group.
- Include a variety of heights and trunk sizes.
- Use a variety of colors. The smaller branches with newer bark tend to be the most colorful.
- If you have only a few trees in the group, an odd number usually works best.

Groups of Winter Deciduous Trees

DIFFERENT SPECIES

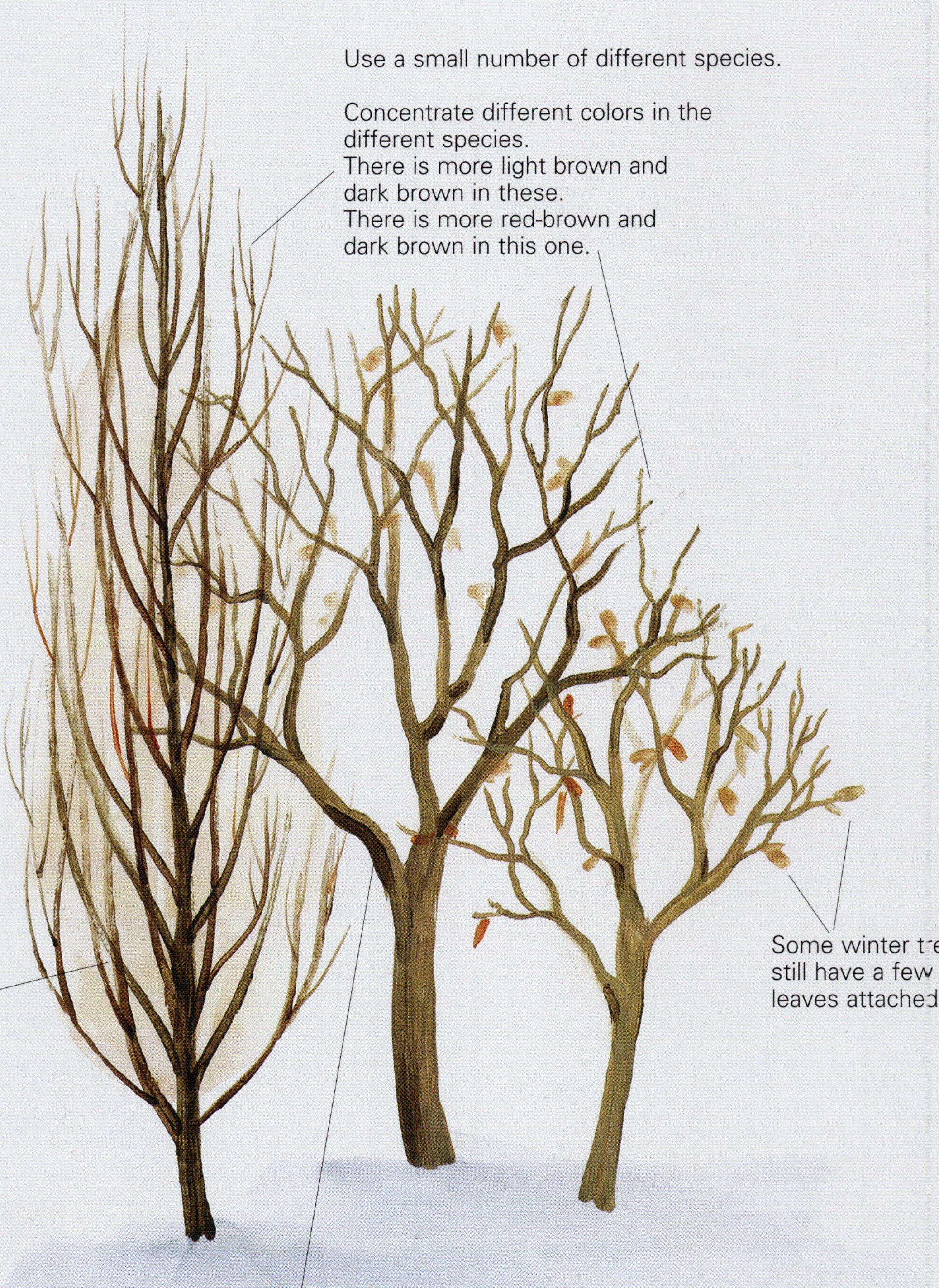

Spring Deciduous Tree

For the foliage, mix the medium, light, and very light colors in the Sap Green sequence. Spring foliage is very light, so you don't need the darker colors. This series is transparent and warm.

Sap Green Sequence

Refer to Page 27 for mixing instructions.

medium:
Sap Green
+ Cadmium
Yellow Dark

light:
medium mix
+ Cadmium
Yellow Light

very light:
light mix
+ Titanium
White

Trunk & branches
#1 Liner
Burnt Umber
Raw Umber
Burnt Sienna

Begin with the trunk, branches, and shadow.

Shadow
#3 Round
Glaze mix
Ultramarine Blue/Burnt Umber

The mottled ring is the shadow of foliage. For a soft look, dampen surface first with clear water.

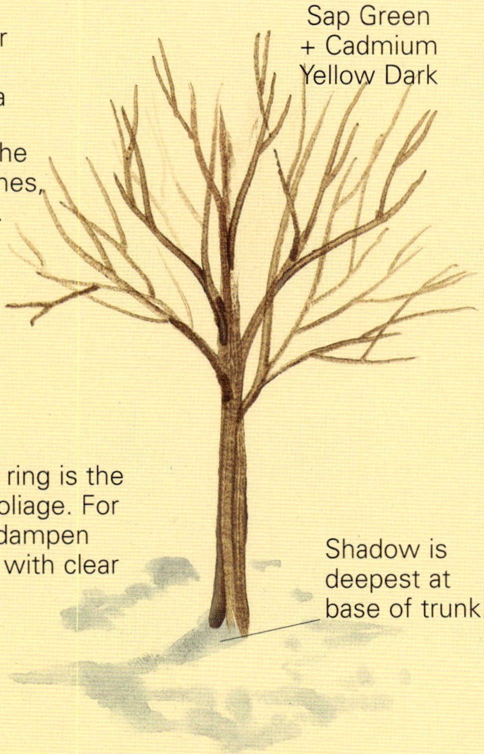

Shadow is deepest at base of trunk.

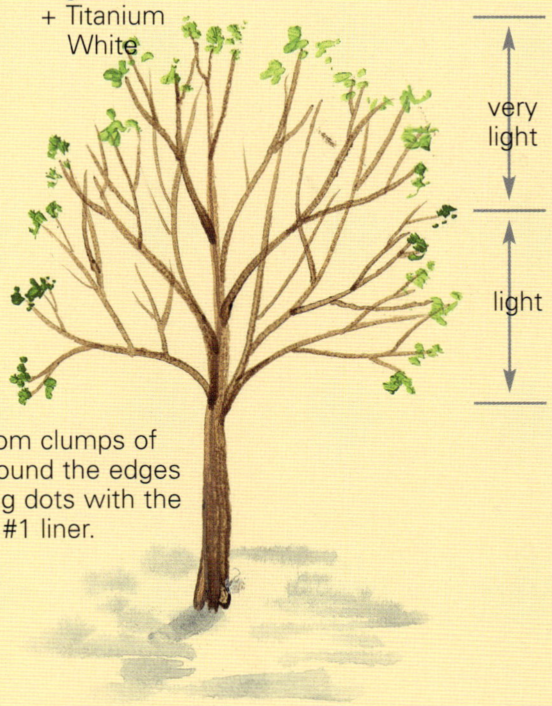

Add random clumps of foliage around the edges by painting dots with the tip of the #1 liner.

Fill in center with random foliage clumps.

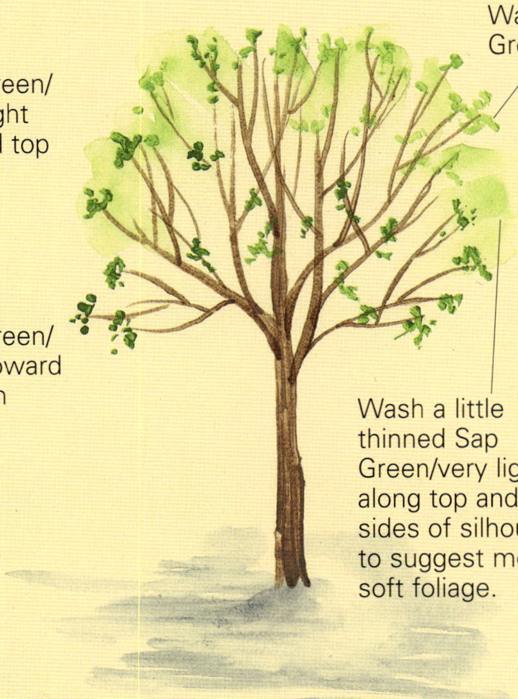

Sap Green/very light toward top

Sap Green/light toward bottom

Wash of Sap Green/light

Wash a little thinned Sap Green/very light along top and sides of silhouette to suggest more soft foliage.

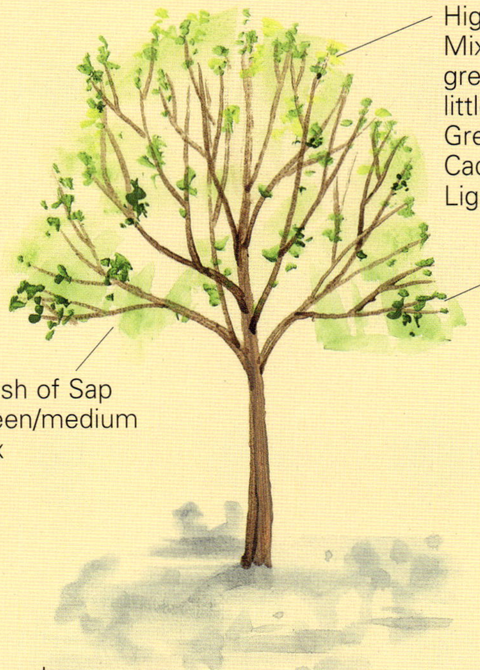

Highlight dots
Mix a very yellow green by adding a little of the Sap Green/very light to Cadmium Yellow Light.

Dots
Sap Green/medium mix

Wash of Sap Green/medium mix

Increase value range:
- Add a light wash of Sap Green/medium toward the bottom.
- Add dots of Sap Green/medium foliage here and there.
- Add highlight dots along the top, toward the light source.

A Selection of Spring Trees

To paint new spring foliage tinged with other colors, begin by dabbing in the greens with a scumbler brush. When the greens are dry, wash over them with very thin brown, red, or orange. Side-load the brush with the wash and paint short, uneven strokes, keeping the loaded side of the brush toward the outside of the tree.

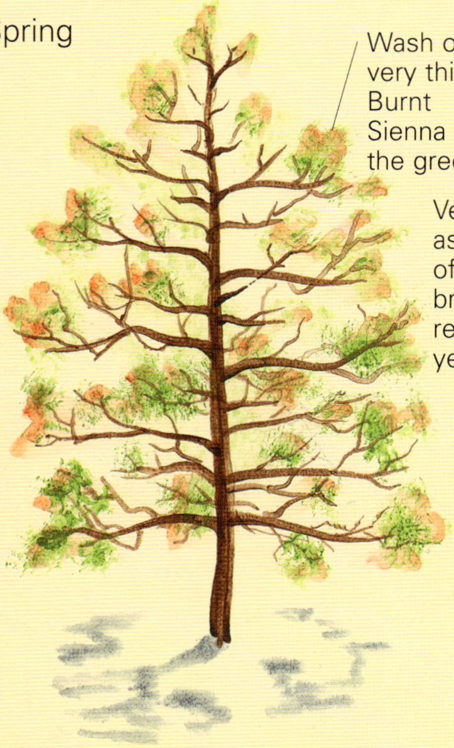

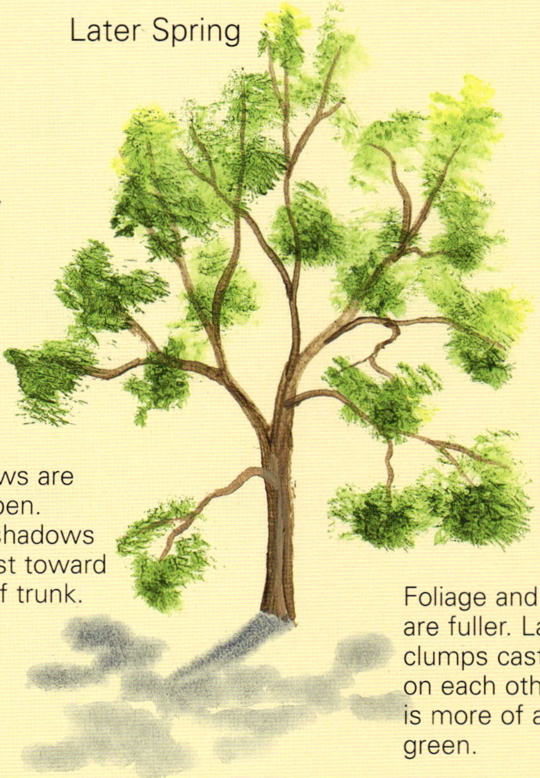

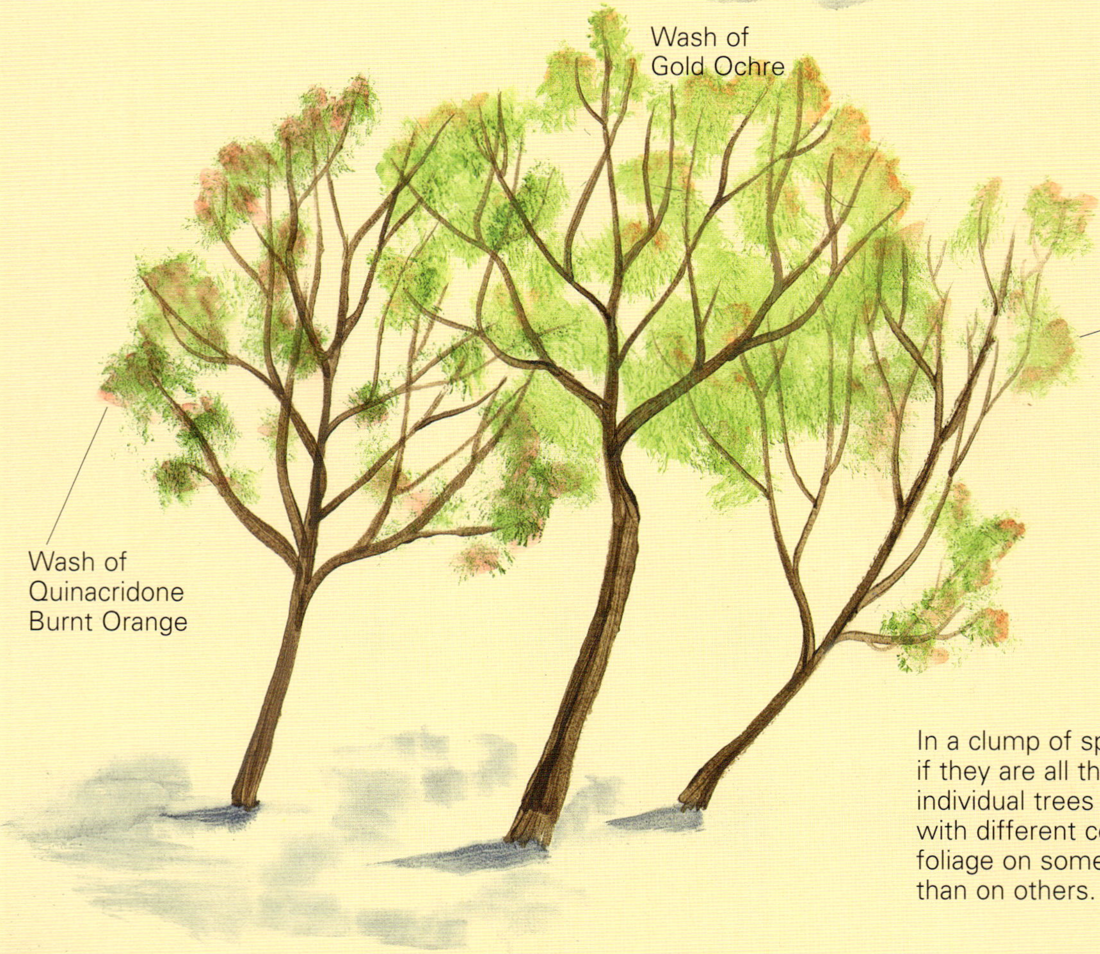

Spring Fruit Trees

Blooming fruit trees provide spectacular displays of white, pink, or coral blossoms. Many species bloom before the leaves come out, and the trees appear as clouds of color. In orchards, trees grow in neat rows rather than in the random patterns of the wild.

Fruit trees are pruned to an even, open form and are usually kept relatively small.

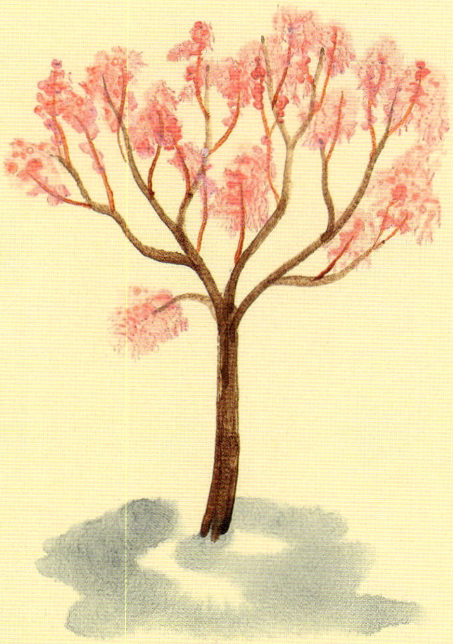

Some, like peaches, bloom before the leaves emerge.

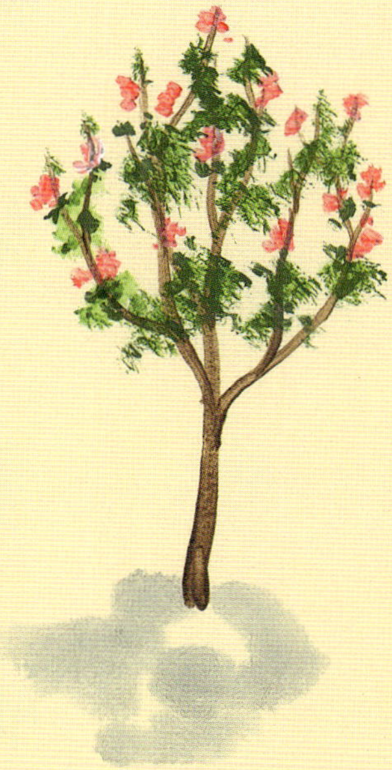

Others, like apples, bloom while the leaves are small.

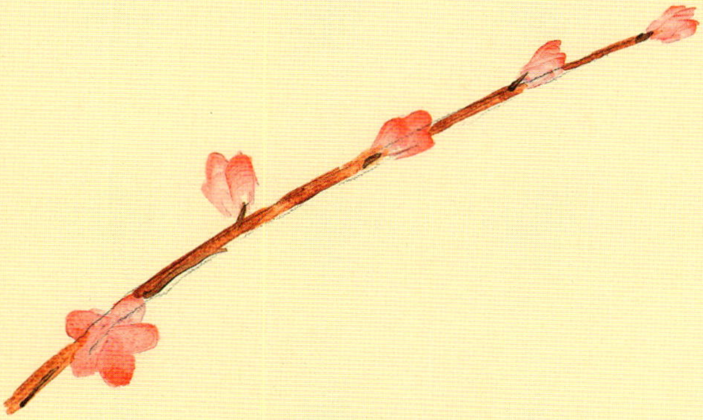

Some, like peaches, bloom singly, evenly, and only on wood that was new the previous season.

The color of the flowers seems to coat the ends of the branches.

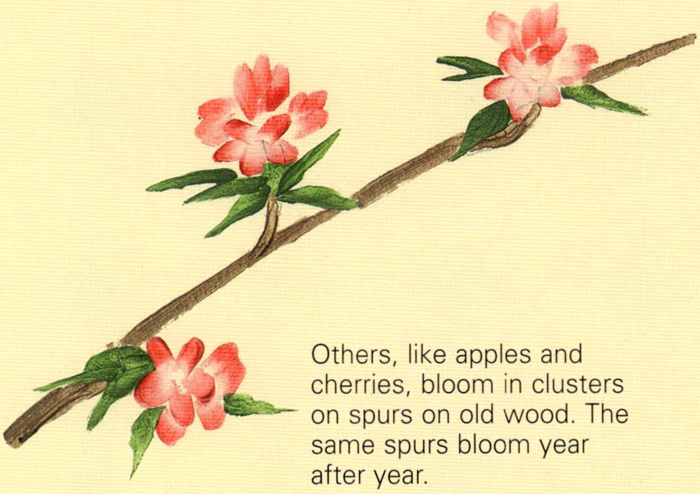

Others, like apples and cherries, bloom in clusters on spurs on old wood. The same spurs bloom year after year.

Summer Tree

Summer foliage reveals only the trunk and small sections of branches. Tree forms are clumps of rich, full foliage in tones of green, varied only by bright highlights on the sunny side and deep shadows on the dark side. This is a season saturated with green, but with rich value contrast. To paint the foliage, mix the Chromium Oxide Green sequence because it is the most opaque.

Chromium Oxide Green Sequence

Refer to page 24 for mixing instructions.

very dark:	dark:	medium:	light:	very light:
dark mix + Mars Black	Chromium Oxide Green + Cadmium Red Deep	Sap Green + Cadmium Yellow Dark	medium mix + Cadmium Yellow Light	light mix + Titanium White

Trunk & branches
Burnt Umber
Raw Umber
Burnt Sienna

Shadow
Glaze mix
Ultramarine Blue/
Burnt Umber

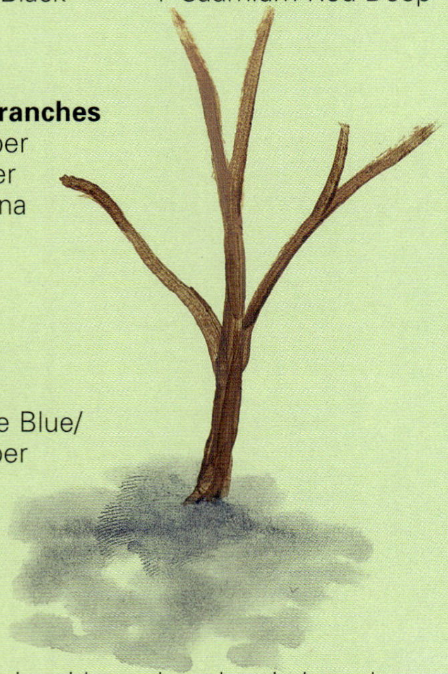

- Begin with trunk and main branches.
- Make shadow dark, with few light spots.

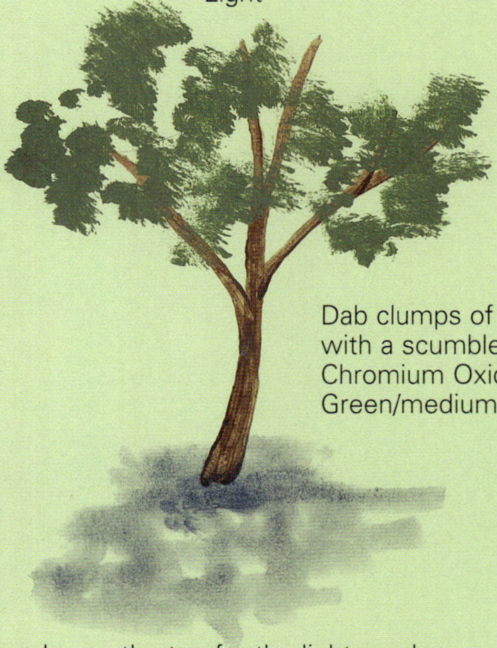

Dab clumps of foliage with a scumbler and Chromium Oxide Green/medium

Leave the top for the lighter color, and leave plenty of "sky holes."

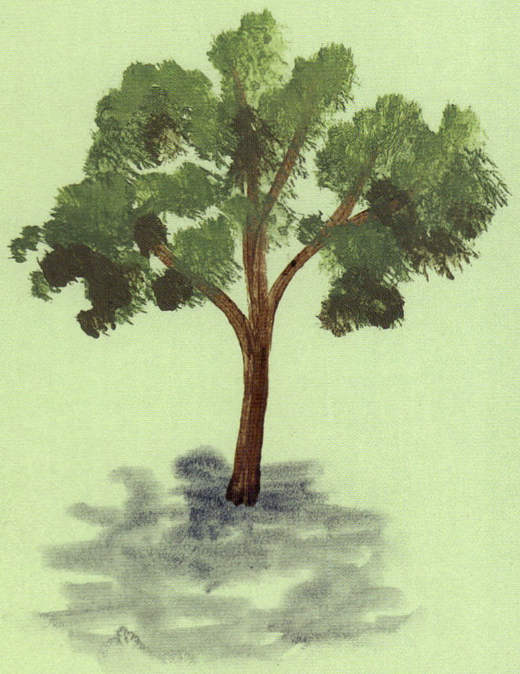

- While wet, scumble Chromium Oxide Green/light at top of tree and at tops of large foliage clumps.
- Scumble Chromium Oxide Green/dark to shade bottoms of clumps.
- Foliage clumps should appear rounded.

Add a few small branches with a liner.

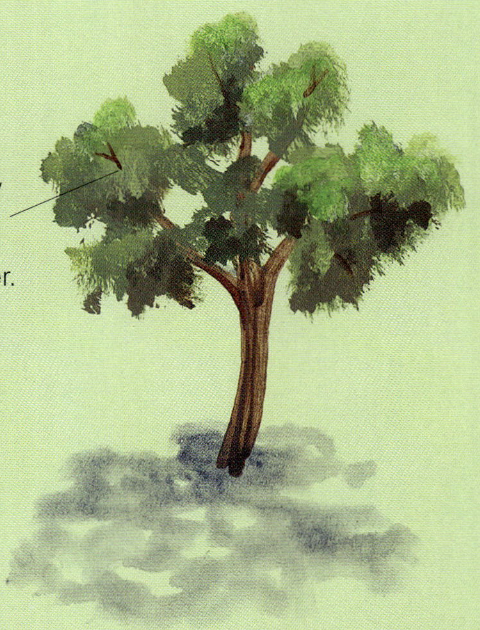

- Lighten brightest highlights by scumbling with Chromium Oxide Green/very light.
- Deepen darkest shadows by scumbling with Chromium Oxide Green/very dark.

Selection of Summer Trees

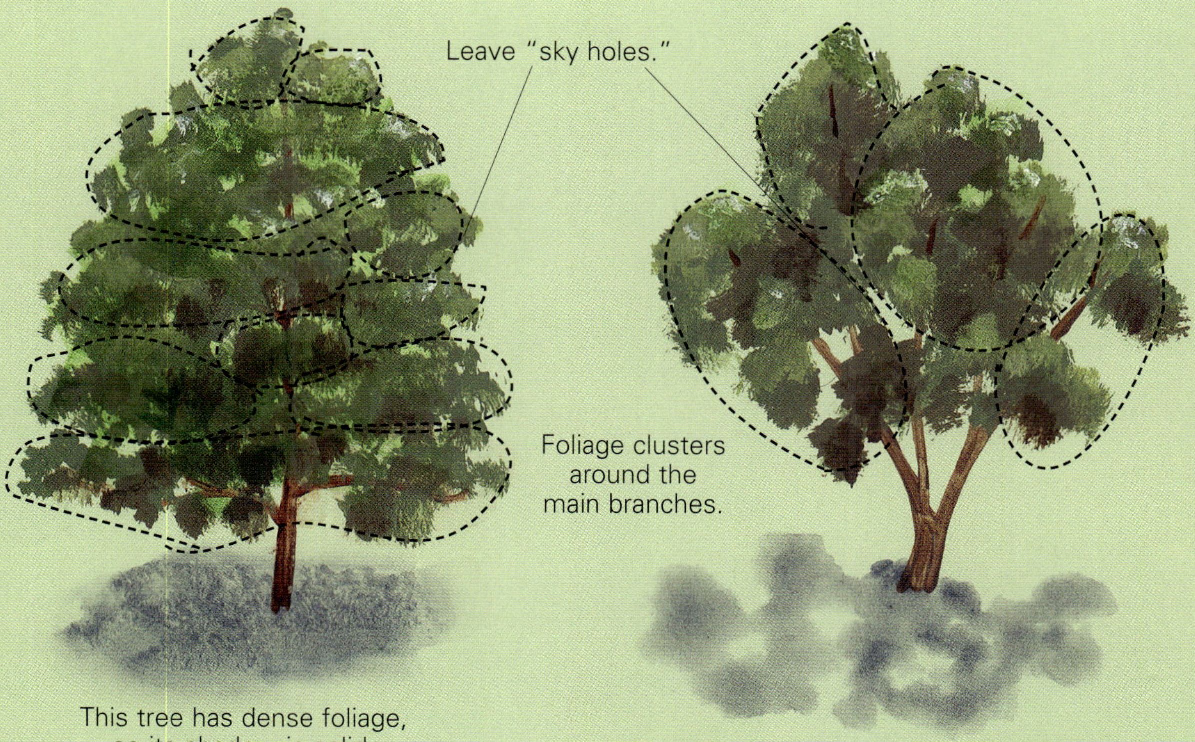

This tree has dense foliage, so its shadow is solid.

This tree has open spaces between foliage clusters, so the shadow is mottled.

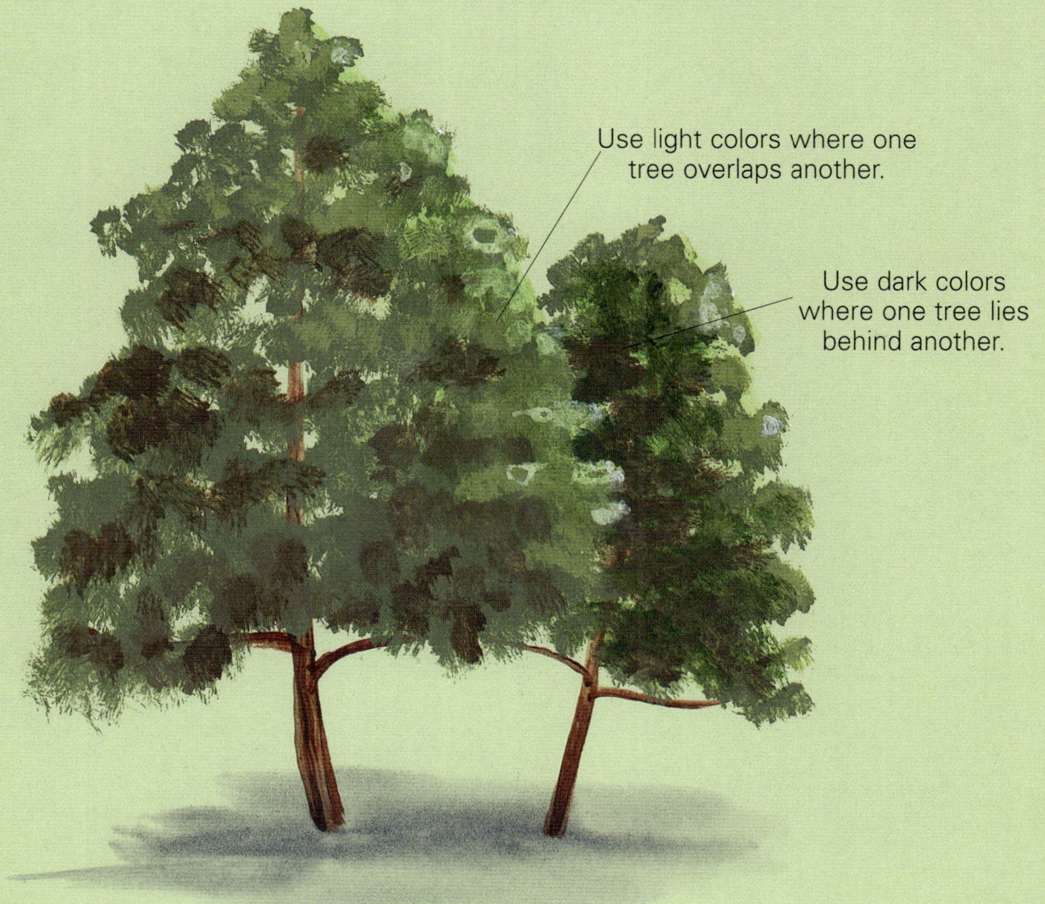

Autumn Tree

Leaves turn autumn colors when green chlorophyll recedes as trees go dormant for winter - the yellows of oaks, ash, and hickory; the reds, oranges, and yellows of maples. On some species, berries ripen and add even more color.

All the trees of a species turn the same general color, but individuals may show variation. For example, some ashes may be a pale yellow and others a golden yellow. There is color variation within the same tree. Some leaves turn color more quickly than others, and shadows and highlights come into play.

Mixing Colors for Autumn Trees

Select the main foliage color and dull it slightly with its complementary color. Starting from the dulled main foliage color, mix a few darker and lighter color variations.

Mix the medium shade from the Phthalo Green sequence. *(Refer to Page 25 for mixing instructions.)* Autumn foliage often has some green in it. The green mixes with the foliage color to give a dark color, shading the clumps of leaves.

Trunk & branches
Burnt Umber
Raw Umber
Burnt Sienna

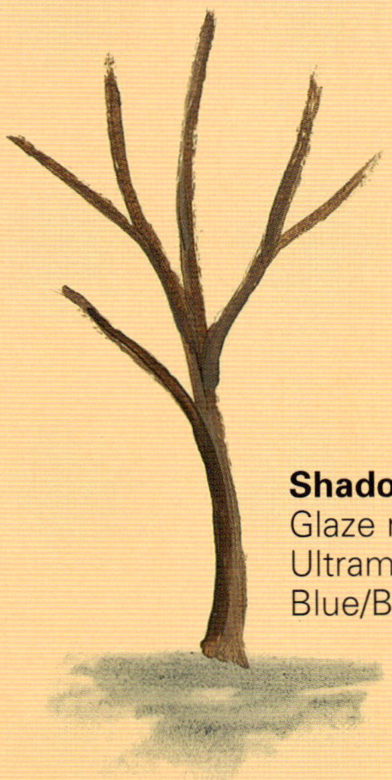

The process for painting an autumn tree is the same as for painting a summer tree except for the foliage colors.

Shadow
Glaze mix
Ultramarine Blue/Burnt Umber

Begin with the trunk, main branches, and shadow.

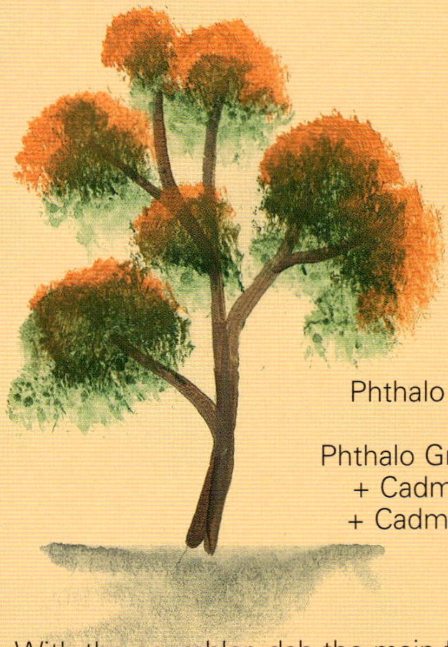

Dulled Orange:

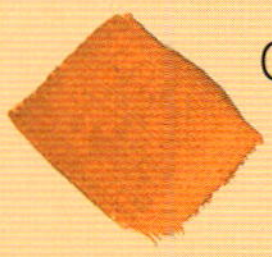

Cadmium Orange + Ultramarine Blue

Phthalo Green Sequence medium:
Phthalo Green (Yellow Shade) + Cadmium Yellow Light + Cadmium Red Medium

With the scumbler, dab the main foliage color (orange) at the top of the foliage clumps, and green at the bottom. Dab repeatedly to blend where colors overlap.

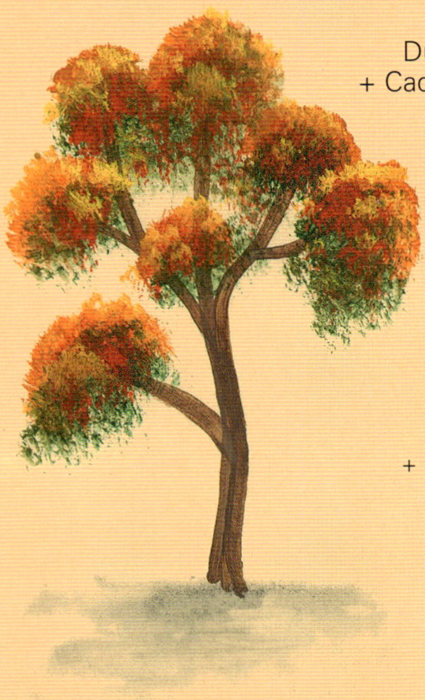

Red-Orange:
Dulled orange mix + Cadmium Red Medium

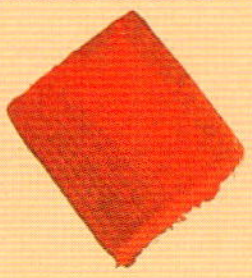

Yellow-Orange:
Dulled orange mix + Cadmium Yellow Deep

- Dab darker foliage color (red-orange) around bottoms of foliage clumps, covering much, but not all of the green.
- Highlight upper edges of clumps, and some random areas within them, with light foliage color (yellow-orange).

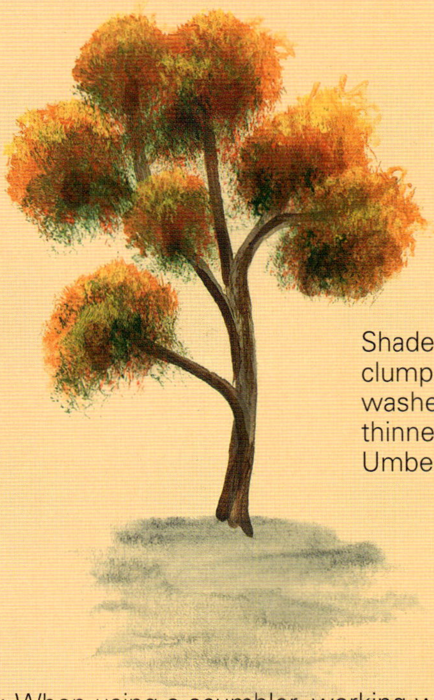

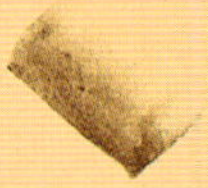

Burnt Umber wash

Shade foliage clumps with washes of thinned Burnt Umber.

Tip: When using a scumbler, working wet-in-wet blends the colors. If you are getting too much "mud," let one color dry before applying the next.

A Selection of Autumn Trees

These tree colors are based on the mixed colors from Page 46.

Yellow Version

- Base foliage color is yellow-orange mix.
- Dab in Burnt Umber for dark areas.

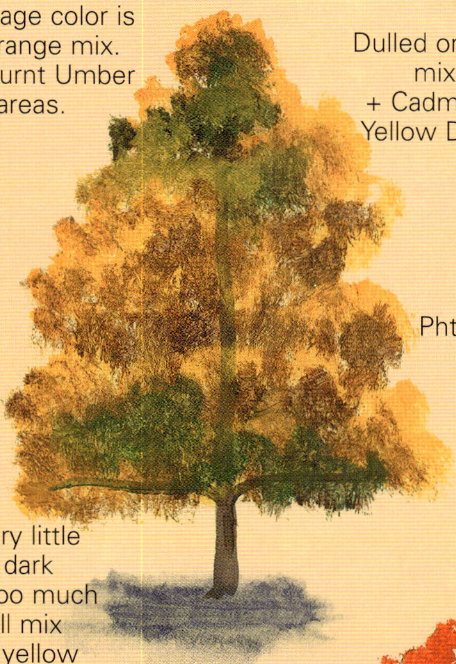

- Add a very little green to dark areas. (Too much green will mix with the yellow and give a yellow-green, which isn't a fall color.)

Yellow-Orange:

Dulled orange mix + Cadmium Yellow Deep

Burnt Umber

Phthalo Green/medium

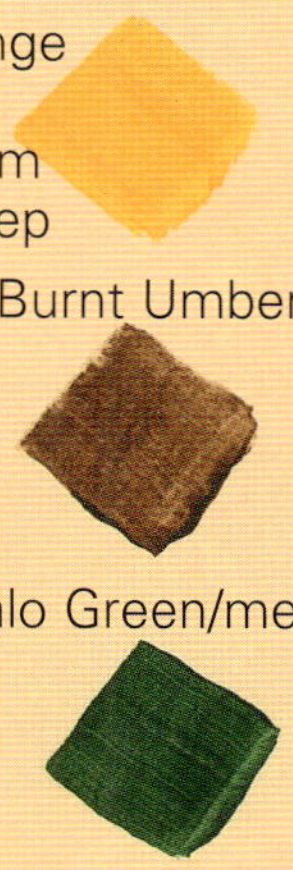

Red Version

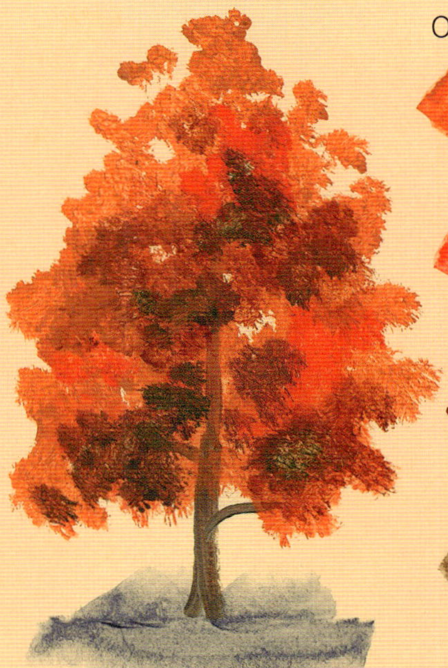

Red-Orange: Dulled orange mix + Cadmium Red Medium

Deeper Red-Orange: Red-orange mix + Cadmium

Burnt Sienna

Burnt Umber

Phthalo Green/ medium

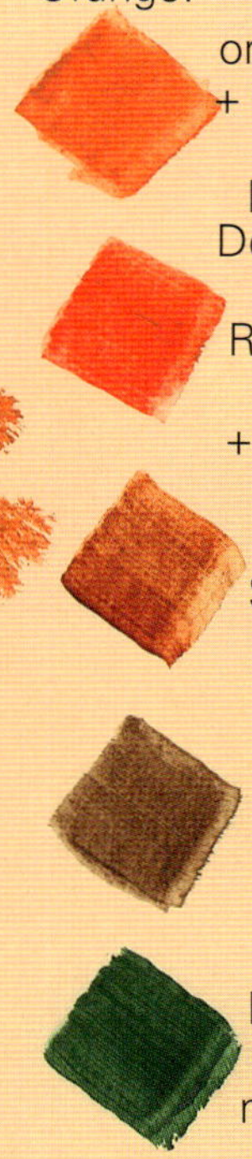

- Base foliage color is red-orange mix.
- Add a deeper red-orange here and there for color variation.
- Dab in Burnt Sienna, Burnt Umber, and Phthalo Green/medium for dark areas.

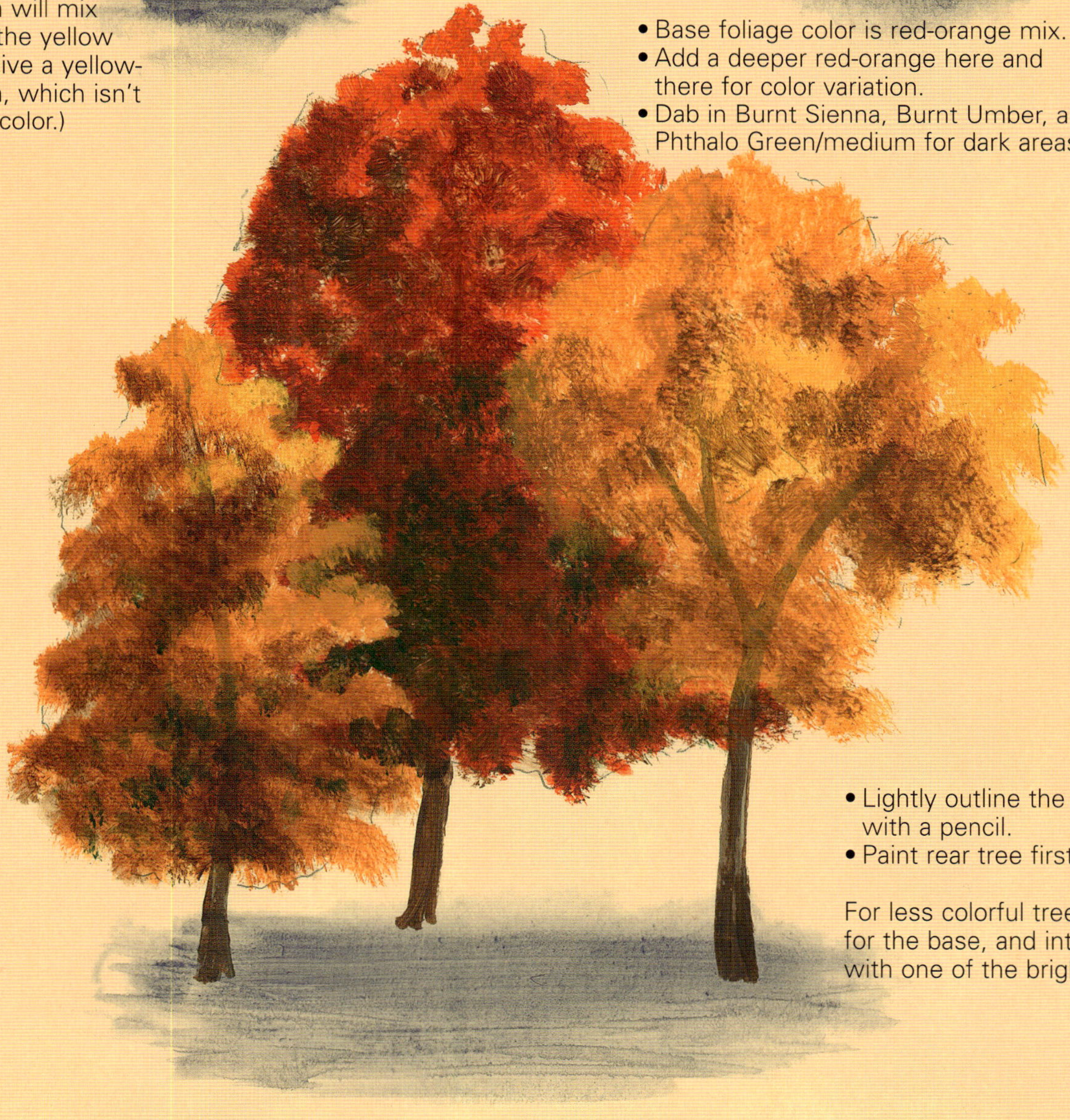

- Lightly outline the clumps of foliage with a pencil.
- Paint rear tree first.

For less colorful trees, use a light brown for the base, and intersperse it sparingly with one of the brighter colors.

Evergreen Tree

To paint a typical evergreen, mix the Cool Green sequence.
Refer to Page 25 for mixing instructions.

very dark:
dark mix
+ Mars Black

dark:
Cobalt Green Deep
+ Ultramarine Blue
+ Cadmium Red Deep

medium:
Cobalt Green Deep

light:
Cobalt Green Light

very light:
Titanium White
+ Cobalt Green Light
+ Cadmium Yellow
Light

Trunk & branches
Burnt Umber
Raw Umber
Burnt Sienna

Shadow
Glaze mixof
Ultramarine
Blue/
Burnt Umber

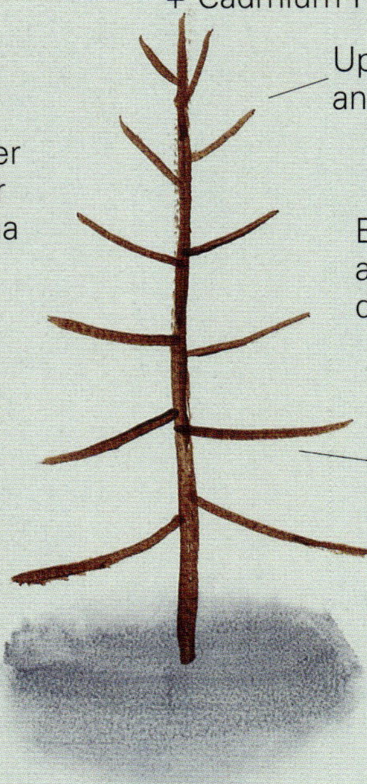

Upper branches angle upward.

Begin with the trunk and side branches to define the silhouette.

Bottom branches droop.

The shadow is dense, as is the foliage.

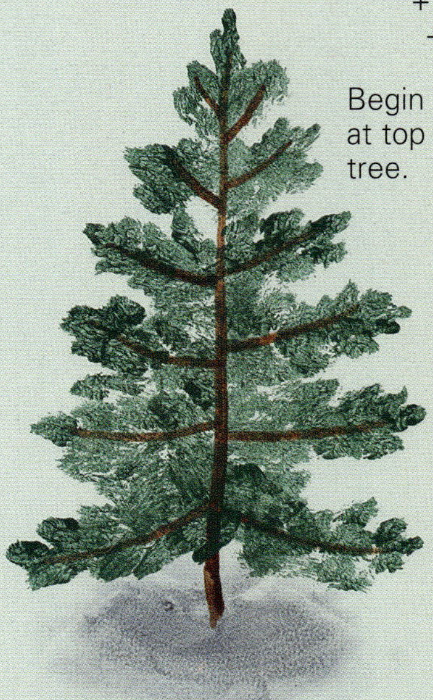

Begin at top of tree.

Leave some open space.

Dab in foliage with a scumbler and Cool Green/medium, following the branch structure.

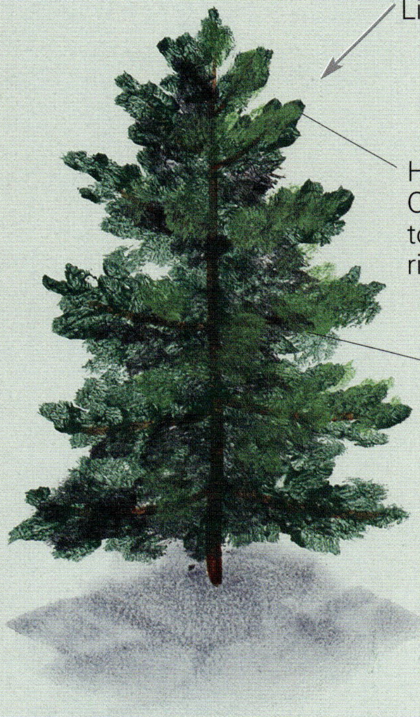

Light source

Highlight with Cool Green/light toward top and right side.

Shade with Cool Green/dark.

Concentrate shadows at bottom of tree and along undersides of branches.

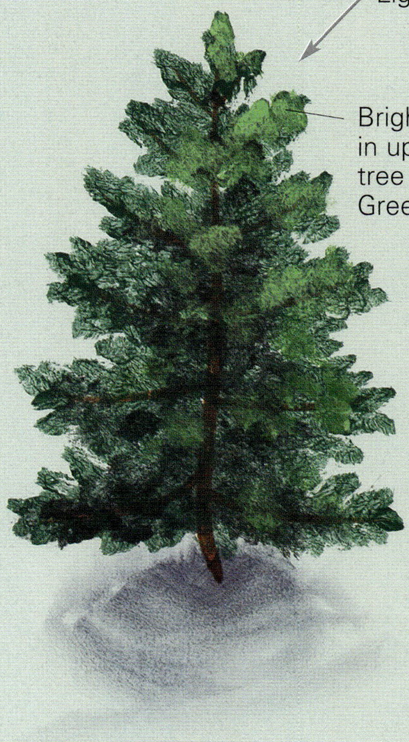

Light scurce

Brighten highlights in upper part of tree with Cool Green/very light.

Deepen darkest shadows with Cool Green/very dark.

Use highlights and shadows to form the shape of the tree and suggest branches.

Evergreens in Snow and Spring

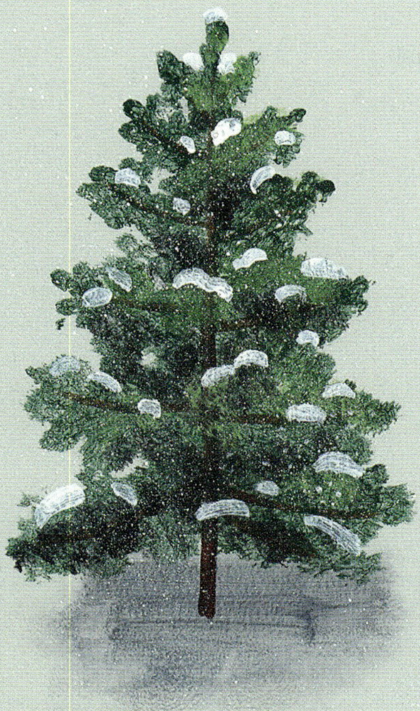

Snow clumps on the branches.

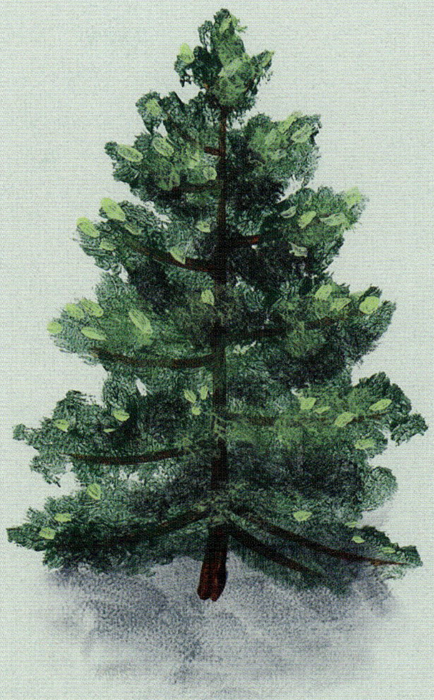

In spring, light green needle clusters – the year's new growth – appear at the tips of the branches.

Some pines have very open branch structures and long needles that grow in clumps. The needles begin high on the tree. A few lower, dead branches remain on the trunk.

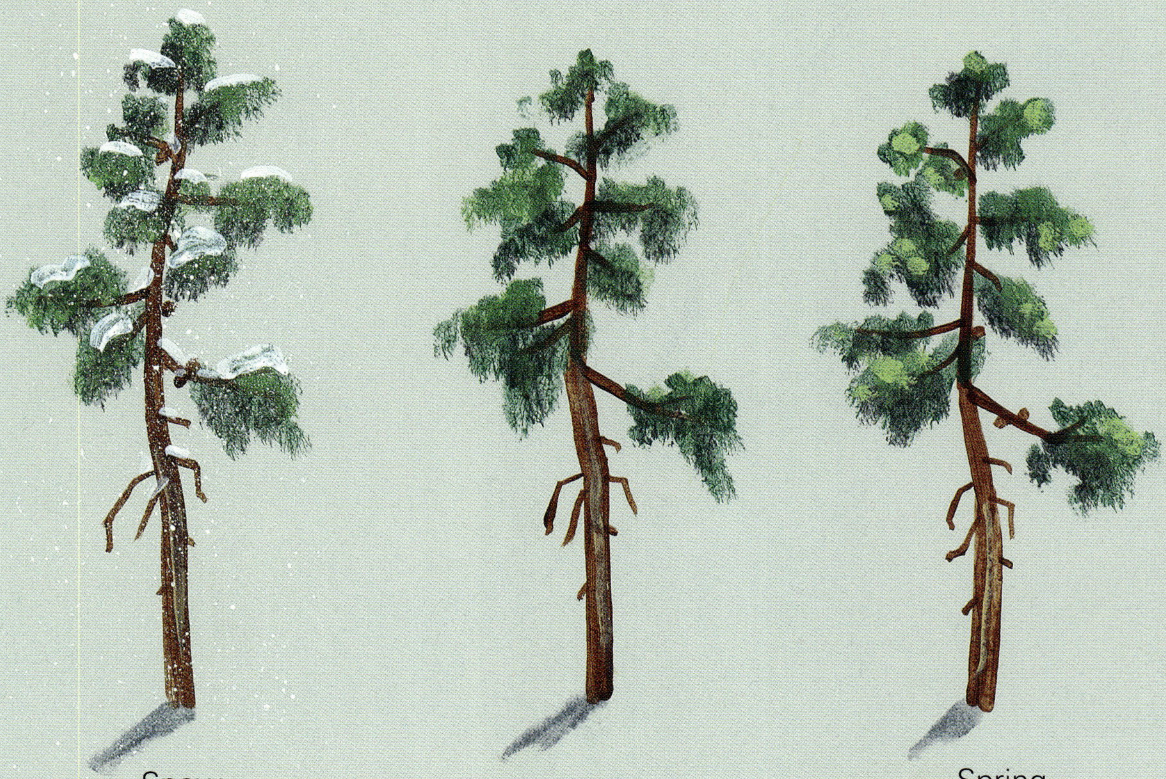

Snow

Spring

A Group of Pines

Work on the farthest tree first and the nearest tree last.

Use highlights and shadows to form and separate individual trees.

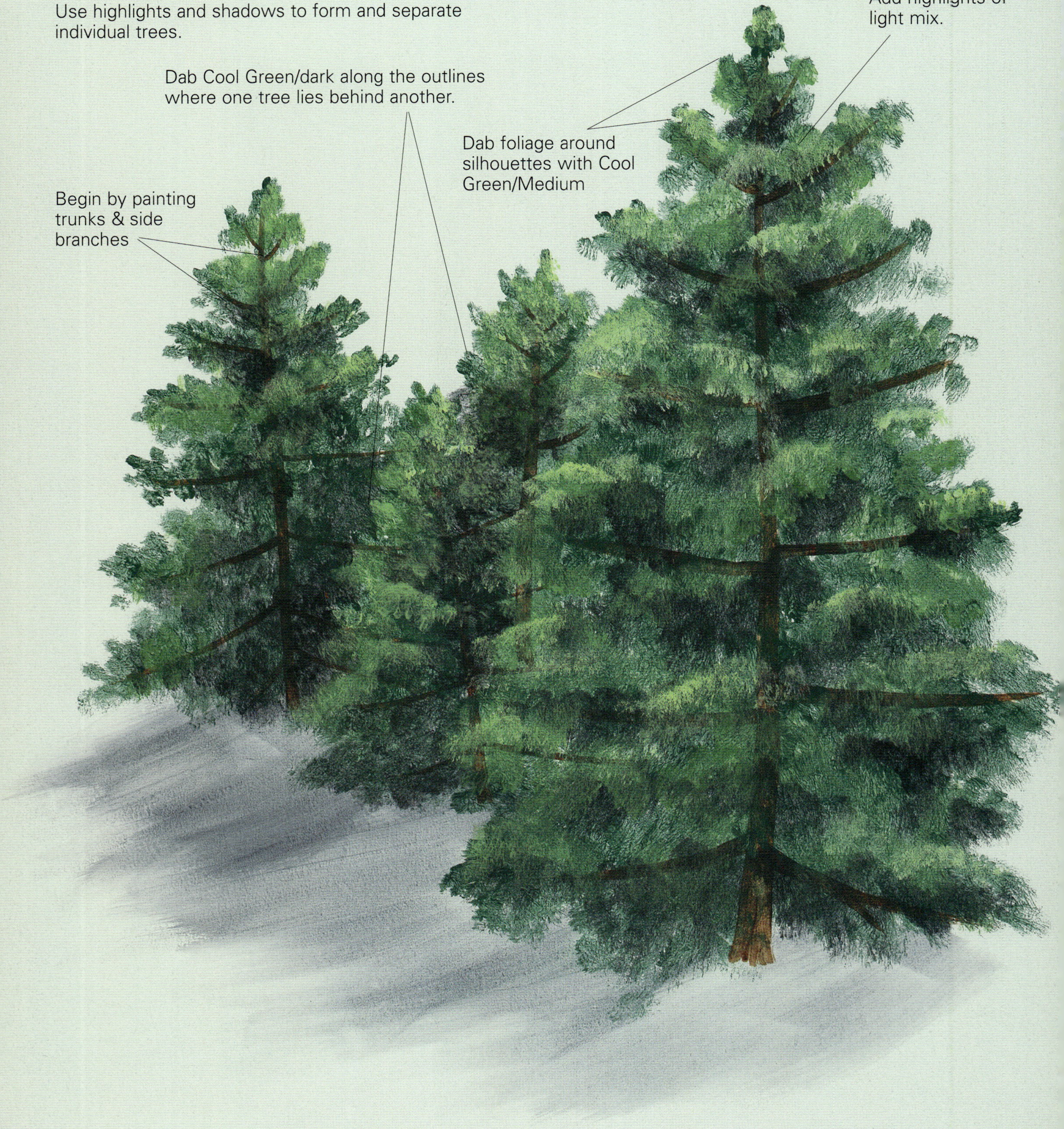

Brambles

The arched shapes and rough textures of brambles add interest to a landscape.

Shadow
Glaze mix
Ultramarine Blue/
Burnt Umber

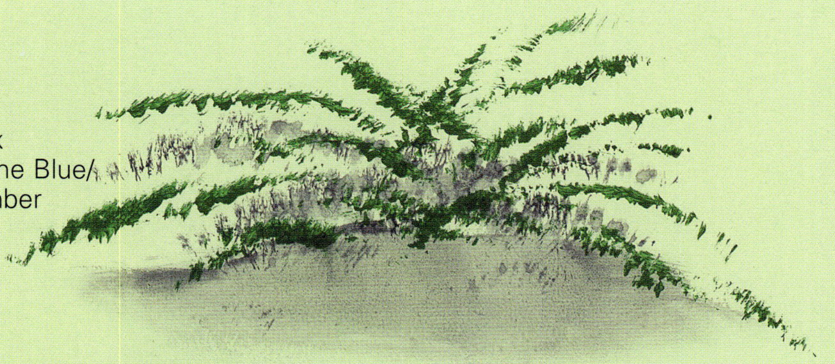

- With fan brush and medium green, paint arched lines in an irregular fan shape.
- Paint the shadow with a round brush.
- With the fan brush, add a few branches of the shadow color.

Fan Brush

The arched shape of the brush gives a rough, curved line of paint.

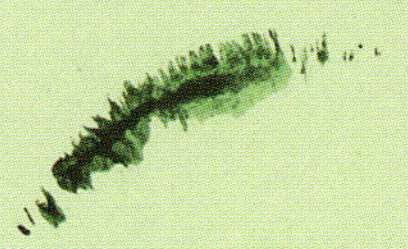

To paint an arching branch, touch tip of fan brush to surface.

Use a scumbler and a very dark green to thicken foliage at center and base of bramble.

Scumble some branches with the light green.

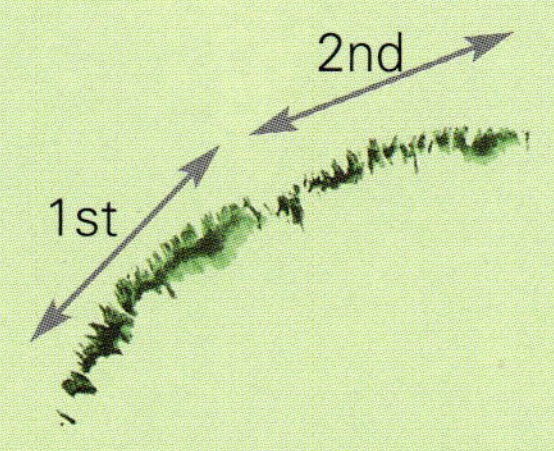

To lengthen the branch, touch brush tip to surface again, continuing the curved shape.

Indicate some branch stems with a #00 liner and Burnt Umber.

Dot berries with tip of liner.

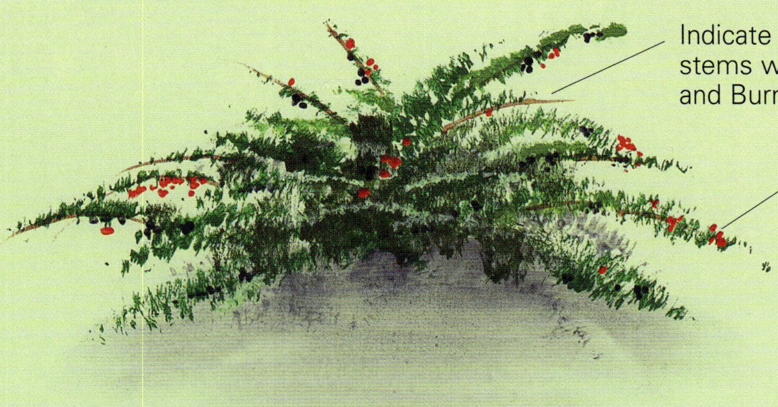

Use a fan brush and a very light green to paint some branches over the light area.

Shrubs

Some shrubs look like miniature trees, with single or multiple trunks. Others appear as clumps of foliage at ground level. Scumblers or fan brushes do a good job with shrub foliage. The fan is especially good for painting even, rounded shapes, as in rows of lavender plants.

Shrub with Visible Trunks

Trunks
Burnt Umber
Raw Umber
Burnt Sienna
Use randomly; variation adds interest.

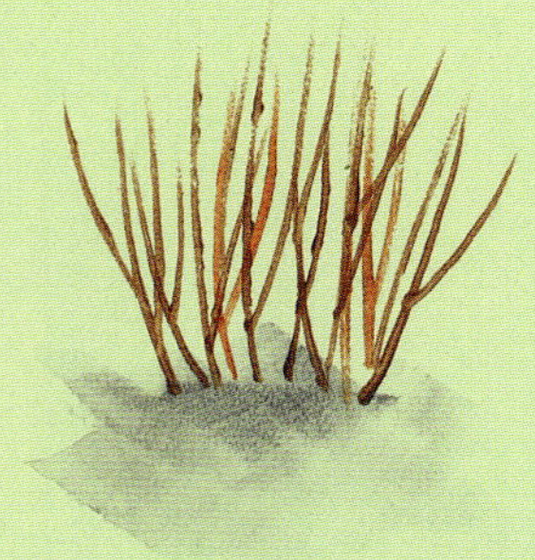

- Paint trunk or trunks with the liner. Begin at base and pull up.
- Paint shadow with a round brush.

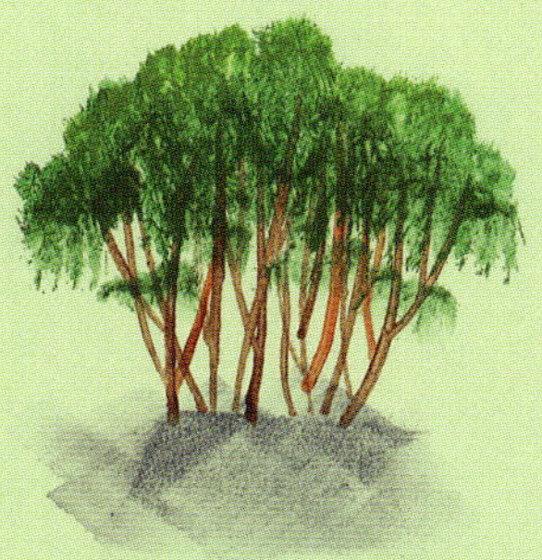

- Use a scumbler to dab on foliage with a medium green.
- Shade with a dark green.
- Highlight with a light green.

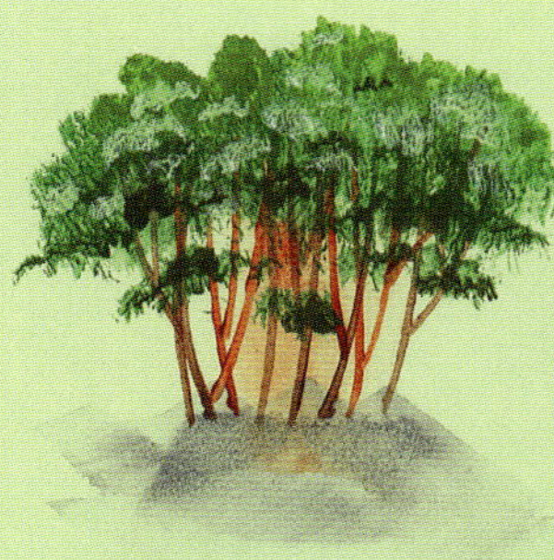

Shadow
Glaze mix
Ultramarine Blue/Burnt Umber

- Scumble lightest highlights with a very light green.
- Scumble deepest shadows with a very dark green.

Low-Growing Shrub

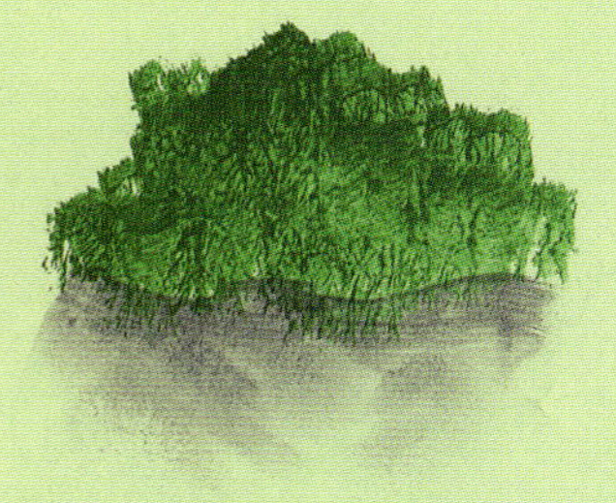

- Scumble foliage with a medium green.
- Paint shadow with a round brush.

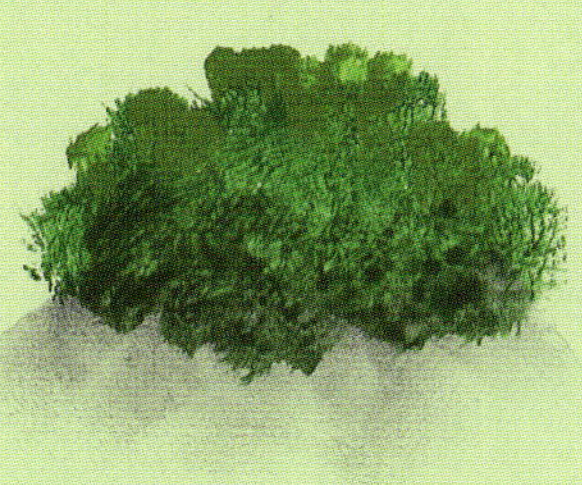

- Scumble highlights with a light green.
- Scumble shading with a dark green.

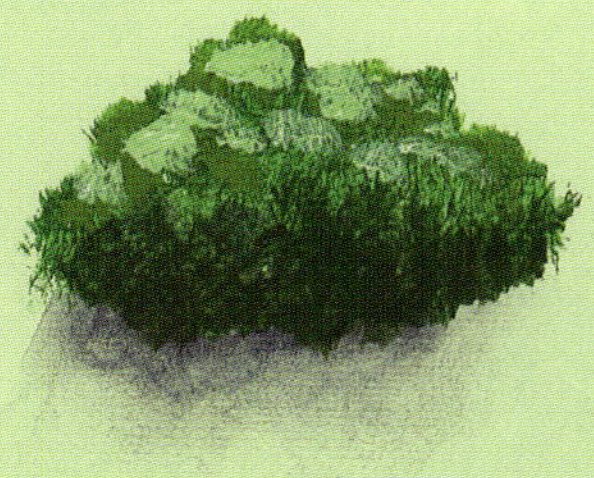

- Scumble lightest highlights with a very light green.
- Scumble deepest shadows with a very dark green.

Lavender

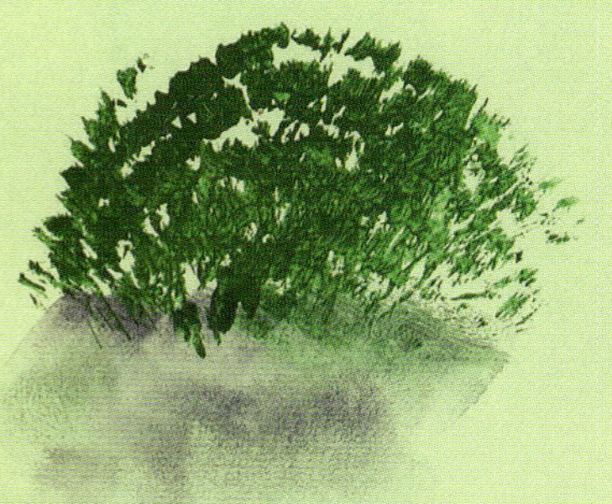

- Dab foliage with the fan brush and a medium green.
- Paint shadow with a round brush.

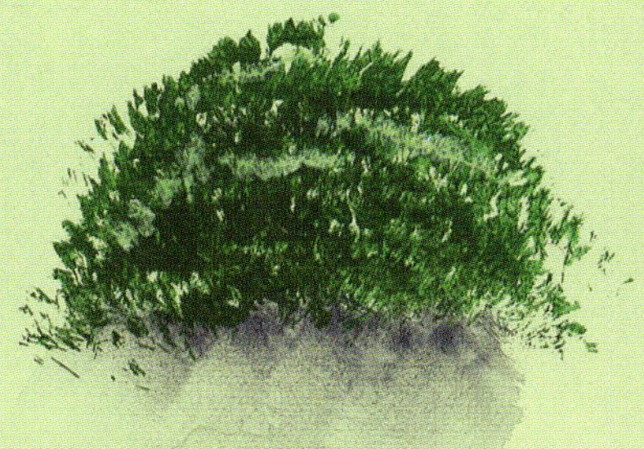

- Dab highlights with the fan brush and a very light green.
- Deepen shadows with the fan brush and a very dark green.

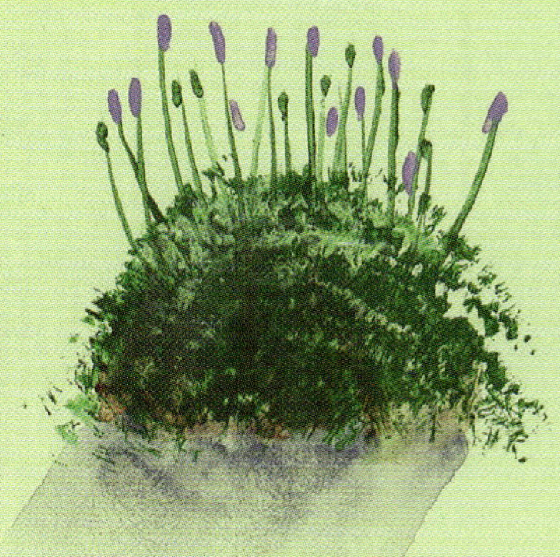

- Paint flower stems with a #00 liner. Begin at top of foliage and pull up. There is some variation in the green of the stems.
- Paint flowers with a touch of the liner tip. Note that immature flowers are green.
- Darken base of plant with a wash of Burnt Umber.

Grape Vines

Vineyard grapes typically have a single trunk, with two "laterals" trained along a wire. Each year's growth comes from them. At the end of each season, the vine is pruned back to the two laterals. With age, the trunks become thick and gnarled. In contrast, the new season's growth has gracefully arching canes.

Trunks & posts
Burnt Umber
Raw Umber
Burnt Sienna
Use randomly; variation adds interest.

Wires
#00 liner
Thinned
Burnt Umber

Trunks & main branches twisted and gnarled

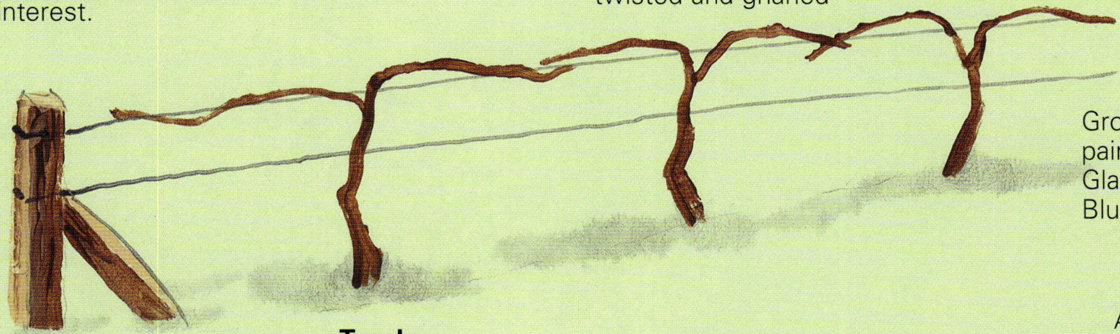

Ground the vines by painting shadows. Glaze mix of Ultramarine Blue/Burnt Umber

End post is braced with another post to help support the weight of the vines.

Trunks
#1 liner
Side-by-side strokes

Arching canes (new growth)
Fan brush
Medium green

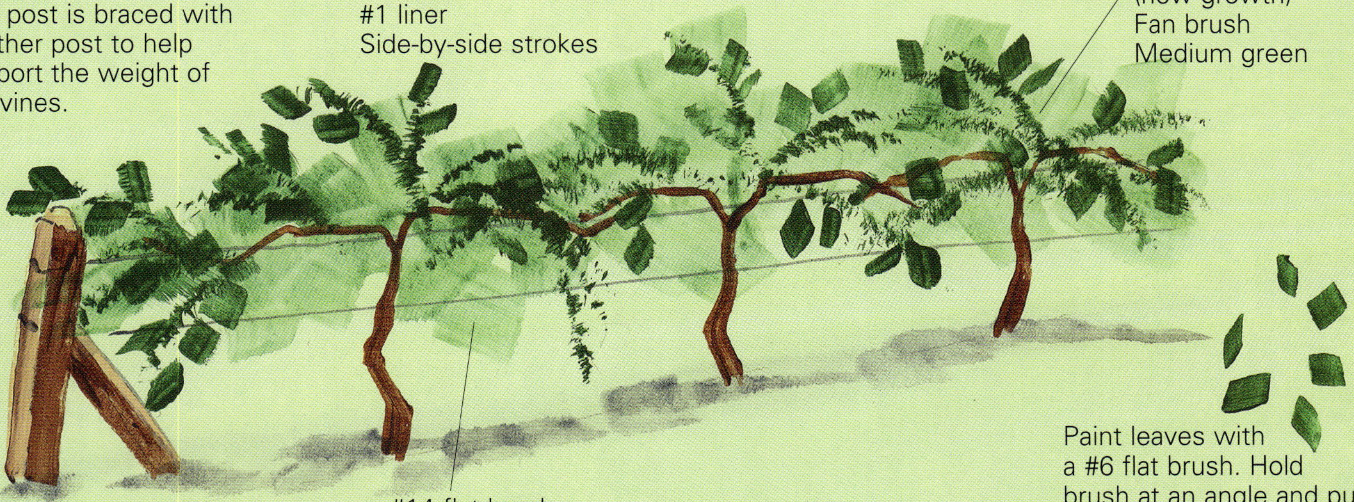

Paint leaves with a #6 flat brush. Hold brush at an angle and pull a short, straight stroke to get a diamond shape. Paint loose clusters.

#14 flat brush
Washes of medium green

Pull a few vines
#00 liner
Burnt Umber

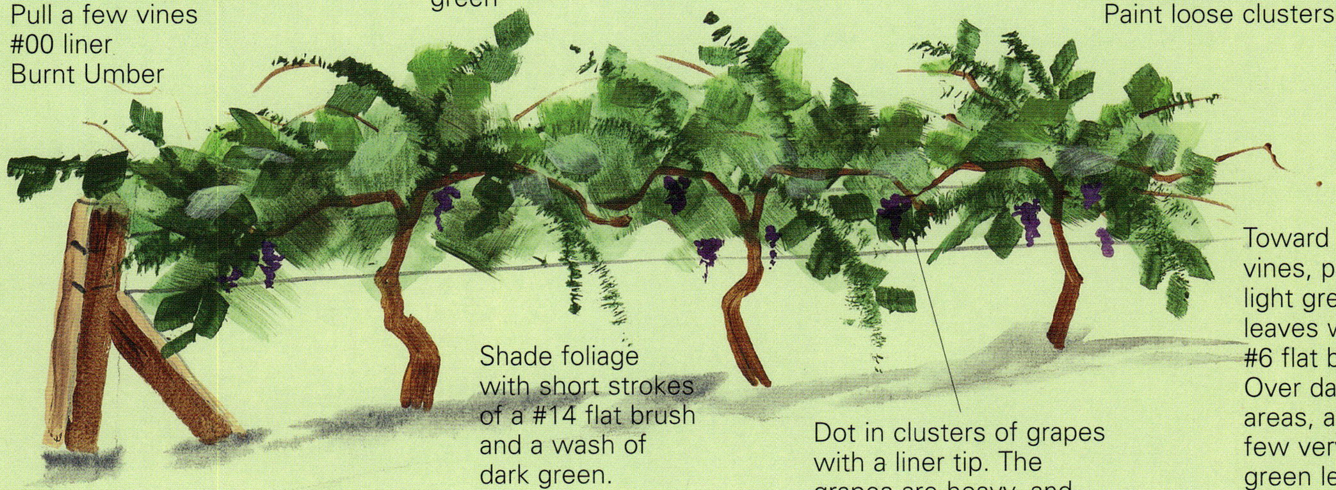

Toward tops of vines, paint light green leaves with the #6 flat brush. Over darkest areas, add a few very light green leaves.

Shade foliage with short strokes of a #14 flat brush and a wash of dark green.

Dot in clusters of grapes with a liner tip. The grapes are heavy, and hang from the bottom of the foliage.

Outside of vineyards, grape vines take other shapes. An untended vine can grow very large, rambling freely through trees. Grape vines can be trained to cover an arbor - a lovely element in a landscape.

Basic Sky

Paint the sky as an even gradation of color. Even if the sky is cloudy, a smooth, graduated color is its foundation.

Use Titanium White (not Mixing White) to get opaque color.

Mix a sequence of 3 colors: medium, light, and very light.

This example was painted with a #20 flat brush.

Use a large brush and work quickly, wet-in-wet. Option: use an extender to slow the paint's drying time.

Cerulean Blue
+ Cobalt Blue
+ Titanium White

Cerulean Blue

Clear Sky

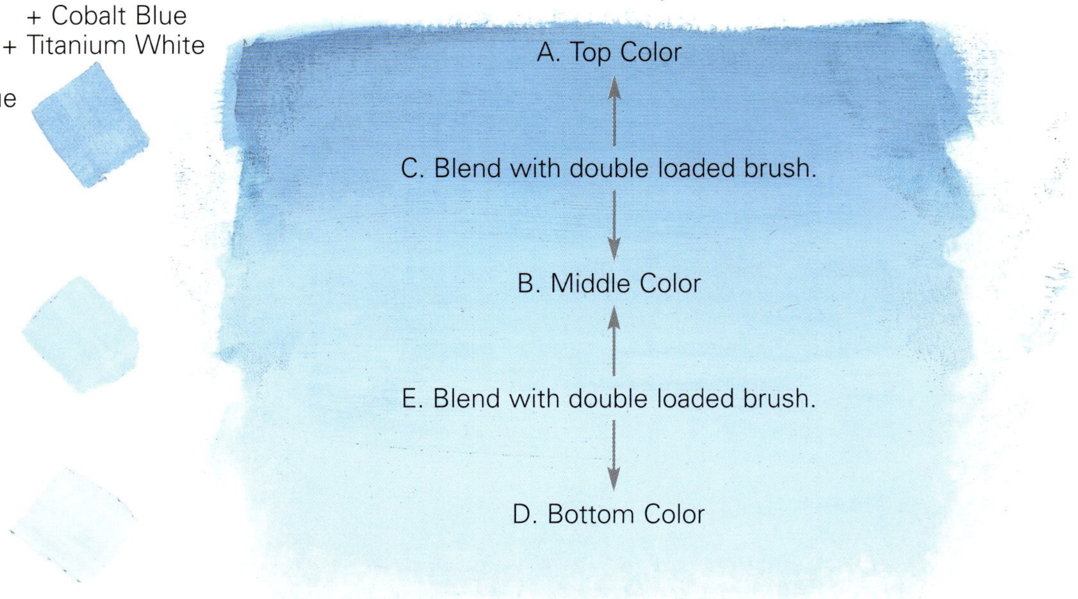

A clear sky is most intense overhead, and lighter at the horizon.

Procedure

1. Begin at the top. Stroke a wide band of the top color, laying down plenty of paint.
2. Stroke brush on clean paper towel to remove most of the paint. Load brush with the middle color.
3. Lay a band of the middle color just beneath the top color, using plenty of paint.
4. Double load brush with top color and middle color. Stroke back and forth over the "seam" between the two colors to blend them on the surface.
5. Proceed in the same manner to the bottom color.

Rainy Sky

Graphite Gray
+ Titanium White

A rainy sky is darker at the horizon.

Clouds

High Clouds

Wispy high clouds are often seen as a background to puffy cumulus clouds.

- Paint a smoothly graduated clear sky.
- While sky is wet, load a fan brush with the cloud color and stroke lightly into the wet paint.

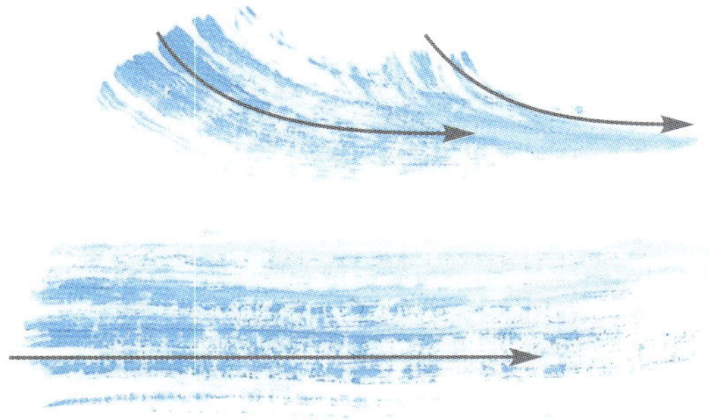

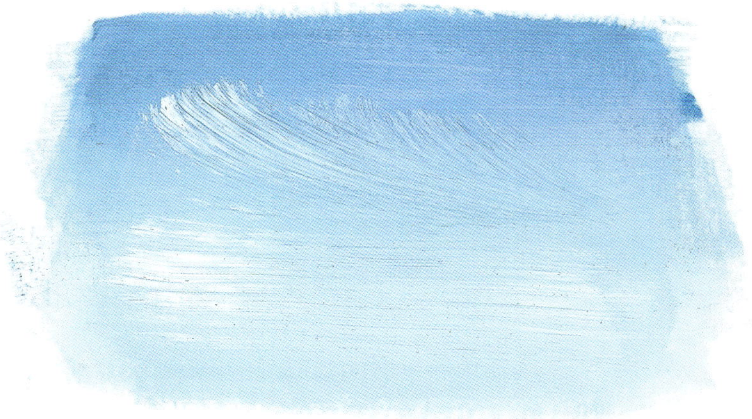

Puffy Cumulus Clouds

Paint a smoothly graduated clear sky. Let it dry before painting the clouds.

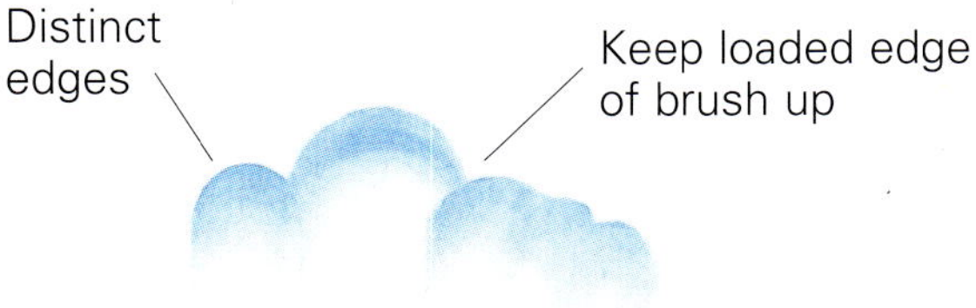

Side-load a large flat brush. Paint top edges of clouds as a series of sideways "C" strokes.

Side-load with Titanium White. Establish tops of clouds. Vary size and height of strokes to make cloud tops uneven.

Add more puffs - fill in clouds with more sideways "C" strokes.

- Lighten tops of clouds with more side-loaded Titanium White.
- Bottoms of cumulus clouds are flat. With a large round brush, stroke Titanium White across bottom edges of clouds. Repeat if needed, drying after each layer.
- Streak a little light gray along flat bottoms of clouds.
- Glaze tops with a very thin wash of Cadmium Yellow Medium.

Stormy Sky

When it rains, the sky is a light to medium-light gray. The raindrops tend to even out the color. But before the rain begins, the gathering storm is dark and dramatic. There are often layers of clouds of different types - distant, puffy clouds toward the horizon, streaky clouds higher up, and very dark, waterlogged clouds directly above with uneven, almost misty bottoms.

When the storm clouds are overhead, there may be an area of blue at the horizon. Or the horizon may be very dark, signaling stormy weather moving in. The possibilities seem endless, but here is one way of painting a stormy sky.

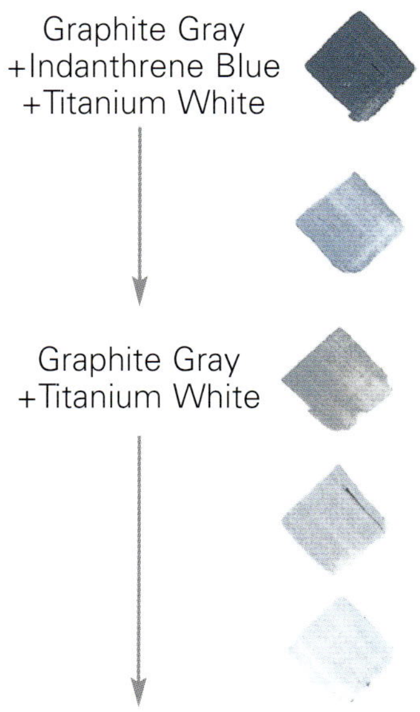

- Paint an evenly graduated sky. Let dry.
- Streak a little light blue at the bottom.

The wider the range of darks and light, the more dramatic the sky. The upper part of the sky is very dark, filled with clouds that are heavy with water.

- Add distant, puffy, light clouds close to the horizon.
- Add horizontal streaks for darker clouds a little higher up.

- Dampen the upper portion of the sky - not so wet that it is shiny.
- Side-load a large flat brush with dark gray-blue. Keeping the loaded edge of the brush up, paint horizontal streaks.

The paint should fuzz slightly on the dampened surface, giving a misty bottom edge to the clouds.

Sunset

The use of sunsets in landscape painting is limited because the light is dim and few features of the landscape are visible. But they are dramatic, and it is fun to paint the range of colors, from deep blue-violet to turquoises, greens, corals, pinks, and yellows. Small clouds may be silhouetted against the intense sky, the moon may begin to show, and a few of the brightest stars may be visible. Here is an example of a sunset.

Dioxazine Purple
+ Mars Black

Phthalo Blue (Red Shade)
+ Mars Black

Titanium White
+ previous mix

Titanium White
+Phthalo Green (Yellow Shade)

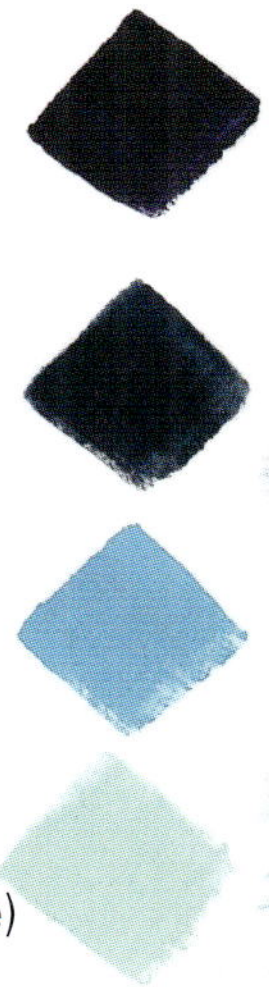

- Paint sky, blending colors wet-in-wet, starting at the top. Not a smooth gradation, but allowing streaks of color.
- When dry, streak in some white, wispy clouds.

Warning: Complementary Colors

When choosing sky colors, remember that you will be glazing yellow and orange over the bottom. Be careful to keep purples out of the area that will be glazed with yellow, and keep blues out of the area that will be glazed with orange. Glazing a color over its complement will dull the color, resulting in gray or brown.

Side-load a large flat brush with thinned Cadmium Yellow Medium. Keeping the loaded side down, lightly glaze the bottom portion of the sky.

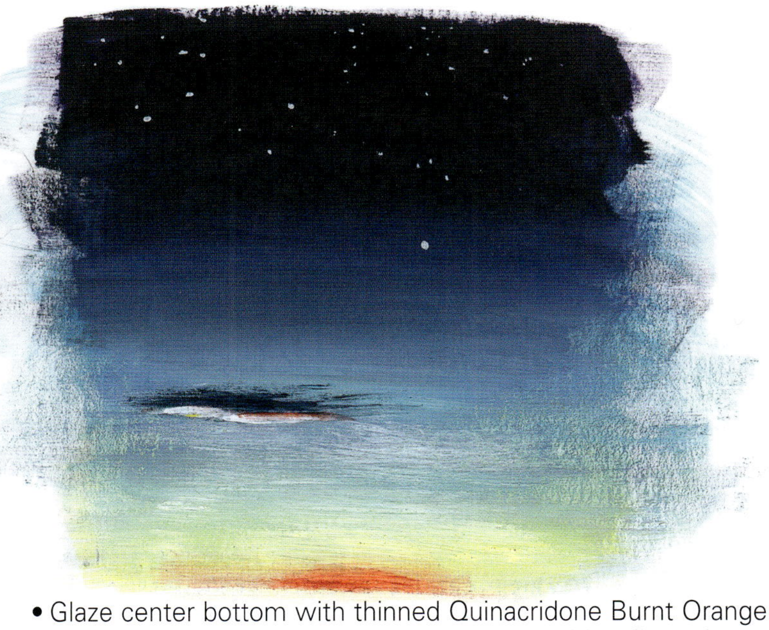

- Glaze center bottom with thinned Quinacridone Burnt Orange.
- Highlight the underside of any dark clouds with reflected sun color.
- Dot stars.

Wet-in-Wet Blending

Notice that although the three steps in this example were painted with the same colors, they all came out different because of the wet-in-wet blending. It is not a completely controllable technique, but it can present some lovely surprises.

Mountains

Except for the sky, mountains are the most distant objects in the landscape. They have indistinct edges and dull colors, and merge to form the single shape of a ridge. There is little, if any, vegetation at the rocky tops of tall mountains. Instead, their craggy shapes are defined with blotches of highlight and shadow. Details are not necessary.

- Paint the craggy shape of the mountain range with a dull color - purplish, bluish, brownish, or gray depending on the color scheme of the painting. For a more natural look, make top edge uneven and jagged. Avoid regularly repeating shapes.
- With a flat brush, block in jagged areas of highlight (a lighter tint of the base color) and shadow (a darker shade of the base color).
- Darken mountains at the base. Side-load a large flat brush with thinned Raw Umber. Keeping the loaded side of the brush down to concentrate the color toward the bottom, wash over the bottom portion of the mountains.

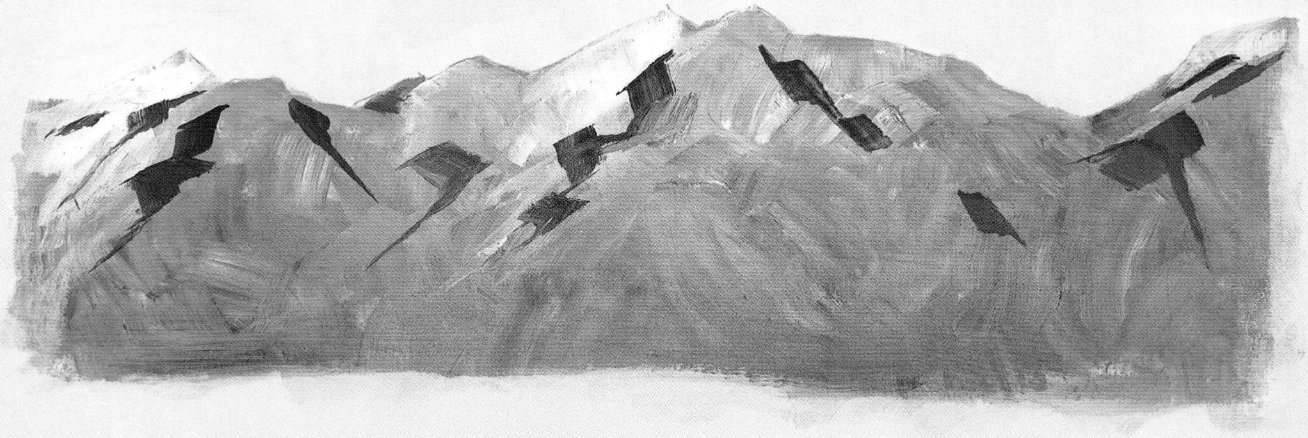

- For an uneven texture that suggests rock, use a paint mixture that is not completely mixed and short, choppy brush strokes.
- Darken mountains at the base with a side-loaded wash of thinned Raw Umber.

Snow-Capped Mountains

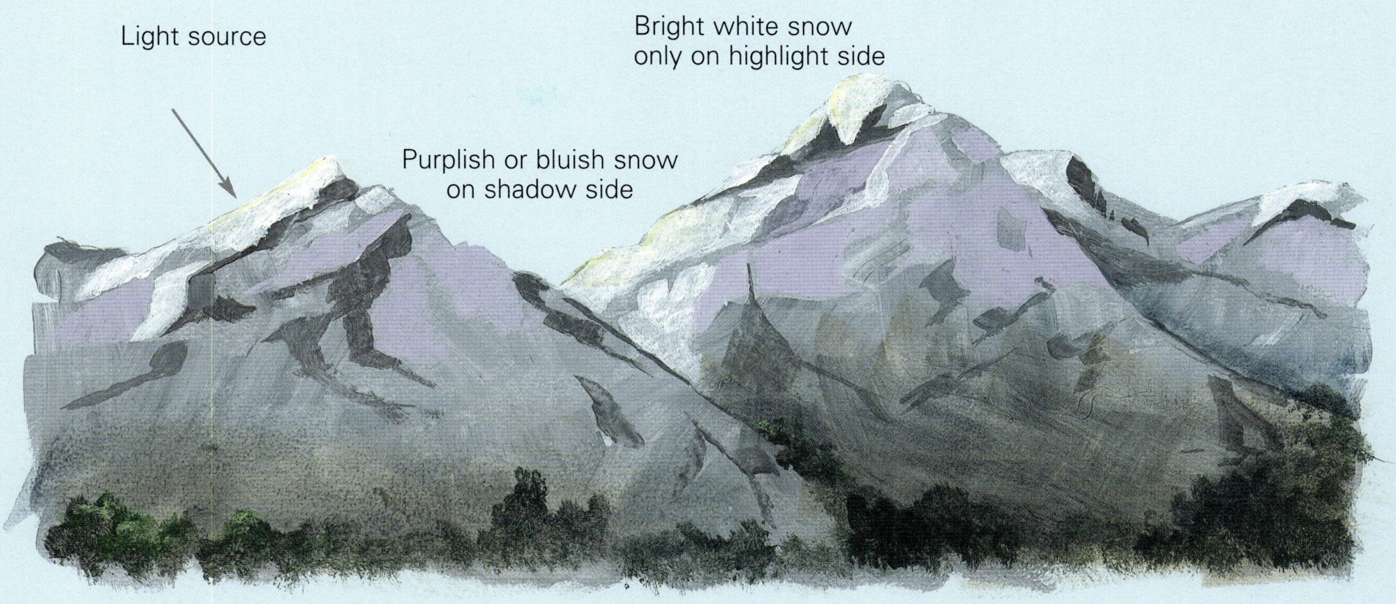

- Paint bright white snow on the highlight side of peaks.
- Wash brightest highlights with very thin Cadmium Yellow Medium.
- Paint purplish or bluish snow on the shadow side. Dull the colors slightly because the mountains are distant.

There are no trees above a certain altitude. At their highest range, trees cluster in valleys where the conditions are less harsh.

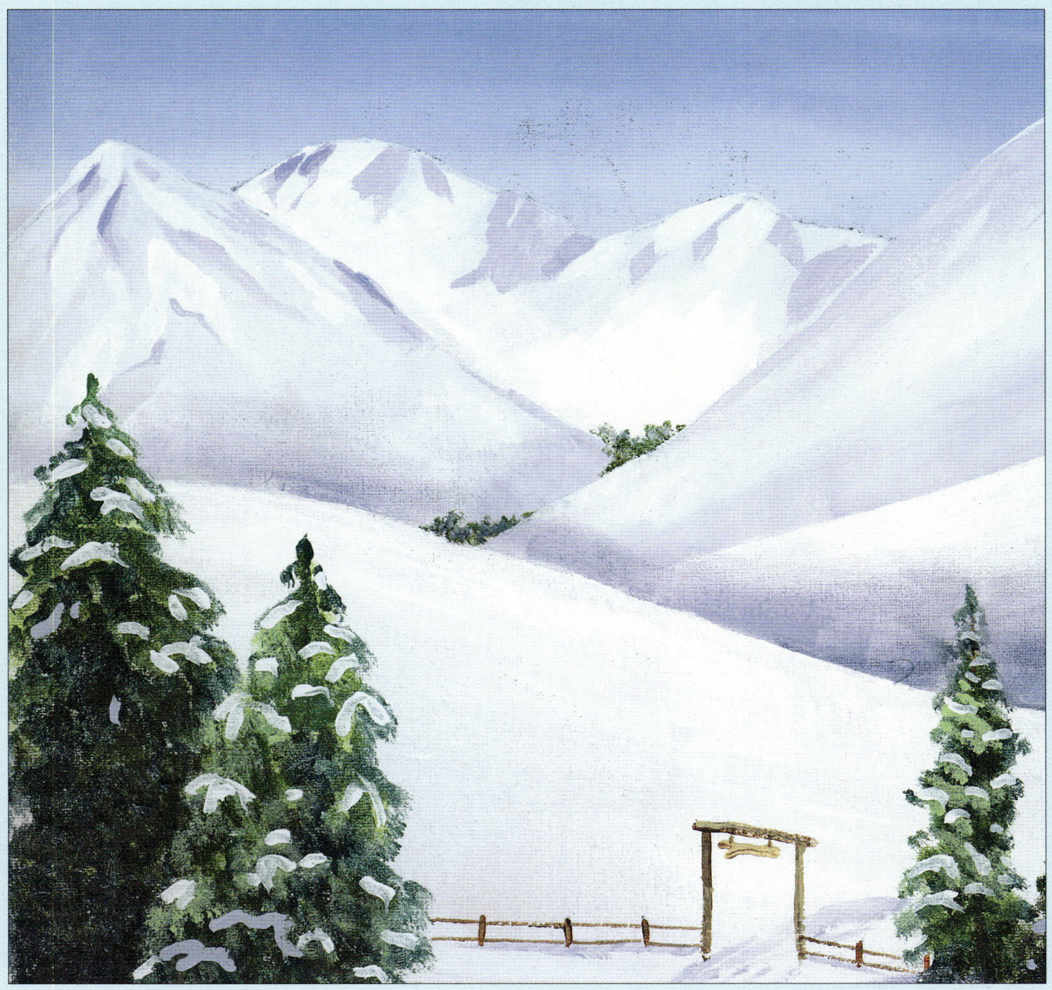

Cluster of Hills

Hills can play a key role in a painting's composition, as they overlap each other and create lines that direct the eye through the painting. Paint the more distant hills in lighter, somewhat duller colors than the nearer ones.

GRASSY HILLS

Use a flat brush to paint grassy hills.

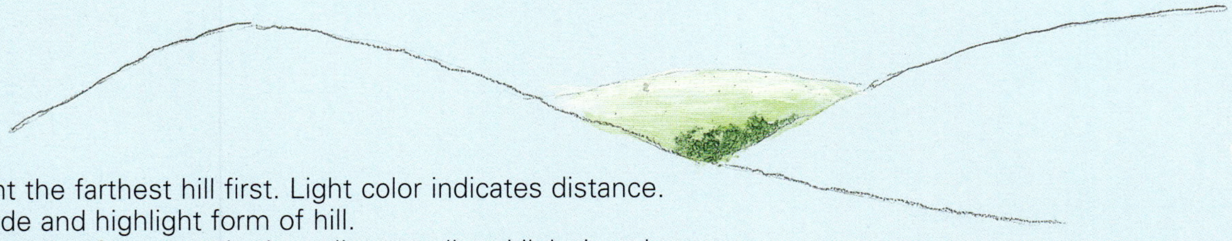

- Paint the farthest hill first. Light color indicates distance.
- Shade and highlight form of hill.
- Scumble a few trees in the valley, small and light in color.

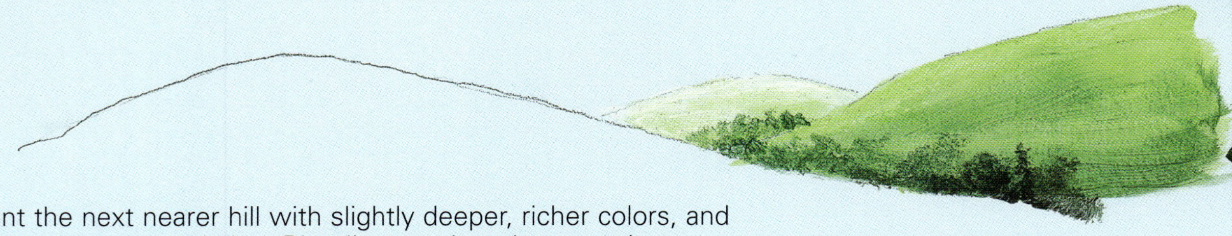

- Paint the next nearer hill with slightly deeper, richer colors, and with more color variation. Blending need not be smooth.
- Scumble trees in the valley. These are larger and have more color because they are closer to the viewer.

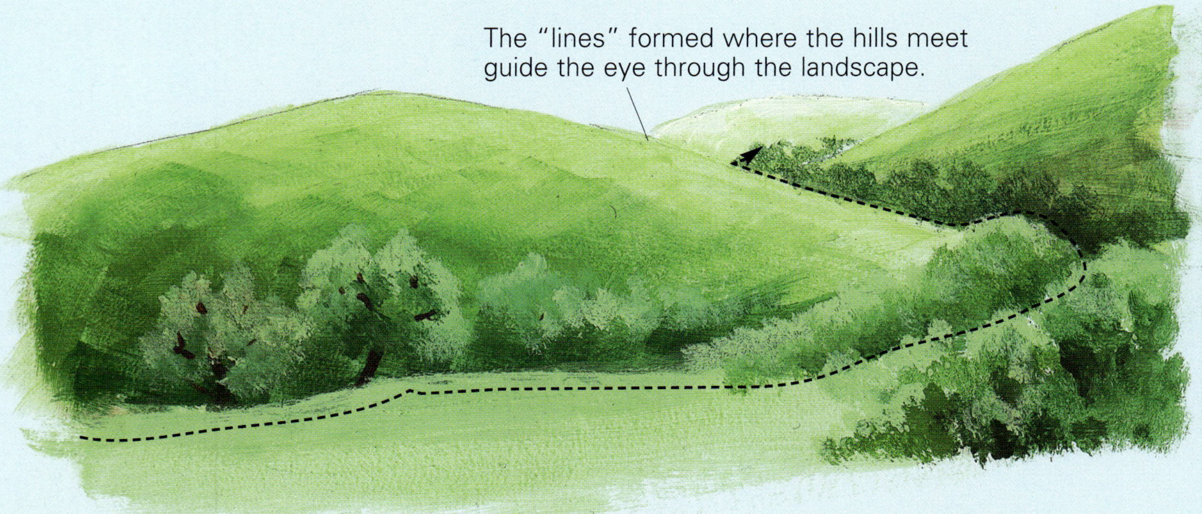

- Paint the nearest hill with the richest color. Use short, choppy strokes of different colors for variation. Wet-in-wet technique blends colors on the canvas.
- Build form with highlights, shadows, and clusters of scumbled trees.
- Scumble largest trees in foreground indicated by dotted line. Suggest a few trunks and branches with a liner.

Tree-Covered Hills

- Paint tree-covered hills in the same sequence, but dab in the color with a scumbler instead of stroking with a flat brush.
- Move between colors to develop highlights and shadows.
- Work wet-in-wet to blend the colors.

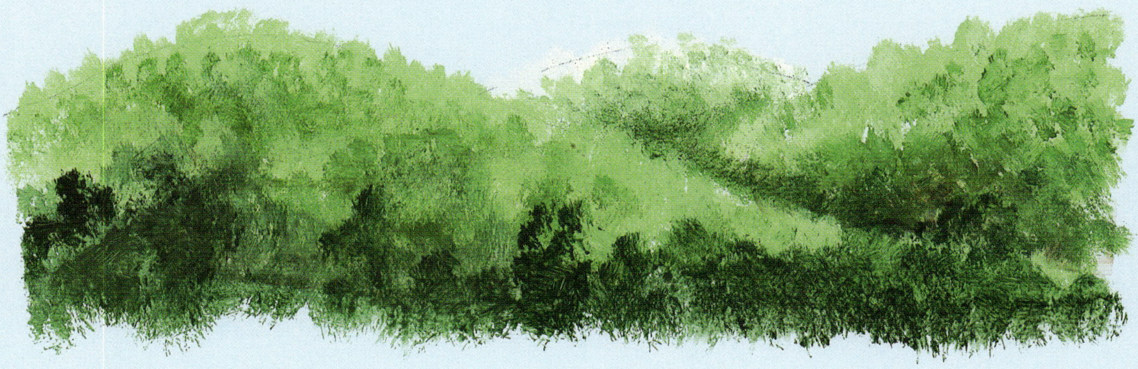

Meadow

Meadows are fairly flat, but rich color variations can come from wildflowers, patches of different types of vegetation, or cloud shadows. Most often, use lighter, duller colors farther away (toward the top) and brighter, deeper colors closer to the viewer (toward the bottom). In some landscapes this sequence could be reversed to have darker, duller colors farther away and lighter, brighter colors closer to the viewer. Look closely at the individual landscape to decide.

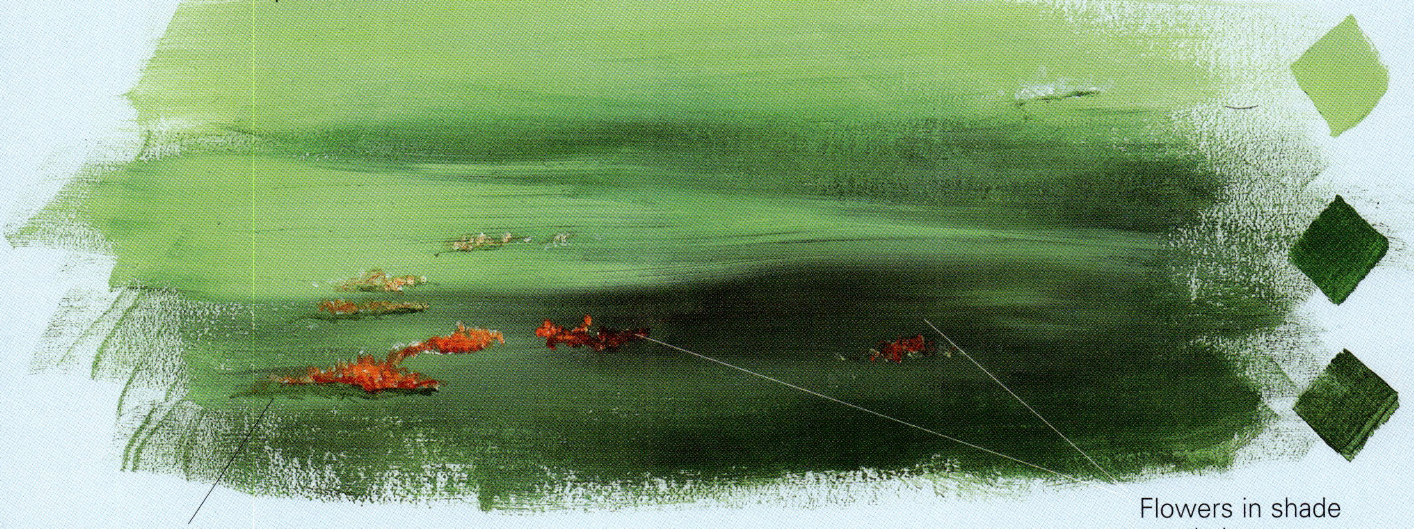

Flowers in shade are darker.

Flower patches have small shadows.

- Paint meadows wet-in-wet. Use a large flat brush and horizontal strokes.
- When meadow is dry, paint shadows of flower patches.
- When shadow is dry, underpaint flower clusters with Titanium White.
- Let white underpainting dry before painting flower colors. Without underpainting, the flower colors will appear dull over the meadow greens.

Water

It's all about reflections.

When painting water, simplify. Be concerned with shape and color. For the shape, water is flat. For the color consider objects underneath the water contributing to murkiness; water may contain algae and be greenish; reflections of the sky and mountains affect the color; movement on the water affects the color.

Paint the water an even color. Add reflections. On a lake or pond the reflections are horizontal streaks - smaller when far away, larger when close. Far away reflections are the color of the lowest part of the sky. Close reflections are the color of the sky overhead.

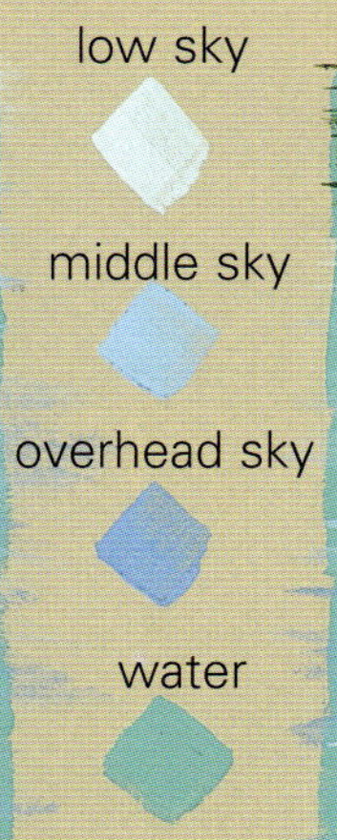

This patch of water reflects trees on the far side and small clouds overhead. All shapes have broken edges.
On glass-smooth water, all you see is reflections. Rougher water shows more of the water color.

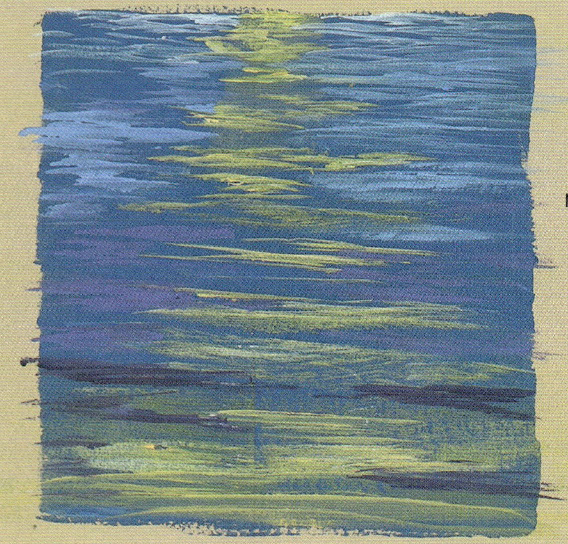

In dim light you see the color of the water. The reflection of a rising or setting sun begins as a small area on the horizon then fans out towards the viewer.

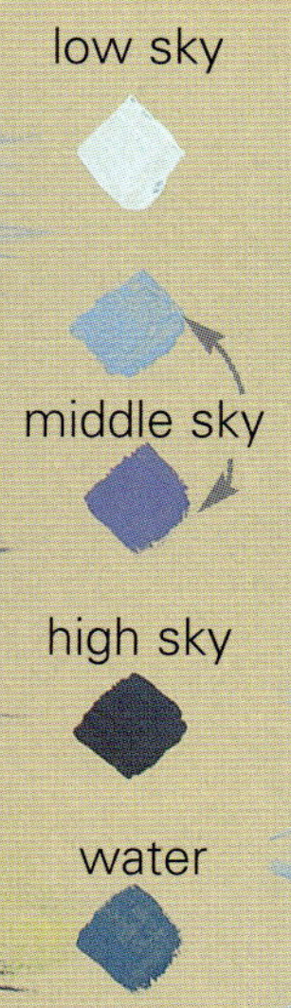

Reflections on choppy water are painted with wider, slightly angled short strokes, but are horizontal.

Painting a Stream

The top edge where the stream disappears into the distance is horizontal.

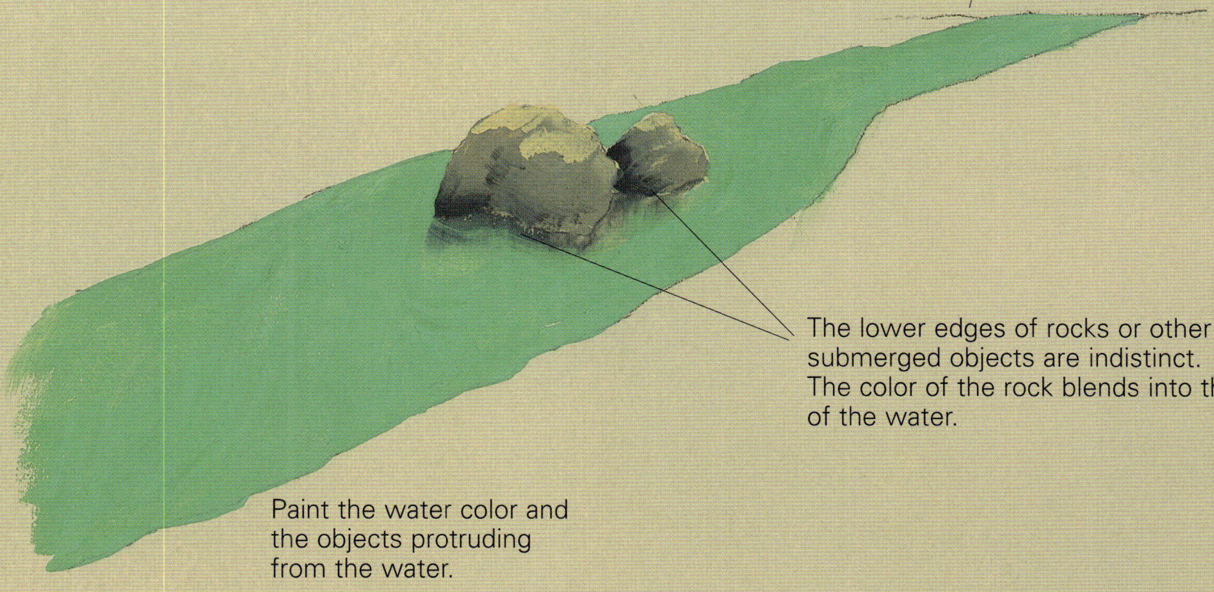

The lower edges of rocks or other partially submerged objects are indistinct.
The color of the rock blends into the color of the water.

Paint the water color and the objects protruding from the water.

flow of water

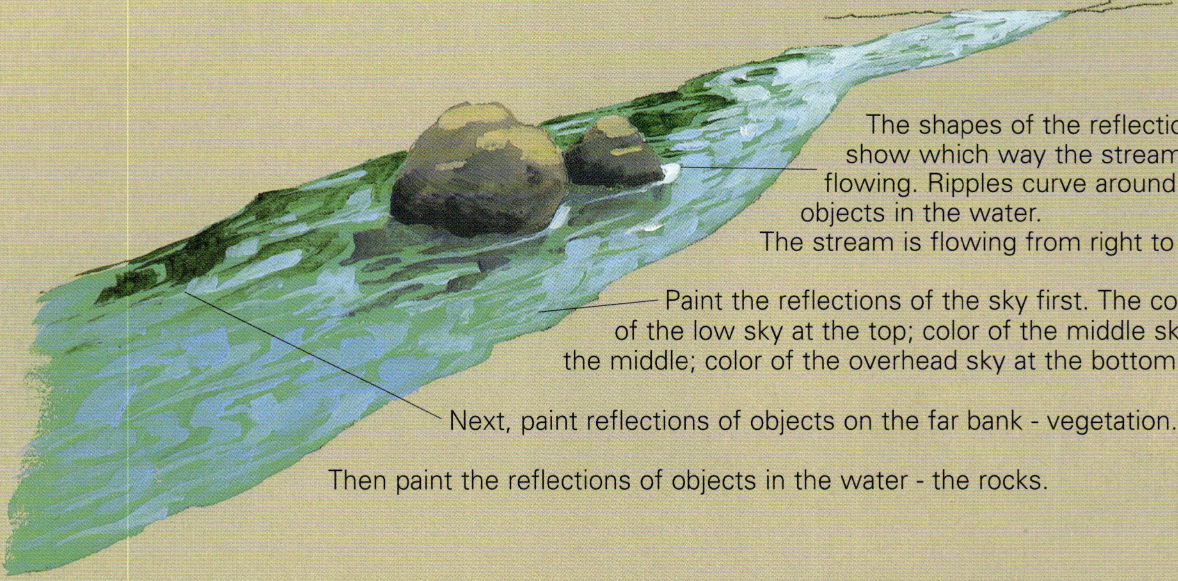

The shapes of the reflections show which way the stream is flowing. Ripples curve around objects in the water.
The stream is flowing from right to left.

Paint the reflections of the sky first. The color of the low sky at the top; color of the middle sky in the middle; color of the overhead sky at the bottom.

Next, paint reflections of objects on the far bank - vegetation.

Then paint the reflections of objects in the water - the rocks.

There is a difference between reflections and shadows. The placement of shadows depends on the relation between the light source and the object casting the shadow. Reflections depend on the position of the viewer. Reflections always stretch towards the viewer. Shadows and reflections may extend in different directions.

Snow

White is rarely used in paintings of snow. It is more effective to portray snow with blues, purples, and greens. Highlights can be warm yellows or yellow-oranges.

Paint snowy landscapes wet-in-wet with a variety of light "snow" colors. Strokes are generally horizontal, but may angle slightly to indicate hills and valleys. Color patches are larger in the foreground and smaller in the background. Most often, paint the background darker than the foreground. However, this may be reversed depending on the composition and the mood of the painting.

Snow colors mixed from Titanium White, Graphite Gray, Dioxazine Purple, and Ultramarine Blue.

Each clump of snow mounded on horizontal surfaces has highlights and shading to define its shape. In the distance, these highlights and shadows may not be visible, but in the foreground they give the landscape a realistic look.

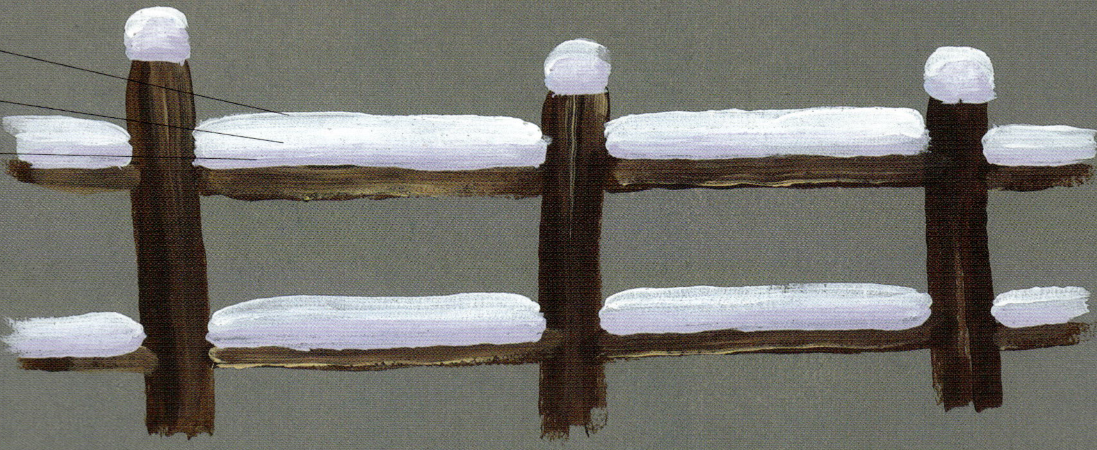

Falling Snow

Falling snow is fun to paint, but the snow obscures much of the detail in the painting. Spatter in stages, keeping in mind that we are looking through more falling snow when we look at an object farther away.

- Paint the background - in this case the sky.
- Spatter with light gray.

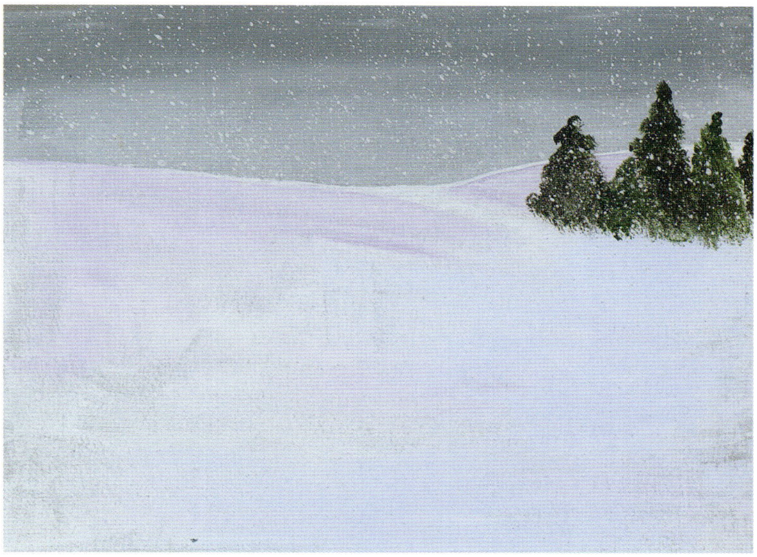

- Paint the middle ground - snow and far trees. Bring snow down to bottom of canvas.
- Spatter entire canvas with lighter gray. The background now has two spattered coats.

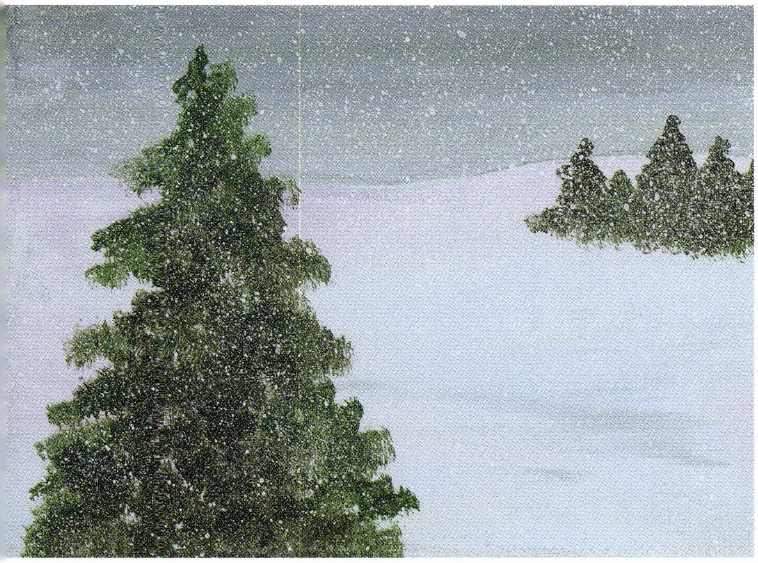

- Paint the foreground - large tree.
- Spatter entire canvas with very light gray. Background now has three spattered coats, middle ground two, and foreground one.

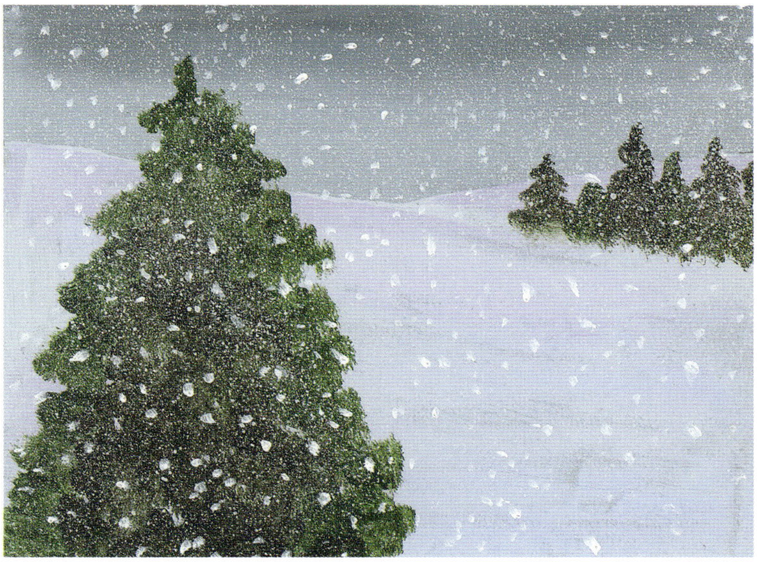

Using the #1 liner and Titanium White, dot larger white flakes over entire canvas.

Simple Barn

Keys to Painting Realistic Buildings

(See the "Linear Perspective" section of "Putting it Together.")

1. Draw the structure in correct linear perspective.
2. Place the building correctly relative to the horizon. For example, a building viewed from above must sit below the horizon.
3. Use landscape elements such as shrubs and trees to create a smooth transition between the building and the other objects in the painting.
4. Values of walls and roof must be consistent with the light source in the painting.

Simple Structure

The simplest building is essentially a box with a roof.

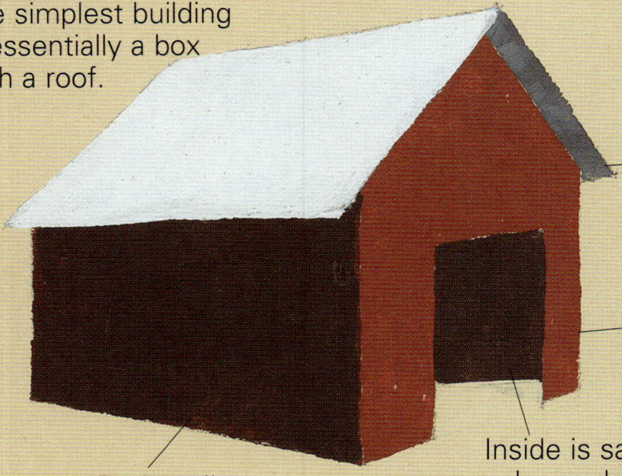

Begin by placing wall and roof colors consistent with the light source.

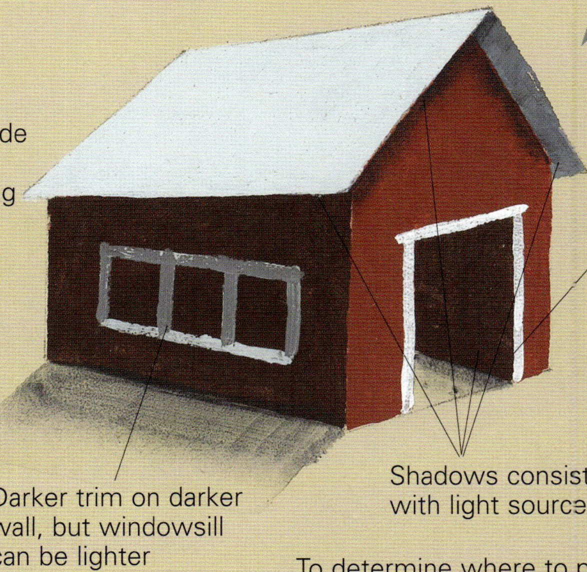

To determine where to paint shadows, imagine the arrow from the light source as a flashlight beam casting shadows.

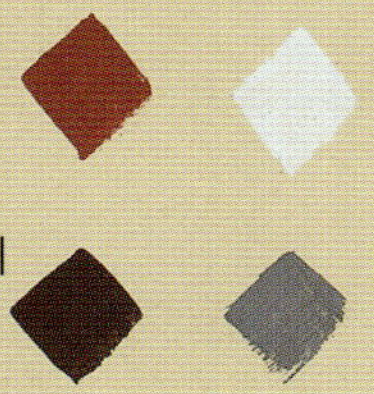

A More Complicated Structure

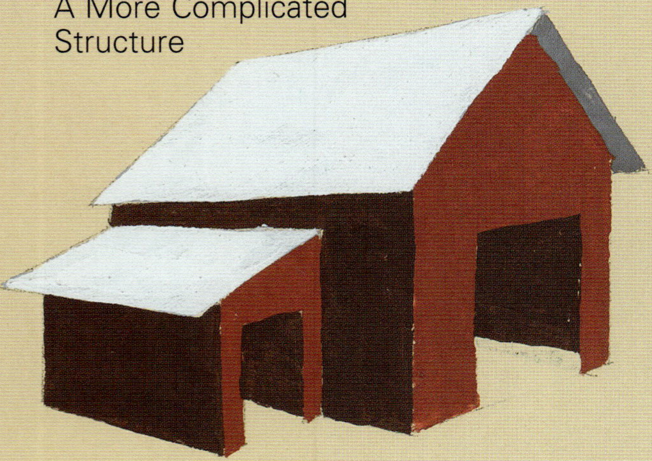

Place wall and roof colors consistent with light source. Placement on the two "boxes" should be consistent.

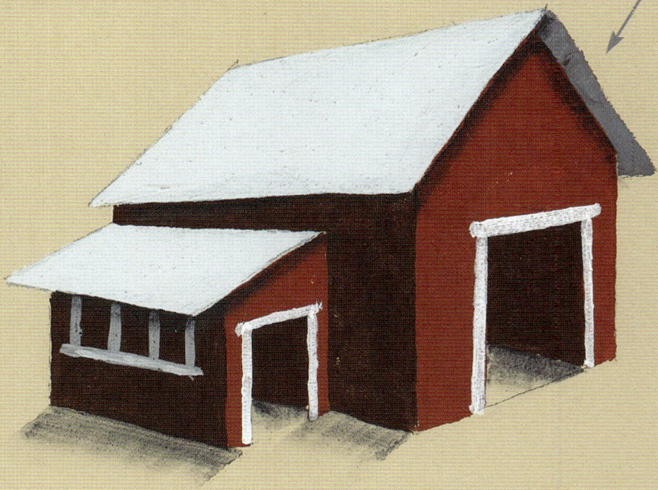

Add shadows and details.

Other Barns

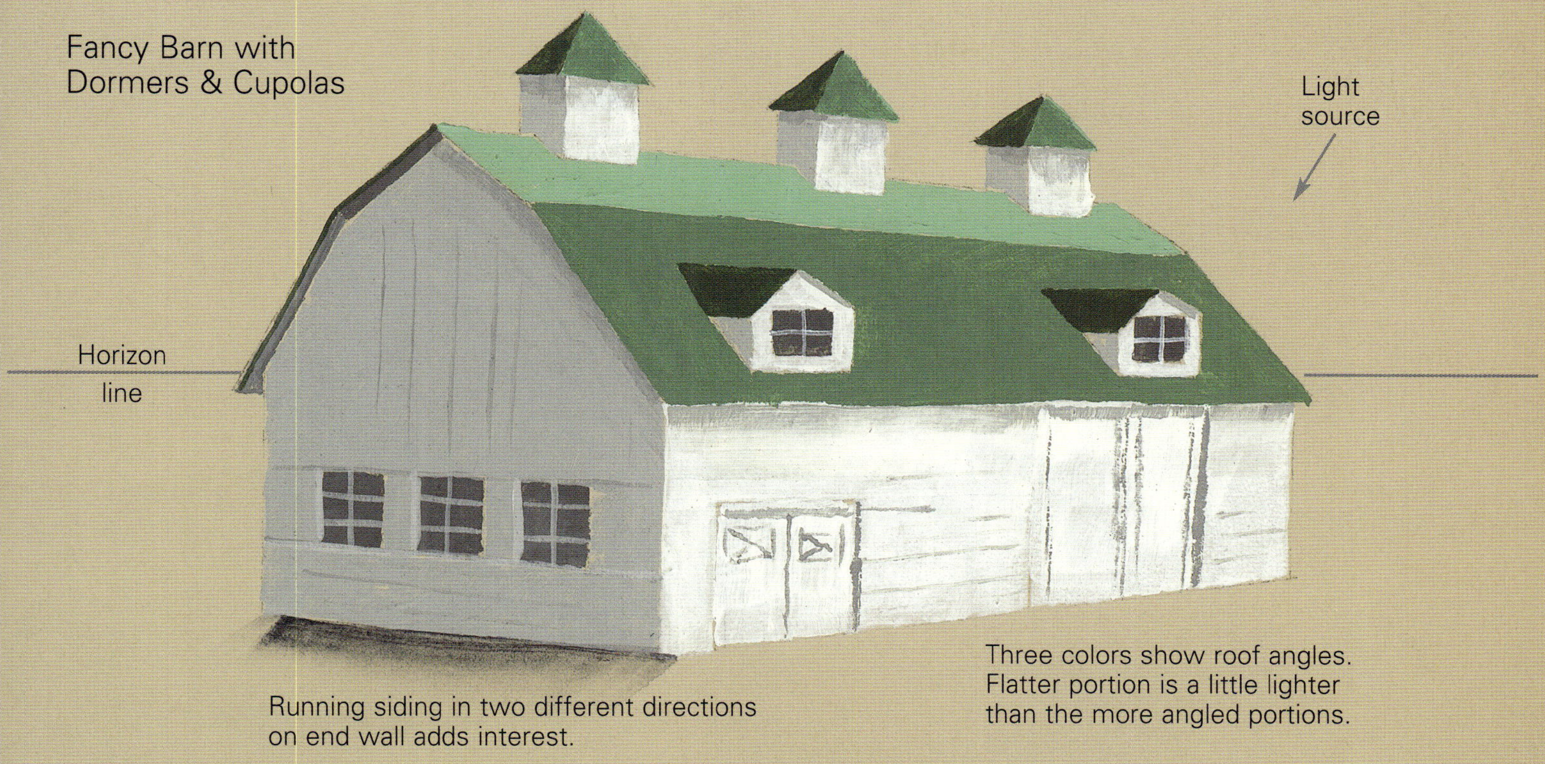

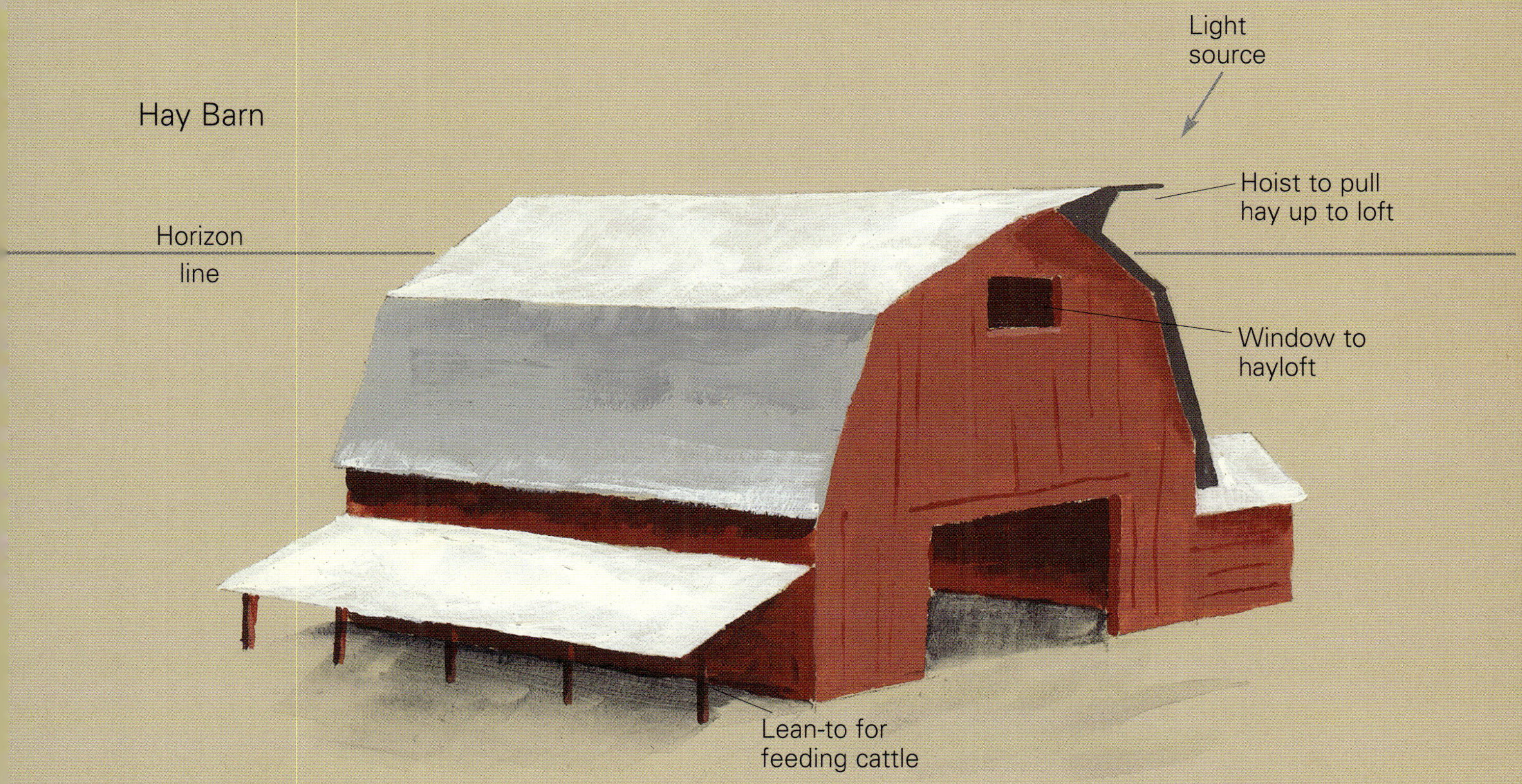

The most complex building is still just a group of box shapes. As long as you shade and highlight consistently, your buildings should be successful. Remember these basics:

- A wall facing the light source is light in value.
- A wall facing away from the light source is darker.
- Trim on a light wall is light.
- Trim on a darker wall is darker.
- The roof overhang casts shadows on all the walls.
- On the wall with the roof peak - whether light or dark - the roof casts a shadow on both upper angled edges of the wall if the sun is high in the sky. If the sun is low in the sky it may cast a shadow on only one edge, the one closest to the light source.

Farmhouse & Barn

Farmhouse

Although roof is green, underside of overhang is a shade of yellow to match the walls.

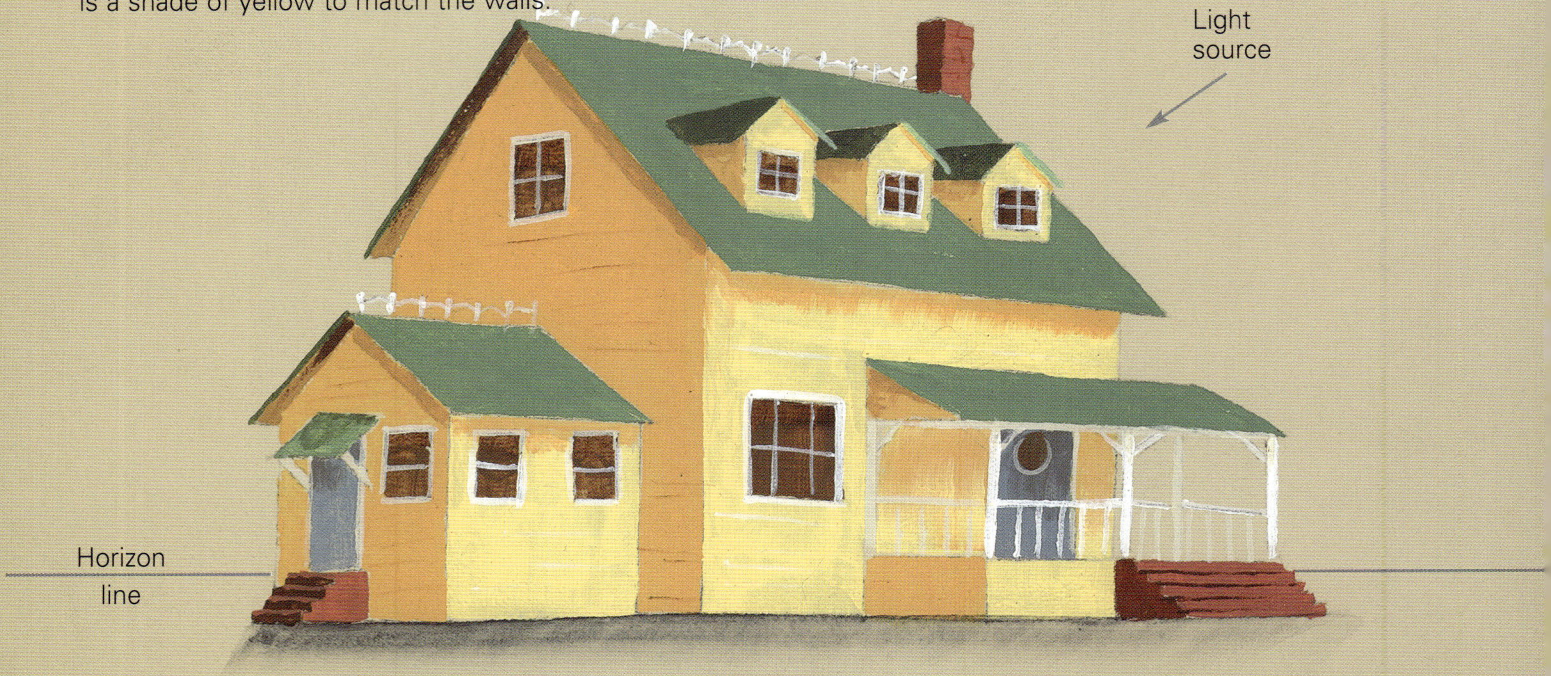

A few simple details, like the trim on the roof peaks and the porch railing, dress up this simple house.

Barn with Silo

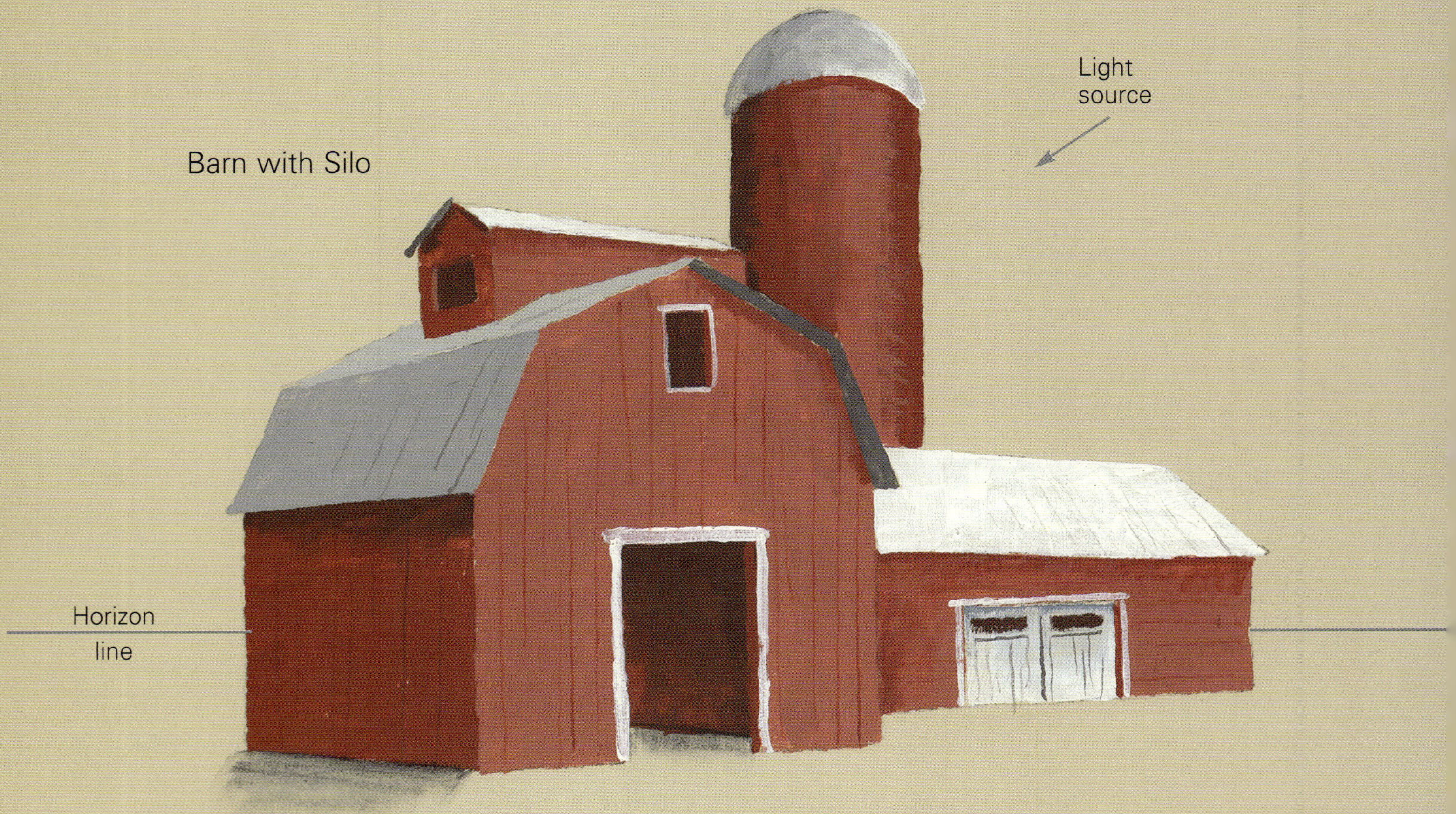

The cross-wise loft is an interesting variation.

Other Buildings

Windows and doors may be the only details on the simplest buildings. More complex buildings include lines indicating individual siding boards, bricks or rocks in chimneys, shingles, or porch railings. A nearer building has more detail than one that is farther away. A building that is a focal point has more detail than one that is playing a supporting role.

Rustic Cabin with Tin Roof

Porch roof adds interest to a simple shape.

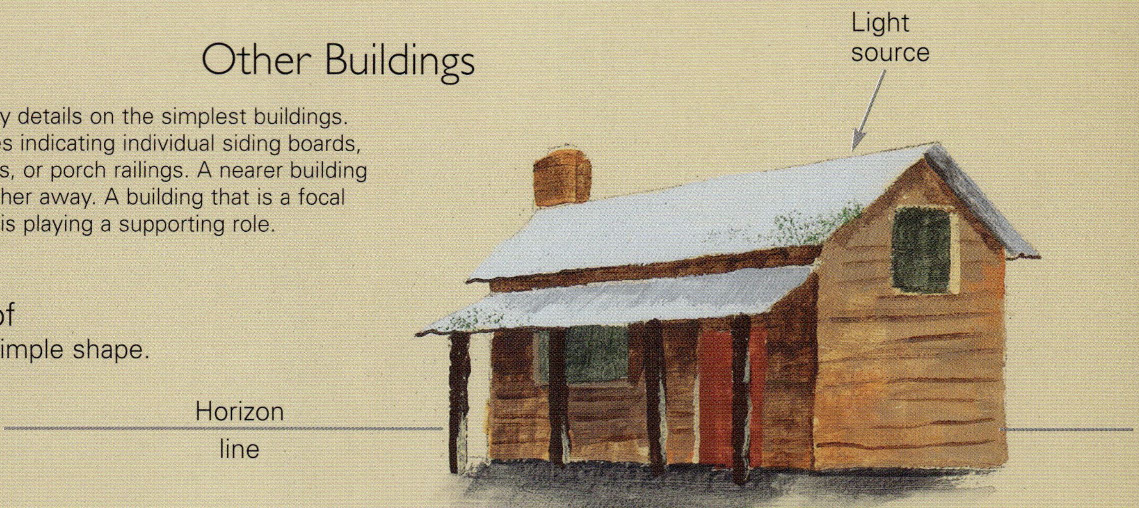

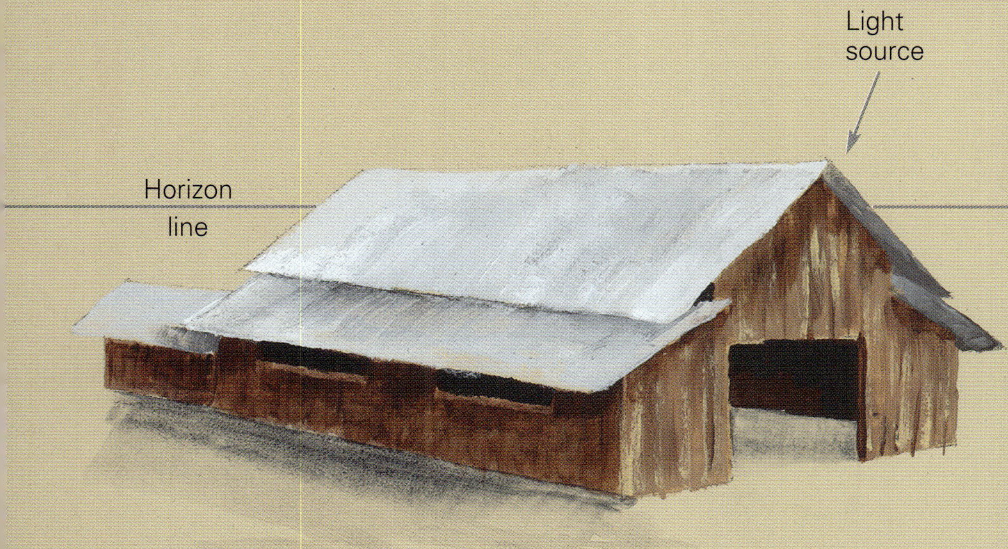

Old Barn with Tin Roof

Double roof is typical of old cattle barns. Wood is aged and rough.

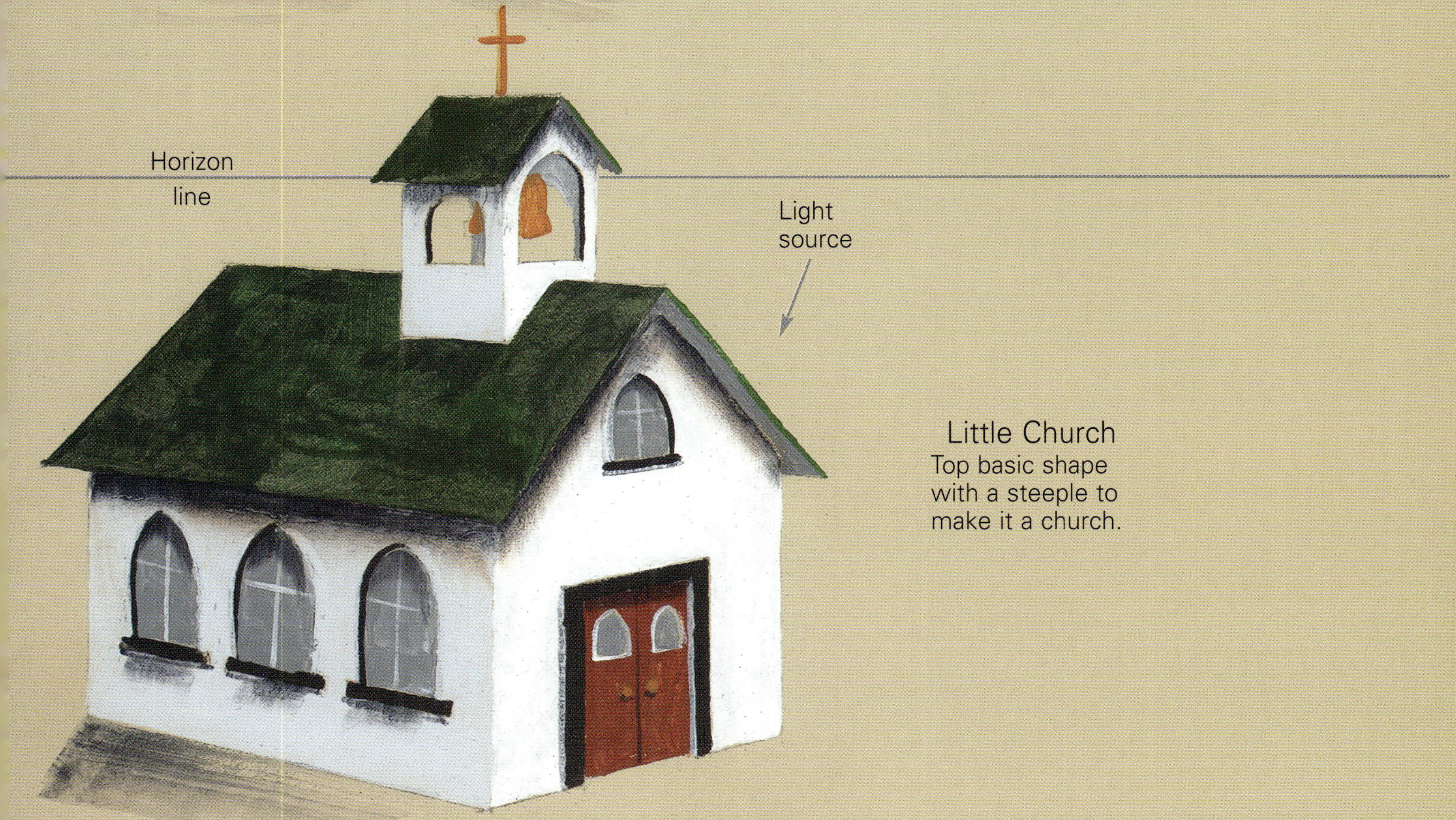

Little Church

Top basic shape with a steeple to make it a church.

Fences

Fences and walls are right at home in the landscape and can greatly contribute to a composition. The line of a fence can guide the viewer's eye to the focal point.

Post & Rail

Can be natural or painted wood

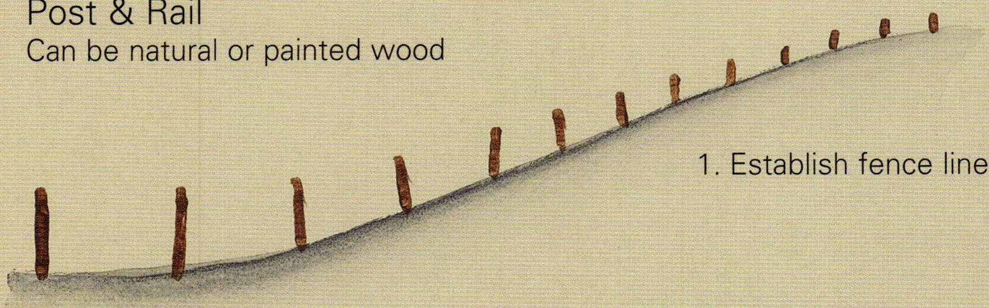

1. Establish fence line with a light shadow.

2. Paint posts.
- Angle posts randomly for a more rustic look.
- Posts are taller and farther apart close to viewer, shorter and closer together farther from viewer.
- A white fence will transition to gray as it recedes into the distance.

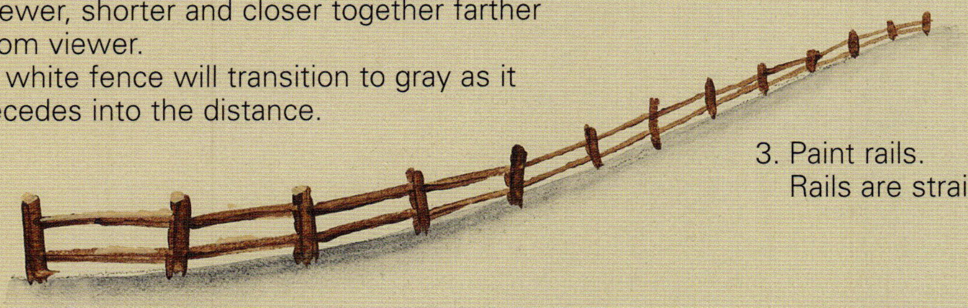

3. Paint rails.
   Rails are straight, not curved.

4. Add a few highlights (light lines) and shadows (dark lines) on fence closest to viewer.

If fence is large enough, you can make posts square or round.

Square post

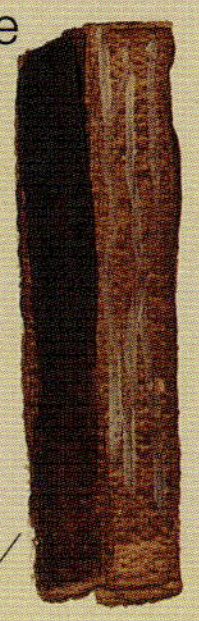

Sharp transition between light and shadow

Round post

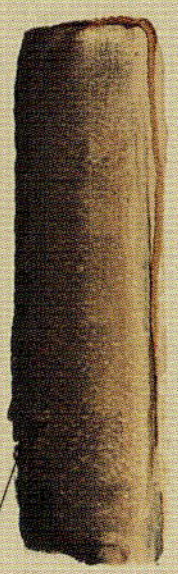

Smooth transition between light and shadow

Livestock Fence

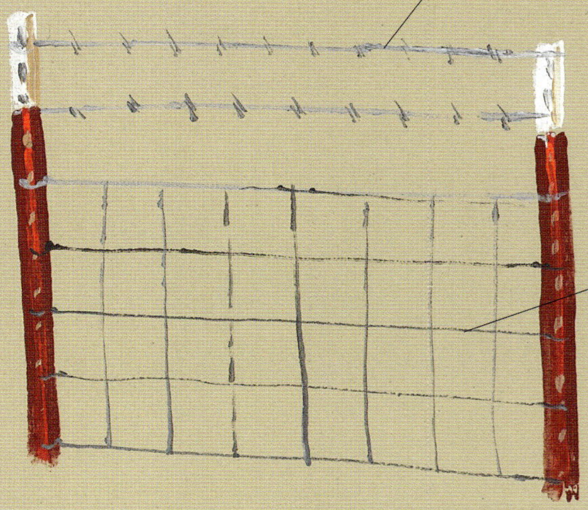

Livestock fence is made of metal posts and wire. Posts are usually red or green and have white tops.

Stacked Fence

This rustic fence is built by stacking squared timbers in a criss-cross pattern. There are no posts, and nails are not used. This type of fence works well in an old farm scene, with brambles growing over it. It would convincingly fence sheep but not larger animals.

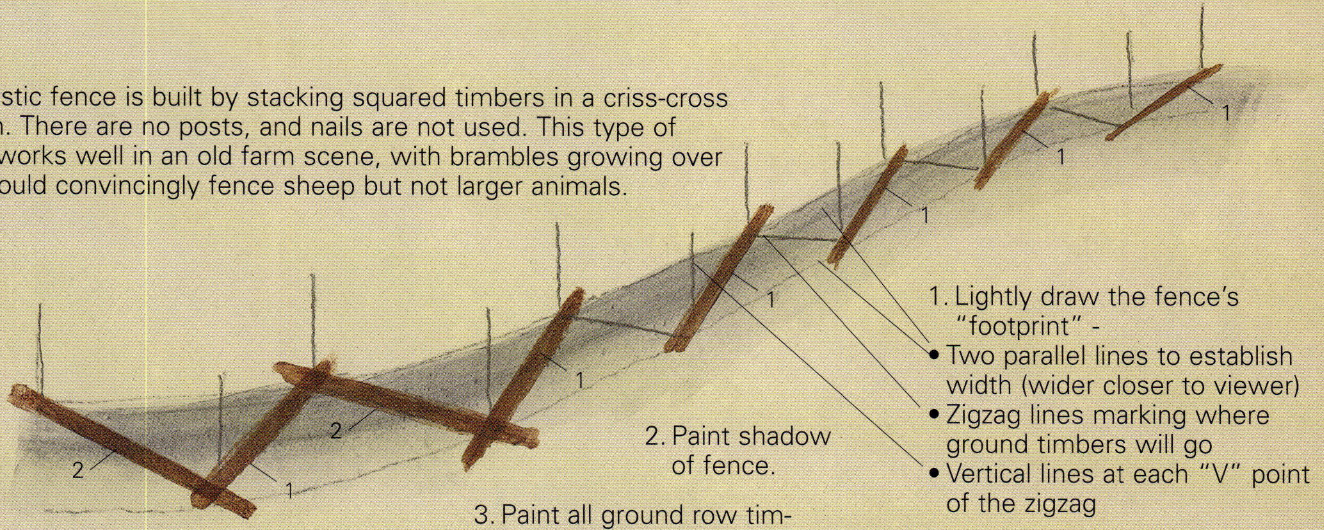

1. Lightly draw the fence's "footprint" -
   - Two parallel lines to establish width (wider closer to viewer)
   - Zigzag lines marking where ground timbers will go
   - Vertical lines at each "V" point of the zigzag
2. Paint shadow of fence.
3. Paint all ground row timbers running at the same angle (timbers #1). Extend each timber slightly beyond the vertical lines.
4. Paint the ground row timbers running at the opposite angle (timbers #2). Extend each timber slightly beyond the vertical lines. Timbers should cross at vertical lines.

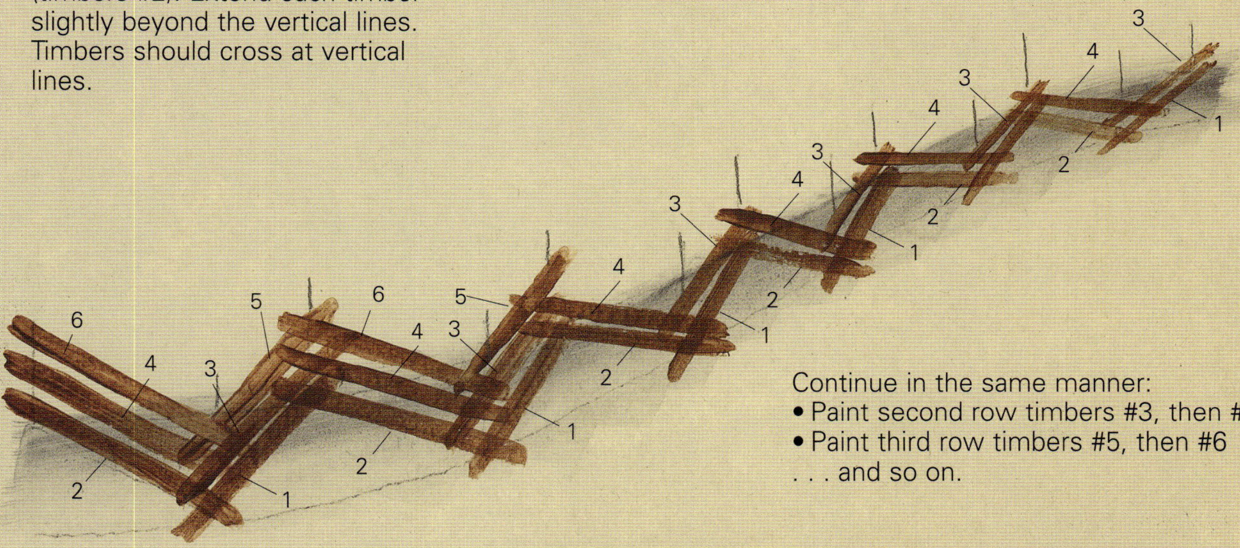

Continue in the same manner:
- Paint second row timbers #3, then #4
- Paint third row timbers #5, then #6

. . . and so on.

Make sure timbers cross at vertical lines to keep fence upright.

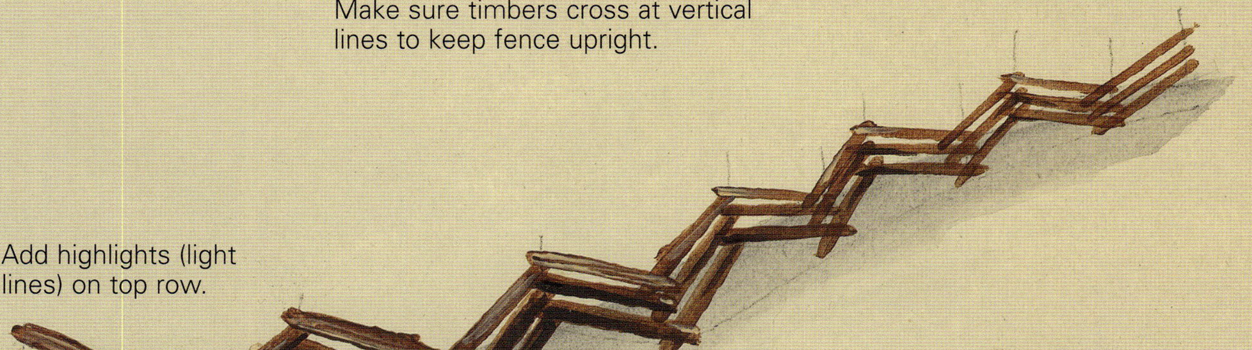

Add highlights (light lines) on top row.

Place shadows on forward edges of timbers.

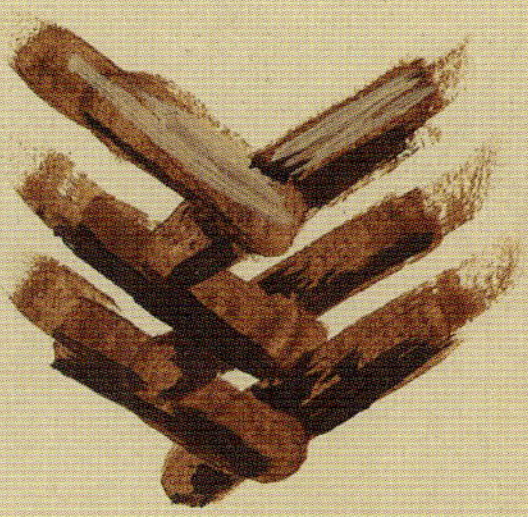

If the fence is large enough, shadows can define the way the ends are stacked.

Rocks with Flowers

Do not strive for an even tone on the rocks. Instead, use the dry-brush technique. The toning color will show through, giving texture to the rocks. The alyssum flowers grow in the gaps between the rocks. Think of where they are rooted when you dab their foliage.

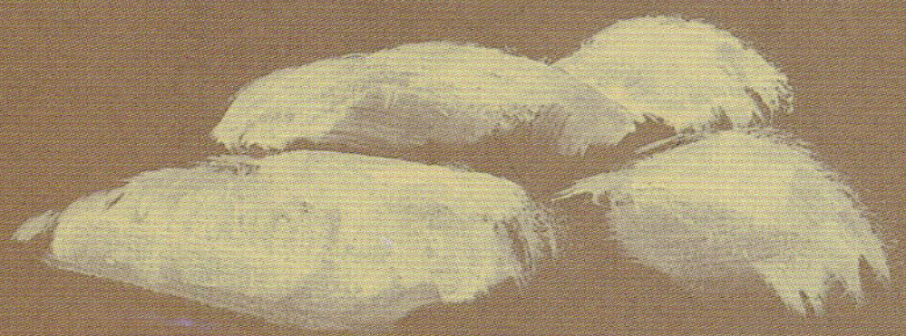

Block in basic shapes with a flat brush and Buff Titanium.

- Concentrate color at tops. Let the toning color of the canvas show at bottoms.
- In the middle of rock shapes, use a dry brush to take advantage of the canvas texture.

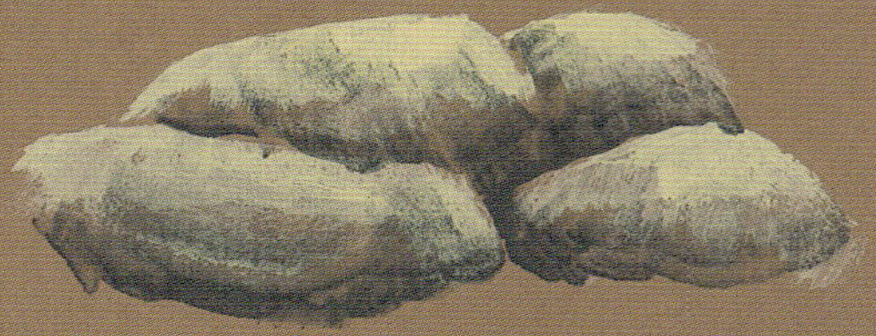

Shade underneath and between rocks.

- Side-load a flat brush with Graphite Gray to get a transition of color across the brush from dark to light.
- Keep loaded side of brush down to shade bottoms of rocks.
- Keep loaded side of brush against the edge of the forward rock to shade between rocks.

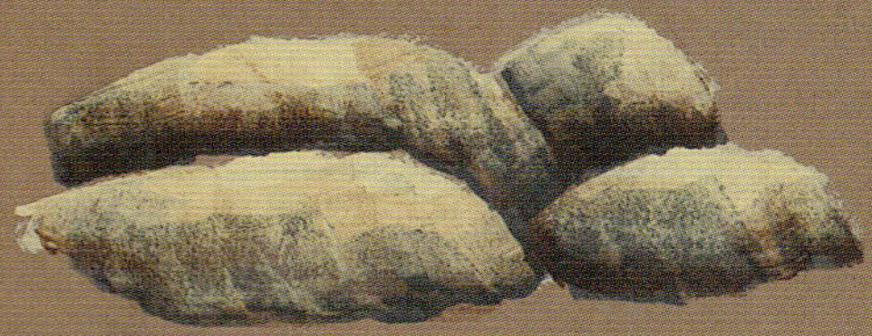

Repeat shading with side-loaded Burnt Umber, painting wider shadow areas.

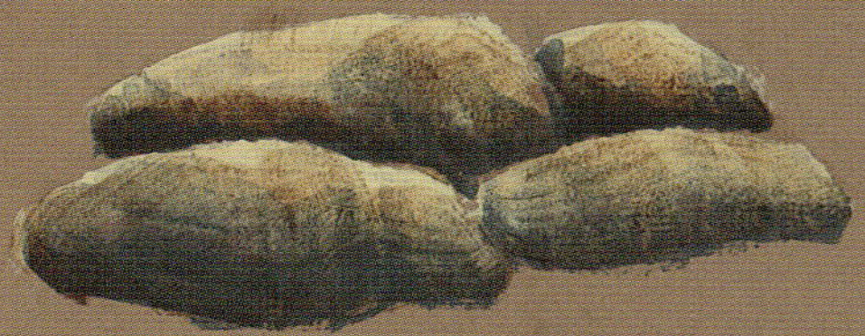

Wash rocks with thinned Burnt Umber. Leave some areas along tops of some rocks untouched, to become brightest highlights.

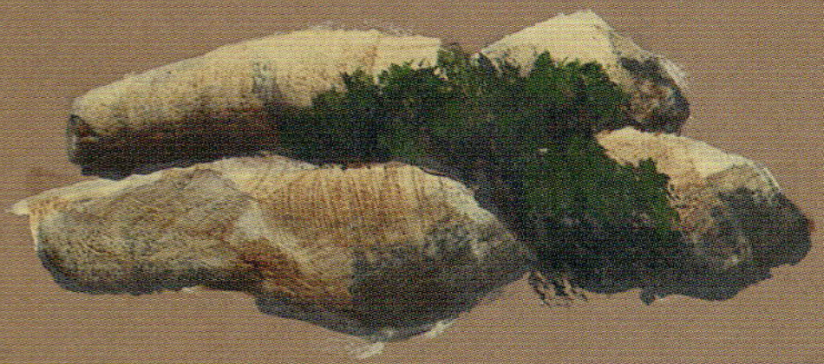

- Scumble patches of dark green foliage between rocks.
- Scumble medium green at tops of foliage clumps.

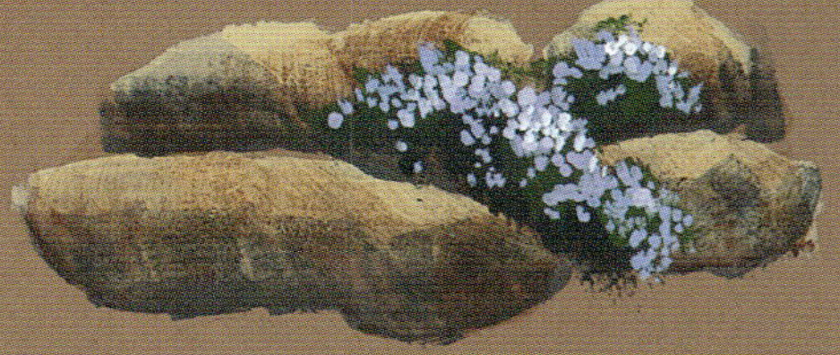

- Dot flowers with the tip of a #1 liner, using several values of lavender.
- Dot lightest values toward tops of flower clusters.
- Dot a few Titanium White highlights.

People

Remember that people are emotionally powerful subjects that draw the eye of the viewer. If you include people in your landscape, keep them small, and few in number. Keep the colors muted and consistent with your color scheme.

Proportion Guidelines

- A typical person is 7-1/2 "heads" tall.
- Hips are midway.
- Spine may curve. The neck is an extension of the spine.
- Include lines for hips and shoulders.
- Elbows are at waist level. Hands fall mid-thigh.

If one shoulder is down, the hip on that side is up.

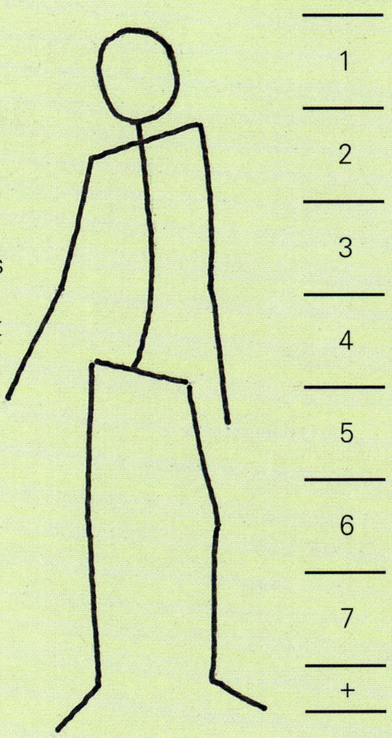

"Blue Jeans" Color Mixes

light	medium	dark	very dark
medium mix + Titanium White	Indanthrene Blue + Graphite Gray + Titanium White	medium mix + Graphite Gray	dark mix + Mars Black

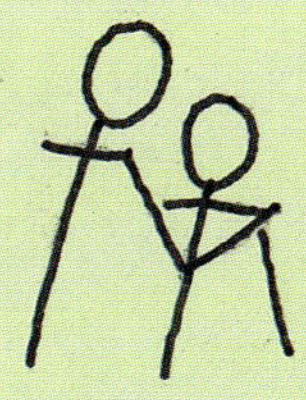

- Draw a stick figure with correct proportions.
- "Flesh out" the stick figure to paint a simple person.

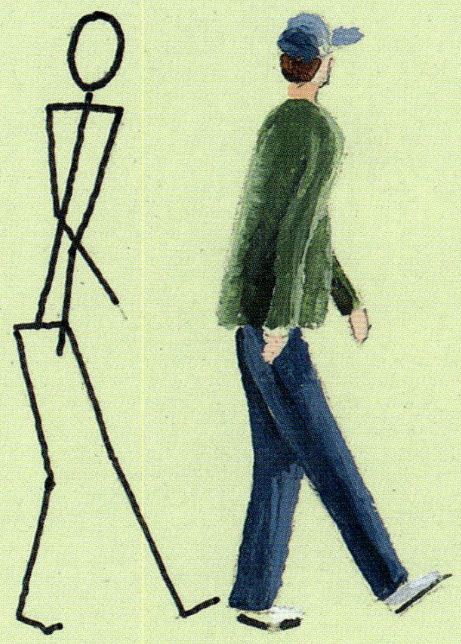

Shoulders forward for walking

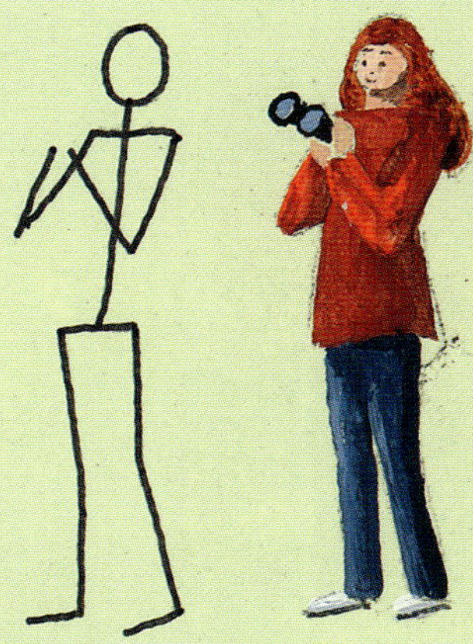

Hips slightly forward for standing

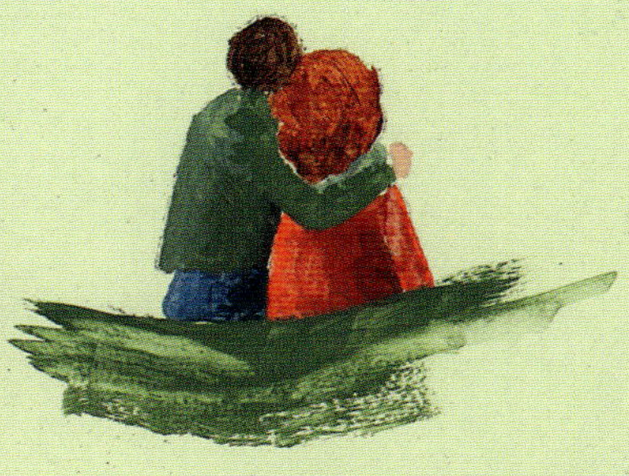

While detail is not important, and may be distracting, some details add character and others are critical. For example, a baseball cap adds character. A tackle box next to a fisherman strengthens the subject.

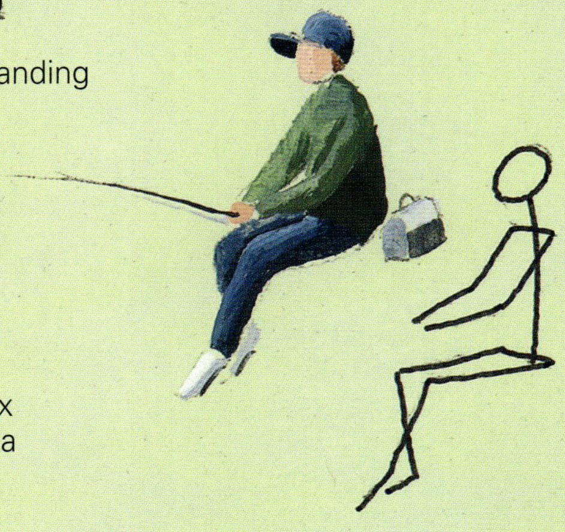

Caucasian Flesh Color Mixes

Light
Titanium White
+ Yellow Ochre
+ Cadmium Red Light

Medium
Light flesh mix
+ Burnt Sienna

Sheep & Cattle

Keep animals small and simple. Paint the shadow first, then paint the colors of the coat. Add shading and highlights to accentuate the form. Indicate the eyes with small dots. Even though the nose is tiny, be accurate with the shape.

SHEEP

Sheep with black faces, ears, and legs are more recognizable than the all-white ones. The typical sheep has a shaggy coat and rounded body. Legs are thin, ears large, and the nose rounded. Grazing sheep occasionally look up to check their surroundings. They add charm, a sense of peace, and an old-fashioned look to a landscape.

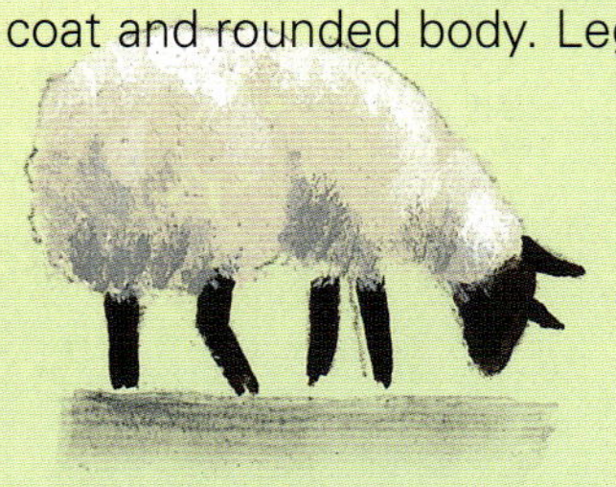
Grazing

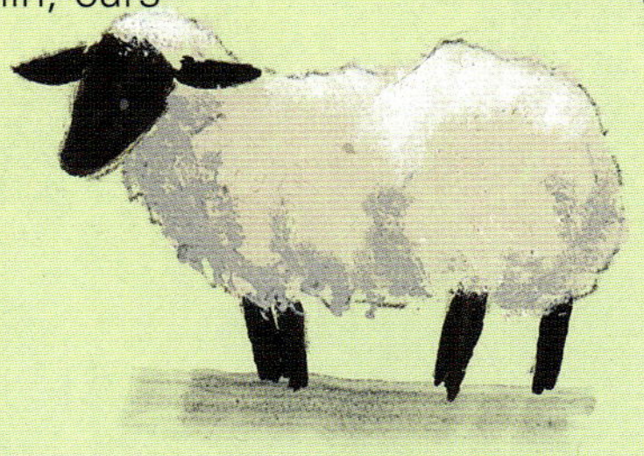
Standing

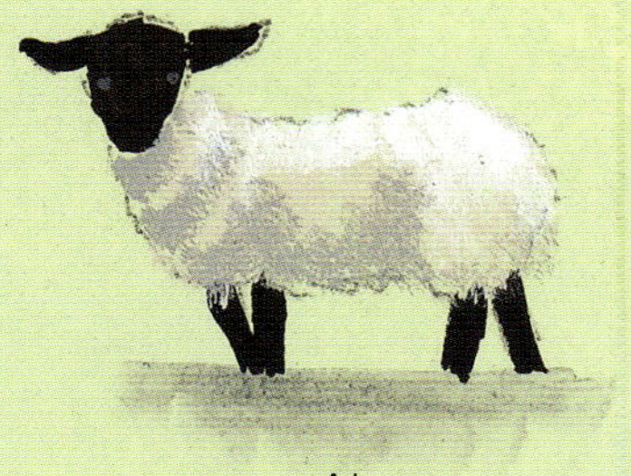
Alert

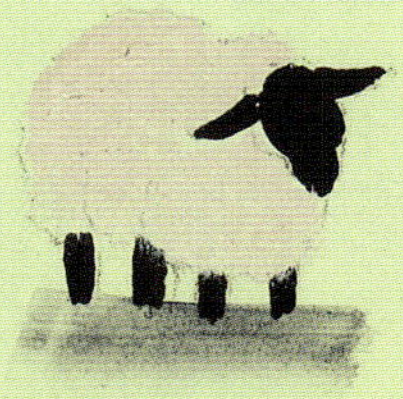

- Paint shadow.
- Paint legs, face, and ears.
- With a scumbler, dab off-white over body for a fluffy look.

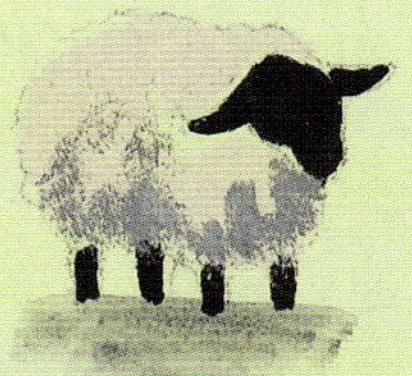
With a scumbler, dab shadows with a medium gray.

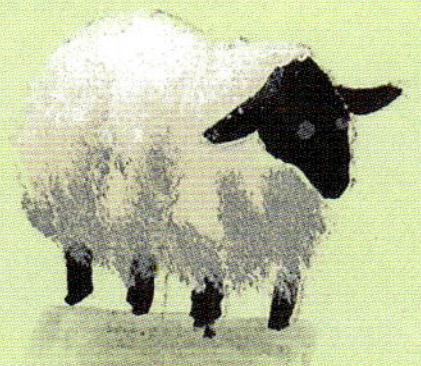
Dab highlights with Titanium White.

CATTLE

Cattle have boxy heads, flat backs, bony hips, and sturdy legs. Some breeds are uniform in color - black, brown, tan or cream - but others have patches of brown and white or black and white. Both males and females may have horns. Dairy cattle graze on rich pasture, but beef cattle are often seen on rangelands. In groups, cattle generally face in the same direction.

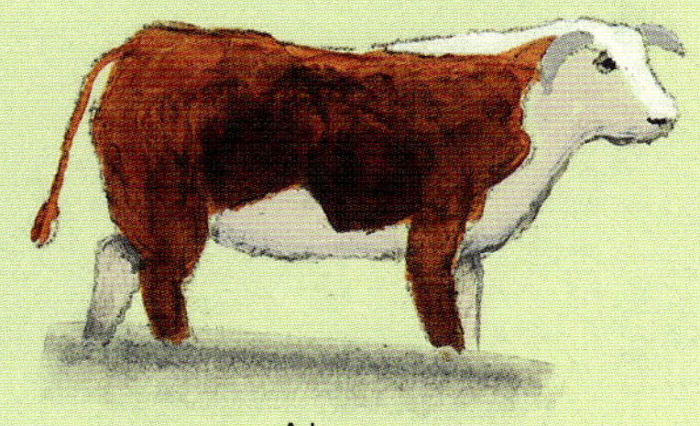
Alert

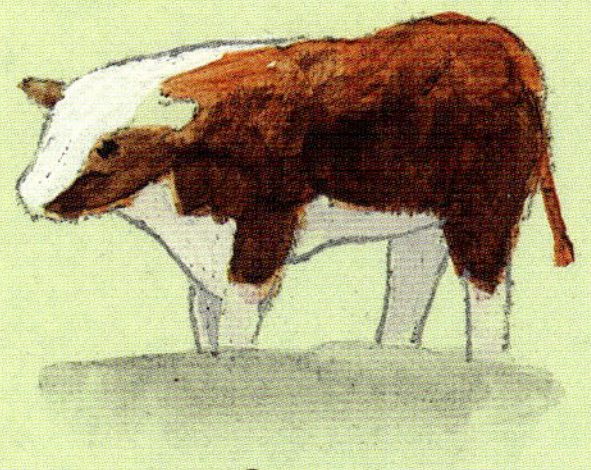
Standing

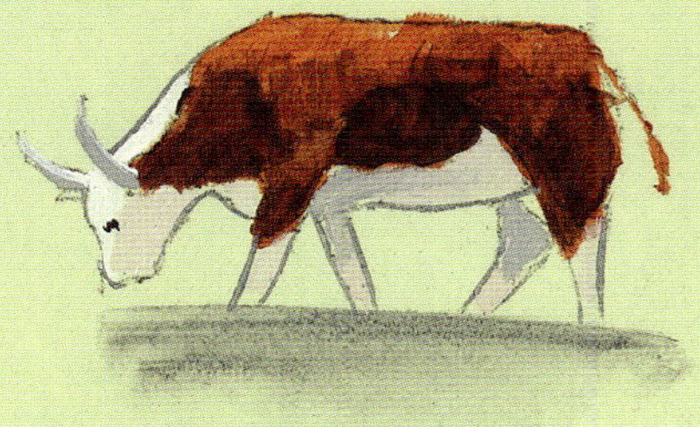
Grazing

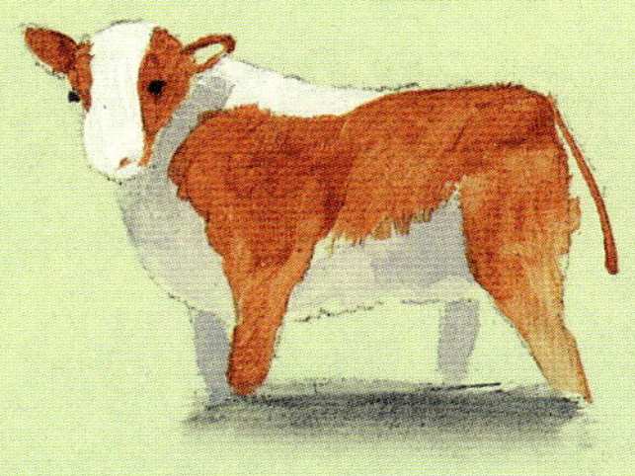

- Highlight white areas with light cream.
- Shade white areas with dark cream and light gray.
- Paint brown areas with Burnt Sienna.

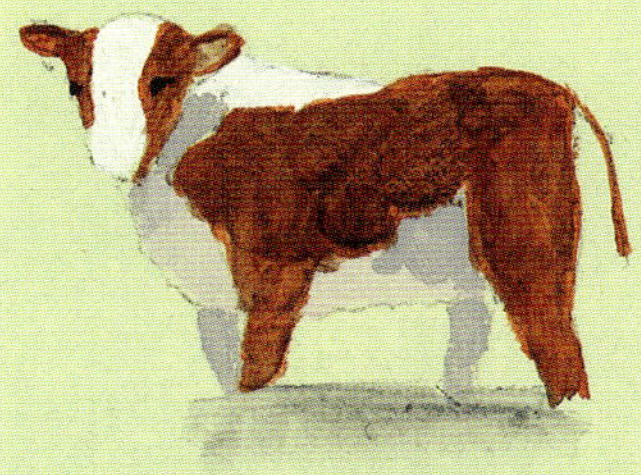
Paint Burnt Umber over the Burnt Sienna.

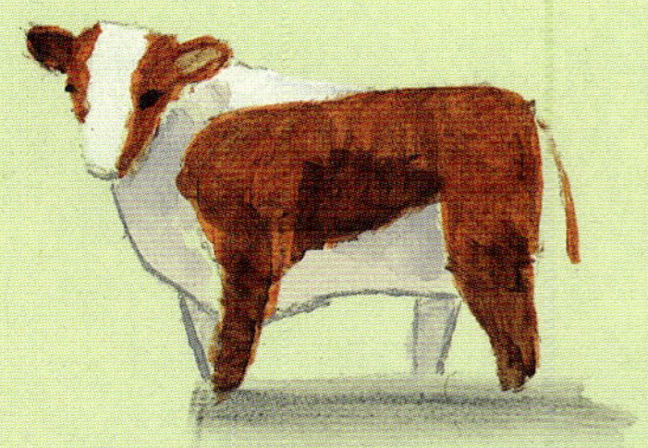
Deepen shadows on brown areas with additional layers of Burnt Umber.

Burnt Sienna and Burnt Umber are transparent colors. Build depth with layers, drying after each layer.

More Animals

Horses

Horses add elegance to the landscape. The bodies are boxy, the legs long and slender, the heads somewhat pointed with large rounded cheek muscles, and the manes and tails flowing.

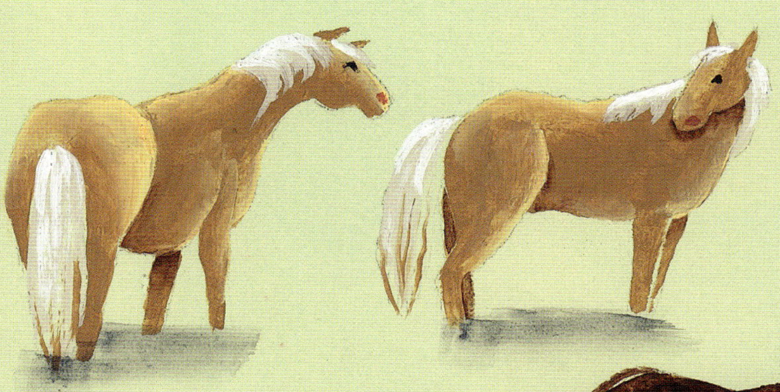

Horses are often seen in groups.

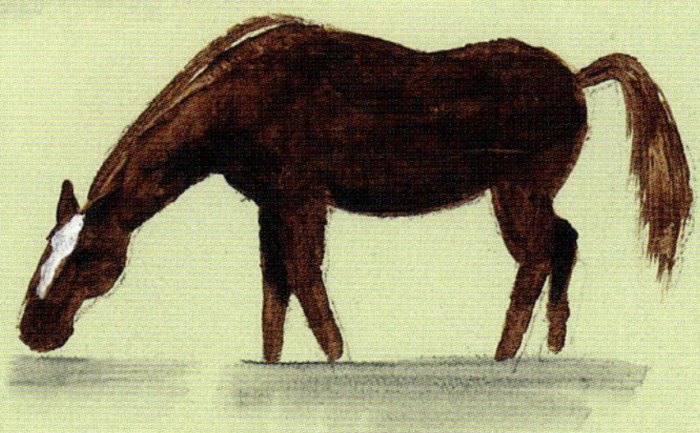

Deer

Deer have large ears, thick bodies, and slender legs. The males have distinctive antlers.

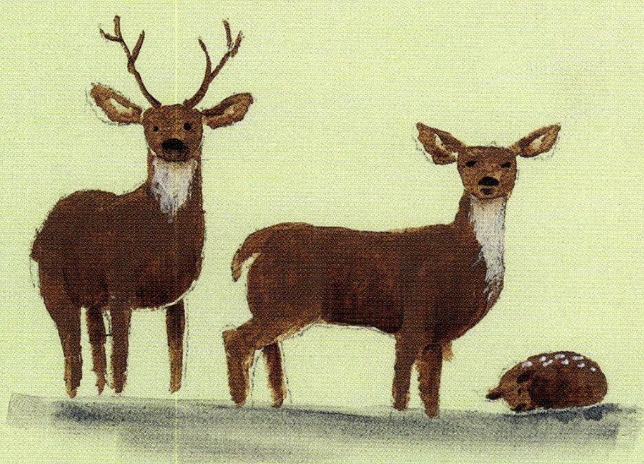

- Poses are alert-deer will frequently be looking at the viewer.
- Fawns are tiny, curled-up shapes with light dots along their backs.

Birds

Distant birds are seen as little "V" shapes. Vary their angles and sizes slightly.

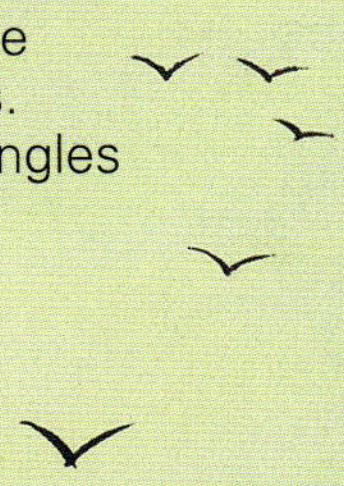

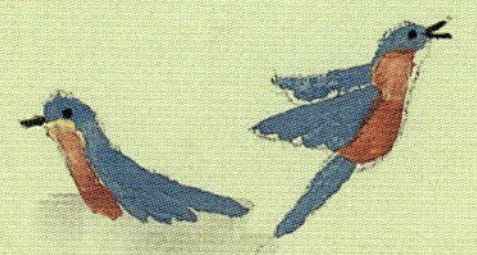

Birds in foreground vegetation can be more detailed.

Foxes

Foxes have pointy ears and noses, slender bodies and legs, and long fluffy tails. The black legs and ear tips, as well as the white chest and tail tip, are distinctive.

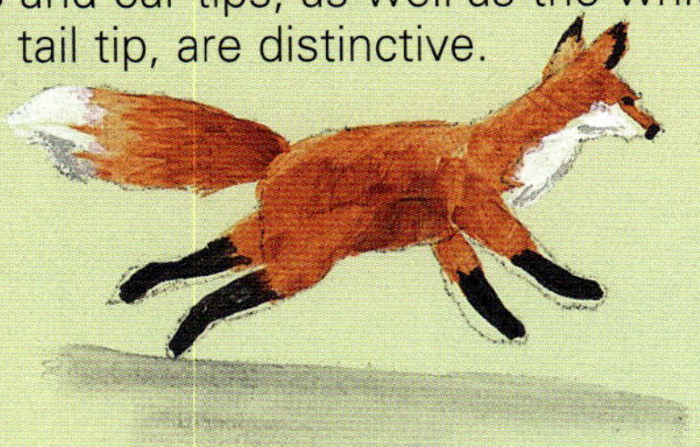

A fox may run through a wilderness scene.

Dogs

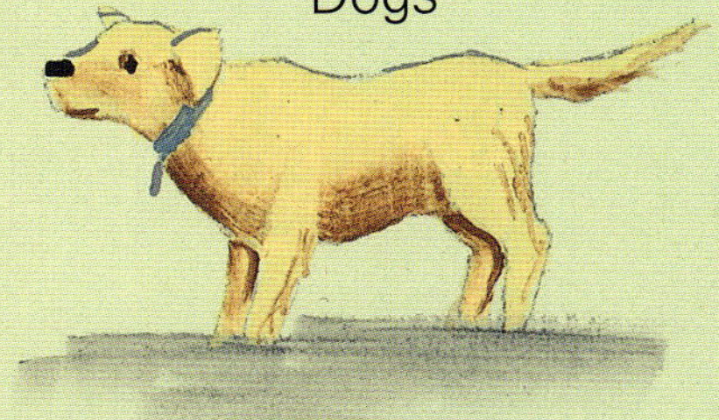

Dogs enjoy the fields.

Cats

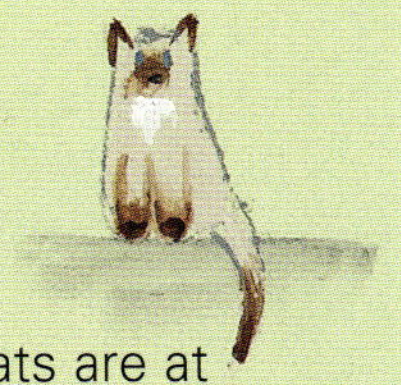

Cats are at home in a garden.

Boat & Chair

A simple boat can add a splash of color to your landscape.

Its pointed shape can direct attention to another element in your composition.

The boat could be drawn up on the shore of a lake or tied to a dock.

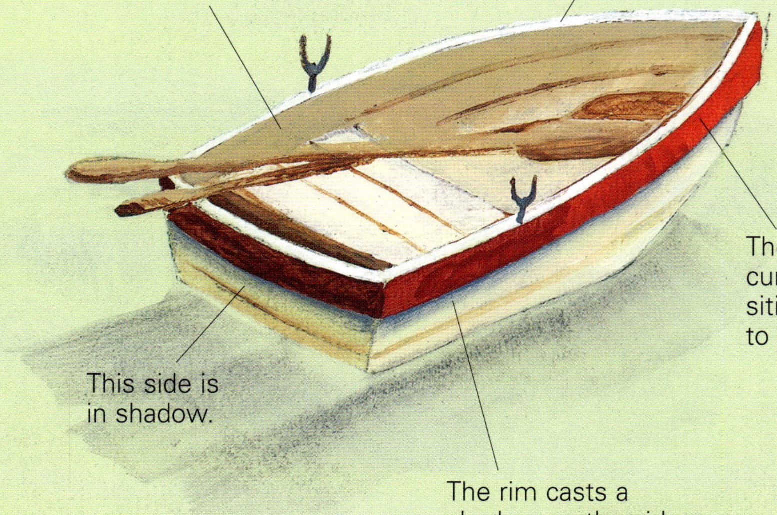

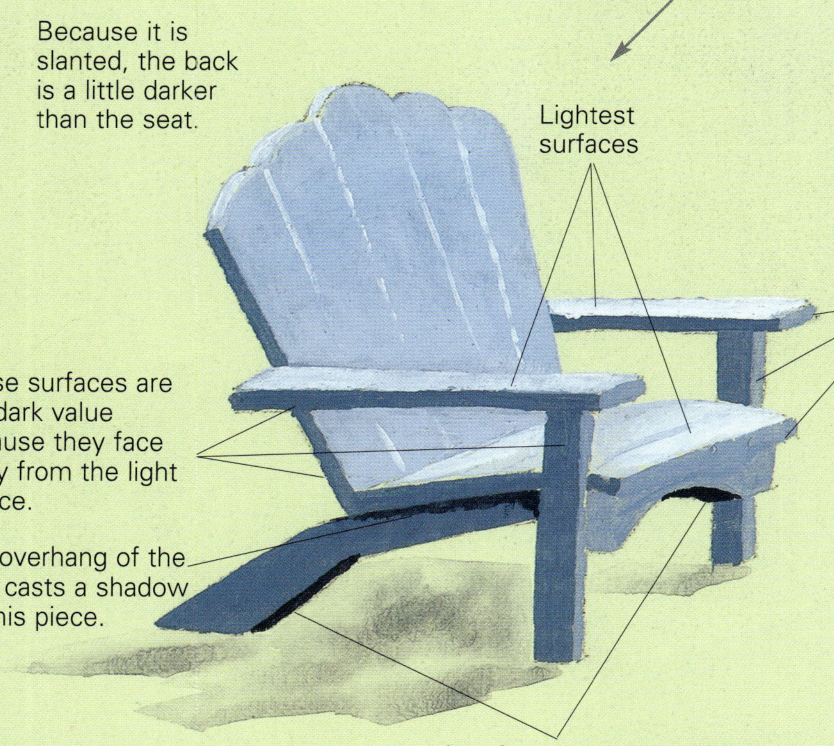

Lawn chairs add a comfortable, homey touch, and they can be colorful.

When painting objects made of wood, be sure to portray the thickness of the boards.

Concrete Items

Light source

A simple concrete bench may become a focal point in a garden scene. A sleeping cat makes it that much more interesting.

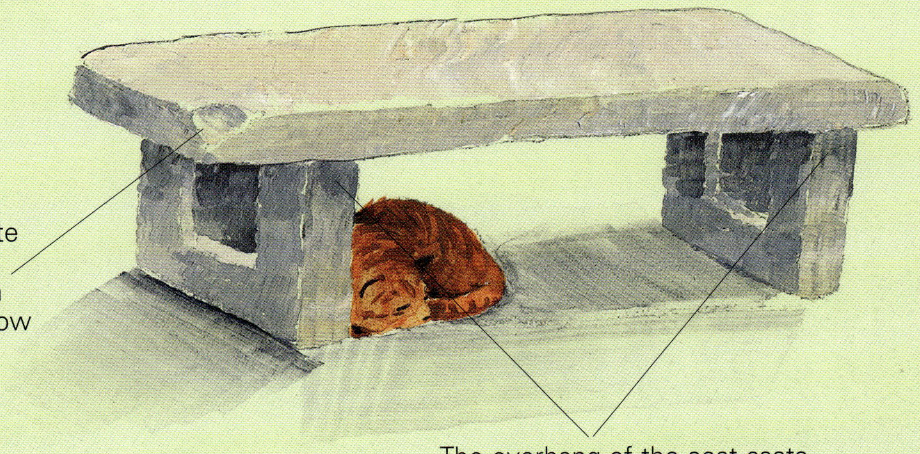

A chip adds a note of authenticity. Note the position of light and shadow within the chip.

The overhang of the seat casts shadows on the leg pieces.

A decorative concrete pot

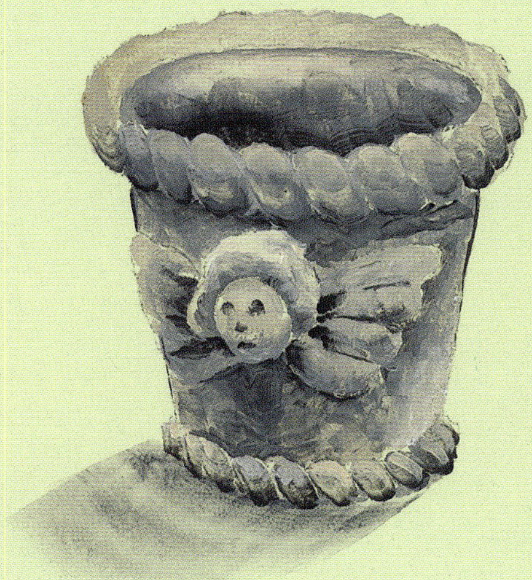

To paint rough, textured concrete shapes:

1. Prepare dark, medium, and light value mixes of Titanium White, Buff Titanium, and Graphite Gray. Only *partially* mix them, so there is color variation within each mix.

2. Working with a #4 flat brush and very short strokes, move among the dark, medium, and light mixes to form the object with light and shadow.

Chapter 5

PUTTING IT TOGETHER

Where is the viewer standing in relation to the painting?

Where is the horizon line?

What is the focal point?

Designing a painting is an orderly process. Working out the perspective and arrangement of elements in a full-size sketch gives me a road map to follow as I paint. If my design includes a building, animal, or person, or some other feature where the perspective must be correct, I continue working on my sketch until I have drawn these elements in their final form.

Creating the Illusion of Depth

In landscape painting we are depicting three-dimensional space in a two-dimensional medium. In the real landscape, the various elements - trees, shrubs, hills, buildings - occupy continuous space. To create the illusion of depth in your painting, it is helpful to group elements into a series of planes that recede into space, to overlap objects, and to suggest distance by the relative size of objects. The rules of perspective provide guidelines for drawing convincing objects made up of straight lines, such as buildings, fences, or fields with rows.

FOREGROUND/MIDDLE GROUND/BACKGROUND

A typical landscape painting has four planes:

1. The elements closest to the viewer occupy the *foreground.* Objects in the foreground tend to be large and detailed. Trees may extend the full height of the canvas.
2. The *middle ground* lies behind the foreground. Objects are still fairly large and some detail is apparent. Individual objects may merge into clusters.
3. Objects in the distance occupy the *background.* They are small and not detailed. In fact, the shapes are just indicated and individual elements merge together. In the background, we see the "forest" and not the "trees."
4. The *sky* occupies the farthest plane.

Figure 1
Background/
Middle ground/
Foreground

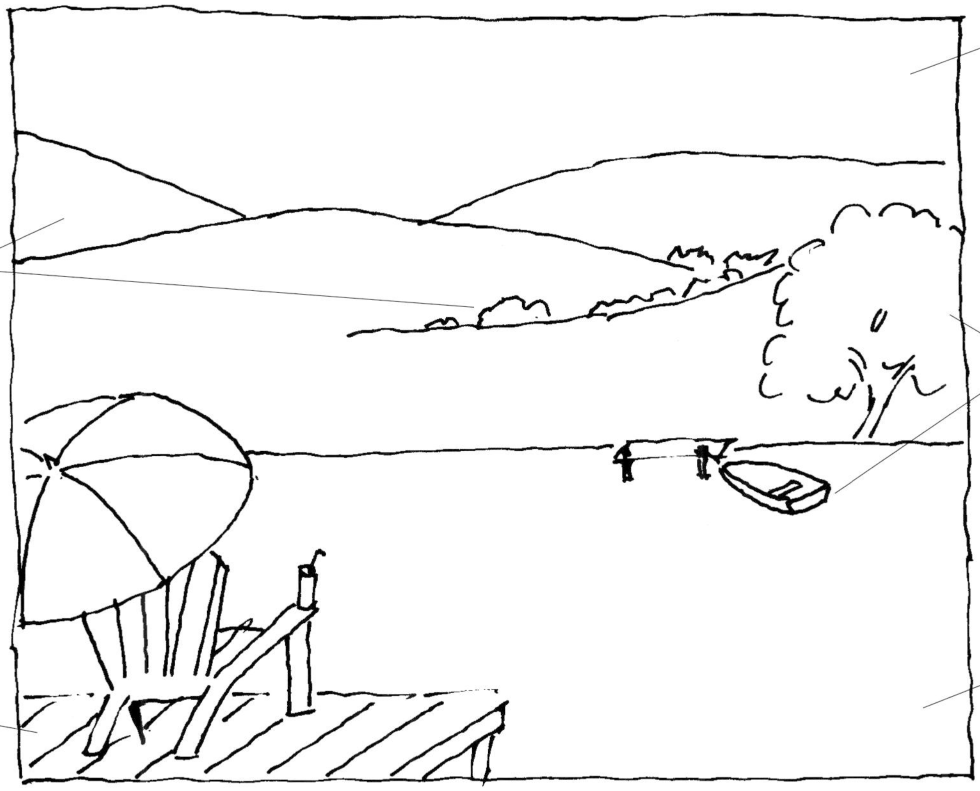

OVERLAPPING OBJECTS

The concepts of "in front of" and "behind" are key to providing the illusion of depth. We use line, value, and color to make nearer objects appear to overlap farther objects.

Figure 2
Overlapping Objects

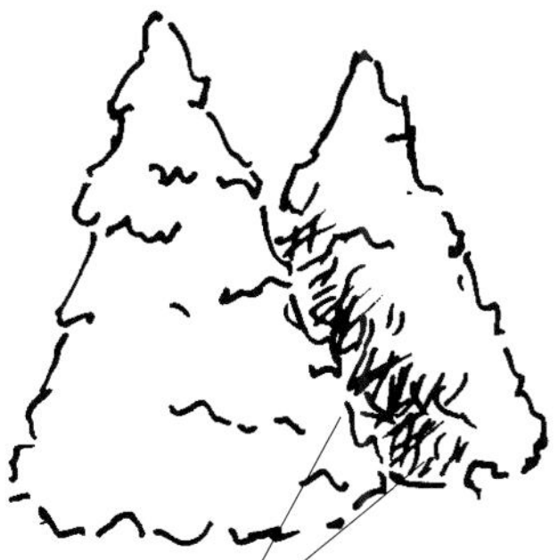

This line and this shadow indicate that the left tree is in front of the right tree.

RELATIVE SIZE

Larger objects appear to be nearer, and smaller objects appear to be farther away. For example, trees in the foreground of a painting are larger than trees in the background. The greater the difference in their size, the greater the distance portrayed. In the case of a fence receding into the background, the posts nearer the viewer appear taller and farther apart than the ones farther from the viewer. Generally, objects closer to the viewer are placed lower on the canvas, and objects farther away, higher.

Figure 3
Relative Size

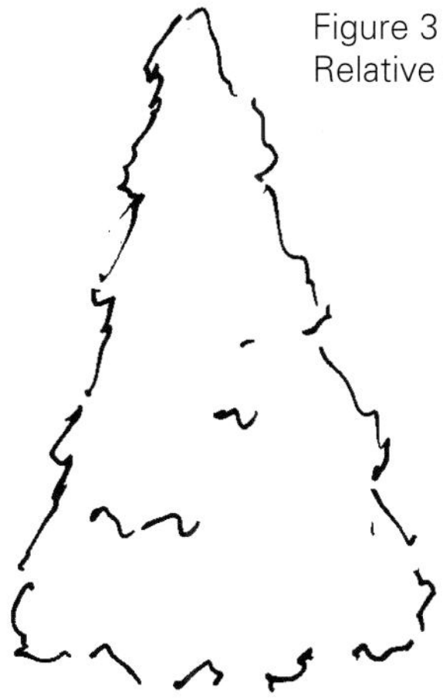

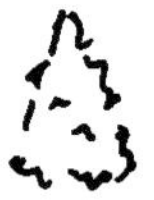

The farther tree is smaller and higher in the plane.

The nearer tree is larger and lower in the plane.

Perspective

Perspective is a series of guidelines for creating the illusion of depth on a flat surface. It was when these drawing methods were developed during the Renaissance that European painting began to take on a more realistic look. There is no law that art must be realistic, but when that is your goal, the rules of perspective will help you achieve it.

Linear perspective provides methods for drawing objects largely made of straight lines, such as buildings, which appear to have depth. An object is drawn in relation to a specific vanishing point (or points) on a specific horizon line. You cannot move the building up or down without re-drawing it, or it will look out of place in your landscape.

Aerial perspective is a set of guidelines that describe the cumulative effects of tiny atmospheric particles on the appearance of distant versus near objects.

Near objects	Far objects
Sharp edges	Fuzzy edges
Lots of detail	Very little detail
Wide range of value	Narrow range of value – darks are lighter, lights are darker
Bright colors	Duller colors
True colors	Bluish or grayish colors

Figure 4
One Point Linear Perspective

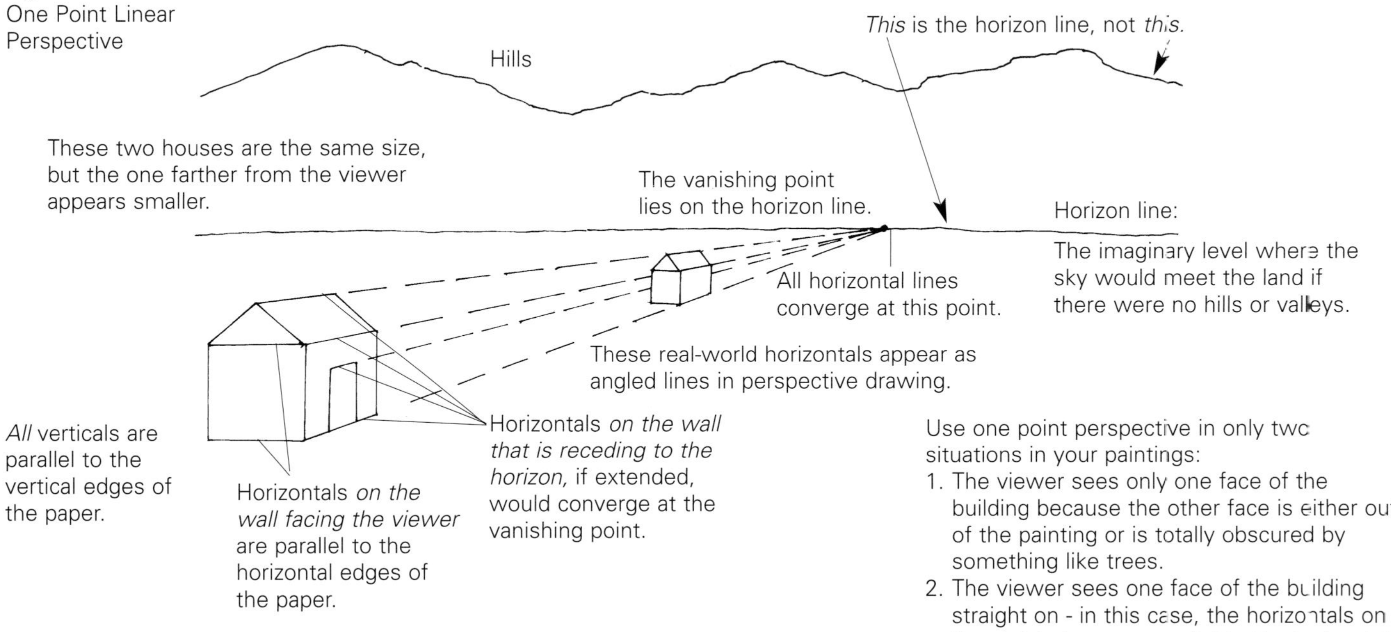

Use one point perspective in only two situations in your paintings:

1. The viewer sees only one face of the building because the other face is either out of the painting or is totally obscured by something like trees.
2. The viewer sees one face of the building straight on - in this case, the horizontals on the visible face are parallel to the horizontal edges of your canvas.

Use two point perspective in all other situations.

Figure 5
Two Point Linear Perspective

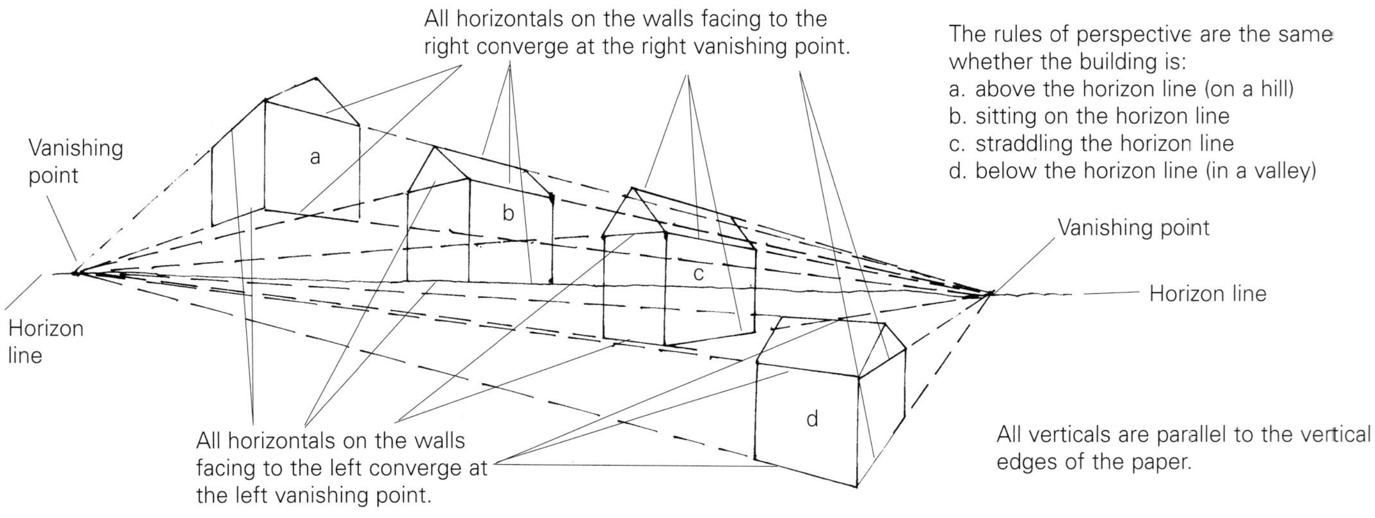

The rules of perspective are the same whether the building is:

a. above the horizon line (on a hill)
b. sitting on the horizon line
c. straddling the horizon line
d. below the horizon line (in a valley)

Figure 6
Draw a Simple Building with Two Point Perspective

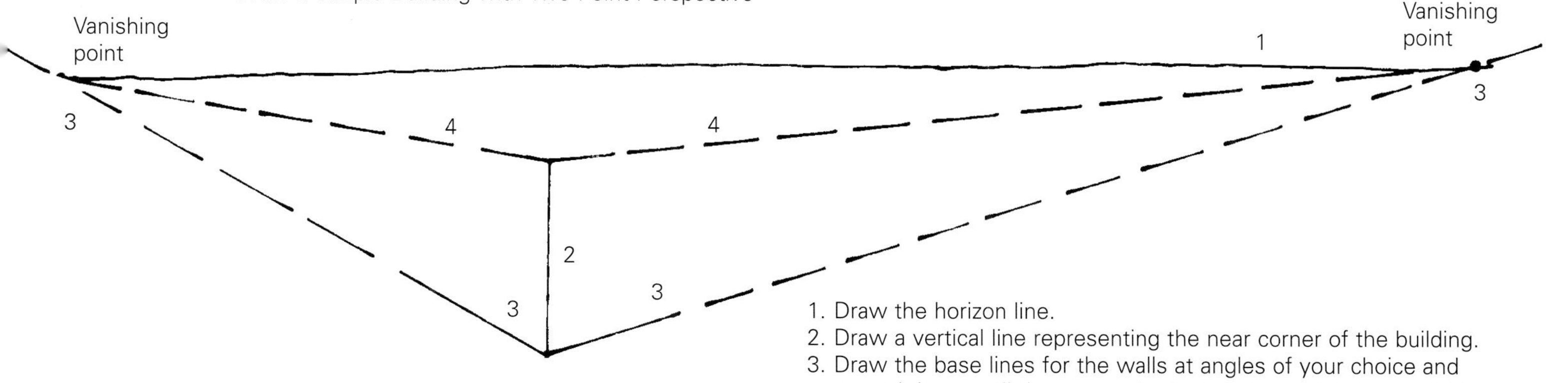

1. Draw the horizon line.
2. Draw a vertical line representing the near corner of the building.
3. Draw the base lines for the walls at angles of your choice and extend them until they cross the horizon line. Mark the vanishing points where these lines cross the horizon line.
4. Draw lines from the top of the vertical to the vanishing points.

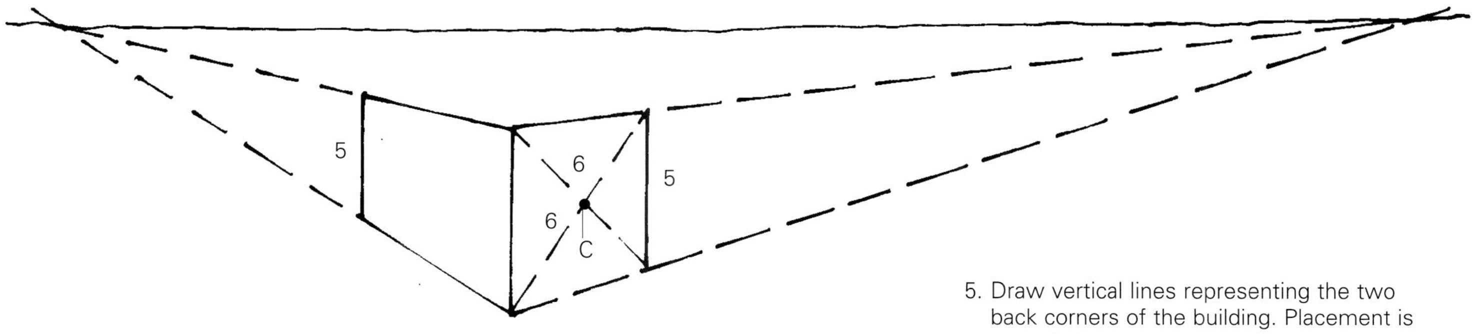

5. Draw vertical lines representing the two back corners of the building. Placement is your choice.
6. Draw diagonals from opposite corners of the wall where the roof peak will be. This locates the center (C).

These two lines would eventually meet.

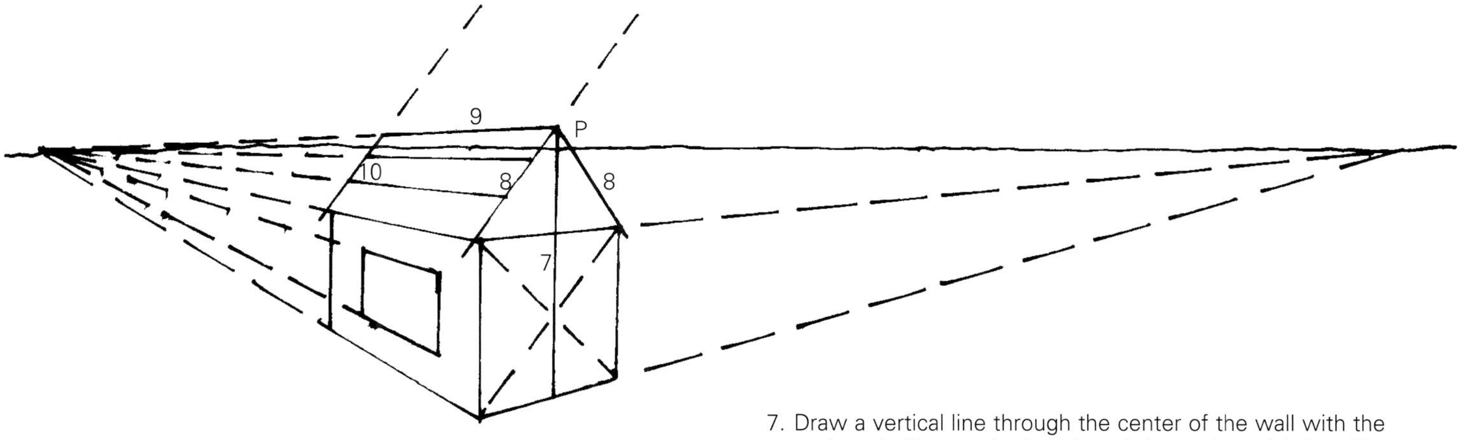

All horizontal lines-such as the tops and bottoms of windows and doors, shingle rows on the roof, or siding lines on the walls-converge at the vanishing points.

7. Draw a vertical line through the center of the wall with the roof peak. Choose the location of the peak on this line (P).
8. Draw lines connecting the peak to the upper corners of the wall.
9. Draw a line from the peak to the left vanishing point. This is the ridge of the roof.
10. Draw a line from the upper corner of the left-facing wall to the ridge line, approximately parallel to the line at the front. These two lines, if extended upward, would eventually meet.

Composition

The *composition* of a painting is the way the individual elements are arranged into the whole. Good composition is pleasing to the eye, draws the viewer into and around the painting, and has an emotional impact that is consistent with the painting's subject.

Tip: If you will be framing your painting, keep in mind that the outer 3/8" of your canvas will be hidden by the frame.

Figure 7
More Lines & Stops

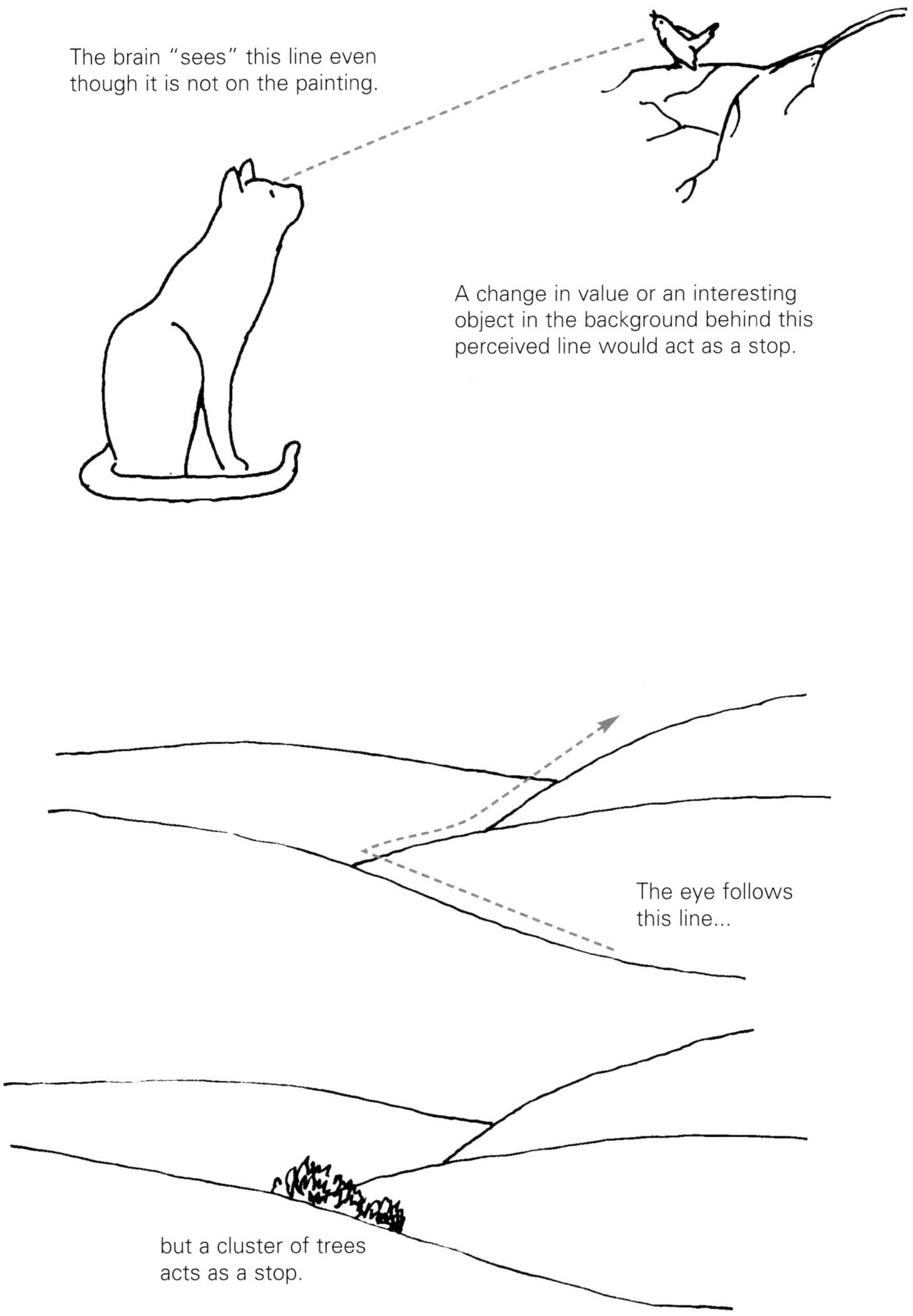

Focal Point

The *focal point* is the part of the painting that naturally draws the eye. Select an interesting element and use composition and contrast to strengthen its impact. In landscapes, examples of focal points are a large rock in a stream where the water breaks dramatically, an animal drinking from a pond, the open door of a barn, or the gate in a stone wall.

One way to place your focal point is to sketch light lines dividing your canvas in thirds horizontally and vertically. Placing your focal point at any of the four intersections where these lines cross is a safe choice; the human eye naturally gravitates to them. This is called the *thirds rule,* but despite its name it is only a guideline.

Avoid placing your focal point along the horizontal or vertical center of your canvas, or too near an edge. Dividing the canvas in half can make for a boring composition, and a focal point near an edge can lead the eye out of the painting.

Contrast attracts the eye and emphasizes the focal point. Some ways to create contrast:

- Have the lightest light and the darkest dark in your painting meet at the focal point.
- Have complementary colors meet at the focal point.
- If the painting is primarily cool, use a bit of a warm color at the focal point, and vice versa.
- Place more detail in and around the focal point than in other parts of the painting.

Lines & Stops

Lines draw the eye into and around the painting, and "stops" stop it. The stronger the line, the more determined the motion. The stronger the stop, the longer the interruption in eye movement.

Lead the viewer to the focal point - the strongest stop - and gently beyond. The eye should not be drawn out of the painting never to return, nor strongly fixed on the focal point.

Figure 8
Drawing the Viewer into the Painting

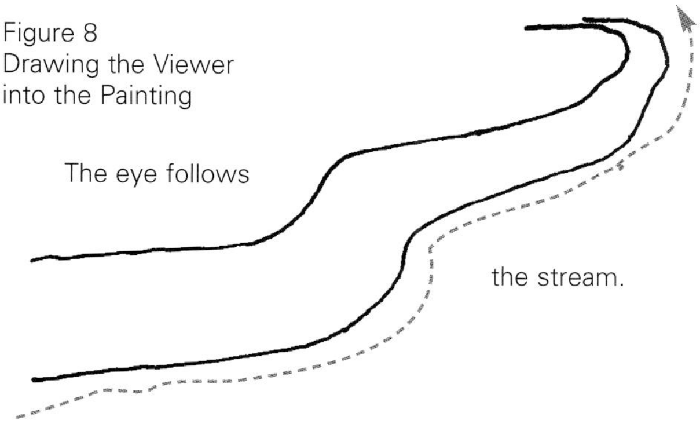

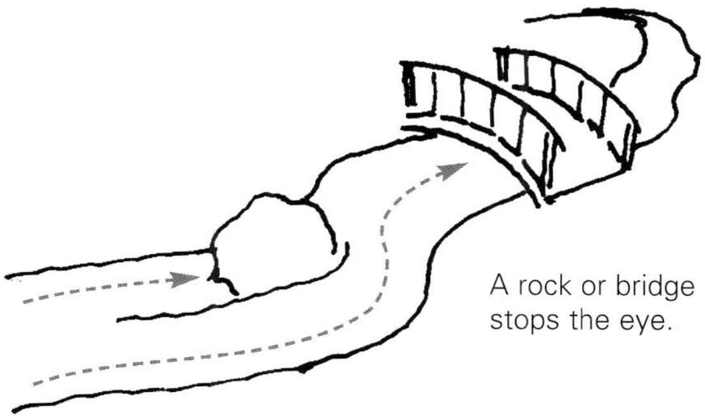

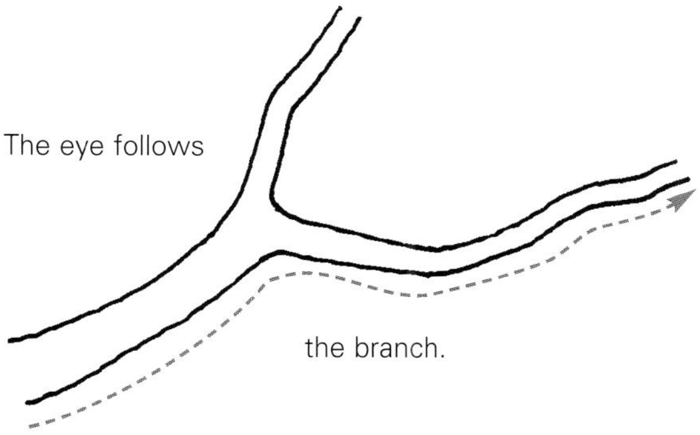

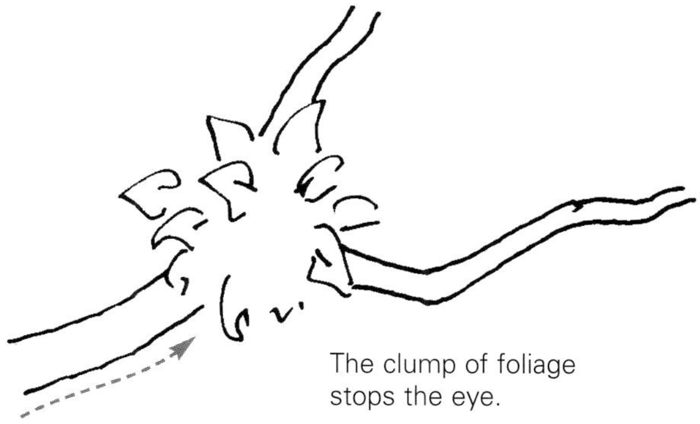

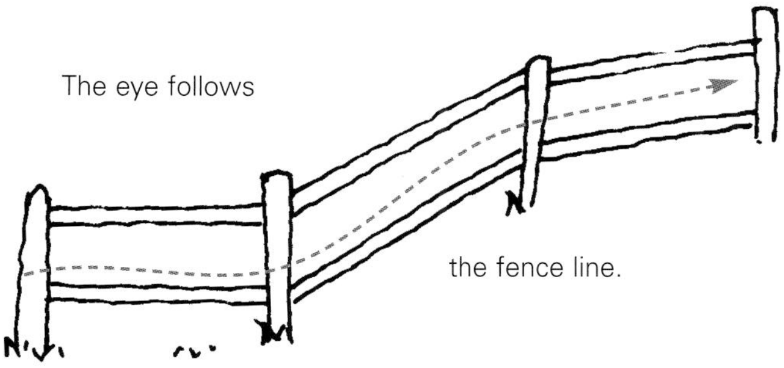

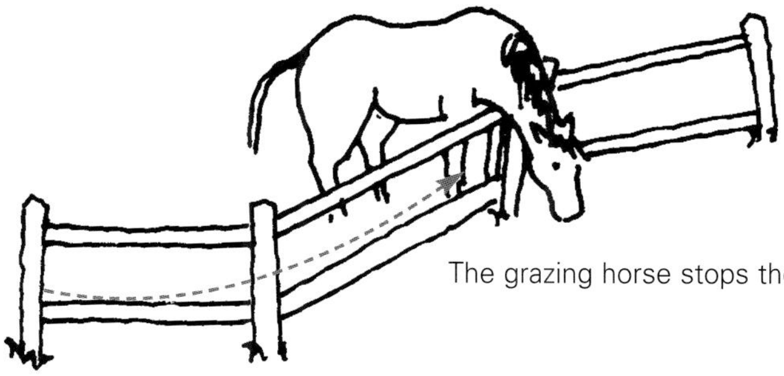

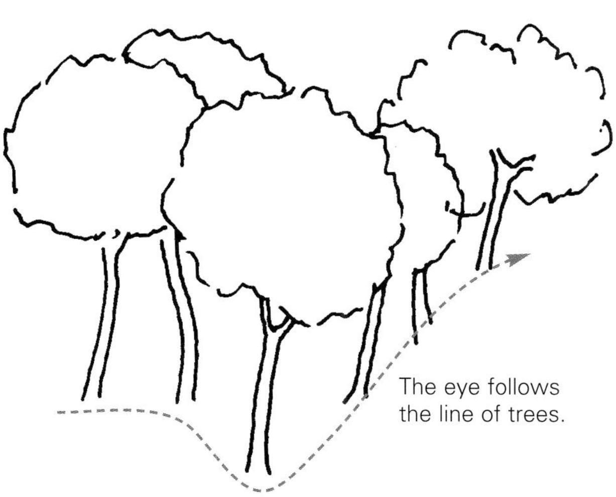

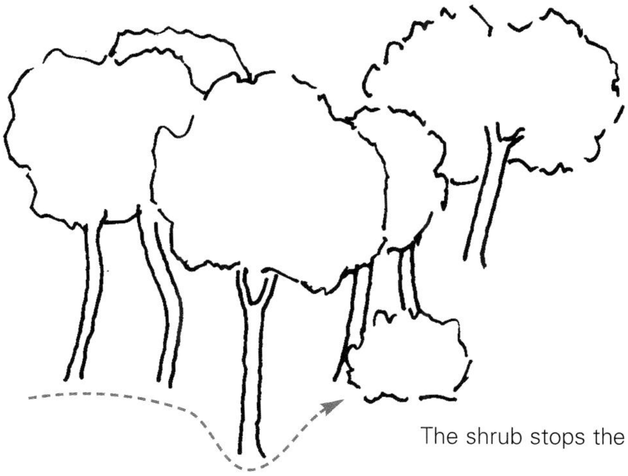

The Elements of Light

Light, expressed through the values in highlights and shadows, is the element of a painting that creates the strongest visual impact.
It is critical that the source of light in a painting be consistent. Select the location of your light source and be sure that every highlight and shadow is correct. An object will look quite different with different light sources, so consider a variety of possibilities and select the one that works best with your composition.

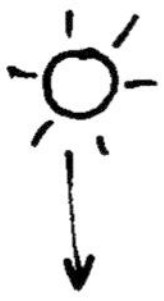

When the light source is high (mid-day):
- Shadows are short
- Highlights are at the top

Fig. 9
Shadows & Highlights

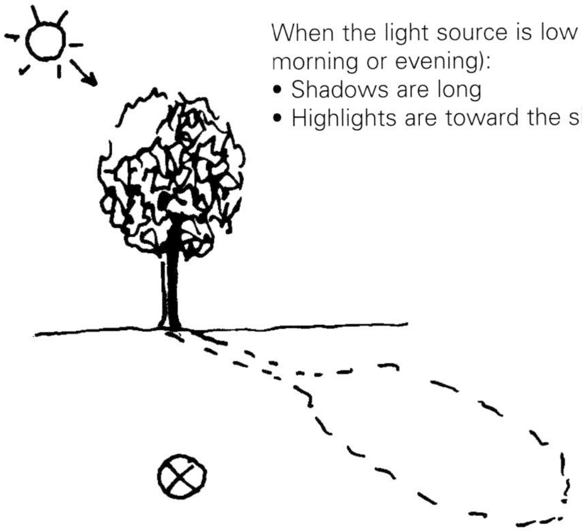

When the light source is low (early morning or evening):
- Shadows are long
- Highlights are toward the side

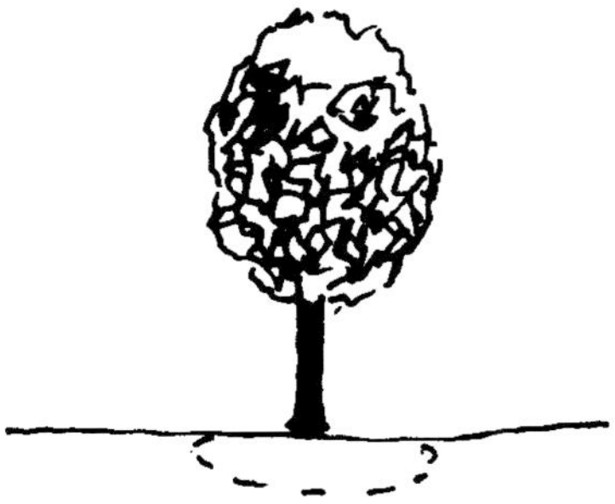

When the light source is in front of the viewer:
- Object is dark with a halo effect
- Shadows stretch straight toward the viewer

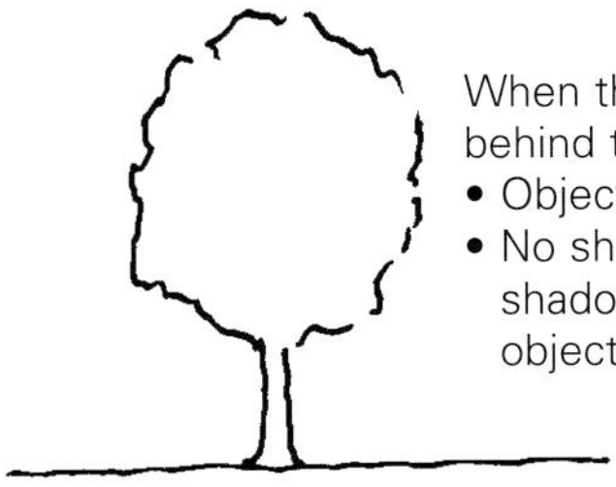

When the light source is behind the viewer:
- Object is bright
- No shadow is visible- shadows are behind objects

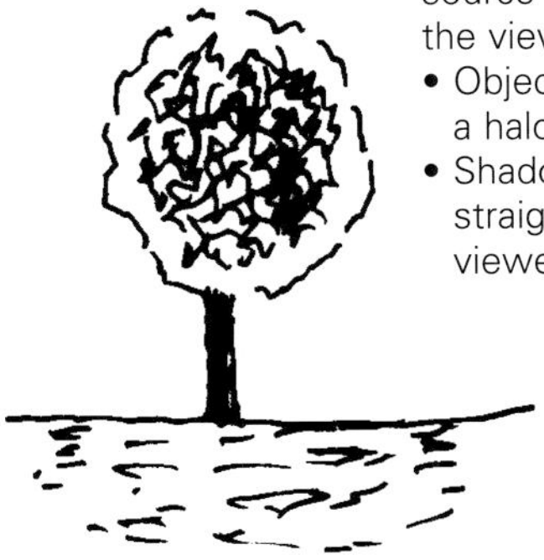

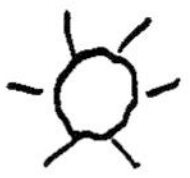

If the light source is to the left, shadows fall to the right of an object and the highlight is on the left side.

If the light source is to the right, shadows fall to the left and the highlight is on the right.

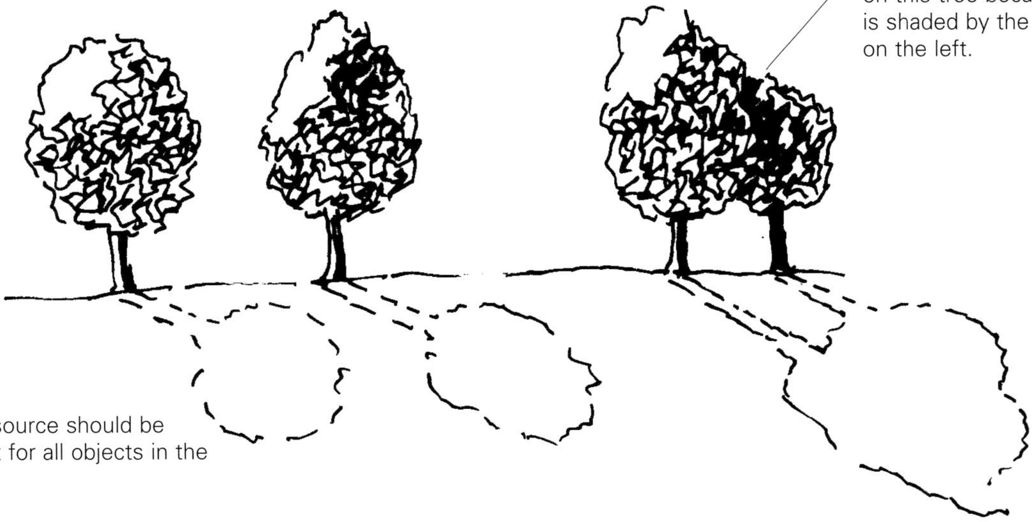

There is no highlight on this tree because it is shaded by the tree on the left.

The light source should be consistent for all objects in the painting.

Figure 10
The Element of Light

Light source in center of painting is appropriate only at sunrise or sunset.

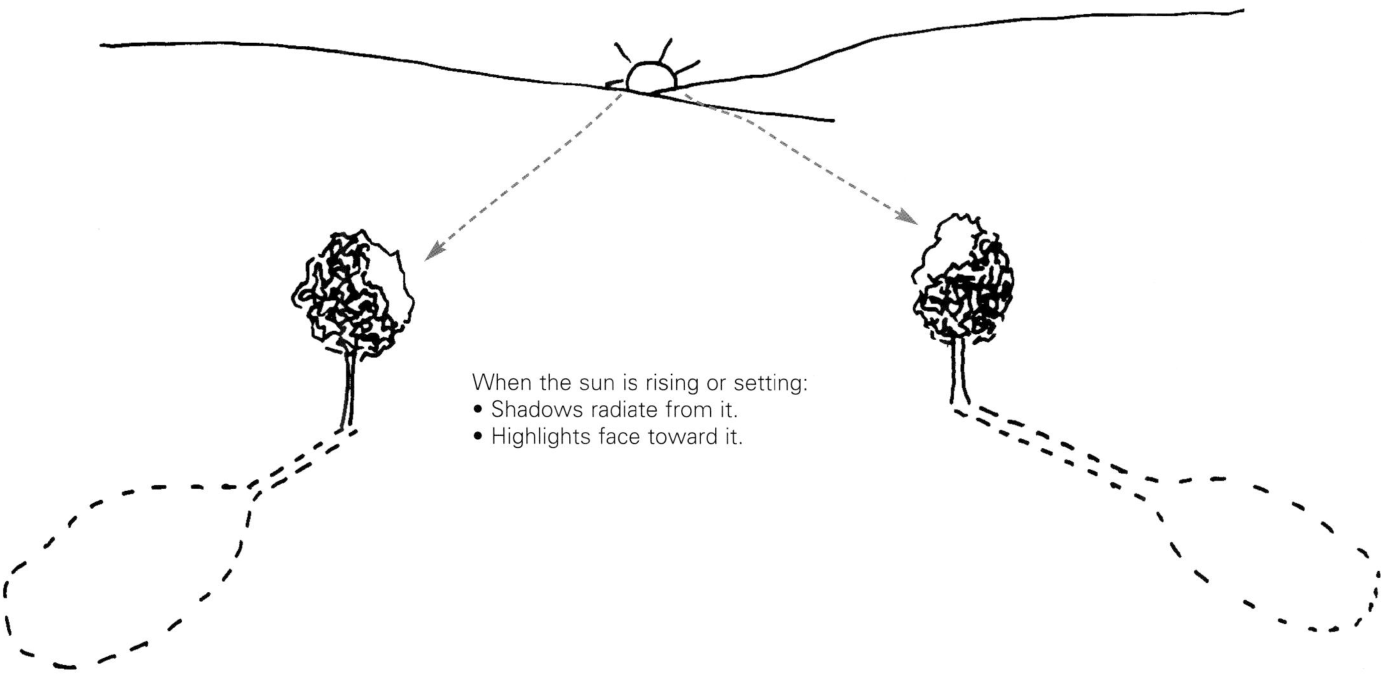

Shadows follow the contour of the ground:
- Straight shadows suggest flat ground.
- This wavy shadow suggests rolling ground.

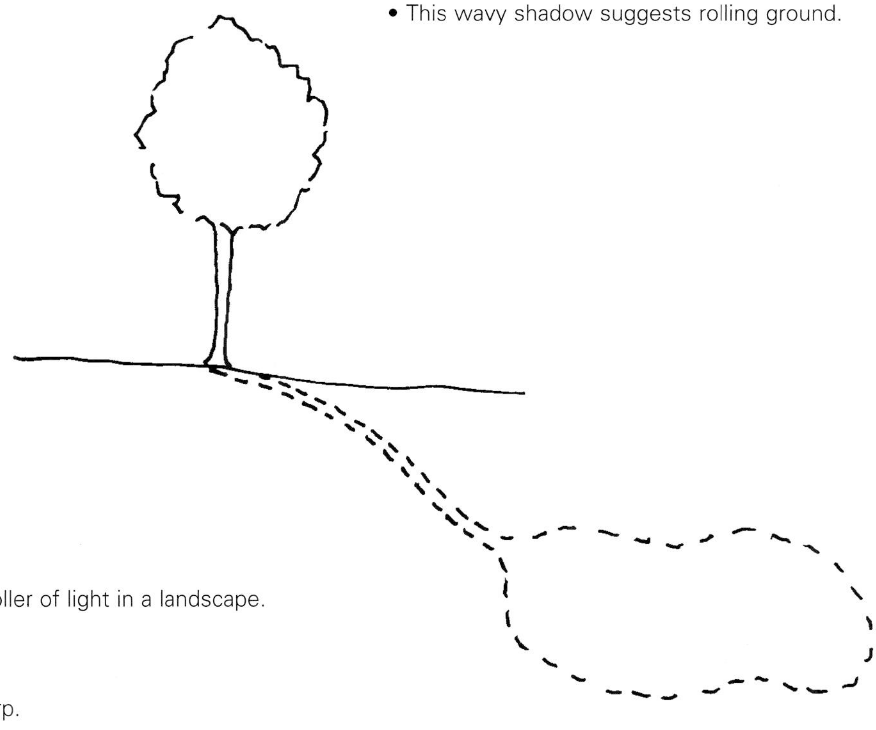

WEATHER & LIGHT

The weather is the primary controller of light in a landscape.

Sunny days:
- Colors are bright and warm.
- Shadows are very dark and sharp.
- Highlights are very bright.
- Edges of shadows are sharp nearest the object and get fuzzier farther away.
- Deep shadows obscure detail, and highlights wash them out.
- Detail shows best in mid-tone areas.

Overcast days:
- Less value contrast than on sunny days.
- Shadows are lighter and highlights are less bright.
- Edges of both highlights and shadows are softer.
- More detail is visible in shadow and highlight areas.
- Colors are cooler and duller.

Cloudy days:
- There can be dramatic differences between areas in sun and areas shaded by clouds.
- The high-contrast areas of sun and shadow create a composition on their own. Be sure that it works within the overall intent of the painting.

Chapter 6

LET'S PAINT LANDSCAPES

Here are eight painting demonstrations, with instructions, color palettes, and photographs of the stages in their development. You can follow the instructions and refer to the step-by-step worksheets to paint these landscapes for yourself, applying the techniques I have described in this book. Enjoy!

Successful paintings don't begin with the first brushstroke-they begin with ideas, sketches, and thoughtful choices. I encourage you to design and paint your own landscapes, breaking down the process into steps that build on each other.

My Design Process

1. The first step is the idea. What do I want to paint and how do I want to convey it? I have three sources for ideas - imagination, memory, and my photographs.
2. I decide what elements will convey my idea. From my imagination, I can create places I would love to be. I freely add, subtract, or rearrange elements from a photograph as well as a memory.
3. I select a canvas size and rough out a full-size sketch, arranging the elements into a composition that supports the focal point. This is largely a process of trial and error, and I may evaluate several sketches in order to choose the composition that works best.
4. Now I turn my attention to value - the lights and darks of the elements. For me, value is the single most important element in a painting. I first do a "value sketch" that is 5" x 7" - although most of the demonstration paintings in this book are 11" by 14". I draw lines on my full-size sketch to divide it in fourths vertically and horizontally, then do the same on my 5" x 7" paper. I copy the drawing square by square to get a reasonably accurate reduction of my sketch. I "color" this small copy with my pencil, placing my darks and lights. At this point, the design really seems to come to life.
5. The final step in developing my compositional sketch is to look at it with fresh eyes. I put it away for a day or two, then come back to it. After some time away from it, I often see new things.

Preparing to Paint

A color scheme will often be strongly suggested by the subject itself. Even if I'm working from a photograph where I already have the colors, it's helpful to think through the color scheme. Having a color scheme guides my color choices.

- I find it helpful to work on a colored, rather than a white canvas, so I choose a color with which to tone the canvas. The toning color should complement the colors I envision for the painting and set the mood that will influence me as I paint. A lighter tone works well for a high key (mostly light values) painting, while a darker tone is appropriate for low key (mostly dark values) paintings. Rather than mixing this color, I use bottled acrylic paints for decorative painting.
- If there are any elements in my sketch that I want to transfer to the canvas - rather than sketch freehand on the canvas - I create a full-size tracing. To transfer the drawing to the canvas, I place the tracing over the canvas and position a piece of graphite paper, graphite side down, between the tracing and the canvas. Going over the lines with a stylus transfers them to the canvas. I use both black and white transfer paper - black over light areas, and white over dark areas.
- I am now ready to paint!

General Instructions

- Match a color of bottled decorative acrylic paint to the toning color on the palette page.
- Cover the canvas with the toning color. Allow it to dry thoroughly before you sketch or transfer your drawing to the canvas.
- Read the instructions and mix generous quantities of the colors you will need for an area *before* you begin to paint. For example, mix all the sky and cloud colors, or all the tree and meadow colors. When you are blending wet-in-wet, you won't have time to stop and mix a color-the paint will dry.

REFUGE

6" x 8" Oval

I like painting small. It encourages me to get straight to the point! The focal point of this simple oval composition is the church, emphasized by the contrast between its light walls and the dark surrounding foliage. The reeds and birds in the foreground invite the viewer into the painting, and the threatening storm invites the viewer into the church.

At first glance it seems that I have broken the compositional "rule" against dividing the painting in half. But the values of the lower sky match the values of the pasture, so the eye doesn't perceive a sharp division.

This painting showcases three techniques - wet-in-wet blending, using a fan brush, and using a scumbler brush. By the time you have finished it, you will be comfortable with all three.

The oval canvas, is toned with a middle value gray that fits the mood of the painting. The instructions begin on Page 88.

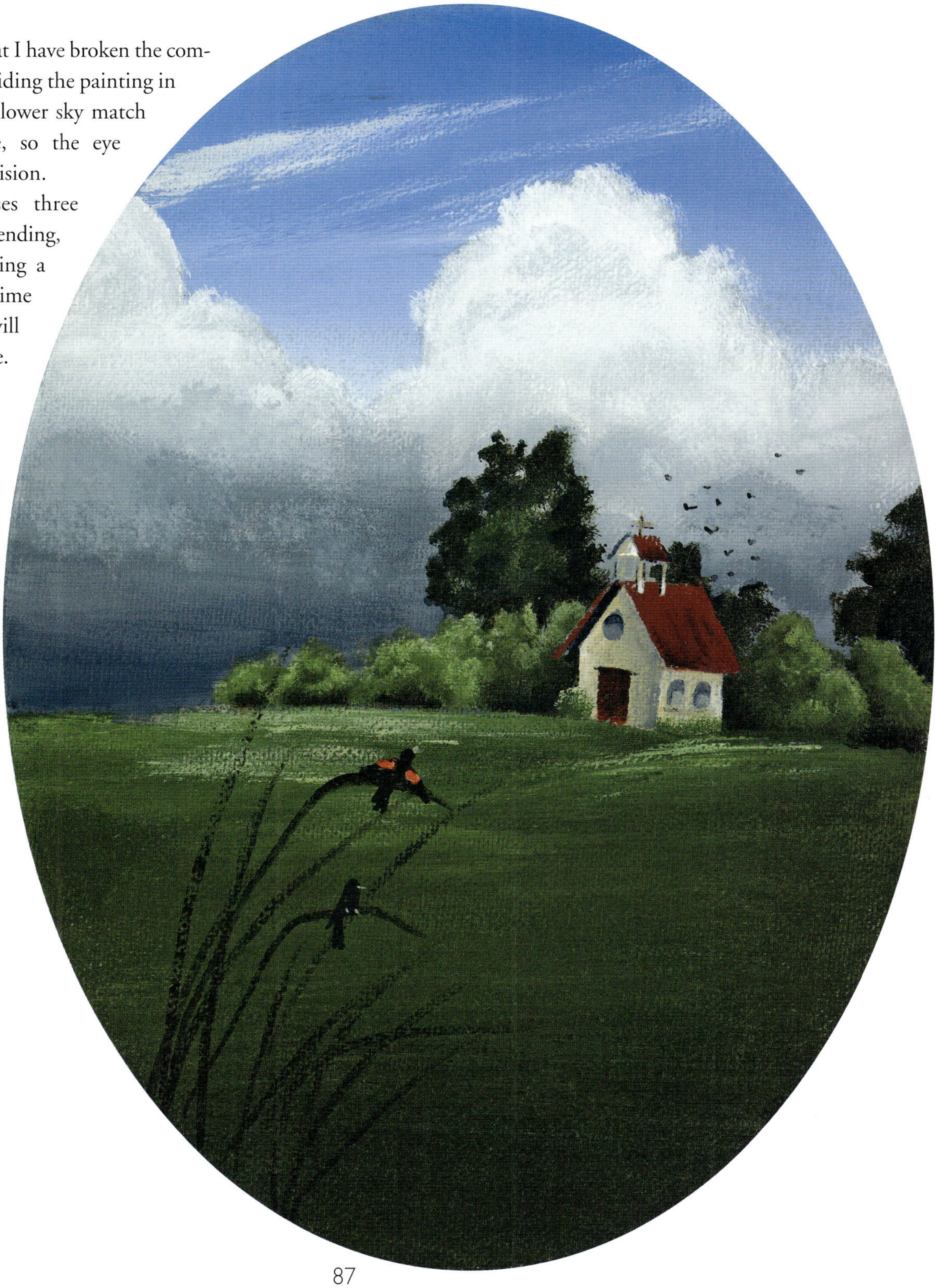

Color Scheme & Palette

This late summer composition calls for lush, deep greens. A storm is threatening, so the sky has deep blues at the top but grays near the horizon. To perk things up, there are red accents on the roof and door of the church, and on the red-winged blackbird.

Start here

S1 Ultramarine Blue + Cobalt Blue Deep + Titanium White

S2 S3 + S1

Start here

S3 Titanium White + Cerulean Blue

Start here

S4 Graphite Gray + Payne's Gray + Titanium White

S5 Titanium White + S4

S6 Titanium White + S5

S7 Titanium White + S6

Used for mixing colors:
Cadmium Red Deep
Cadmium Yellow Deep
Cadmium Yellow Light
Cerulean Blue
Cobalt Blue Deep
Graphite Gray
Mars Black
Payne's Gray
Sap Green
Titanium White
Ultramarine Blue

Sap Green Sequence

Refer to Page 24 for mixing instructions.

very dark, dark, medium, light, very light

G1 Sap Green sequence/very dark + Mars Black

Used straight from the tube:

Buff Titanium

Red Iron Oxide

Burnt Umber

Antique Gold (Metallic)

Toning color:

gray acrylic paint for decorative painting

First Stage

1. Tone canvas with gray. Let dry.
2. Sketch or transfer lines for tops of clouds and hills.
3. Paint blue portion of sky wet-in-wet with a #14 flat brush and back-and-forth horizontal strokes. Start at top with darkest blue S1, transition to S2 at middle, and S3 at bottom. Paint down to tops of clouds.
4. With a small fan brush, streak high clouds with lightest gray S7.
5. Re-transfer line at top of clouds. Paint cloudy sky with a #14 flat brush. Begin at top of hills and work upward, blending wet-in-wet. Start with darkest gray S4 and work a little Payne's Gray into lowest sky area. Transition upward through the grays, through medium S5, through light S6, to very light S7.
6. Tap in top edges of clouds with a #4 scumbler.
7. Paint hillside wet-in-wet with a #20 flat brush. Begin at bottom with Sap Green/very dark. Transition upward to Sap Green/medium at top.
8. While paint is wet, streak in color variations with a small fan brush - a little Sap Green/very light at top of pasture, and a little Sap Green/light in the middle.

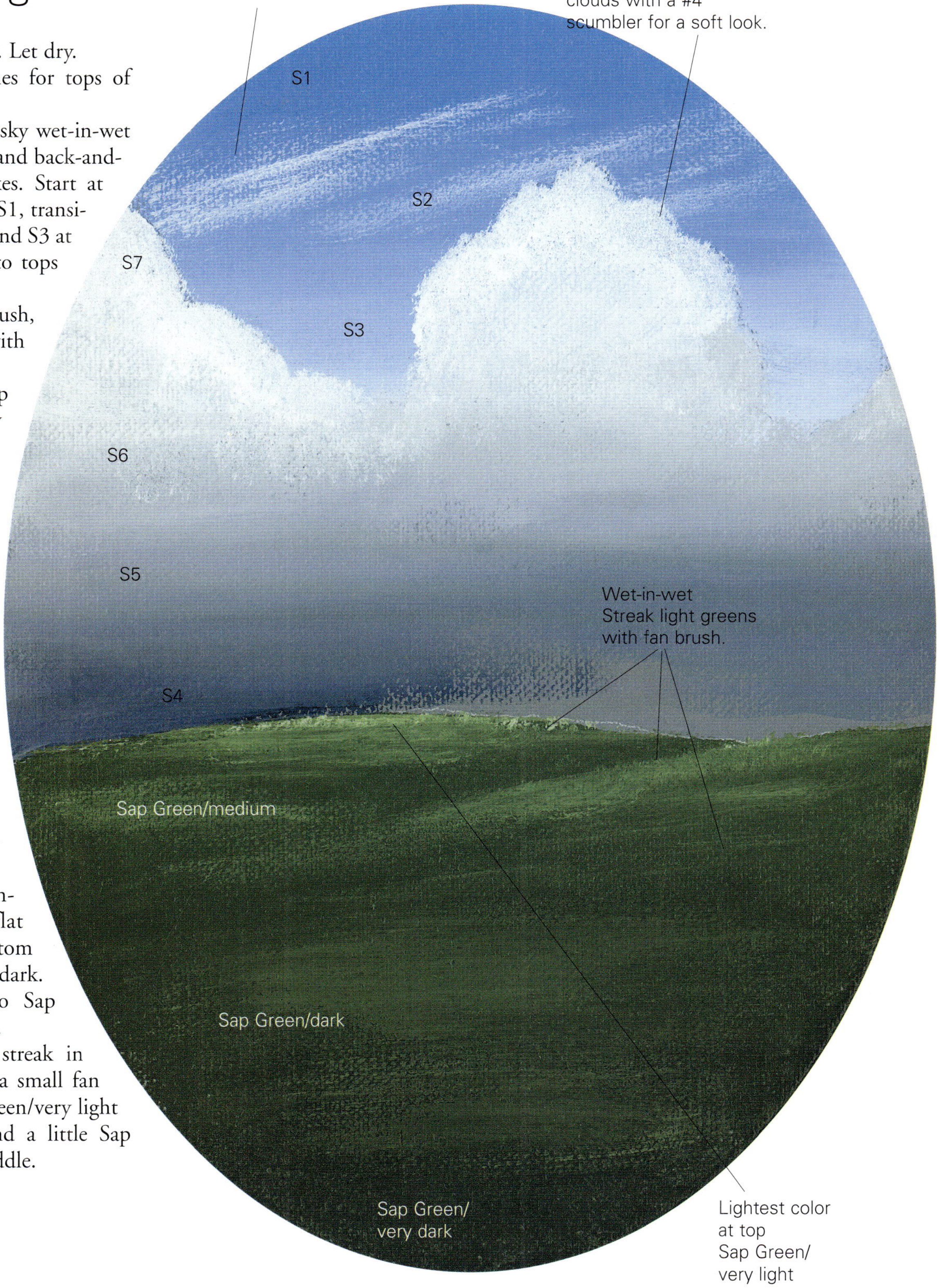

Second Stage

1. Locate a few cloud areas where S6 transitions to S7. Using the #4 scumbler and S6, tap in a few puffs upward from the S6 area into the S7 area. This creates a darker puff over a lighter background.
2. Locate a few areas where S5 transitions into S6. Tap in a few S5 puffs over the S6 area.
3. Tap a few S5 puffs over the darker S4 area. This gives the look of a small, light cloud in front of the larger, darker one.
4. Transfer church outline, so you can place trees properly. Be sure walls are vertical. (If you use the canvas grain as a guide, be sure grain is vertical.)
5. Large, dark trees: Tap in foliage with G1 and Sap Green/very dark, using a #2 scumbler. Tap highlights on middle tree with a little Sap Green/medium.
6. Small trees: Tap in foliage with the medium, light, and very light values of the Sap Green sequence. Tap in a little of the darker shades at the base.
7. With the #1 liner brush and G1, pull strokes upward from lower left to make several tall reeds.

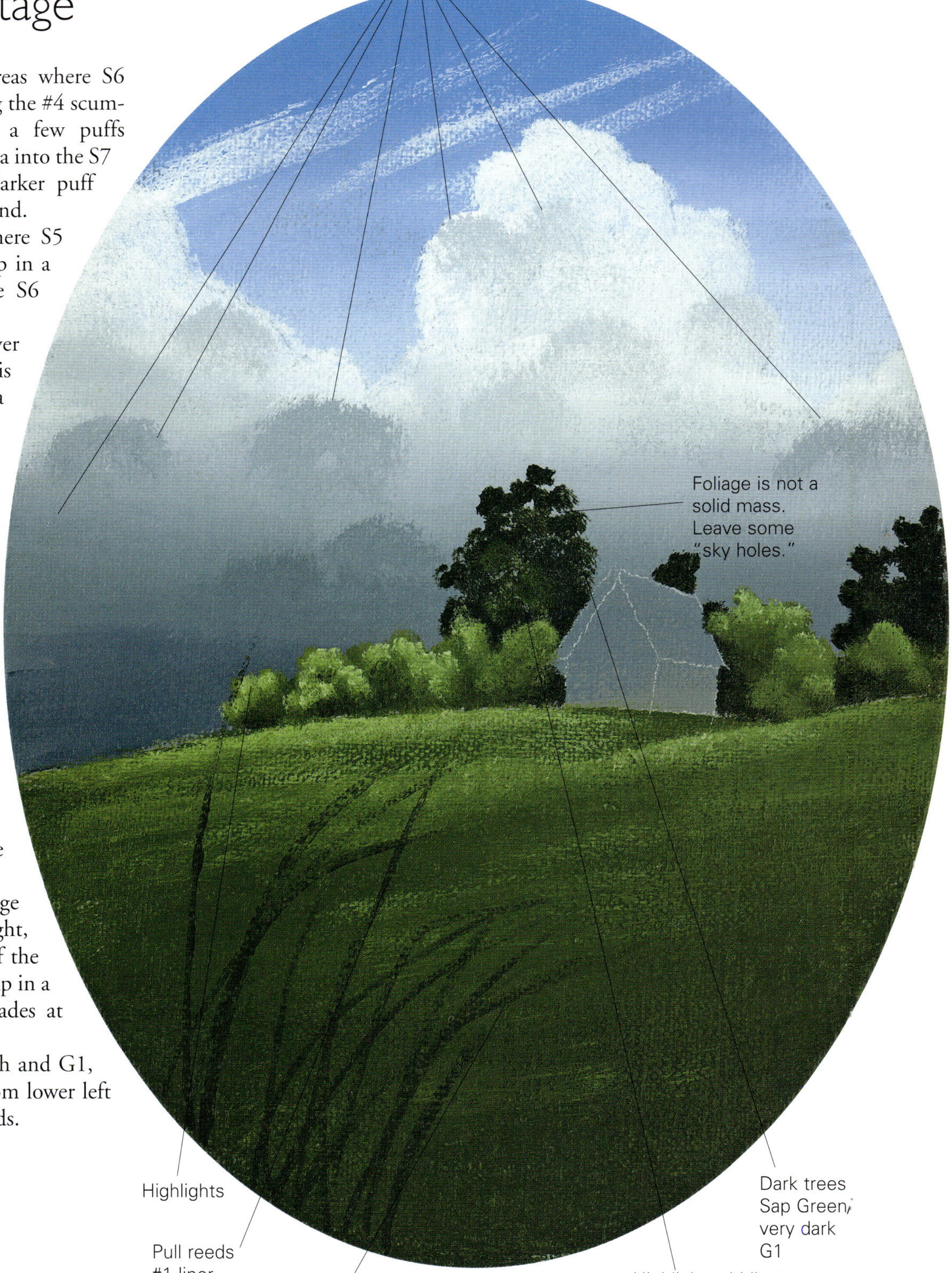

Final Stage

See finished painting.

1. Paint front wall of church (with door) Buff Titanium. While wet, add a little Titanium White at left side, and a little medium gray S5 at right edge, to separate front wall from side wall. Add a little medium gray along angled top edge at right, for shadow cast by roof.
2. Paint side wall Buff Titanium. While wet, add a little Titanium White along both left and right edges.
3. Paint windows medium gray S5. Add dark gray S4 shadows at tops.
4. Paint door Red Iron Oxide. Streak with Burnt Umber, concentrating darker color at top.
5. Paint roof Red Iron Oxide. Streak Burnt Umber upward from bottom edge.
6. Paint underside of roof overhang Payne's Gray.
7. Paint steeple front Buff Titanium. Highlight lower right corner with lines of Titanium White.
8. Paint post supports Buff Titanium. Emphasize bases with a little Titanium White.
9. Paint steeple roof same as church roof.
10. Paint cross with a liner and Antique Gold or Yellow Ochre. To separate it from background, parallel gold lines with very fine Payne's Gray lines.
11. Dab in foundation plantings to soften stark line at bottom of church.
12. Paint foreground birds Mars Black with tiny Buff Titanium beaks and feet. Underpaint red patches on wings with Titanium White, let dry, and paint Cadmium Red Medium.
13. Paint background birds as tiny "V" shapes with a #00 liner and thinned Mars Black. ❑

Value Sketch

Refer to the value sketch to guide placement of darks and lights.

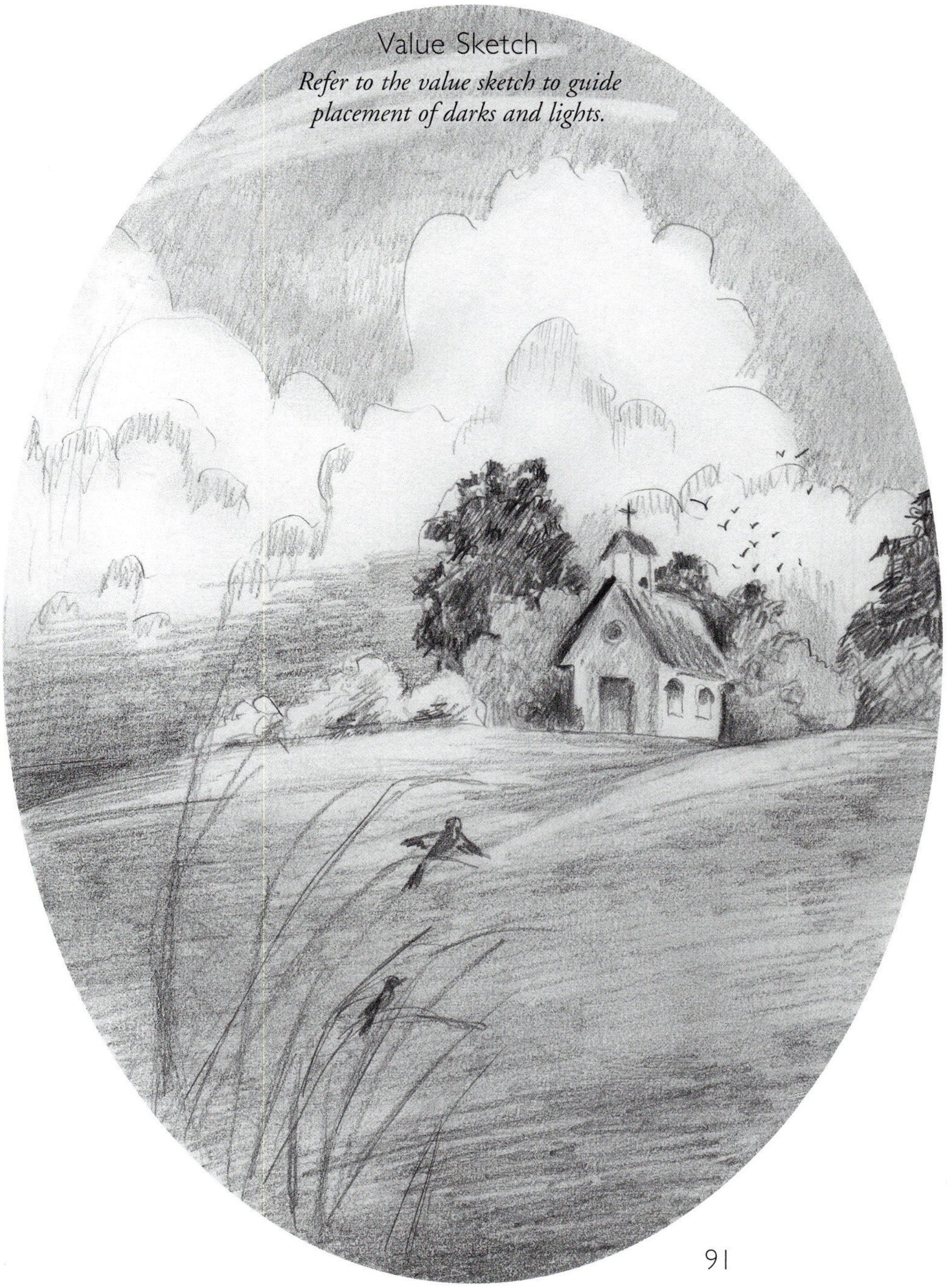

Close-up: Church

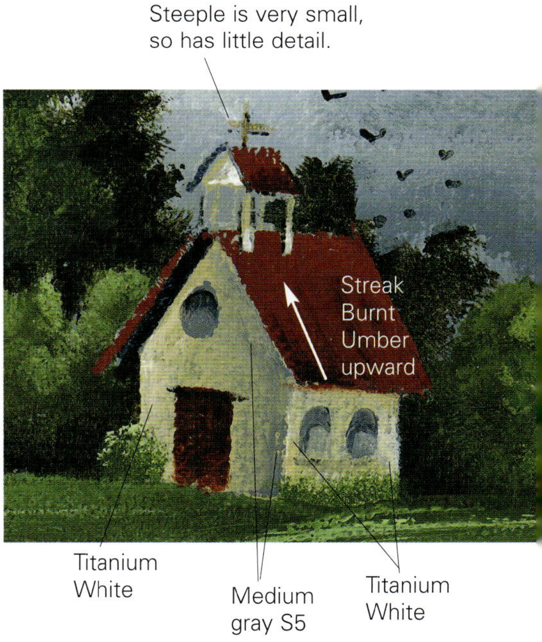

Pattern for Church Actual Size

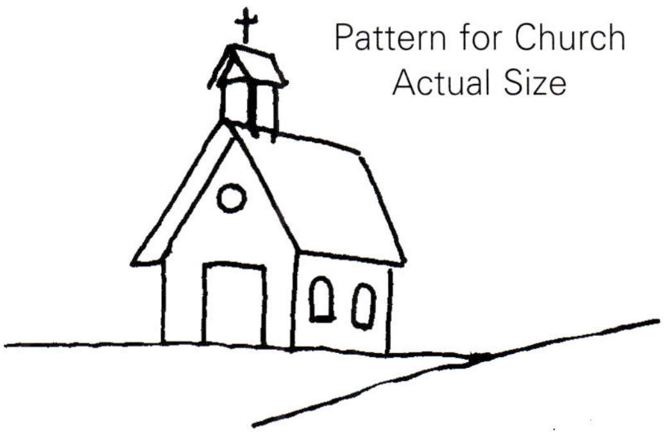

SNOWFALL

5" x 7"

What could be more magical than a thick coat of snow on a quiet landscape?

There is very little difference between sky and ground in this snowy scene. The falling snow suppresses value contrast and mutes colors. Against this background, the far trees almost appear to float. Turquoise shadows ground the foreground trees. The irresistible foxes add life and color. The canvas is toned with a light blue-gray, a good mid-range color for the snow, darker than the highlights and lighter than the shadows.

Small paintings look elegant in very wide frames. A warm gold frame would bring out the color of the foxes.

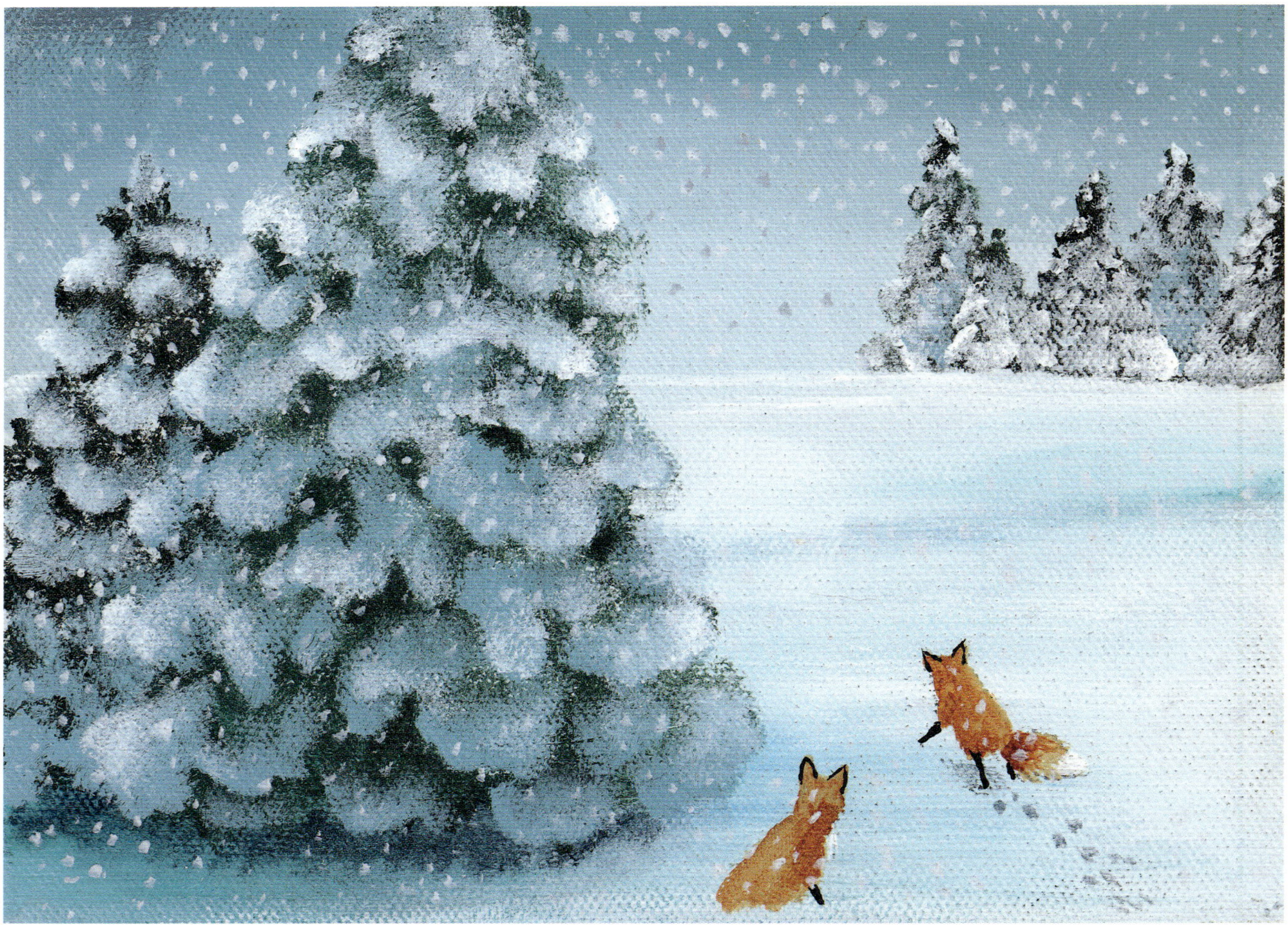

Color Scheme & Palette

This is basically a complementary color scheme - blue-green appears in the snow and trees, and its complement, red-orange, appears only in the foxes. The lack of repetition of the red-orange isolates and draws attention to the foxes.

Used for mixing colors:
Cadmium Red Deep
Cobalt Green Deep
Mars Black
Payne's Gray
Phthalo Turquoise
Titanium White

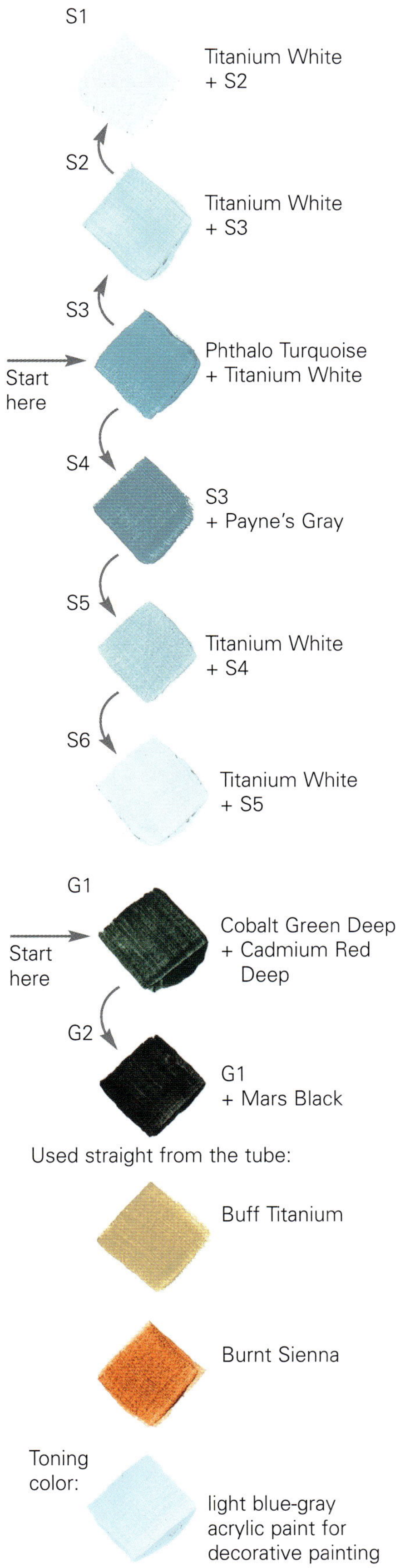

Value Sketch

Refer to the value sketch to guide placement of darks and lights.

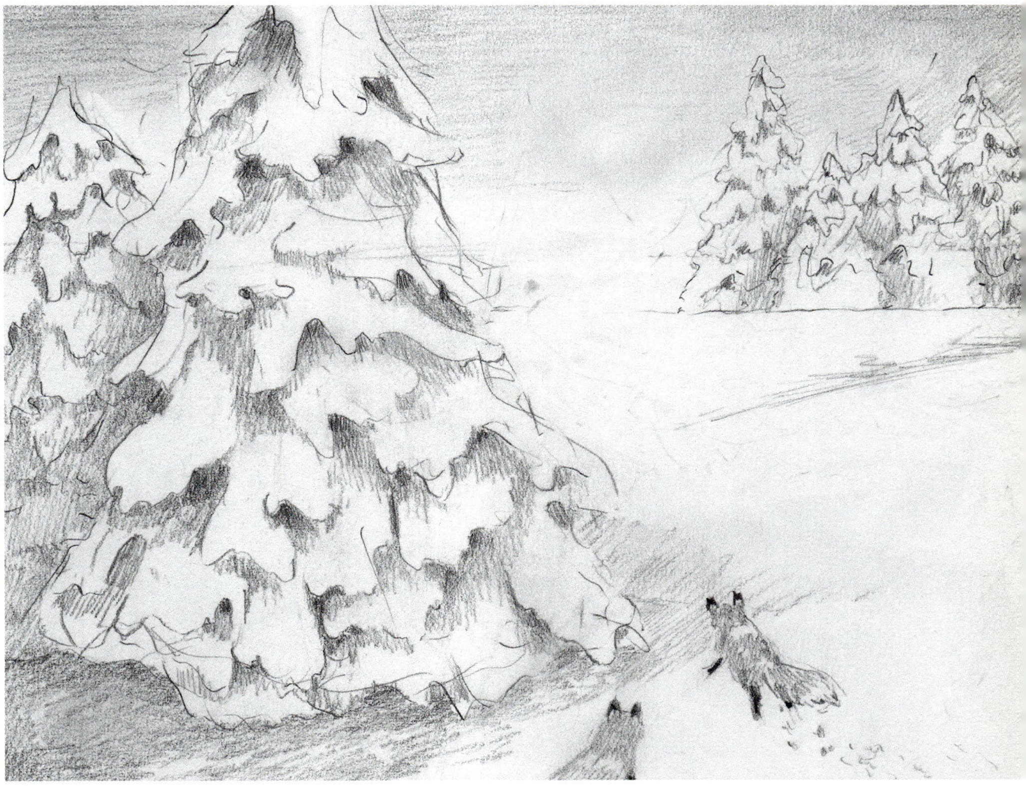

First Stage

1. Tone canvas with light blue-gray. Let dry.
2. Sketch horizon line.
3. Paint sky wet-in-wet with a #14 flat brush and horizontal strokes. Begin at top with S4. Bring this color down on both sides. Work downward and blend colors smoothly with back-and-forth strokes. Transition into S5, then S6, finishing at the horizon line.
4. Paint snow wet-in-wet with a #14 flat brush and horizontal strokes. (No need to paint behind trees at left.) Paint upper portion of snowy ground on the right with very light turquoise S1. Do not blend into sky color S6, but allow a slight division in color at the horizon.
5. Working downward while paint is wet, transition to light turquoise S2.
6. While paint is wet, paint snow under foreground trees medium turquoise S3. Blend into light turquoise at bottom right.
7. While paint is wet, streak a little Phthalo Turquoise with a small fan brush on the right.
8. With the small fan brush, streak Titanium White at horizon and in lightest area at center.

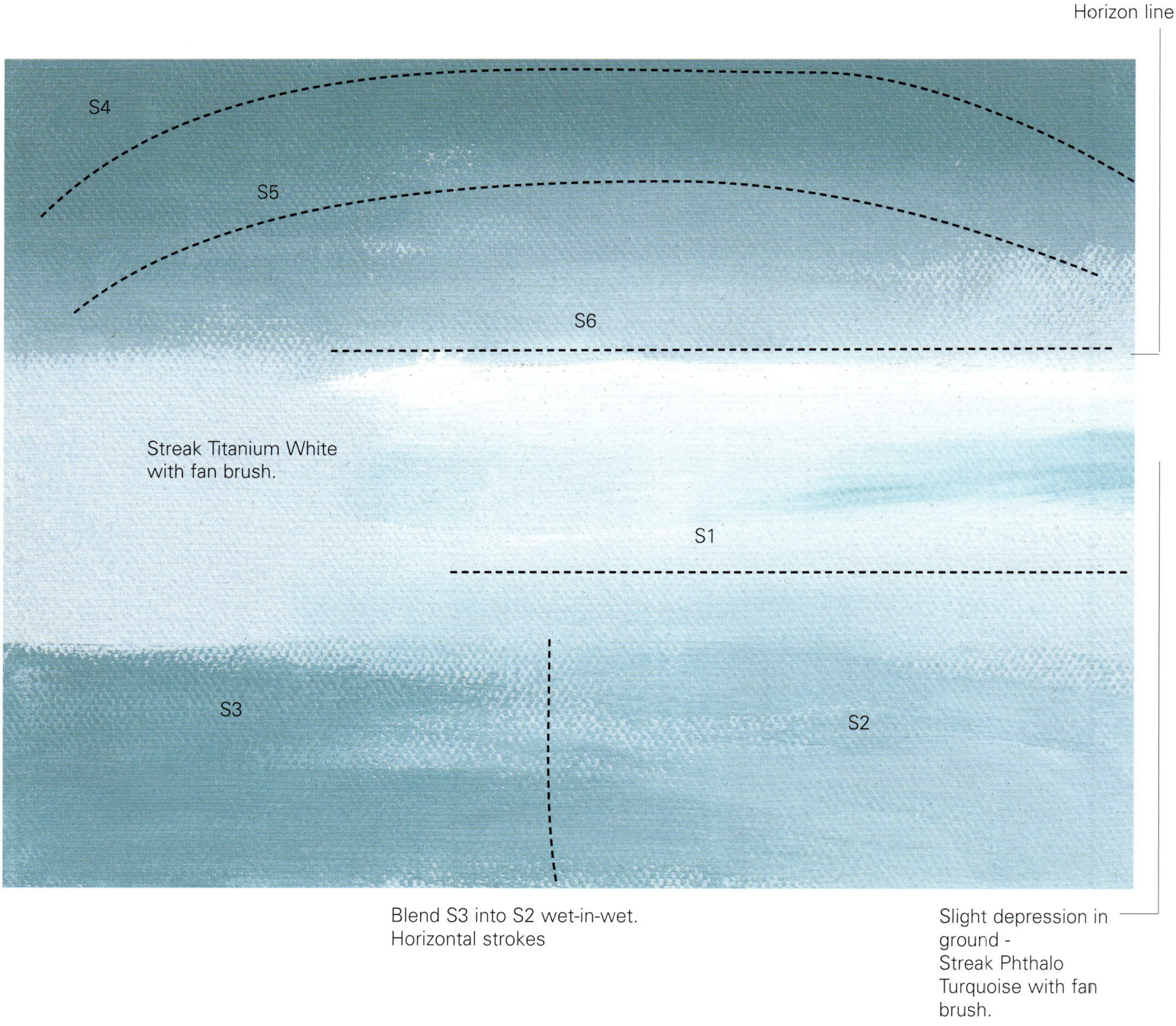

Second Stage

1. Keeping tip of brush pointing upward, tap in background trees with a #2 scumbler and dark green G2.
2. Tap in left foreground tree with a #4 scumbler and dark green G2.
3. Tap in large foreground tree with a #4 scumbler and light green G1.
4. Darken shadows under foreground trees with a #14 flat brush side-loaded with a little thinned Payne's Gray. Stroke next to bottom of tree, with loaded side up against the tree.

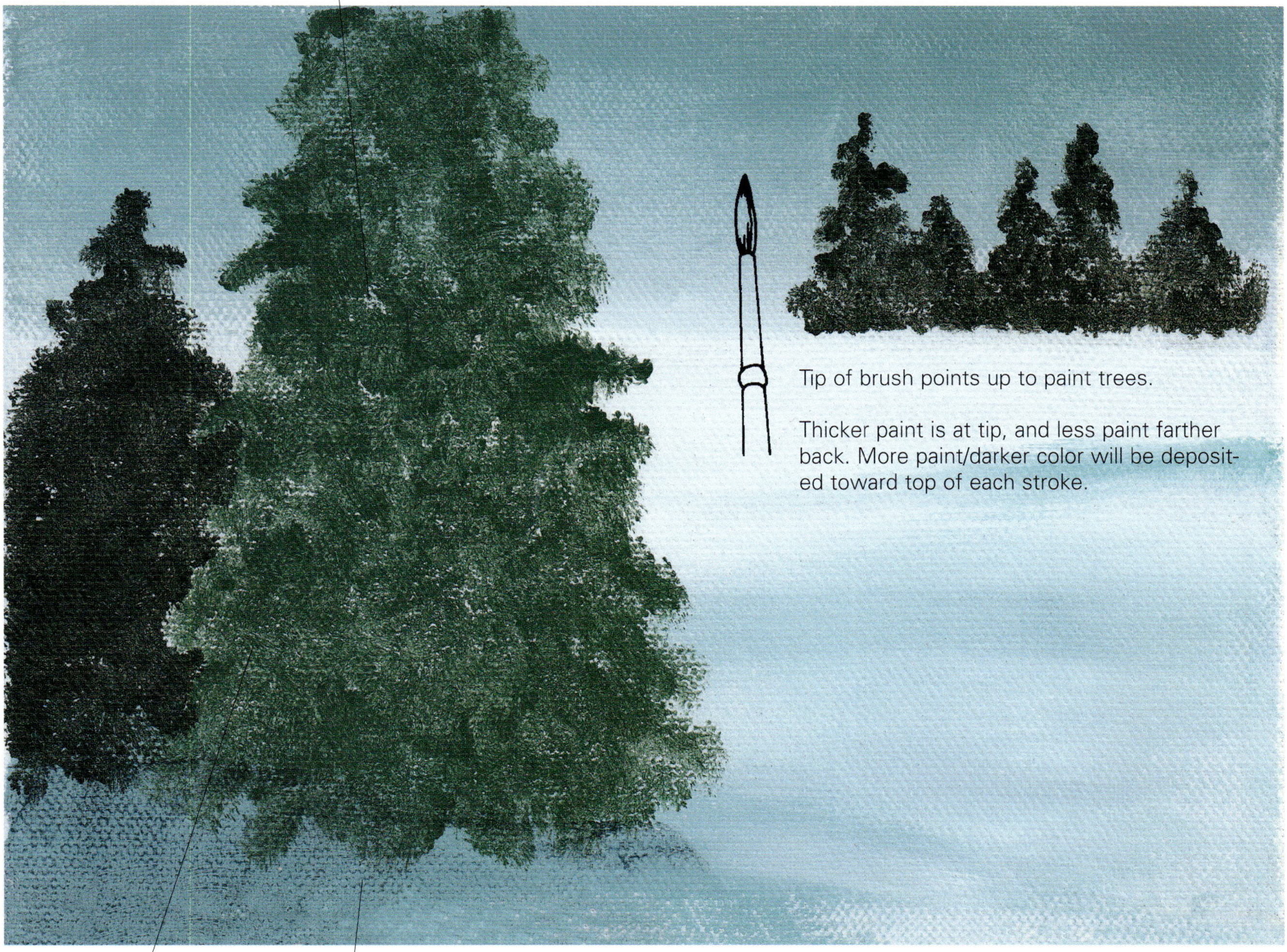

Third Stage

Snow builds up in clumps at the tips of the branches. Keeping this in mind helps you place the clumps.

1. Keeping tip of brush pointing downward, tap in snow clumps on background trees with a #2 scumbler. Use three different values - S1, S2, and S3 - to suggest the roundness of the trees and that some trees are in front of others.
2. Tap in larger snow clumps on foreground trees with a #4 scumbler.

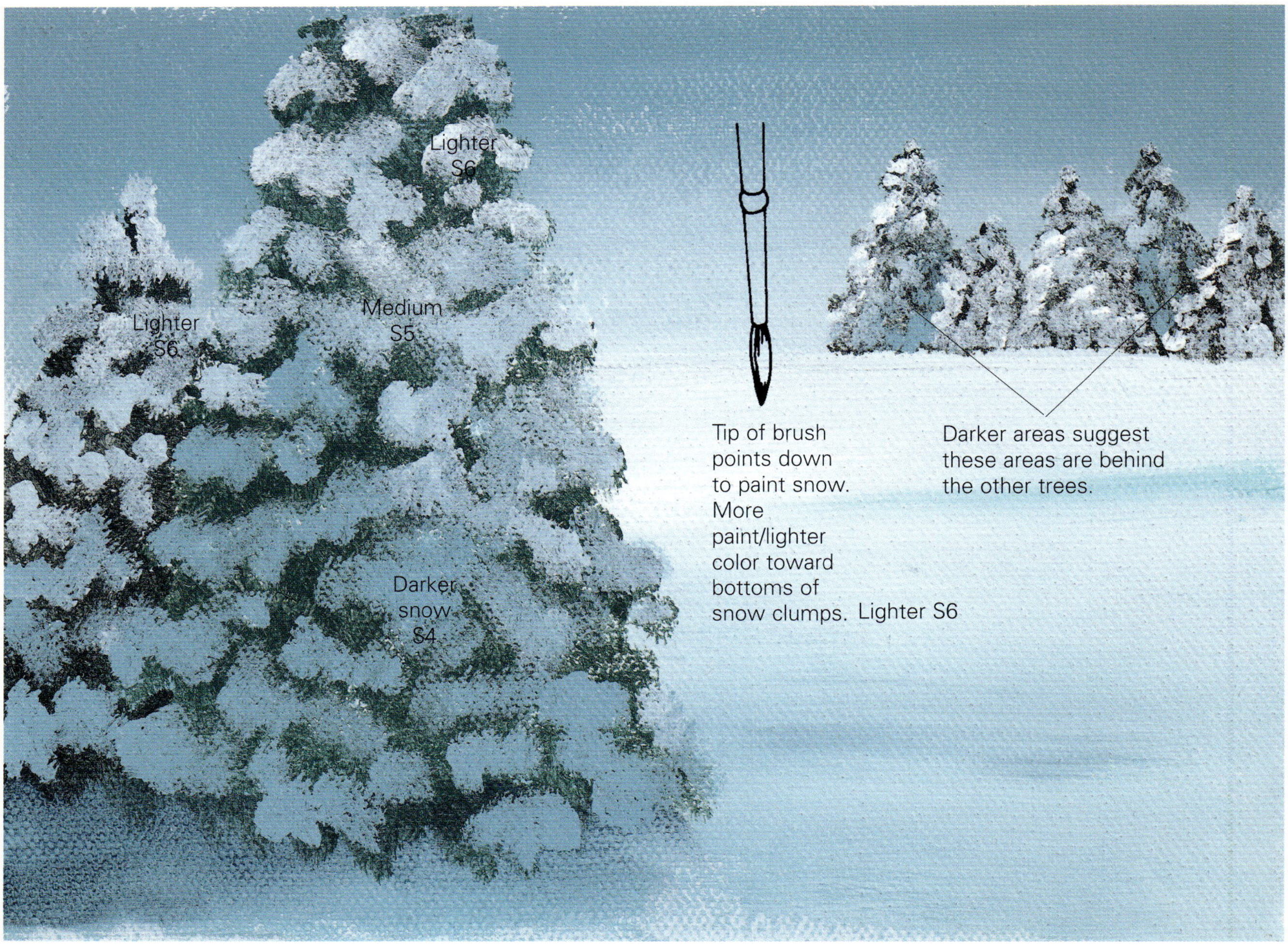

Final Stage

See finished painting.

1. Highlight snow clumps on foreground trees with the #4 scumbler, pointed end downward. Tap lighter value snow color at bottom edges of snow clumps. (Highlights are at bottom of clumps because tops are shaded by branches above.) Give clumps in brighter light more variation than those in shadow.
2. Transfer and paint foxes. Add shadow and paw prints with thinned Payne's Gray.
3. Dot falling snow with the tip of a #1 liner and S1. ❑

Fox Step-by-Step

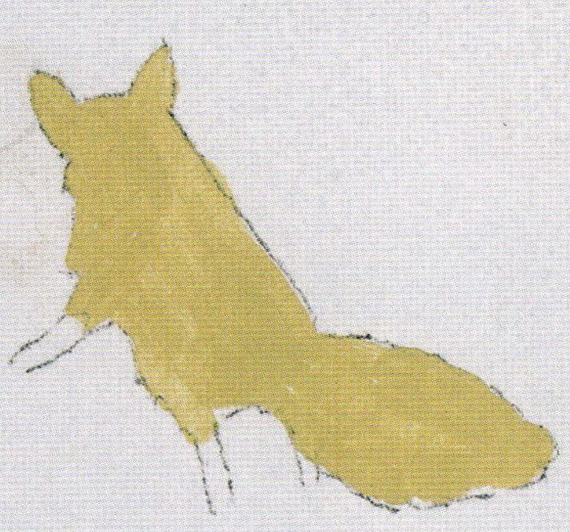

1. Underpaint with Buff Titanium for an even base.

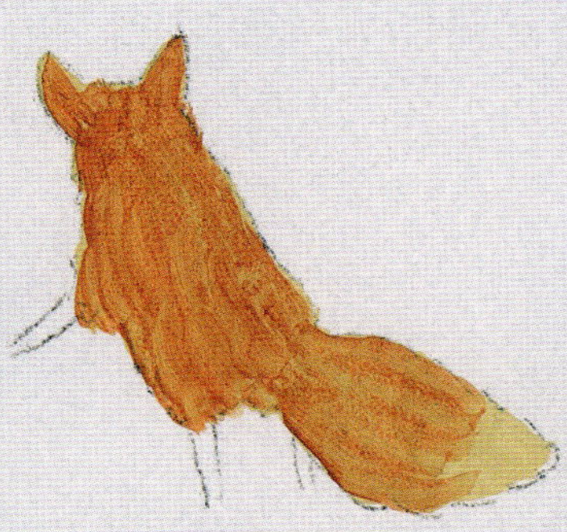

2. Paint red fur with thinned Burnt Sienna and a #3 round brush.
   - Stroke in direction of fur growth.
   - This is a transparent color, so brush strokes may show.

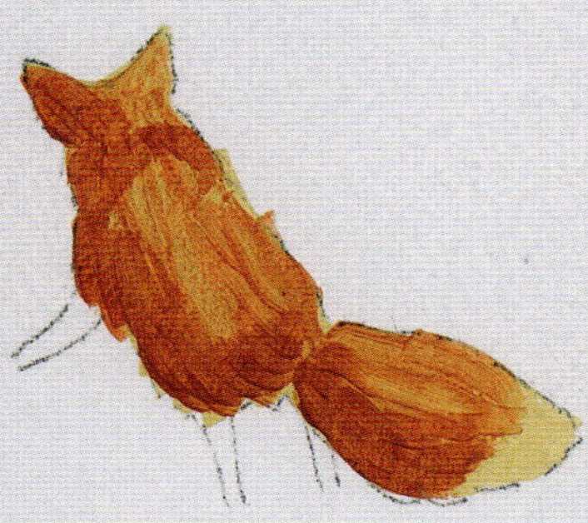

3. Paint over shadow areas with full strength Burnt Sienna.

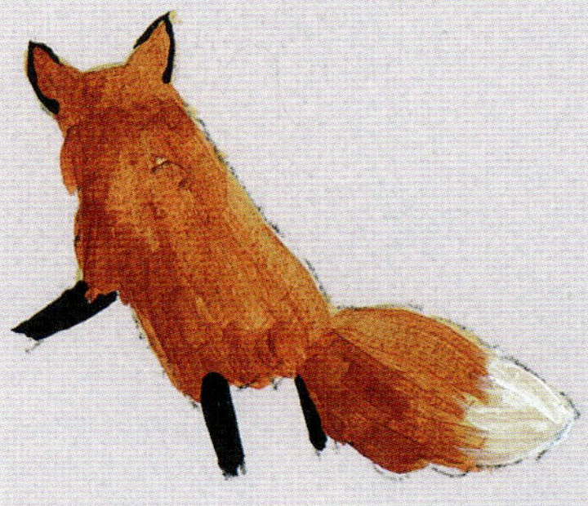

4. Using a #00 liner:
   - Tip ears and paint legs with Mars Black.
   - Tip tail with Titanium White.

FOX PATTERN

The foxes in this painting are very small.

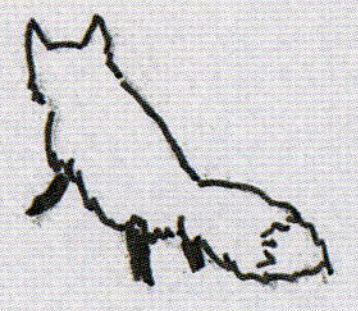

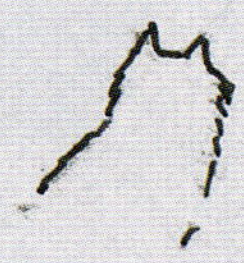

BEAR CROSSING

11" x 14"

I painted these bears in a springtime landscape, emerging from the woods onto the grassy banks of a stream. The bears are a strong focal point, both emotionally and visually - emotionally, because they are the only animals in the scene, and visually, because the brown of their fur is different from the rest of the colors in the landscape. To avoid fixing the viewer's eye on the bears, I deepened the value of the nearby background to blend them into their surroundings. I added a stream to lead the eye through the composition and into the distance. The rocks in the stream briefly catch the eye, and the far hill on the right visually "stops" the stream.

Value Sketch

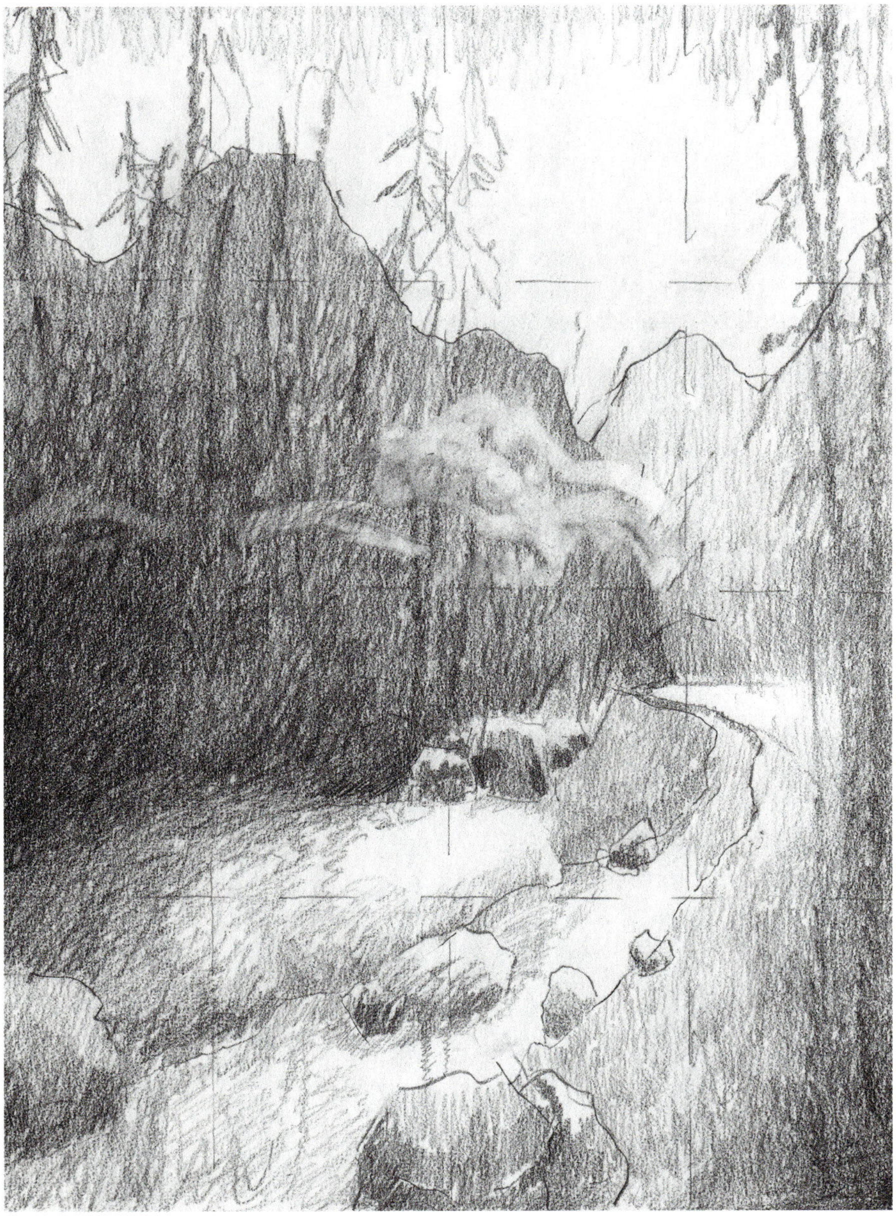

The placement of values is a composition in itself. The far hill on the right is light, to give the impression of an open area out of sight beyond the darker hills. Light values emphasize the stream and its grassy banks, and contrast with the dark woods.

Value Sketch

Refer to the value sketch to guide placement of darks and lights.

Pattern for Bears (actual size)

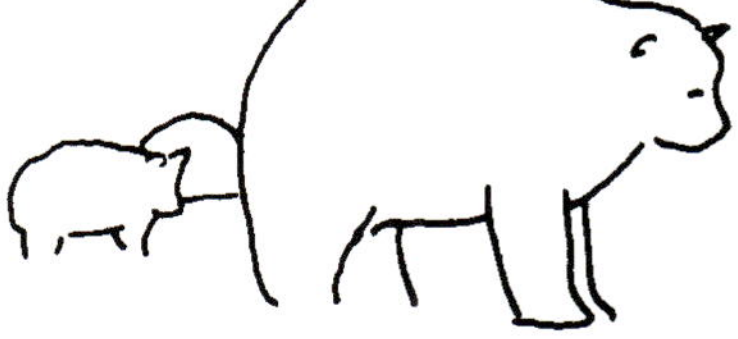

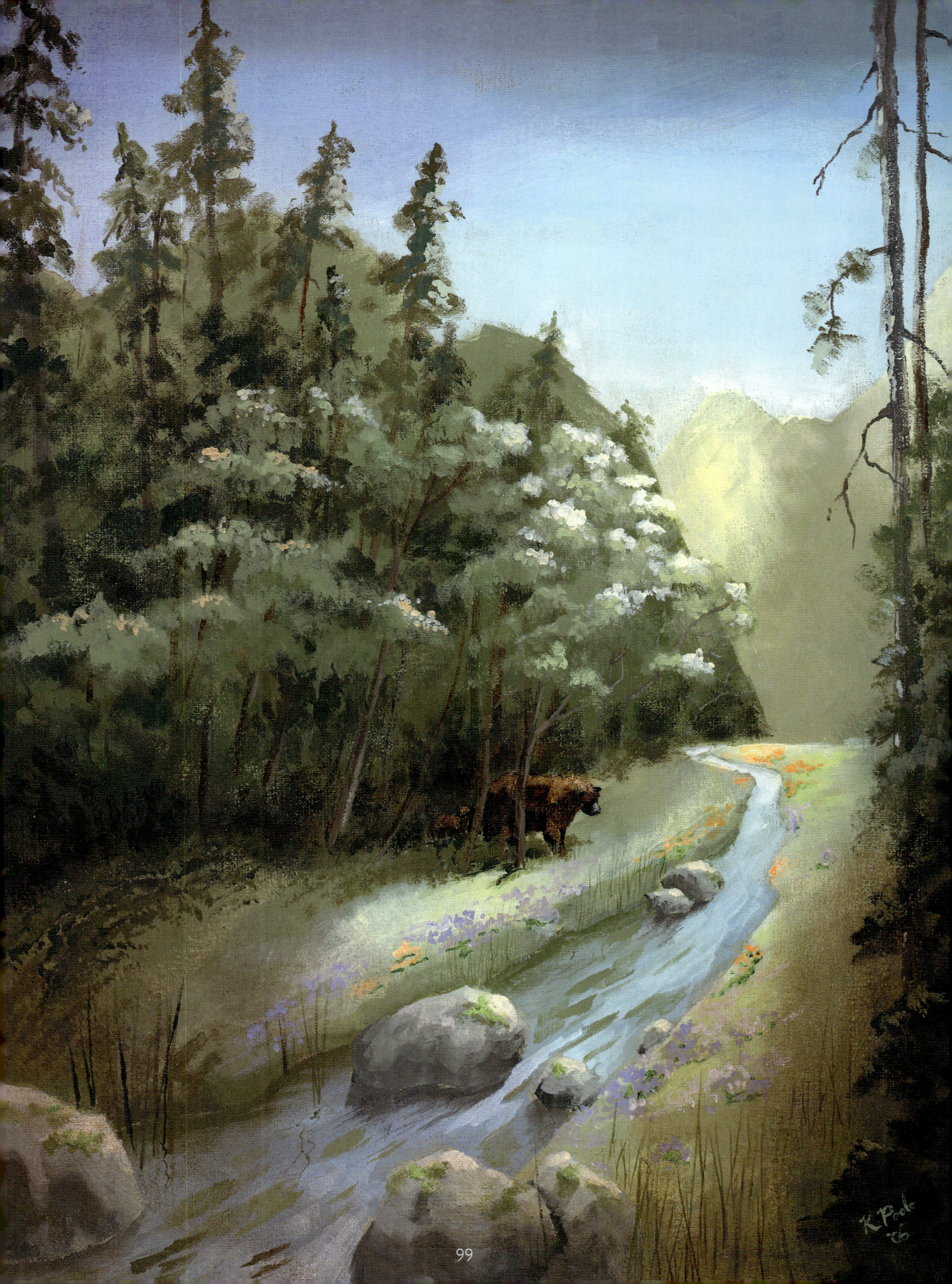

Color Scheme & Palette

Springtime landscapes require a full range of greens. The purples and oranges of the wildflowers complete the secondary triad color scheme (purple, green, and orange).

Used for mixing colors:

Buff Titanium
Burnt Umber
Cadmium Lemon
Cadmium Orange
Cadmium Red Deep
Cadmium Red Medium
Cadmium Yellow Medium
Cerulean Blue
Chromium Oxide Green
Cobalt Blue
Dioxazine Purple
Gold Ochre
Graphite Gray
Mars Black
Titanium White
Ultramarine Blue

B1 — very light Titanium White + B2

B2 (Start here) — light Titanium White + Cerulean Blue

B3 — medium B2 + Cobalt Blue

B4 — dark B3 + Graphite Gray

D1 — D2 + Graphite Gray

D2 (Start here) — Burnt Umber + Graphite Gray + Buff Titanium

O1 — Titanium White + O2

O2 (Start here) — Titanium White + Gold Ochre + Cadmium Red Medium

O3 — Cadmium Orange + Titanium White

V1 — Titanium White + V2

V2 (Start here) — Titanium White + Dioxazine Purple + Ultramarine Blue

Used straight from the tube: Sap Green

R1 — Buff Titanium + Titanium White + Gold Ochre

G1 — Titanium White + G2

G2 — G3 + Cadmium Lemon + Titanium White

G3 — G4 + Buff Titanium

G4 (Start here) — Chromium Oxide Green + Gold Ochre + Cadmium Red Medium

G5 — G4 + Mars Black

G6 — G5 + Cadmium Red Deep

G7 — G6 + Mars Black

P1 — light Titanium White + P2 + Cadmium Yellow Medium

P2 (Start here) — medium Chromium Oxide Green + Ultramarine Blue

P3 — dark P2 + Mars Black

Toning color: jade green acrylic paint for decorative painting

First Stage

1. Tone canvas with jade green. Let dry.
2. Sketch lines for edges of mountains, stream, large rocks, and edge of woods to left of stream. Transfer bear pattern.
3. Using a #20 flat brush, paint sky wet-in-wet, blending colors on the canvas. Begin with very light B1 in the "V" between mountains. Work upward through B2 and B3 to B4. Sky is darkest at top. Bring dark mix lower down at left side.
4. Paint stream in reverse sequence - darkest (B4) at bottom and lightest (B1) at top. Begin at bottom with the #20 flat brush, switching to a #10 flat where stream narrows at top. As you move from one color to the next, streak a little of the new color in the area just painted.
5. Paint main shapes of hills and meadows with a #20 flat brush and greens G1 - G7.
6. Paint rocks, placing R1, B4, and Graphite Gray to form their shapes.

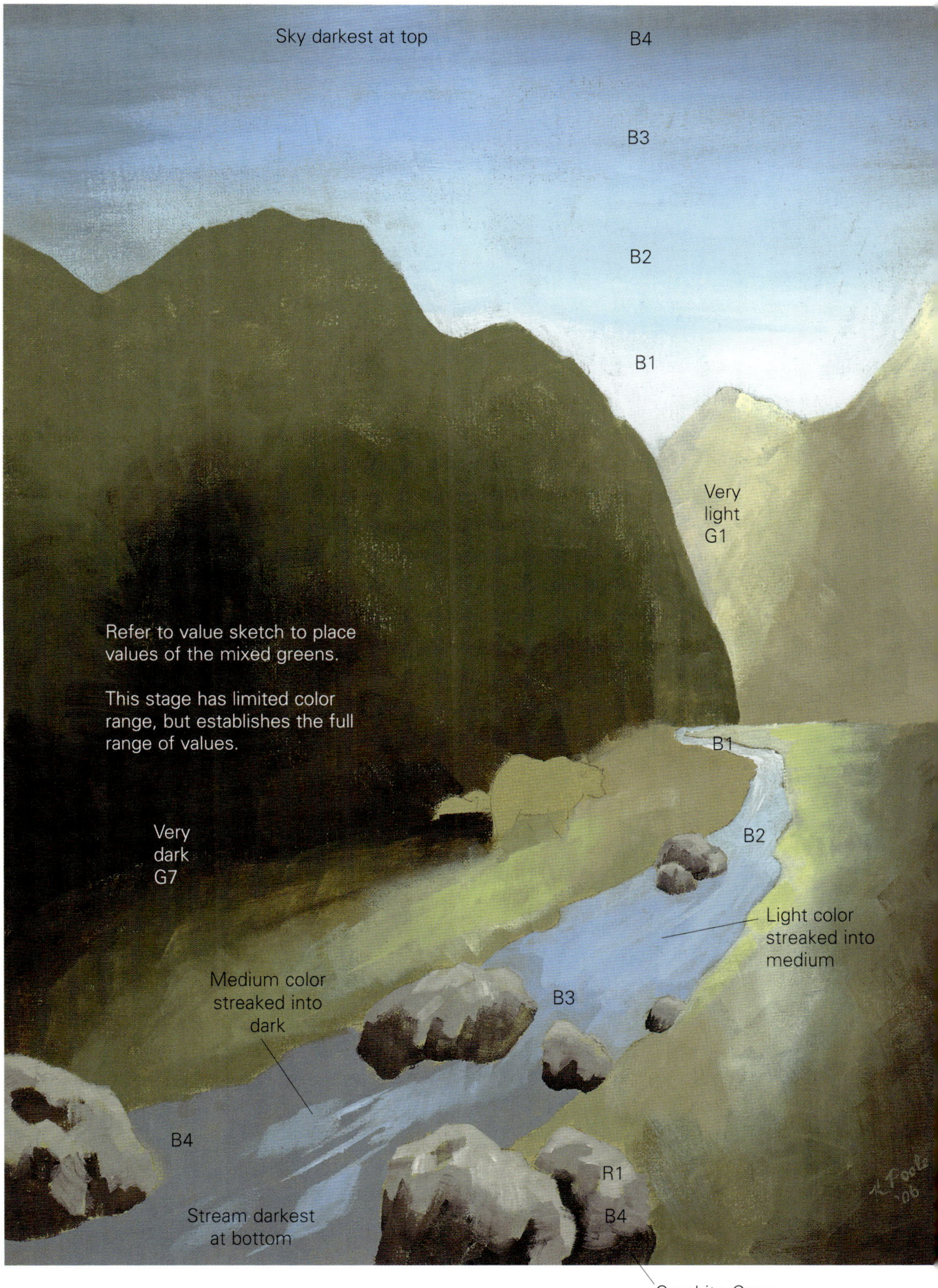

Second Stage

1. Stroke pine trunks with a #3 round brush and browns D1 and D2. With a #1 liner, pull some branches toward tops of trees on right.
2. Dab pine foliage with a #4 scumbler brush. Dab lighter green G4 at tops of trees, and darker green G6 farther down.
3. Highlight sections of trunk on larger tree at right with beige R1.
4. Accent pine trees with bluish greens P1, P2, and P3. Dab the medium color over most of the trees, dark color toward the bottom, and a little light color for highlights. Highlights face the stream.
5. Re-transfer bears. Paint bears with toning color to re-establish their shapes. Let dry.
6. Paint bears Burnt Umber. Shade with Mars Black to establish form. Let dry.
7. Highlight bears with beige R1 along the back, shoulders, hips, and muzzle of the adult, and on the backs of the cubs.
8. Paint reflections in stream with a side-loaded large flat brush, using medium green G4 for the reflection of the far bank, and Graphite Gray for the reflections of the rocks. Note that there is no reflection of the near bank; the viewer wouldn't see it from this angle.
9. Paint rocks with a second coat, smoothing transitions between R1, B4, and Graphite Gray to make them appear rounder.

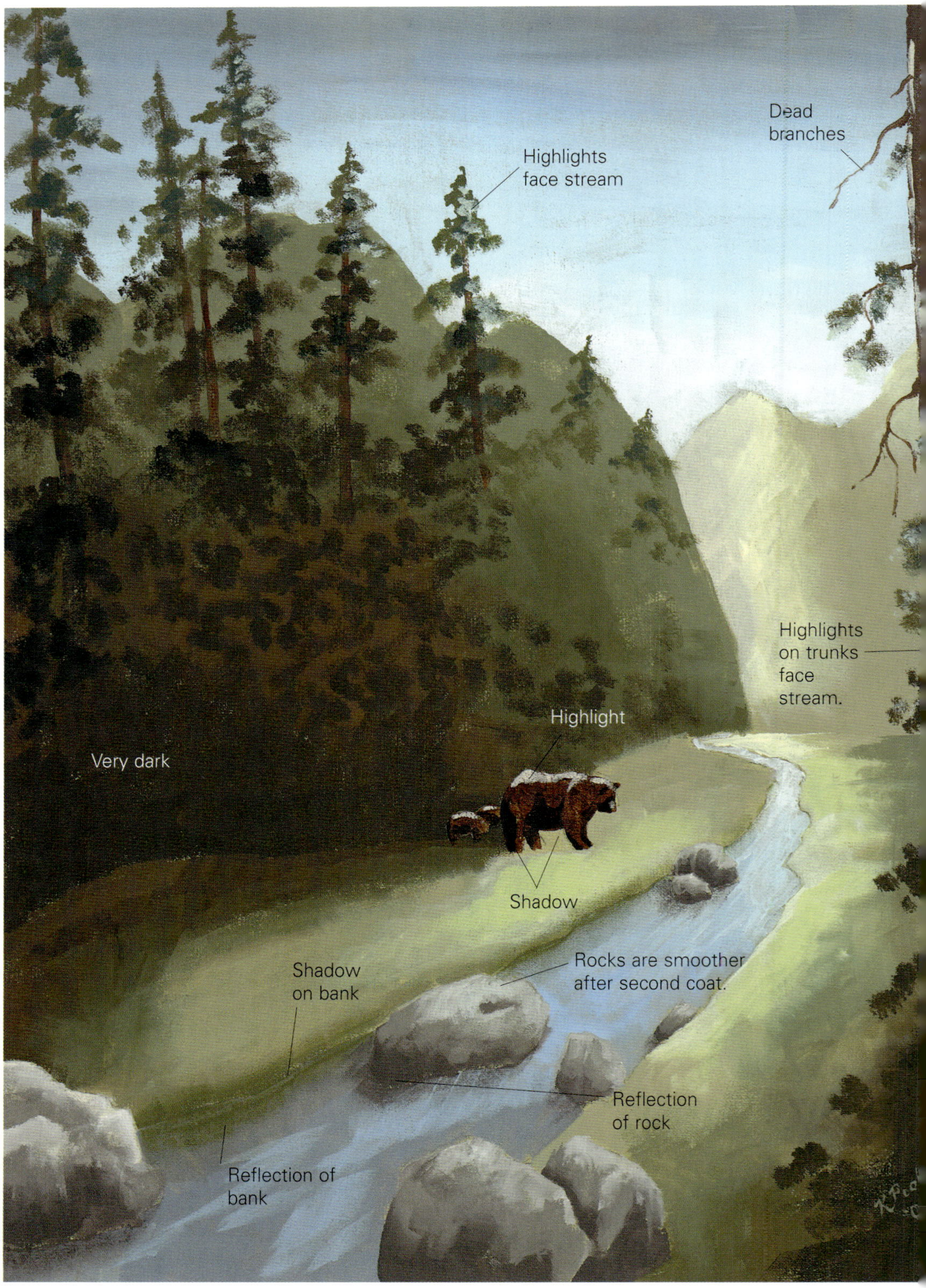

Third Stage

1. Tone down highlights on bears with a wash of thinned Burnt Umber.
2. Paint trunks and branches of deciduous trees with a #3 round brush and browns D1 and D2, beige R1, and Burnt Umber. For color variation, move between colors without washing brush. Highlight some trunks and branches with R1.
3. Dab foliage clumps with a #4 scumbler brush and greens G1 - G7. Form clumps with lighter colors on top and darker colors on bottom.
4. To integrate bears into landscape and tuck them into the woods, dab Mars Black and Burnt Umber along bases of trees to left of bears. Paint a dark green shadow under bears.
5. Using a fan brush and dark green G5, dab brambles below tree line toward left edge of canvas.
6. Highlight tops of rocks with beige R1.
7. Dab Sap Green moss in random patches on rocks. Dab green G2 over centers of patches.

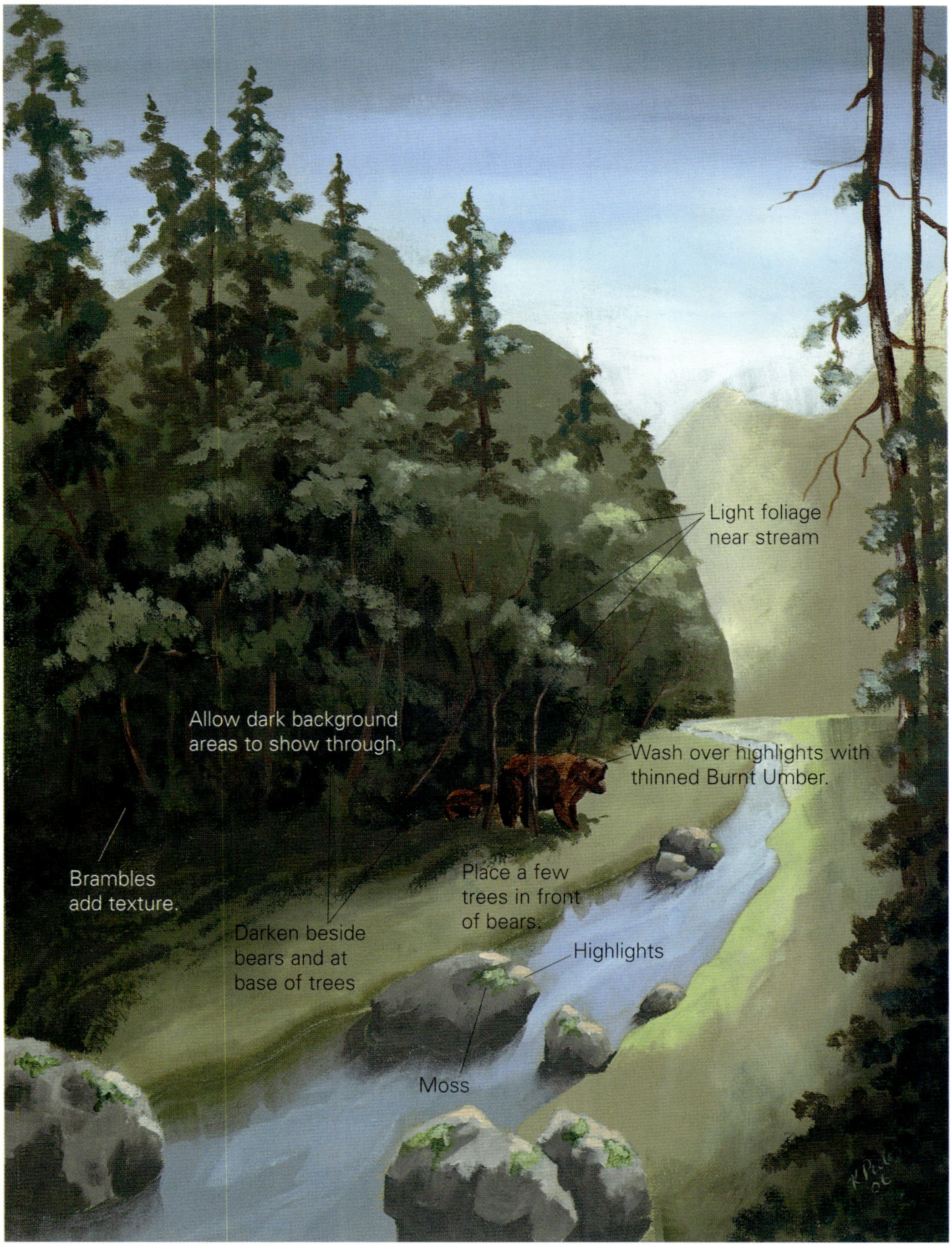

Final Stage

See finished painting.

1. Correct values as needed. Brighten bank below and slightly to left of bears.
2. Add accent colors by dotting in patches of wildflowers along stream banks with oranges O2 and O3, and blue-violets V1 and V2. Add a little foliage to patches for a realistic look.
3. To integrate tree flowers with ground flowers, dot dogwood blooms with light oranges O2 and O1. (Pure white is too stark.) Concentrate lightest color closest to stream.
4. Add depth with foreground details. Pull each grass blade from base upward to tip, with a single stroke of a #0 liner and some darker greens. Vary length and cross some blades.
5. Suggest reflections of forest in stream with strokes of greens here and there. Use a #6 flat brush, stroking on an angle or on the chisel edge.
6. With a #20 flat brush, wash thinned Dioxazine Purple over left side and bottom of painting to darken. (This is a very strong color, so be sure wash is thin. You can always add another wash, but you can't take it away.) Let dry.
7. Darken the bottom few inches of painting with a wash of thinned Burnt Umber.
8. Wash a tiny bit of thinned Cadmium Yellow Medium on light side of far hill. ❑

FEEDING TIME

11" x 14"

The peaceful magic of winter is the subject of this painting of a ranch in the snow. The fence divides the scene into wild and domesticated areas, and the large gate connects them. The buildings are different styles and materials, but unified by painting the trim the same color. The shape of the white building depends on contrasting values.

Value Sketch

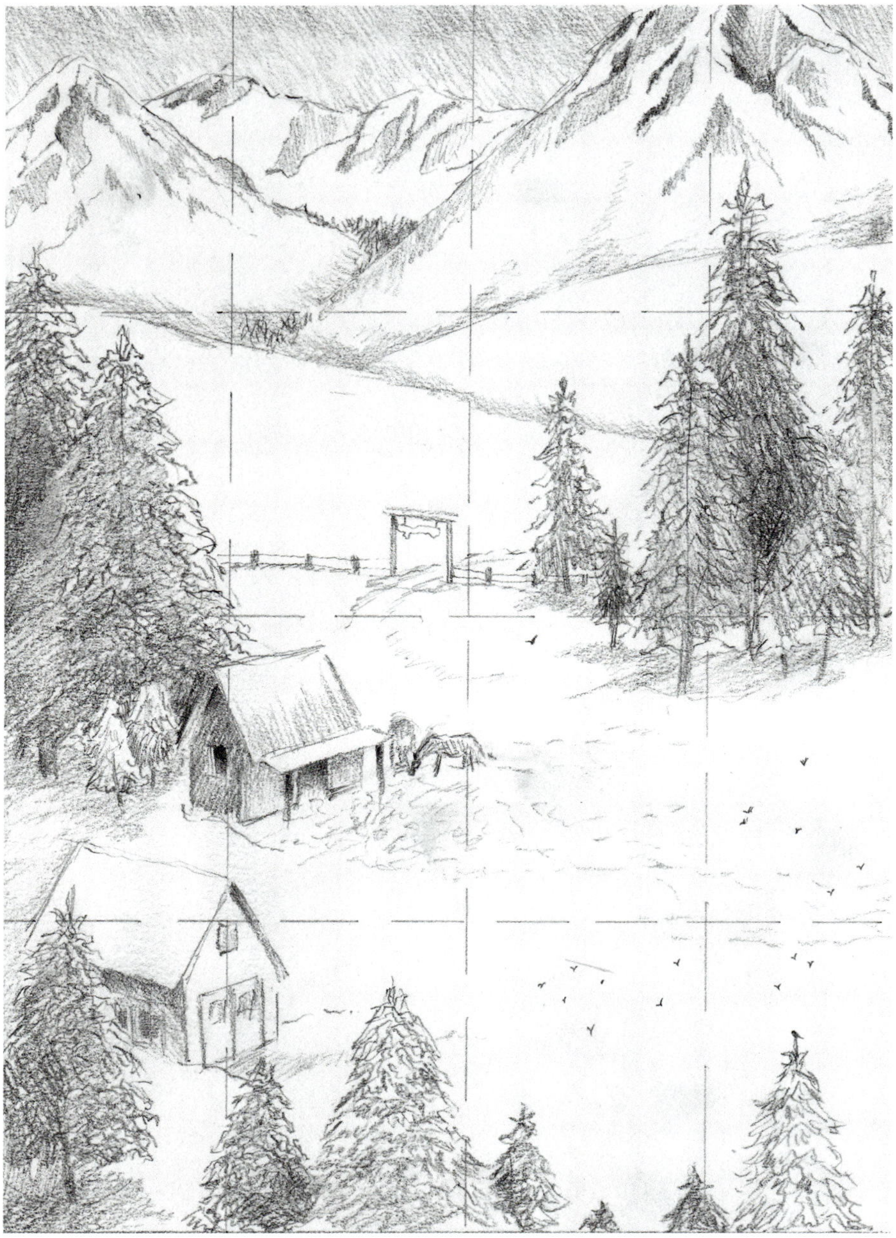

The **focal point** is the horses. Their dark colors contrast with the light snow, and they are positioned consistent with the "thirds rule." A series of elements leads the eye in a zigzag pattern through the painting - the lines of the trees, the curve between the houses, the curved tracks in the snow around the horses and through the gate, and the lines at the bases of the hills and mountains. These lines lead to, and then away from the horses into the background.

Instructions begin on Page 107.

Value Sketch

Refer to the value sketch to guide placement of darks and lights.

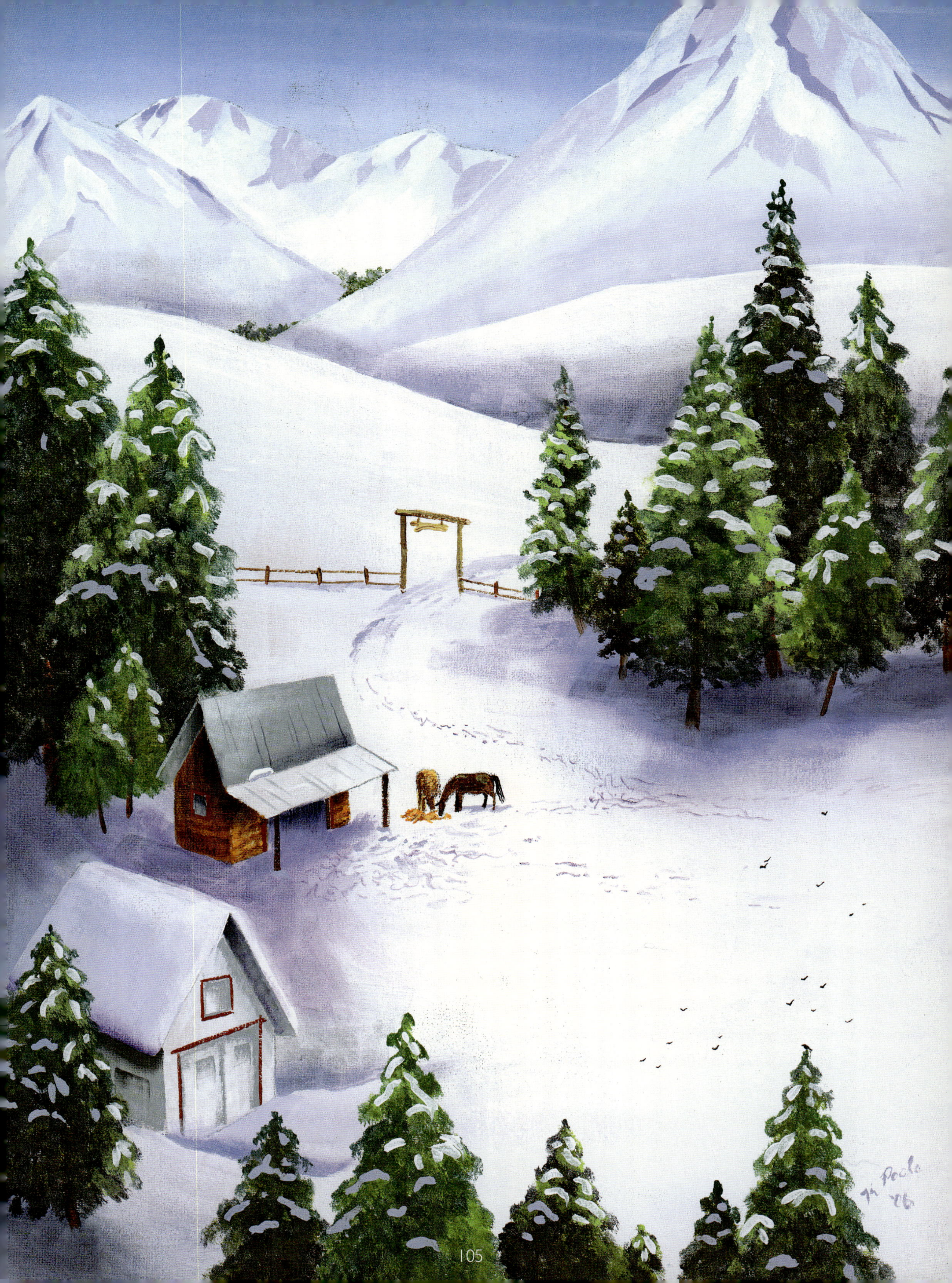

Color Scheme & Palette

The colors in this painting are mainly blue, blue-violet, and blue-green - an analogous color scheme centering on blue. The orange-y browns of the log building, the horses, hay, and fence complement the blue.

Start here

S1 — Cerulean Blue + Dioxazine Purple + Graphite Gray + Titanium White

S2 — S1 + Titanium White

S3 — S1 + Dioxazine Purple

S4 — S3 + Titanium White

S5 — Titanium White + S4

S6 — S5 + Cerulean Blue

Start here

G1 — Payne's Gray + Titanium White

G2 — Titanium White + G1

G3 — Titanium White + G2

R1 — Cadmium Red Deep + Red Iron Oxide

Toning color: gray violet acrylic paint for decorative painting

Sap Green Sequence

Refer to Page 24 for mixing instructions.

dark — medium — very light

Cool Green Sequence

Refer to Page 25 for mixing instructions.

very dark — dark — medium — light

W1 — Dioxazine Purple + Payne's Gray

Used straight from the tube:

- Burnt Sienna
- Burnt Umber
- Gold Ochre
- Buff Titanium
- Cadmium Yellow Medium

Used for mixing colors:

- Cadmium Red Deep
- Cadmium Yellow Deep
- Cadmium Yellow Light
- Cerulean Blue
- Cobalt Green Deep
- Cobalt Green Light
- Dioxazine Purple
- Graphite Gray
- Mars Black
- Payne's Gray
- Red Iron Oxide
- Sap Green
- Titanium White
- Ultramarine Blue

First Stage

1. Tone canvas with gray violet. Let dry.
2. Sketch skyline.
3. Using a #14 flat brush, start sky at top with S1. Place S2 beneath it and blend where the colors meet. Streak some light into the dark and some dark into the light, and re-blend to give the look of high, wispy clouds.
4. Lightly draw mountain outlines. Refer to *Mountains Step-by-Step* to paint mountains.
5. Using a #20 flat brush, paint right hill lavender S5. Highlight top with Titanium White. Shade with S4, then S3.
6. Using a #20 flat brush and lavender S5, paint left hill down to fence line. Highlight top with Titanium White. Streak in some pale blue S6.
7. Transfer outlines of buildings, and sketch lines for tree trunks, so you can place their shadows correctly.
8. Paint remaining snow using Titanium White, lavender S5, and blue S6.
9. Mix a darker, grayer lavender, and paint the shadows with this mix and S4.

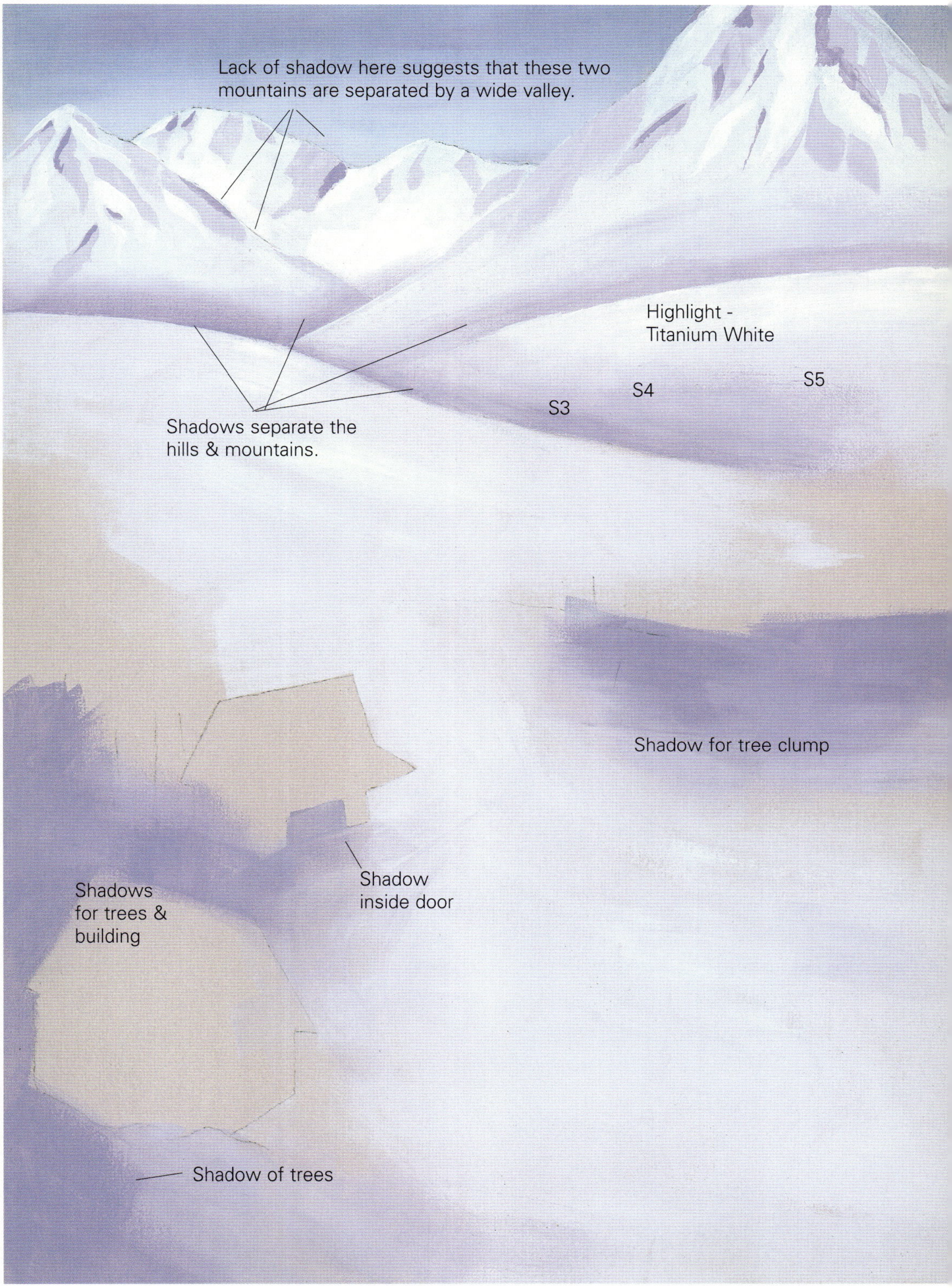

Second Stage

1. Pick up Burnt Umber and Buff Titanium on a #1 liner. Paint fence and gate. Colors will mix randomly on the canvas. Paint fence rails with same colors and a #00 liner.
2. Paint the two clusters of trees in the middle ground, following *Trees Step-by-Step.*
3. Transfer outlines of buildings.
4. Paint log walls Gold Ochre. While paint is wet, wipe away random streaks with the chisel edge of a clean flat brush to divide logs. Following the perspective of each wall, make streaks horizontal on front and on lower portion of side, and vertical on upper portion of side. Let dry.
5. Darken side of log building with a wash of thinned Burnt Umber.
6. On log building, paint front of tin roof dark gray G1.
7. Paint flat roof of log building light gray G3.
8. Paint underside of back of roof G1. While paint is wet, blend in Graphite Gray shadow at the peak.
9. Paint peaked end of white building light gray G3.
10. Paint shadow side of white building G1. Paint underside of roof overhang G1. Blend Graphite Gray wet-in-wet for deepest shadow toward peak.

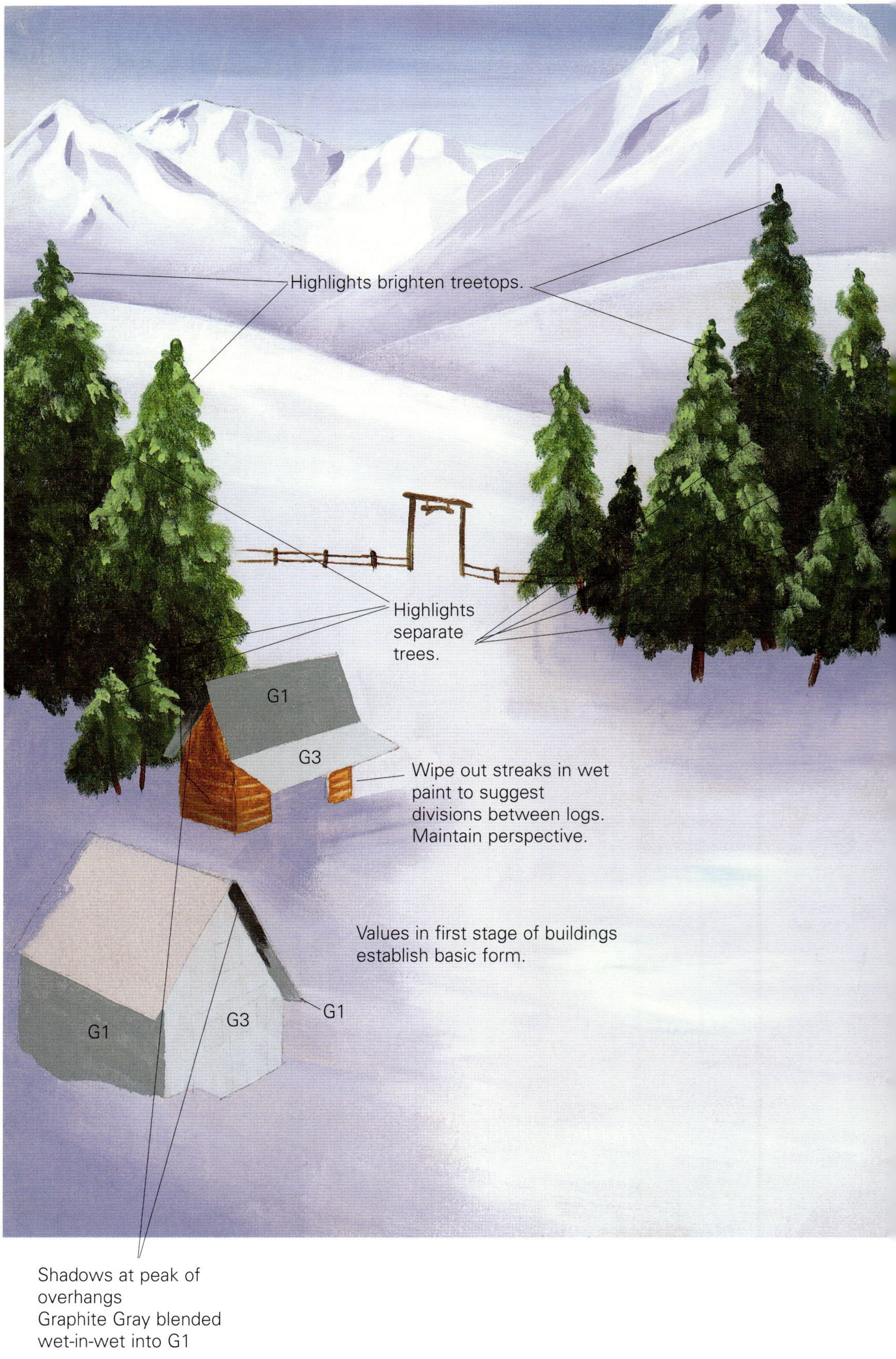

Third Stage

1. Highlight upper left front of log building roof. Side-load a large flat brush with light gray G3. Keeping loaded side of brush up, pull horizontal streaks from left edge of roof to right.
2. Shade lower right of log building roof. Side-load a large flat brush with thinned Payne's Gray. Keeping loaded side of brush along dividing line between the two parts of the roof, pull horizontal streaks from right edge to left.
3. Add detail lines with a #00 liner. Use thinned Payne's Gray on front of roof, and gray G2 on flat part of roof. Keep strokes parallel to edges of roof.
4. Add a thin line of G2 along outer edge of back of roof.
5. Add a thin line of thinned Payne's Gray to edge of flat part of roof.
6. Shadow log walls with Burnt Umber.
7. Paint log building window dark gray G1. Shade with Graphite Gray.
8. Paint shadow inside door with thinned Payne's Gray.
9. Paint posts Burnt Umber.
10. To indicate thickness of walls, add a vertical line of Burnt Umber along right side of door (this edge is in shadow) and a vertical line of Buff Titanium along left side of window (this edge faces the light).

Continued on page 112

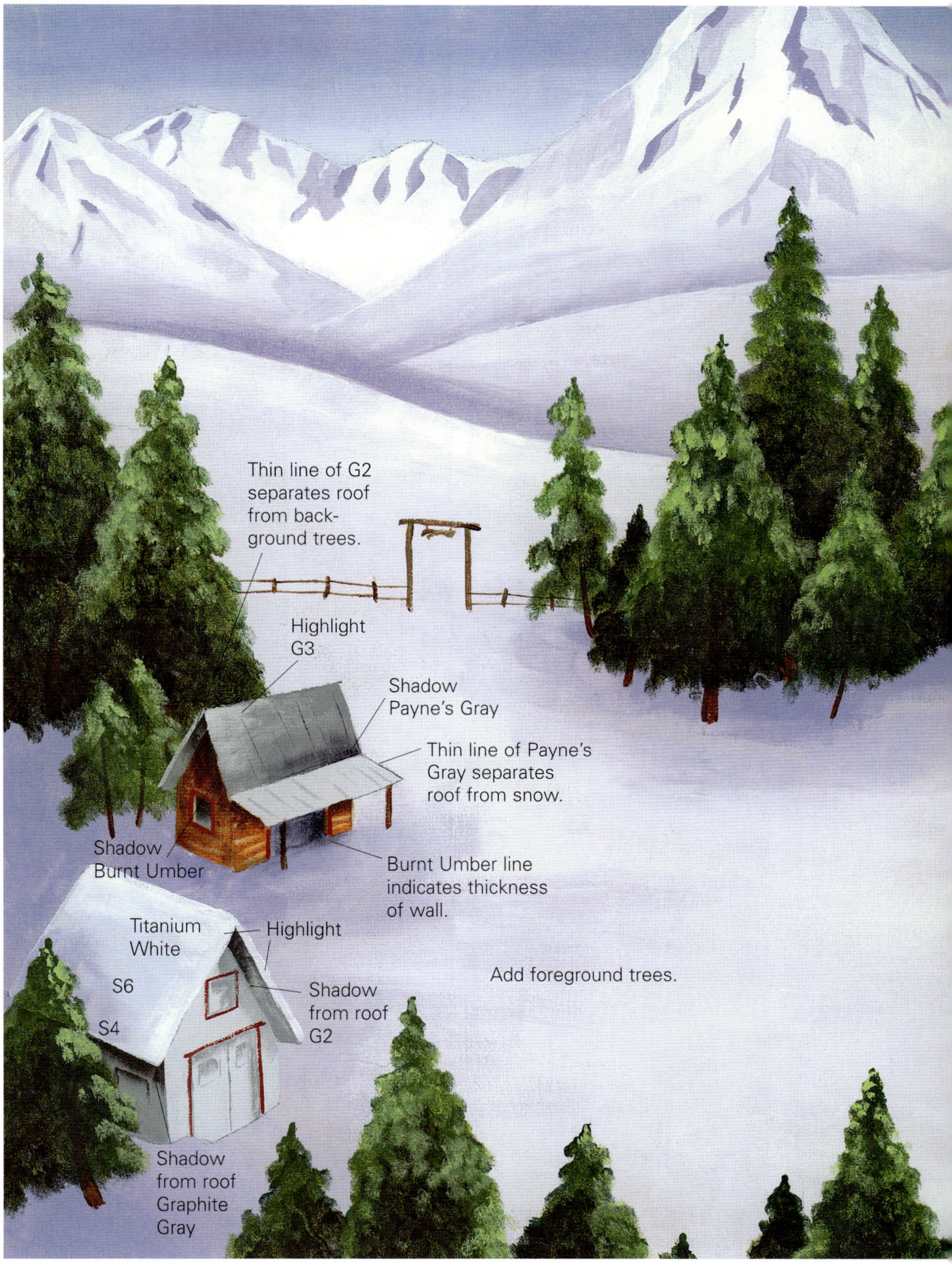

Trees Step-by-Step

(Pre-Snow)

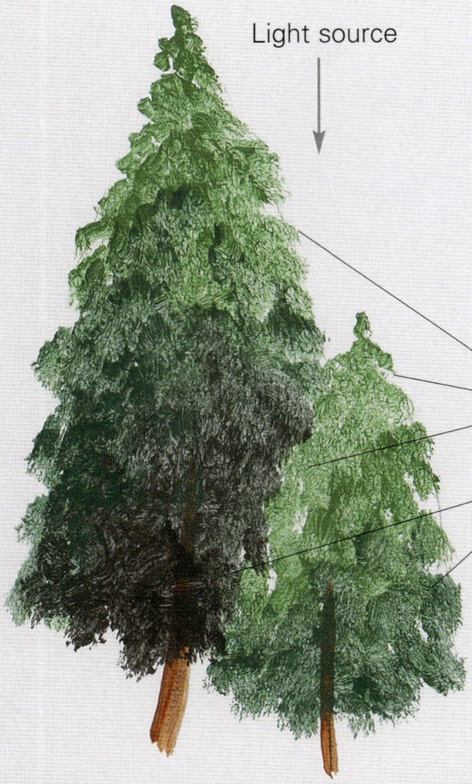

- Establish the conical forms of the trees by correctly placing the values.
- Paint bases of trunks before painting foliage. It is not necessary to paint upper trunks.
- Mix Sap Green sequence (dark, medium, and very light values only).
- Mix Cool Green sequence (very dark, dark, medium, and light values only).
- Use a #2 scumbler toward tops of trees and a larger #4 farther down. These greens are transparent, so paint light values first, then place the darker values around them.
- Dab on pine needles with the colors of the Cool Green sequence.
- Dab lightest value on sides facing the light and on the other side of the forward tree.
- Use dark colors on trees in the rear against the edges of the forward trees.
- Dab darker colors toward bottom of trees.

Trunks
Move between Burnt Umber and Burnt Sienna for color variation.

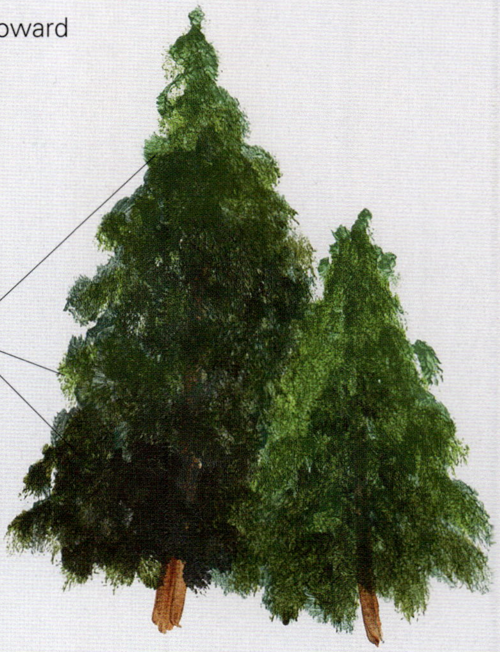

Dab Sap Green/medium on the light portions of the trees.

Dab Sap Green/dark everywhere else.

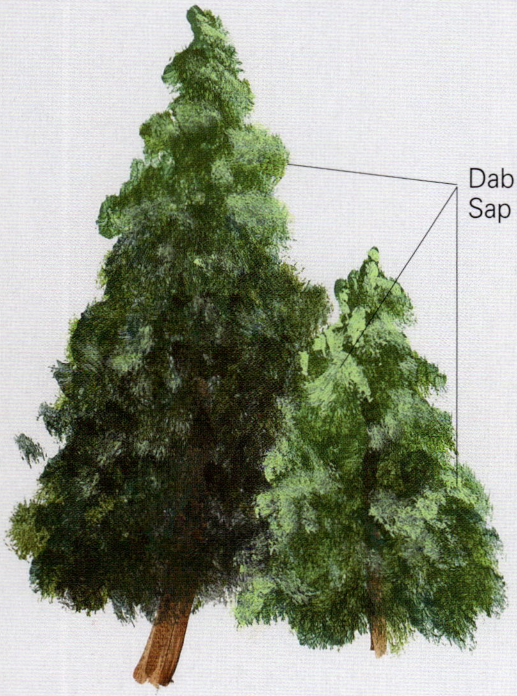

Dab highlights with Sap Green/very light.

Mountains Step-by-Step

Snow-covered mountains are simple shapes with the different values indicating sunlight and shadow. Light source is directly overhead.

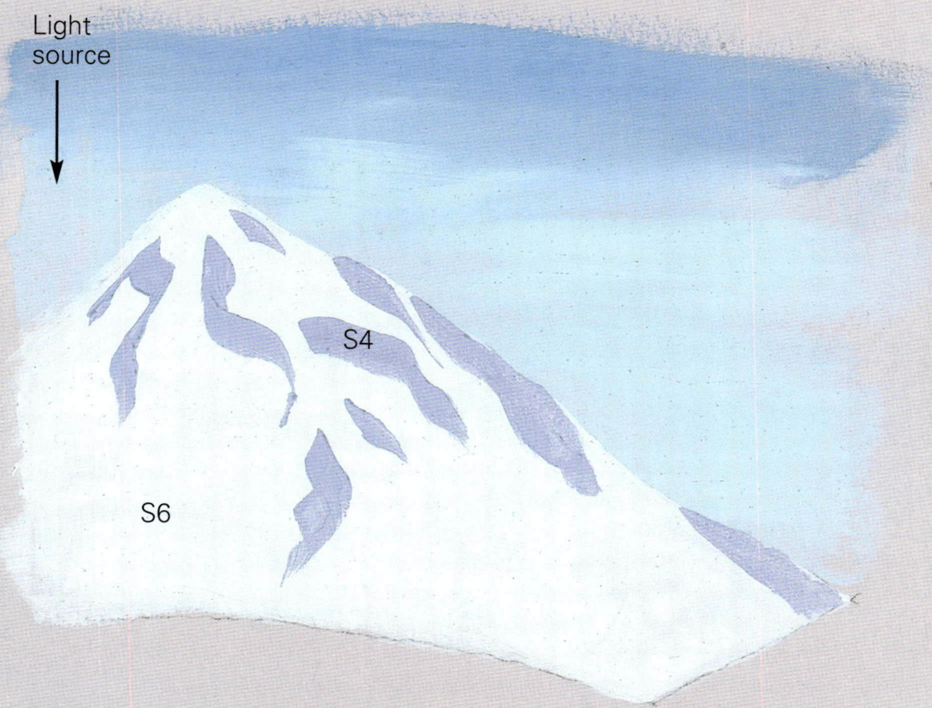

- Paint base color of snow very light blue S6. Using a #14 flat brush, paint far mountain first, then mountain on left. Switch to a #20 flat brush and paint mountain on right.
- Shadows are random shapes, generally radiating from the mountain peak. Paint with a #6 flat brush and light lavender S4.

With the #6 flat brush, add Titanium White highlights alongside some of the shadows. Concentrate highlights on light side of mountain.

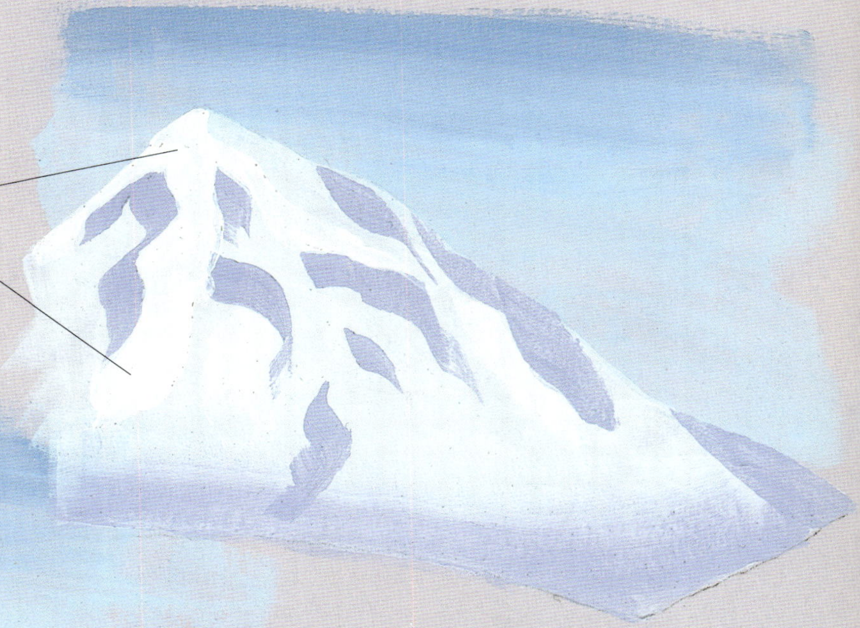

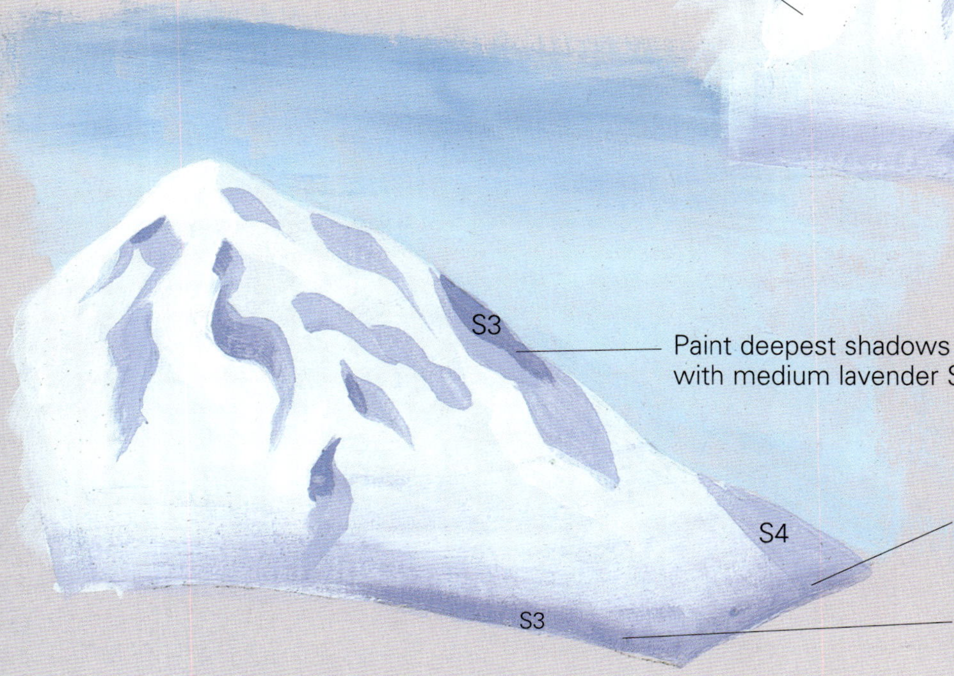

Paint deepest shadows with medium lavender S3.

Separate mountains from each other and from foreground hills with light lavender S4 shadows.

Strengthen separating shadows with medium lavender S3.

Third Stage, continued from page 109

11. Shade under roof on side of white building with a flat brush side-loaded with Graphite Gray.
12. Add shadow of roof on front with side-loaded gray G2.
13. Outline window, doors, and door details with a liner and G2. Shade them with a flat brush side-loaded with G2.
14. Paint side window with side-loaded Graphite Gray.
15. Paint snow on roof with light blue S6. With Titanium White, highlight top and front portions of roof snow, and paint snow built up on other side of roof. Shade snow with lavender S4.
16. Paint trim on both buildings with dull red R1.
17. Paint foreground trees, using the same method as for middle ground trees.

Final Stage

See finished painting.

1. Paint hay with tiny liner brush strokes of Gold Ochre, Burnt Umber, and Buff Titanium.
2. Paint shadow under horse lavender S4.
3. The horses are small; paint only their overall shapes, without details. Paint right horse Burnt Umber, with Mars Black on far legs and tail.
4. Paint left horse Gold Ochre, with Burnt Umber head and shading.
5. Lighten trees by adding clumps of snow. Using the #1 liner, paint Titanium White clumps on highlight sides and medium lavender S4 clumps on shadow sides.
6. Deepen shadows on snow with washes of Payne's Gray and W1. Build up color slowly with additional washes. Wash darkest shadow areas under trees, inside log building, and between and to left of buildings.
7. With thinned W1, add shadow of fence, and streak tracks in the snow around log building and in a curved path leading out through the gate.
8. With a liner and Titanium White, paint a clump of snow in angle of tin roof of log building.
9. With a small scumbler brush, tap in a few clumps of trees in valleys of background mountains.
10. Add a flock of tiny birds with a liner brush and gray G2. Add a tiny bird resting on treetop in right foreground. ❑

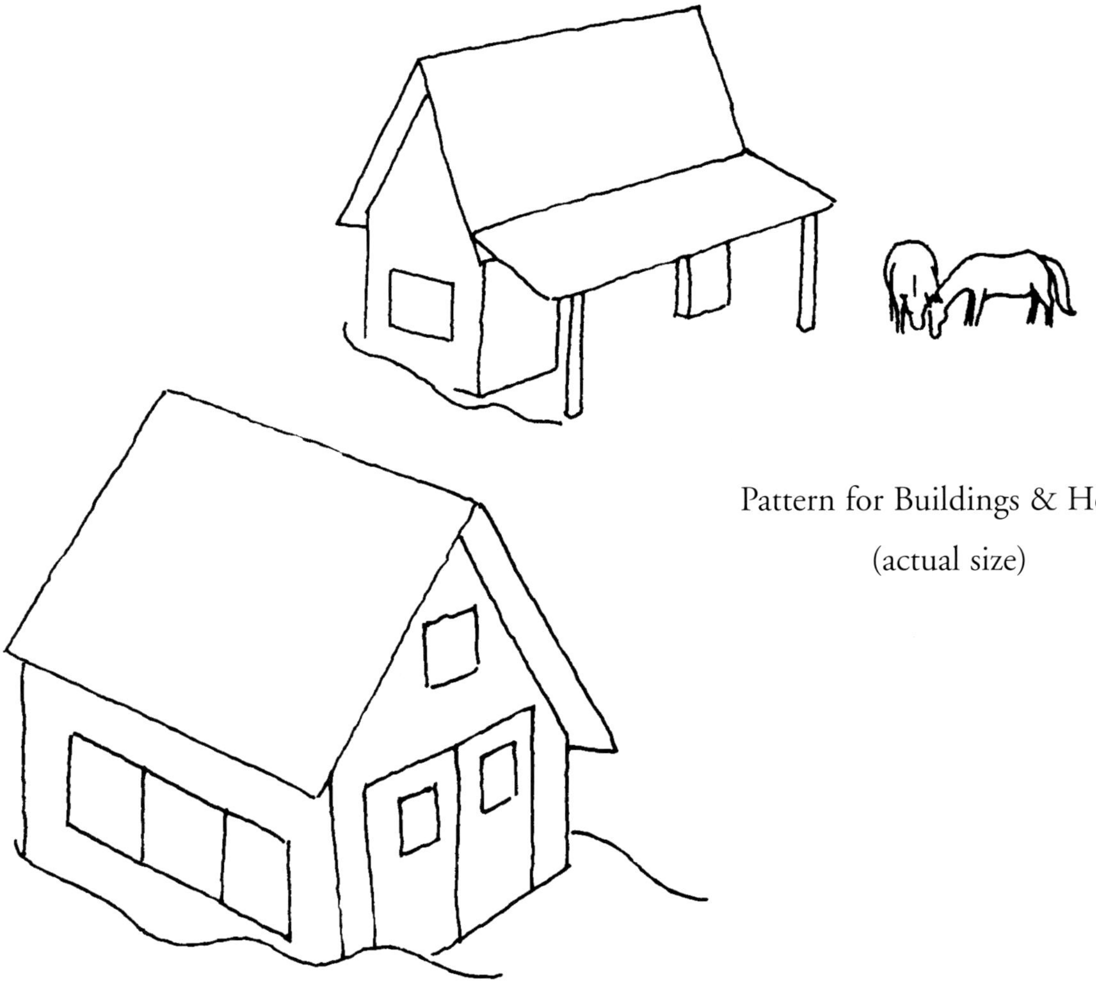

Pattern for Buildings & Horses

(actual size)

Tuscan Gate

Instructions begin on Page 114

Pattern

(actual size)

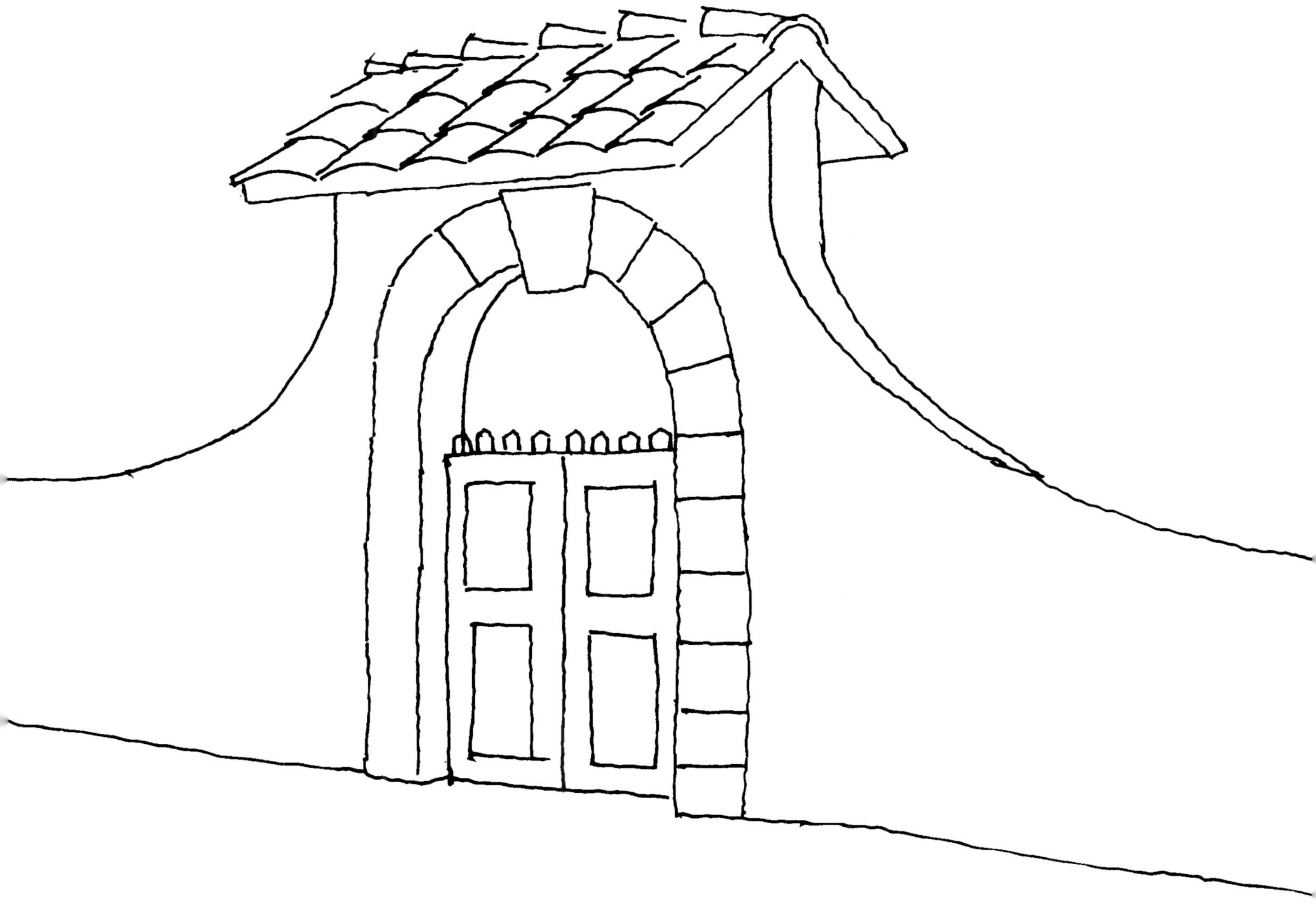

TUSCAN GATE

11" x 14"

I have never been to Tuscany, but I know there are vineyards, distant hills, and luminous skies. The cypresses, with their dark, distinctive silhouettes, are the signature elements of the region's landscape. The opening in the gate is the focal point of this painting. It is framed by the joyous color of the bougainvillea, and backed by the strong verticals of the dark cypress. The opening invites the eye to wander to the vineyard, the far hills, and the tiny background trees pointing upward to the richly colored sky.

Value Sketch

Refer to the value sketch to guide placement of darks and lights.

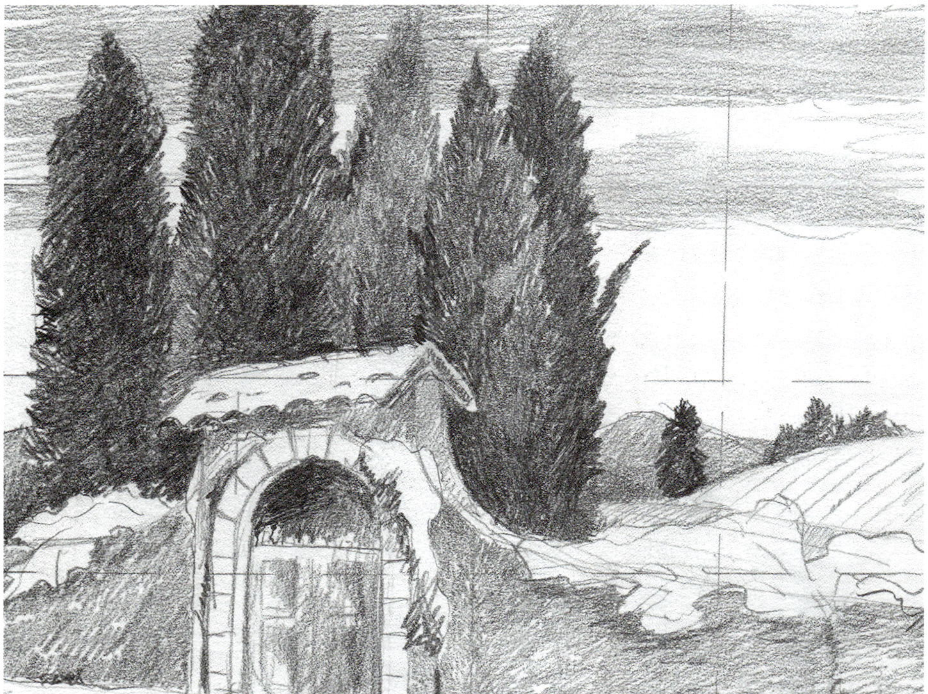

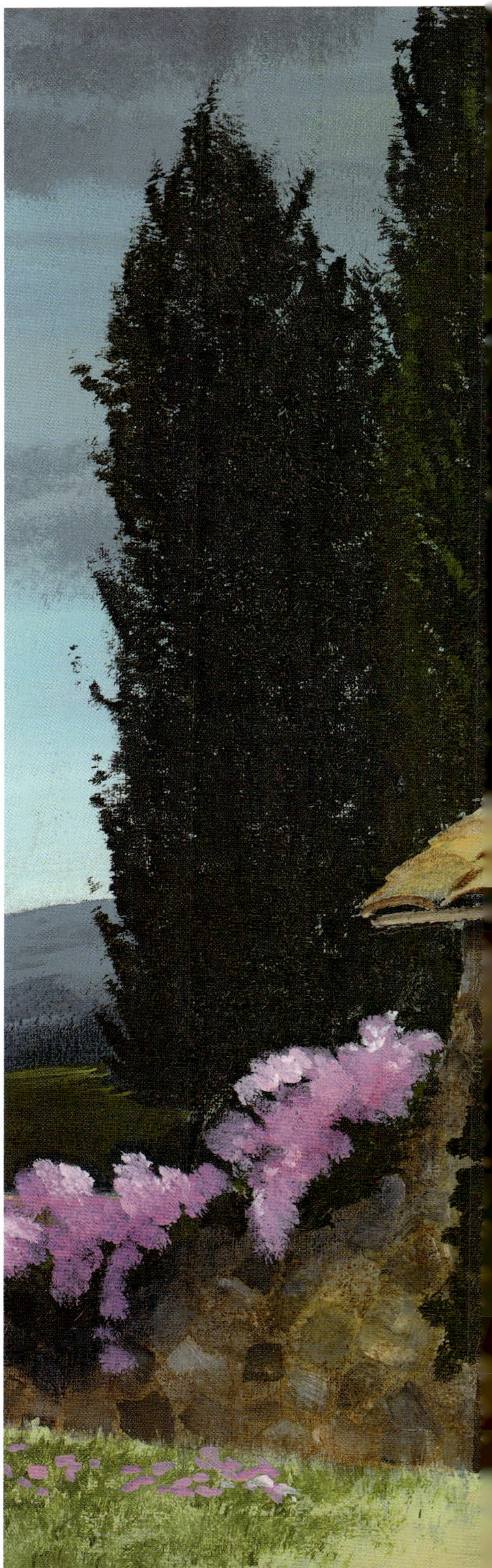

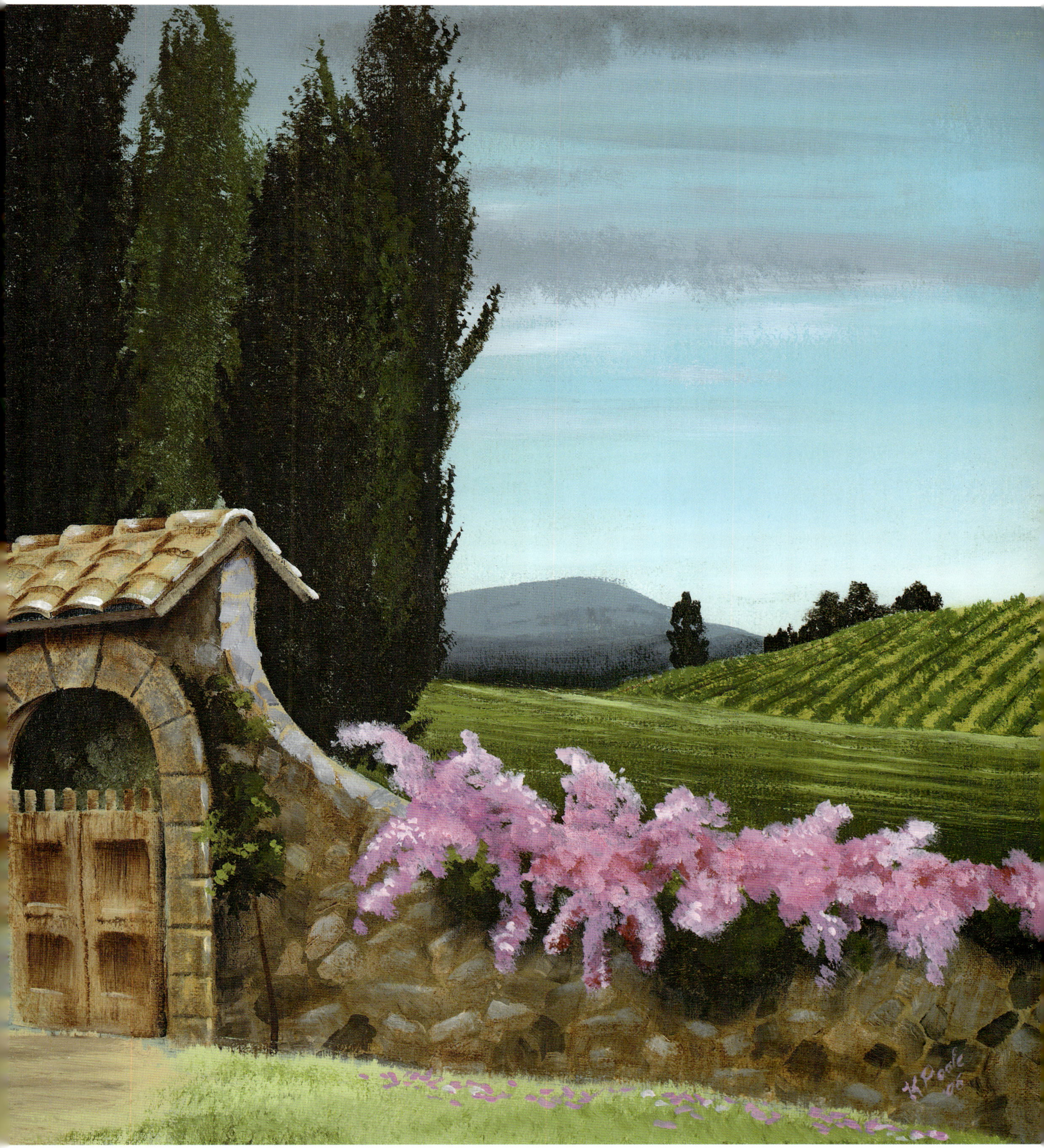

Color Scheme & Palette

S1 Titanium White + Phthalo Green (Yellow Shade)

S2 Titanium White + Cobalt Turquoise

S3 Titanium White + Phthalo Turquoise

S4 Titanium White + S5

S5 Titanium White + S6

S6 Titanium White + Graphite Gray + Phthalo Blue (Green Shade)

H1 S6 + Graphite Gray + Phthalo Blue (Red Shade)

Phthalo Green Sequence

Refer to Page 25 for mixing instructions.

very dark dark medium light

Sap Green Sequence

Refer to Page 24 for mixing instructions.

very dark dark medium light very light

Cool Green Sequence

Refer to Page 25 for mixing instructions.

very dark

Toning color:

medium green acrylic paint for decorative painting

Used straight from the tube:

Buff Titanium

Raw Sienna

Graphite Gray

Payne's Gray

The color scheme is the primary colors of light: red, green, and blue. In this case, "red" becomes a series of bright, cool pinks, but true reds would work equally well. The sky colors lean toward a turquoise blue. Brown is fundamentally a mix of red and green, so it is harmonious in this color scheme.

Used for mixing colors:
Burnt Umber
Cadmium Red Deep
Cadmium Red Light
Cadmium Red Medium
Cadmium Yellow Deep
Cadmium Yellow Light
Cobalt Green Deep
Cobalt Turquoise
Graphite Gray
Mars Black
Permanent Rose
Phthalo Blue (Green Shade)
Phthalo Blue (Red Shade)
Phthalo Green (Yellow Shade)
Phthalo Turquoise
Quinacridone Magenta
Quinacridone Violet
Sap Green
Titanium White
Ultramarine Blue

Titanium White + Quinacridone Magenta

Titanium White + Quinacridone Violet

Titanium White + Permanent Rose

First Stage

1. Sketch horizon line and cypress outlines.
2. Begin at bottom of sky. Paint a band of light green S1. Working upward, smoothly transition to light turquoise S2, then S3. About halfway up, introduce streaky bands of the gray-blues S4, S5 and S6, separated by bands of S3. Finish with streaky band of S6 at top. Let dry.
3. Add scumbled puffs of fluffy texture to some of the gray streaks.
4. Redraw horizon line and cypress outlines. Sketch hills. Transfer gate outline.
5. Paint far hills H1, blending into Cool Green/very dark at bottom. Let dry. Add a little S6 at tops of hills.
6. Paint middle ground hill with the Phthalo Green sequence, the Sap Green sequence, and Cool Green/very dark.
7. Tap in small background trees with a #2 scumbler. Use Cool Green/very dark for single tree, and Sap Green/very dark for the rest.
8. Following *Distant Vineyard Step-by-Step,* paint the vineyard.
9. Paint middle ground hill with Sap Green/medium. While wet, streak in Sap Green/light with a fan brush. Streak Sap Green/very light toward top of hill to right of gate.

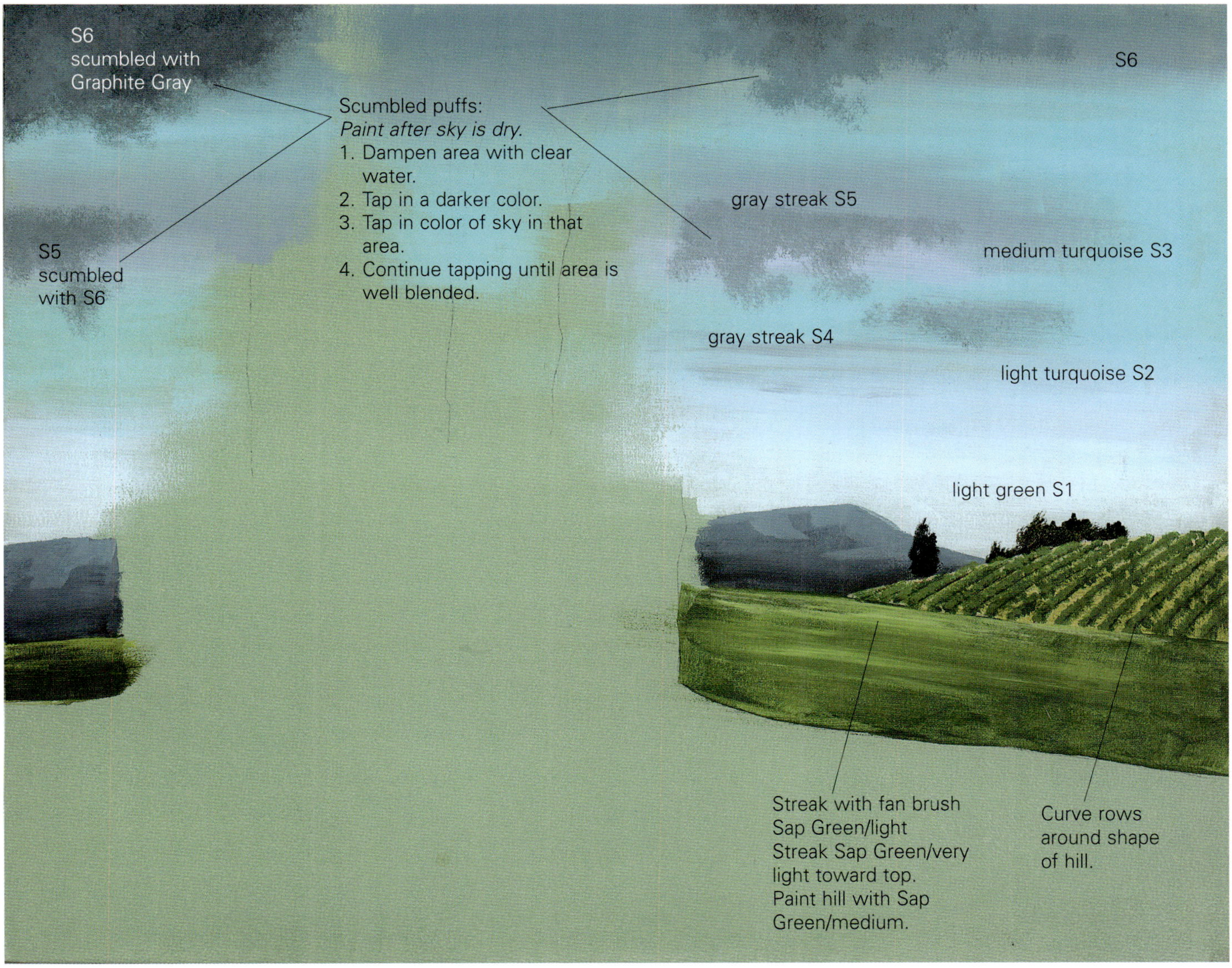

Second Stage

1. Place cypress tree colors according to diagram - very dark colors, separated and given form by sparing use of lighter colors. Complete one tree at a time, beginning in back (#1, #3, #5). Begin at top and work down. Use a fan brush and a tapping motion. On left side of tree, hold brush end pointing down and handle pointing up toward the right to give slightly curved, irregular strokes suggesting a branch angled sharply upward. On right side of tree, hold brush end pointing down and handle pointing up toward the left. Refer to *Tree Details.*
2. Transfer gate outline.
3. Dab in trees that show through opening with a scumbler, Cool Green/very dark on left and top, transitioning to lighter colors in lower right.
4. Lay in roof, stones around arch, and top edge of wall with Buff Titanium.
5. For face of rock wall, follow Step 1 in *Stone Wall Step-by-Step.* Do not paint wall where flowers will overlap.
6. Very lightly load a scumbler with the Buff Titanium/Graphite Gray mixture. Lightly stipple texture on stones forming arch.
7. Basecoat gate with Buff Titanium. While wet, add vertical streaks of Burnt Umber with a small fan brush.
8. Paint end edge of roof with Burnt Umber and a small round brush. While wet, streak with Buff Titanium.

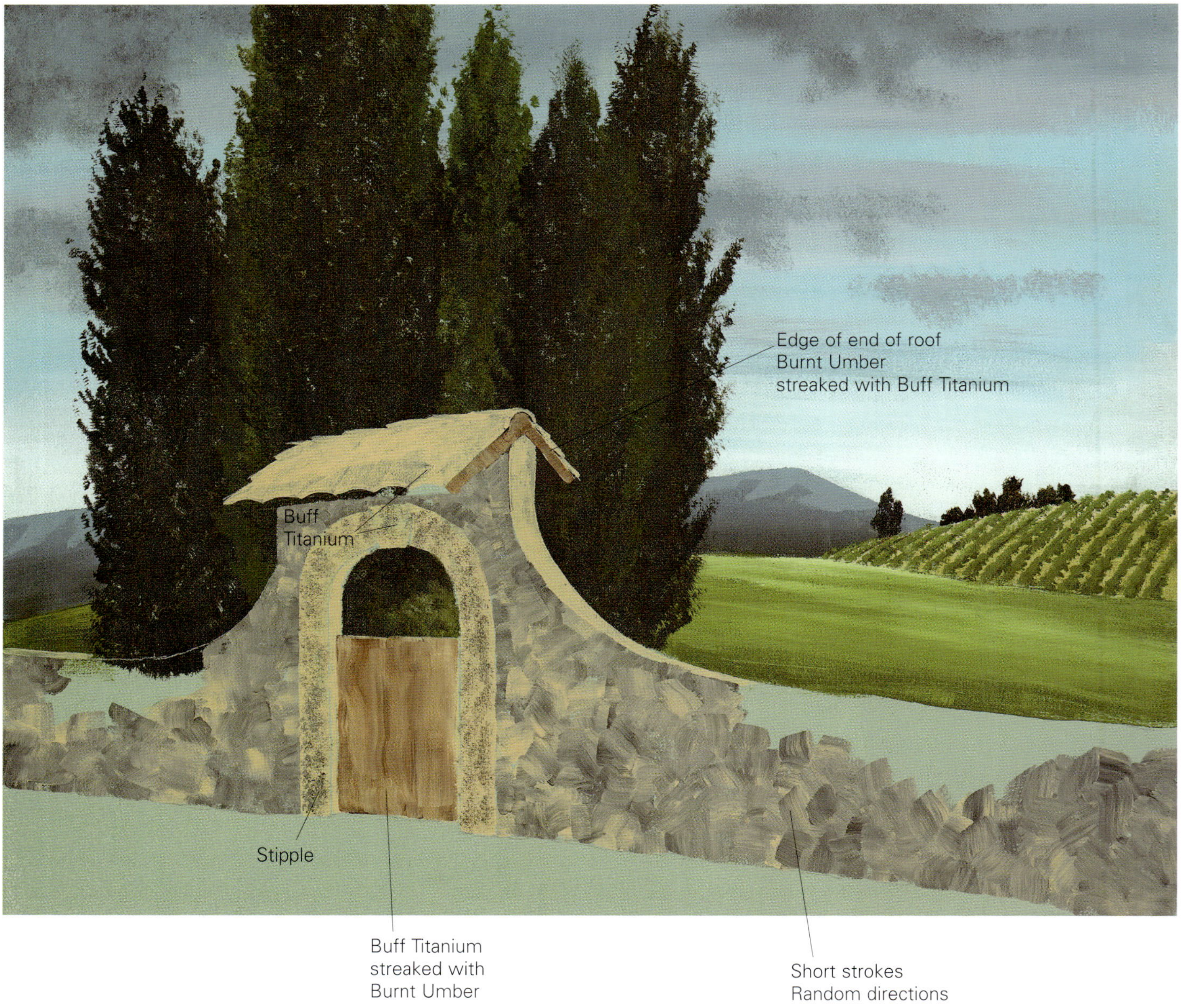

Final Stage

See finished painting.

1. Finish wall following the *Stone Wall Step-by-Step* instructions.
2. Wash gate with thinned Burnt Umber.
3. Shade tops of four inset panels with side-loaded Burnt Umber. Add horizontal highlight lines of Buff Titanium at bottom of panels.
4. Tap in the division between doors with Burnt Umber on the chisel edge of a flat brush.
5. Paint crenellations at top of gate with a #4 flat brush and Burnt Umber. Streak in Buff Titanium toward the top of each one.
6. Paint inner edge of left side of arch with Buff Titanium. Shade at top with Burnt Umber, then a narrower area of Payne's Gray.
7. Follow *Roof Tiles Step-by-Step* to complete the roof.
8. Paint ivy vines on both sides of arch with a scumbler and the Phthalo Green sequence. Paint vine stems with a #1 liner and Burnt Umber.
9. Tap in bougainvillea foliage with Sap Green/very dark and Sap Green/medium .
10. For bougainvillea flowers, mix three tints each of Quinacridone Magenta, Quinacridone Violet, and Permanent Rose. Using a #2 scumbler, tap in sprays of flowers with these tints, also using the pure colors from the tube. Concentrate darker tints and pure colors at bottom of sprays, and lighter tints at top. Finally, add dots of the lightest tints on some sprays. ❑

To paint left sides of trees:

Handle close to horizontal near tops to give a nearly vertical stroke.

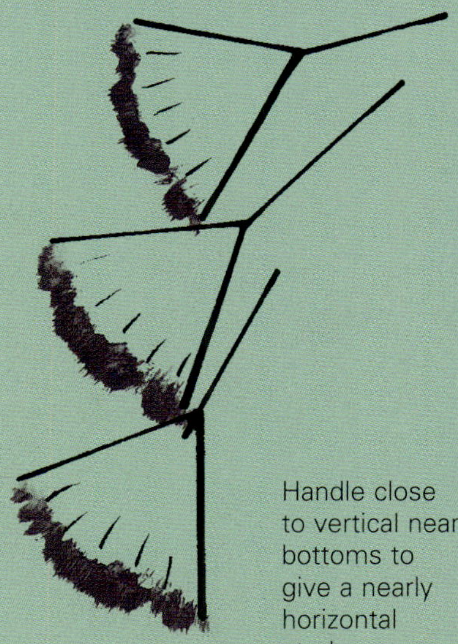

Handle close to vertical near bottoms to give a nearly horizontal stroke.

To paint right sides of trees:

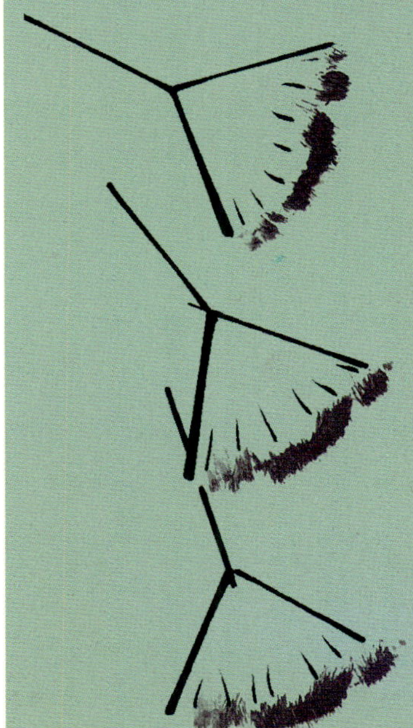

Tree Color Details

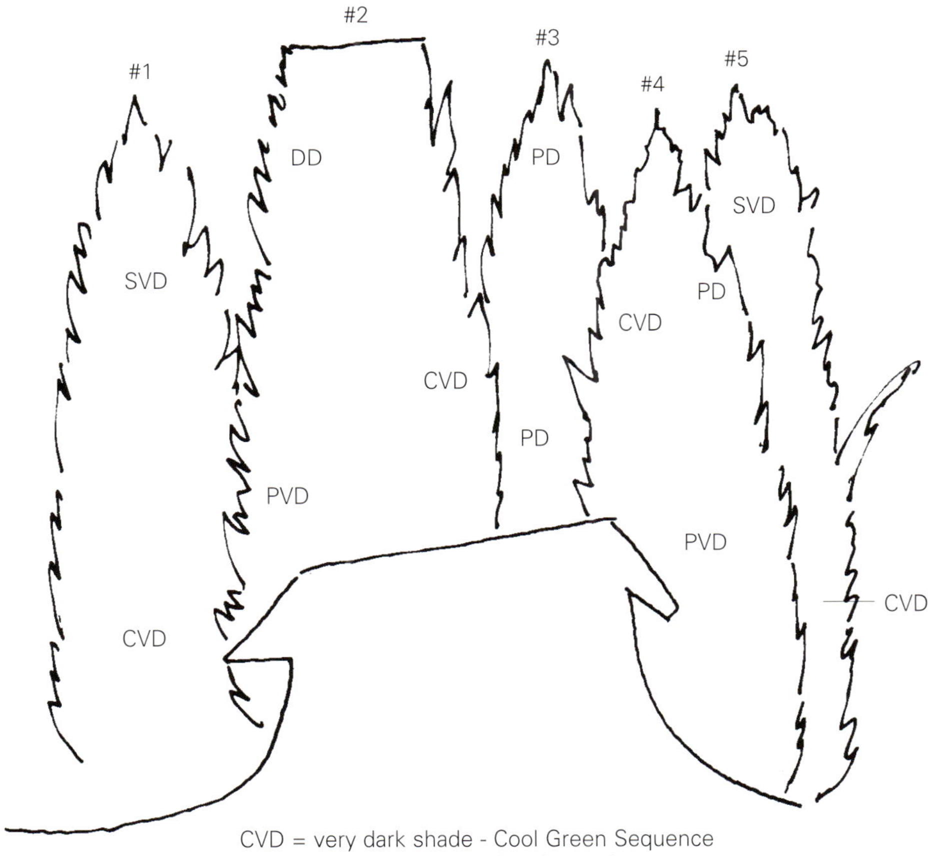

CVD = very dark shade - Cool Green Sequence
SVD = very dark shade - Sap Green Sequence
PD = dark shade - Phthalo Green Sequence
PVD = very dark shade - Phthalo Green Sequence

Stone Wall
Step-by-Step

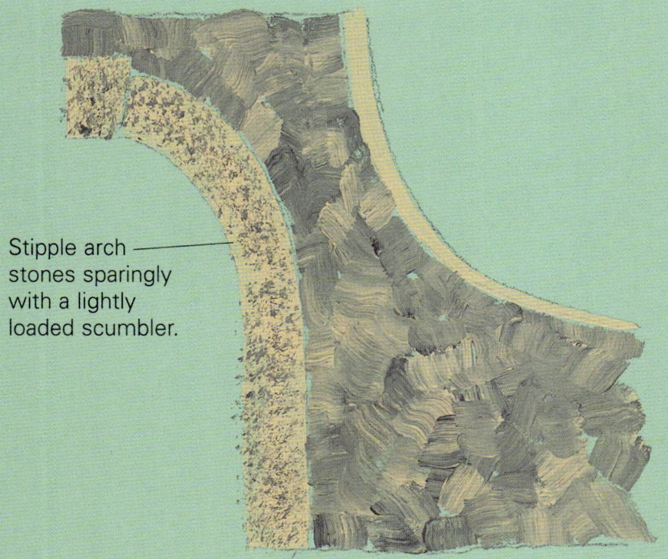

1. Paint wall.
- Prepare a partially mixed blob of Graphite Gray and Buff Titanium.
- Load a #8 flat brush from different portions of the paint blob, for variety of color on the brush. Paint walls with short strokes in random directions.

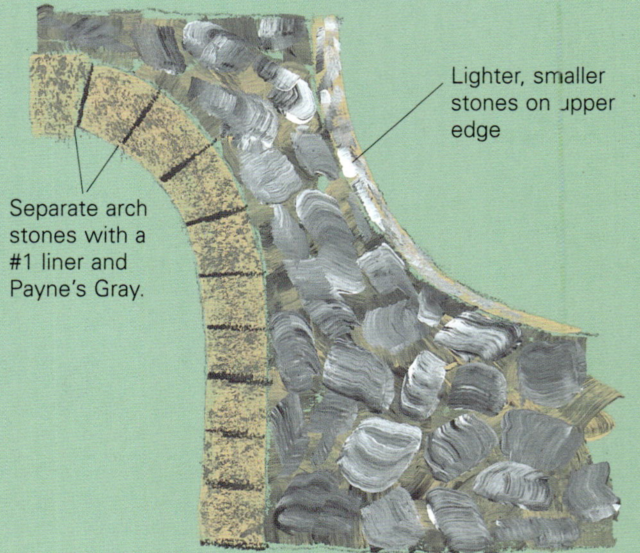

2. Paint individual stones.
- Prepare a partially mixed blob of Graphite Gray and Titanium White.
- Load a #6 round brush from different portions of the paint blob, for variety of color on the brush. Paint individual rounded stones over face of wall.
- Paint lighter, smaller stones on upper edge. Use a smaller brush loaded from lightest areas of paint blob.
- Let paint dry.

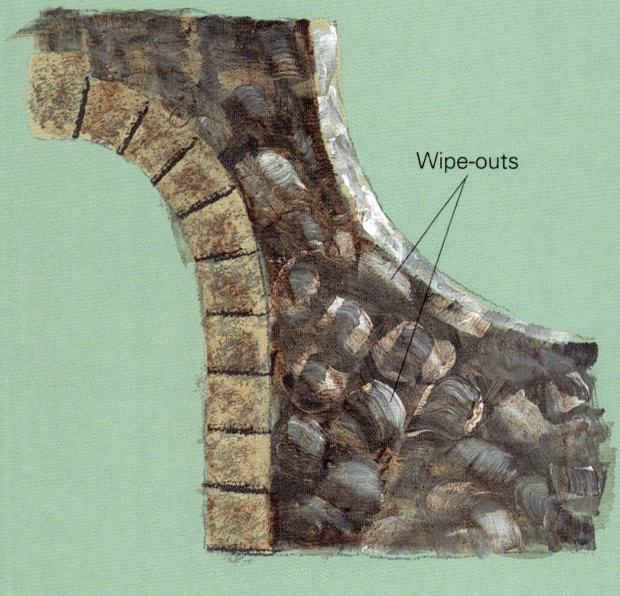

3. Define individual stones.
- Wash wall-except upper edge - and arch stones with thinned Burnt Umber.
- While wet, use a clean, damp brush to wipe out highlights on tops of randomly selected stones.

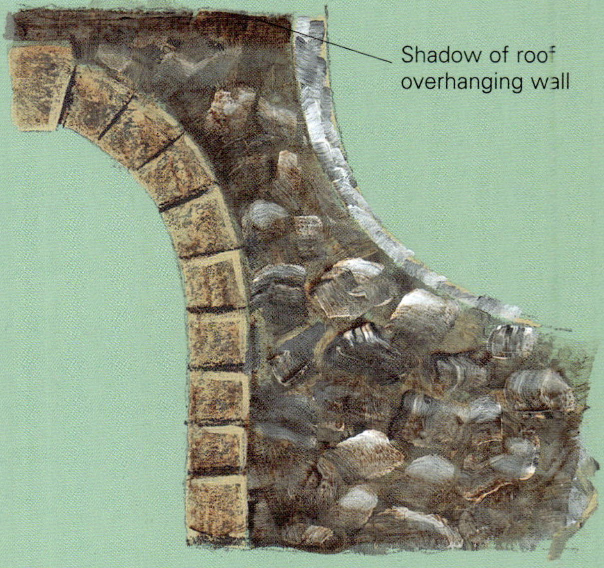

4. Paint details and shadows.
- Using a #1 liner and Buff Titanium, paint highlight lines on right and upper edges of arch stones.
- Paint shadows on wall under roof and to the left of the left side of the arch with a large flat brush side-loaded with Burnt Umber. Repeat with a narrower shadow of Payne's Gray.
- Paint shadows under flowering vine area with Payne's Gray.

Distant Vineyard Step-by-Step

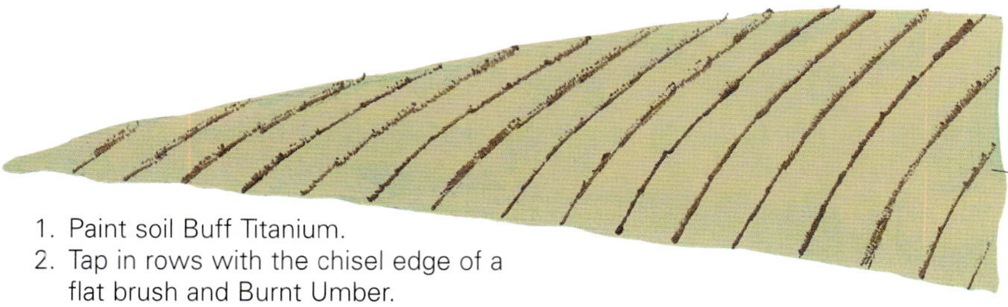

1. Paint soil Buff Titanium.
2. Tap in rows with the chisel edge of a flat brush and Burnt Umber.

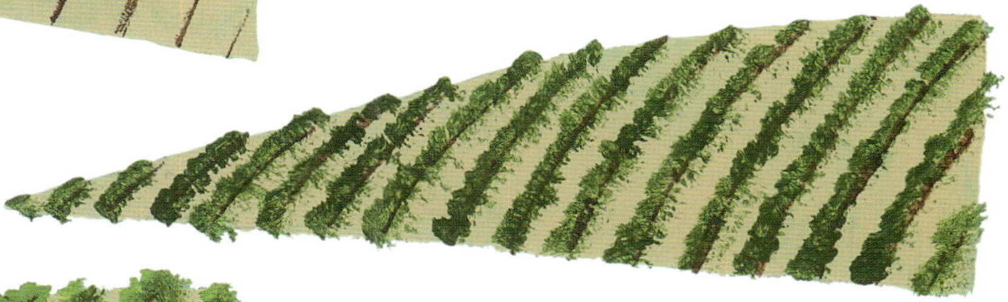

3. Tap in foliage with a #2 scumbler and Sap Green/medium.

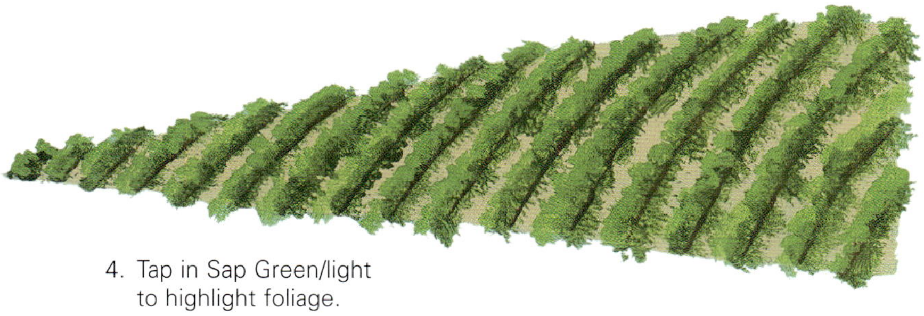

4. Tap in Sap Green/light to highlight foliage.

5. Wash over entire hill with thinned Sap Green/dark to reduce the value contrast. (The farther away an object is, the less the value contrast.)

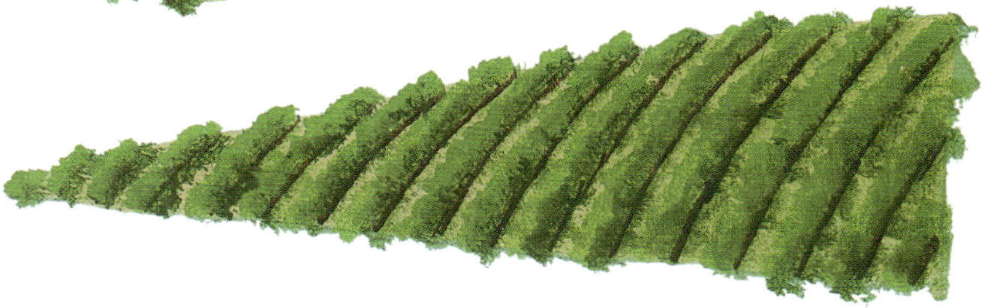

Tile Roof

Step-by-Step

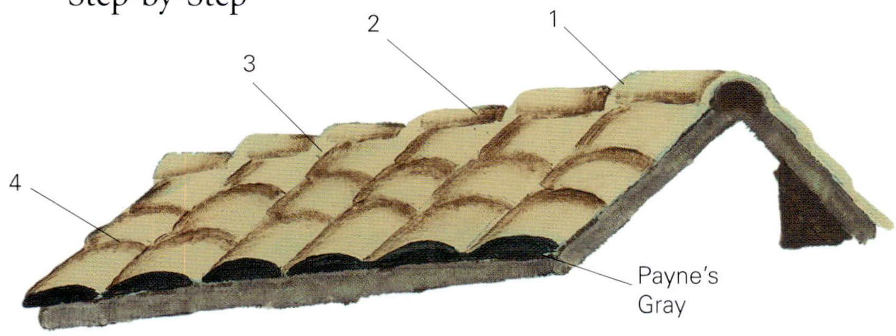

Shade between tiles with side-loaded Burnt Umber:

1. between the peak tiles - loaded edge of brush to right
2. between the peak tiles and top row of roof tiles - loaded edge down
3. between the columns of roof tiles - loaded edge to left
4. between the rows - loaded edge up

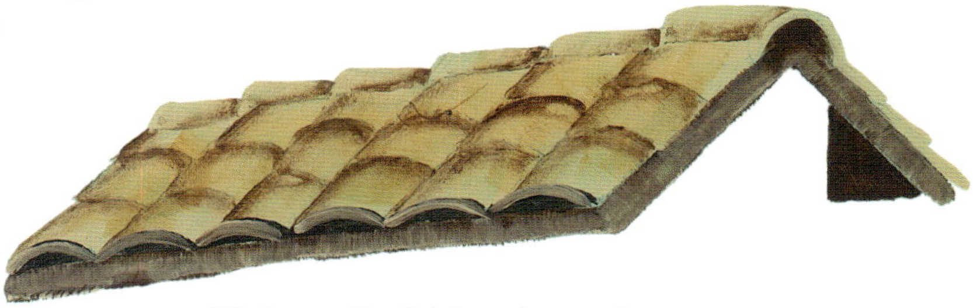

Wash over tiles lightly and unevenly with thinned Raw Sienna.

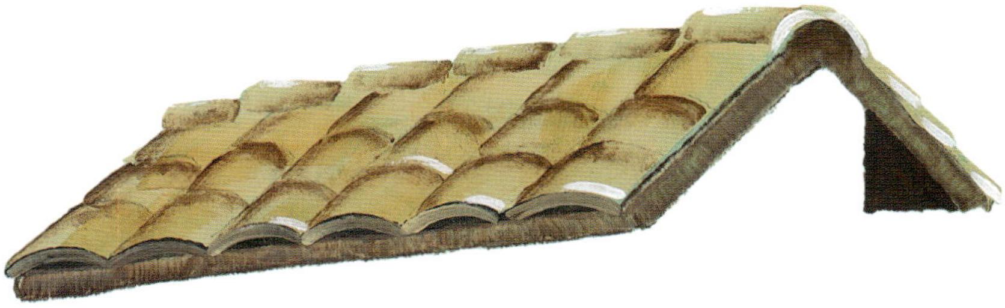

Add a few Titanium White highlights with a #1 liner.

LOVE OF LAVENDER

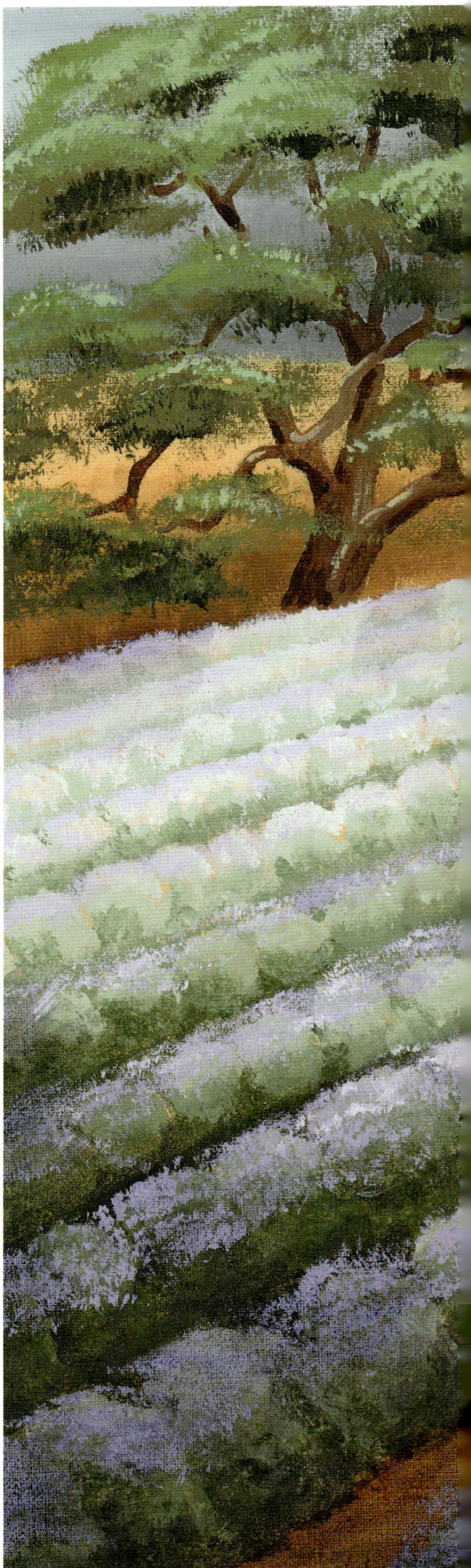

11" x 14"

The marching rows of lavender are the main theme in this painting. The curved rows suggest that the ground is gently rolling, and they also lead the eye in a zigzag pattern from foreground to background. I angled the farmhouse to fit into the zigzag. The front of the house faces into the composition. The large heritage oak on the left balances the house, and the oaks around it integrate it into the landscape. The women and their dog provide emotional and visual interest to oppose the attraction of the house as the focal point. Their poses are balanced, with two women bending toward each other and one standing straight up, taking a break. The grays of the stormy sky are a nice fit with the grayed colors of the lavender. Also, the stormy sky is dramatic and irregular - a contrast to the regular calm of the farm fields. The areas of darker value at the bottom of the painting are shadows, suggesting large trees out of view.

Value Sketch

Refer to the value sketch to guide placement of darks and lights.

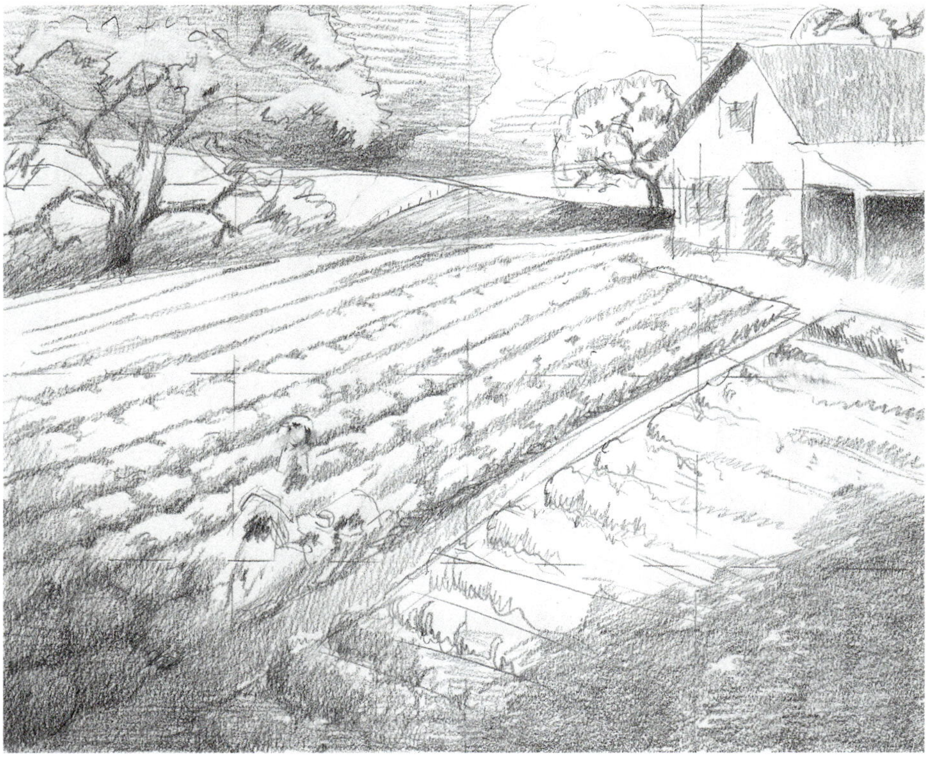

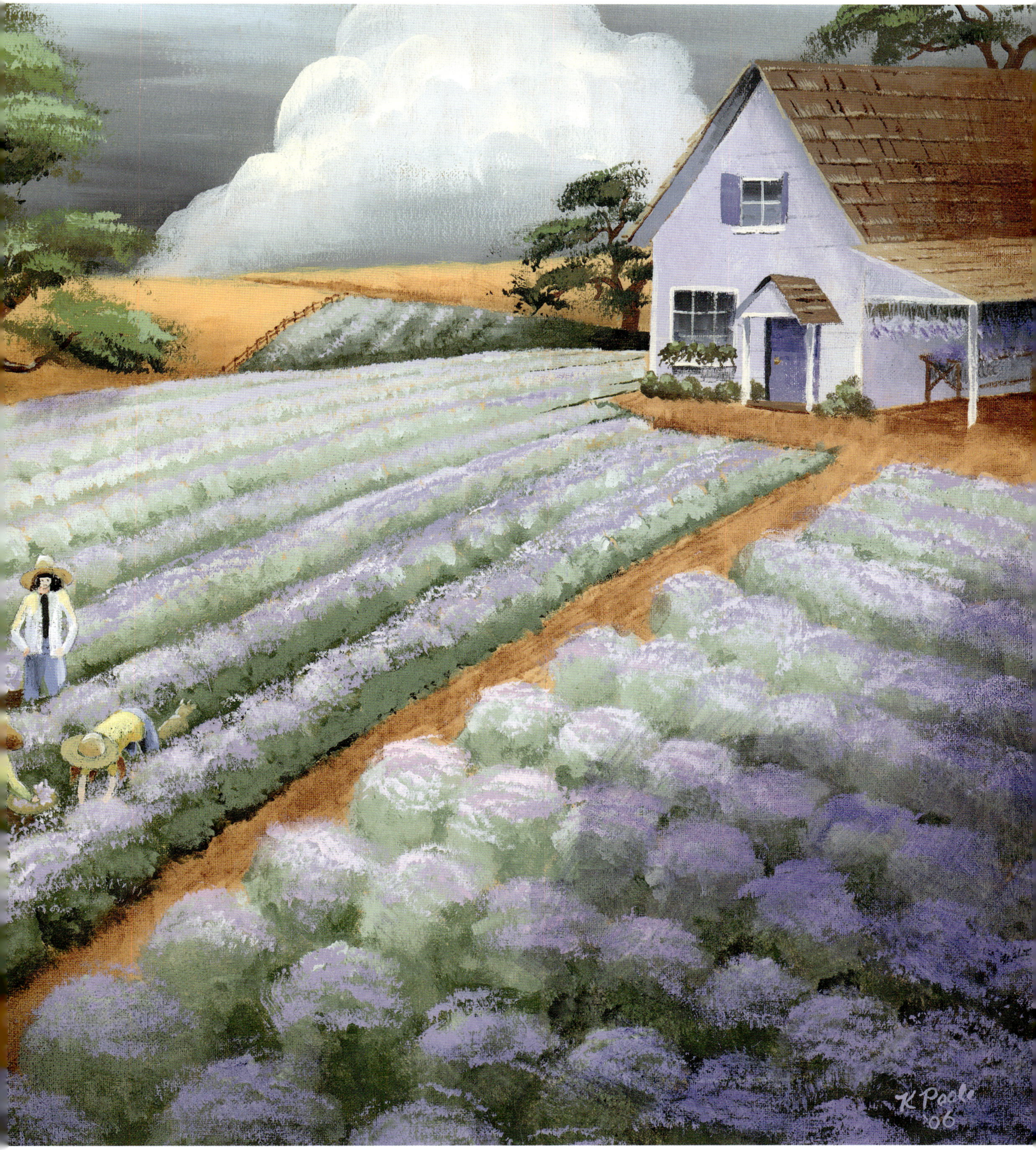
K. Poole
'06

Chromium Oxide Green Sequence

Refer to Page 24 for mixing instructions.

very dark | dark | medium | light | very light

S1 — S2 + Graphite Gray

S2 — S3 + Graphite Gray

S3 — Titanium White + Cerulean Blue (Start here)

S4 — Titanium White + Buff Titanium

S5 — S4 + Graphite Gray

H1 — Naples Yellow + (Titanium White)

H2 — Gold Ochre + Burnt Umber + (Dioxazine Purple)

BG1 — BG2 + Burnt Umber

BG2 — Cobalt Green Light + Cadmium Red Medium (Start here)

BG3 — BG2 + Titanium White

G1 — G2 + Titanium White

G2 — G3 + Titanium White

G3 — G4 + Titanium White

G4 — Cobalt Green Light + (Cadmium Red Medium) (Start here)

G5 — G4 + Mars Black

B1 — Burnt Umber + Buff Titanium (Start here)

B2 — B1 + Buff Titanium

P1 — S5 + Dioxazine Purple

P2 — P1 + (Dioxazine Purple)

P3 — P2 + Graphite Gray

P4 — P5 + Titanium White

P5 — S5 + Dioxazine Purple + Ultramarine Blue

P6 — P7 + Titanium White

P7 — S5 + Dioxazine Purple

P8 — P9 + Titanium White

P9 — S5 + Quinacridone Violet

W1 — Dioxazine Purple + Payne's Gray

Wash of W1

W2 — Dioxazine Purple

Wash of W2

Color Scheme & Palette

This is a complementary color scheme with lavenders and golds playing the leading roles. The greens of lavender plants are grayed and slightly bluish. Because the plants are crowned with blooms, the lavenders dominate the greens.

Used for mixing colors:
Buff Titanium
Burnt Umber
Cadmium Red Deep
Cadmium Red Medium
Cadmium Yellow Medium
Cadmium Yellow Light
Cerulean Blue
Chromium Oxide Green
Cobalt Green Light
Dioxazine Purple
Gold Ochre
Graphite Gray
Indanthrene Blue
Mars Black
Naples Yellow
Payne's Gray
Quinacridone Violet
Titanium White
Ultramarine Blue

NOTE: Parentheses around a color name indicate that you should add just a touch of the color to the mix.

Toning color:
ochre tan
acrylic paint for decorative painting

First Stage

1. Tone canvas with ochre tan. Let dry.
2. Transfer lines of hills and lavender rows, and outline of house and cloud.
3. Paint sky wet-in-wet with a #14 flat brush. Finish each section before proceeding to the next. Sky to left of cloud: Begin at bottom with dark blue gray S1. Blend a little Graphite Gray into lower area toward cloud. Working upward with patchy strokes, transition to blue gray S2, then light blue S3.
4. Sky to right of cloud: Paint in the same manner, but don't use Graphite Gray. This section is higher in the sky.
5. Cloud: Paint base dark gray S1, then quickly transition to light gray S5. Side-load a large flat brush with light cream S4. Paint bright areas with gently curved strokes, keeping loaded side of brush toward top of cloud.
6. Use the #14 flat brush to paint farthest hill light brown H1 at horizon. Blend into dark brown H2 at bottom of hill to give it form.
7. Paint left portion of middle hill with same colors and process. Blend in a little Burnt Umber on darkest portion at left.
8. For lavender patch on middle hill: With a #14 flat brush and short, choppy strokes, blend dull gray-greens BG1 - BG3 wet-in-wet, grading from dark at right, to medium, to light at left. Mottled texture indicates a distant field of relatively large plants. Deepen far right area with a little Mars Black.
9. For lavender plants on main hill: Paint row lines with a #6 round brush and greens G2 - G5. Follow value sketch to place the different values of green along lines.
10. Wash Burnt Umber on path. Use a #20 flat brush and short, criss-crossed strokes to add texture.

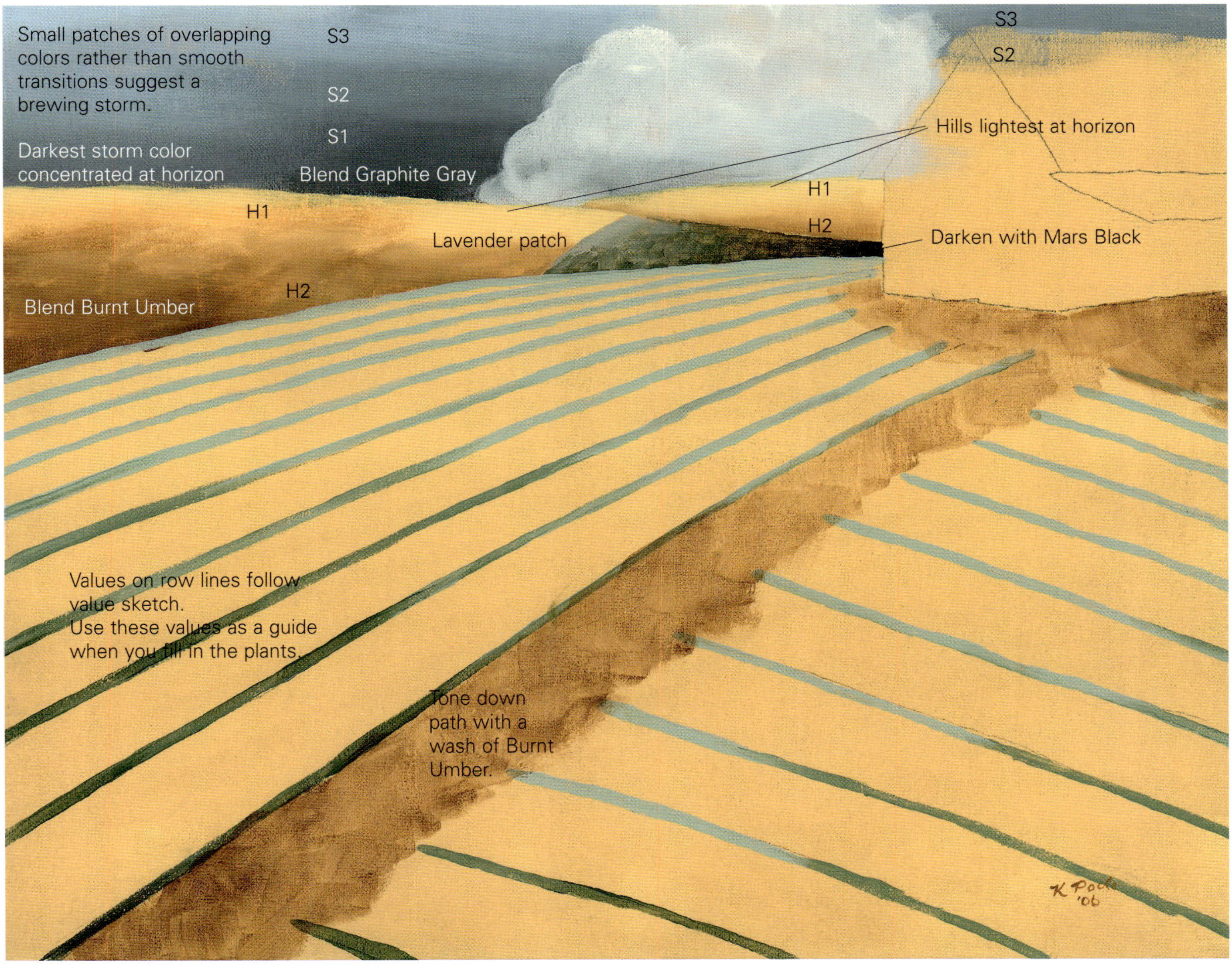

Second Stage

1. Transfer tree trunks and branches. Paint trees following *Heritage Oak Step-by-Step.*
2. Paint lavender foliage following *Lavender Fields Step-by-Step.* Dab in farthest rows with a small scumbler in two steps, green G2 at base and G1 at top. As you near the viewer, switch to a larger scumbler, gradually increase value contrast, and paint foliage clumps in four steps.
3. Block in house front wall with dull lavender P1.
4. Block in upper roof with brown B2. Add Buff Titanium to B2 to lighten, and block in lower roof.
5. Paint underside of roof overhang with P3, blending to Graphite Gray at the peak.
6. Paint roof shadows on front wall with P2, then P3.
7. Paint side wall (under lean-to) beginning with Graphite Gray in upper right area, blending to P3, then to P2 in lower left.

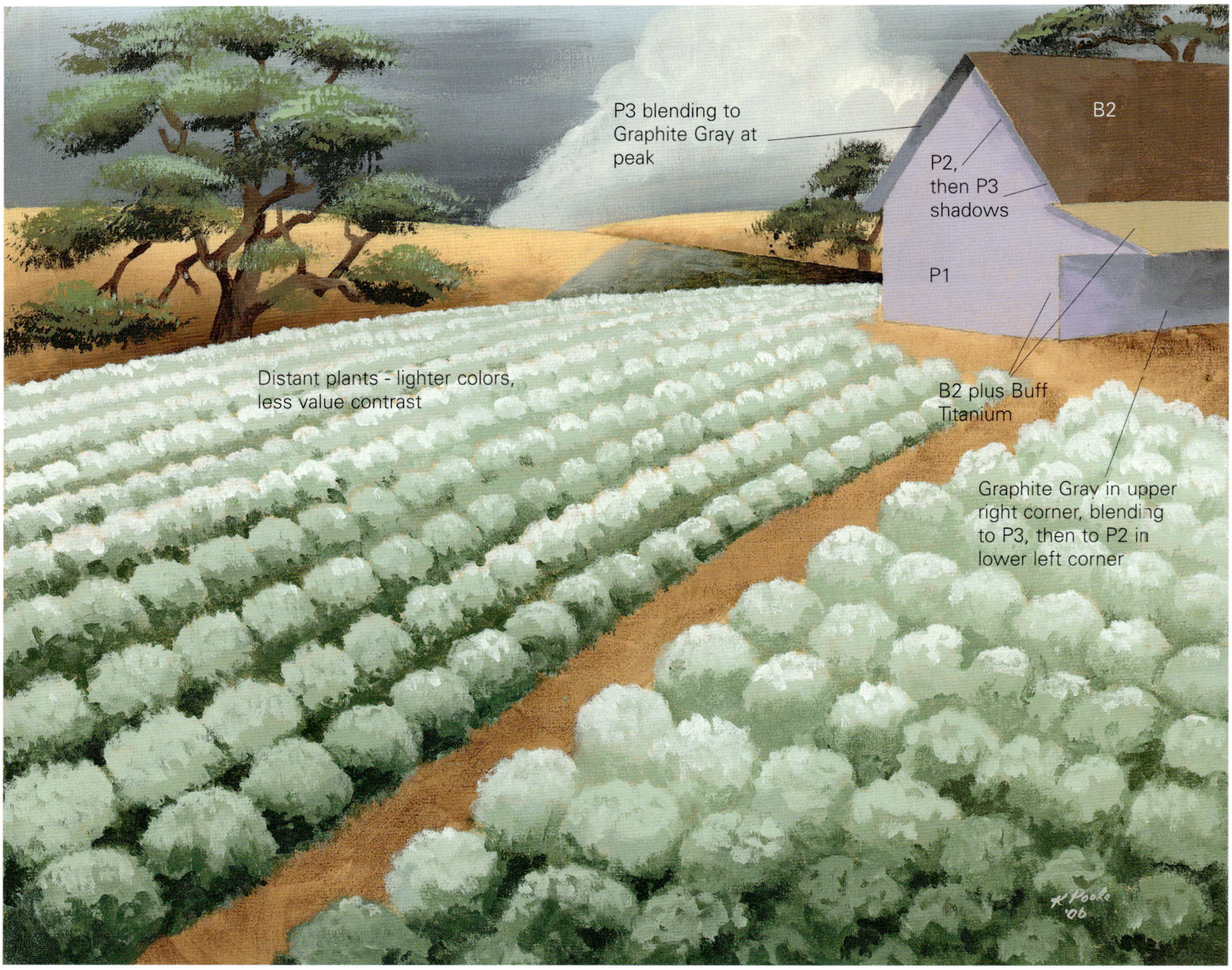

Nearer plants - darker colors, more value contrast

Final Stage

See finished painting.

1. Line in tiny background fence with a #0 liner and Burnt Umber.
2. Suggest flowers on far lavender patch by dabbing in rows with a little lavender P1 on tip of scumbler.
3. Add lavender flowers to plants on main hill, following *Lavender Fields Step-by-Step.*
4. Transfer house details: lines for rows of shingles and outlines of windows, shutters, door, and porch roof.
5. Paint porch roof B2.
6. Tap in shingle details with the tip of a rake brush. Maintain correct perspective; angle divisions between shingles to match pitch of roof.
7. Paint windows dark gray-lavender P3. Blend Graphite Gray at tops.
8. With light cream S4, paint window trim, window box, posts on porch and lean-to, and trim on edges of house.
9. Paint shutters and door P3 brightened with a little Dioxazine Purple.
10. Blend Graphite Gray shadow at top of door. Add a line of Graphite Gray shadow along left edge of door.
11. Using the colors of the Chromium Oxide Green sequence, paint window box plants with the tip of a #3 round brush, and foundation plants with a scumbler.
12. Paint workbench Burnt Umber.
13. Paint harvested lavender on workbench and hanging from lean-to roof. Use a #1 liner for stems, and the tip of a #3 round brush to dot in blossoms.
14. Paint the people as "fleshed out" stick figures. *(See Page 73.)* Paint blue jeans with different value mixtures of Indanthrene Blue, Graphite Gray, and Titanium White.
15. Paint shirts light, warm colors to stay within the color scheme.
16. Paint hats Naples Yellow in shadow areas, Naples Yellow plus Titanium White in highlight areas, and Titanium White for brightest highlights. Paint dog with same colors as hats.
17. Wash Burnt Umber on right, lower portions of house roof and on ground under lean-to.
18. Shade lean-to interior with a wash of Payne's Gray.
19. Deepen shadows in foreground with washes of Dioxazine Purple and W1. Use a #20 flat brush and several light layers of washes. ❑

House Details

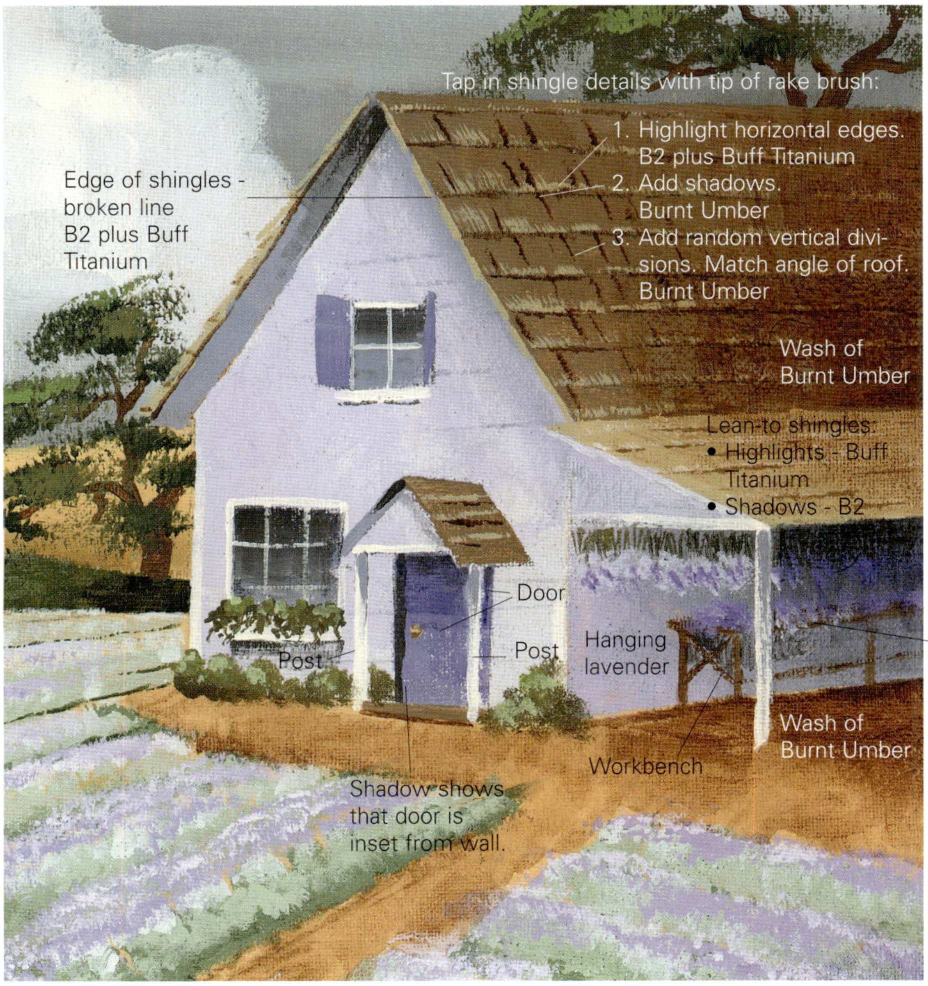

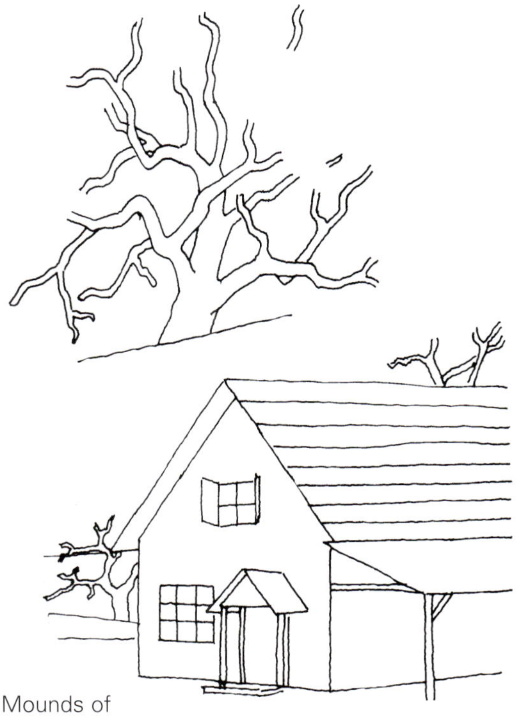

Patterns

Enlarge @200% for actual size.

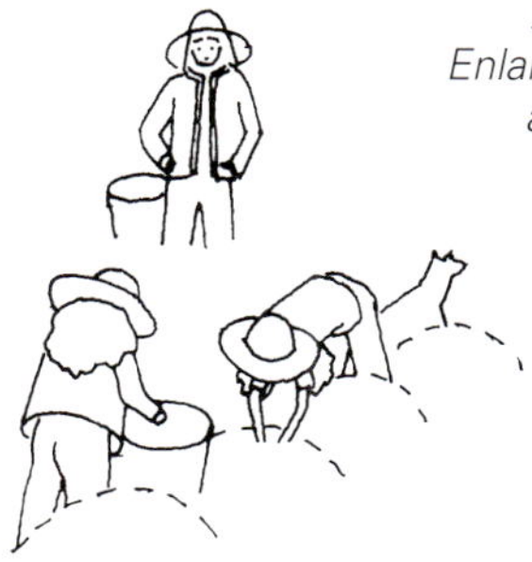

Heritage Oak Step-by-Step

1. Paint trunk and branches.

#3 round brush for larger branches
#1 liner for smaller branches

browns B1 and B2

Burnt Umber in shadows
B2 highlight where branch crosses in front

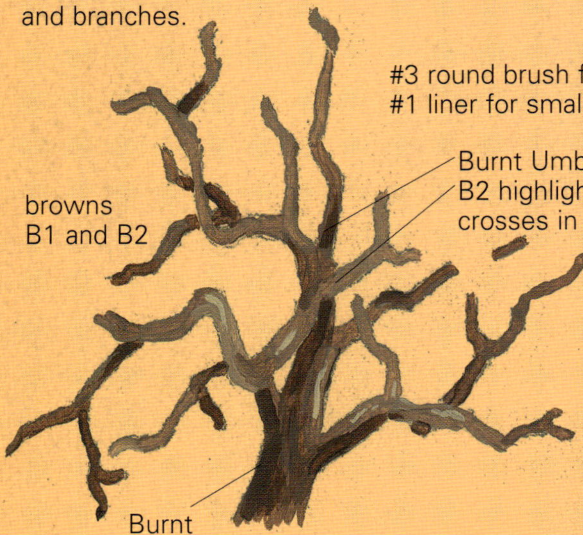

Burnt Umber

Mix Chromium Oxide Green sequence. Tap in foliage clumps with a #1 fan brush.

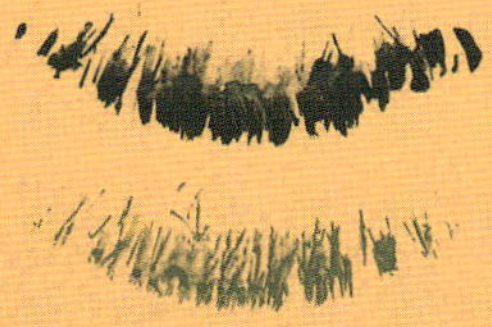

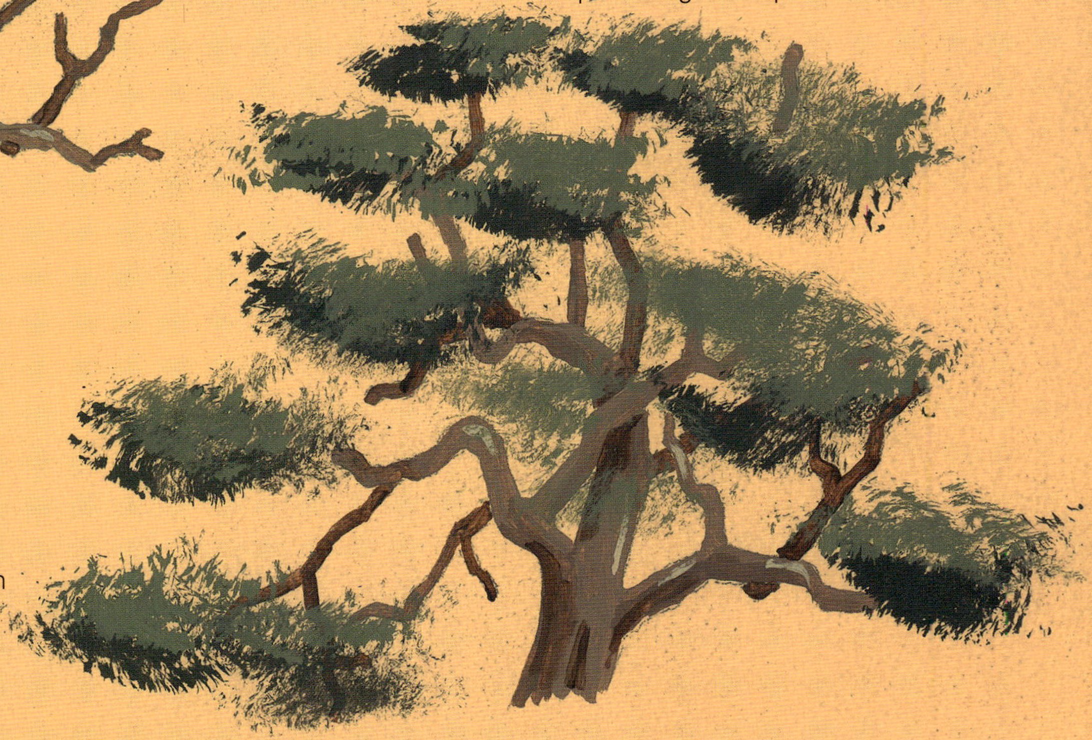

2. Tap in lower portion of foliage clumps with medium and dark values, #1 fan brush pointing down.

3. Tap in upper portion of foliage clumps with medium and light values, #1 fan brush pointing up.

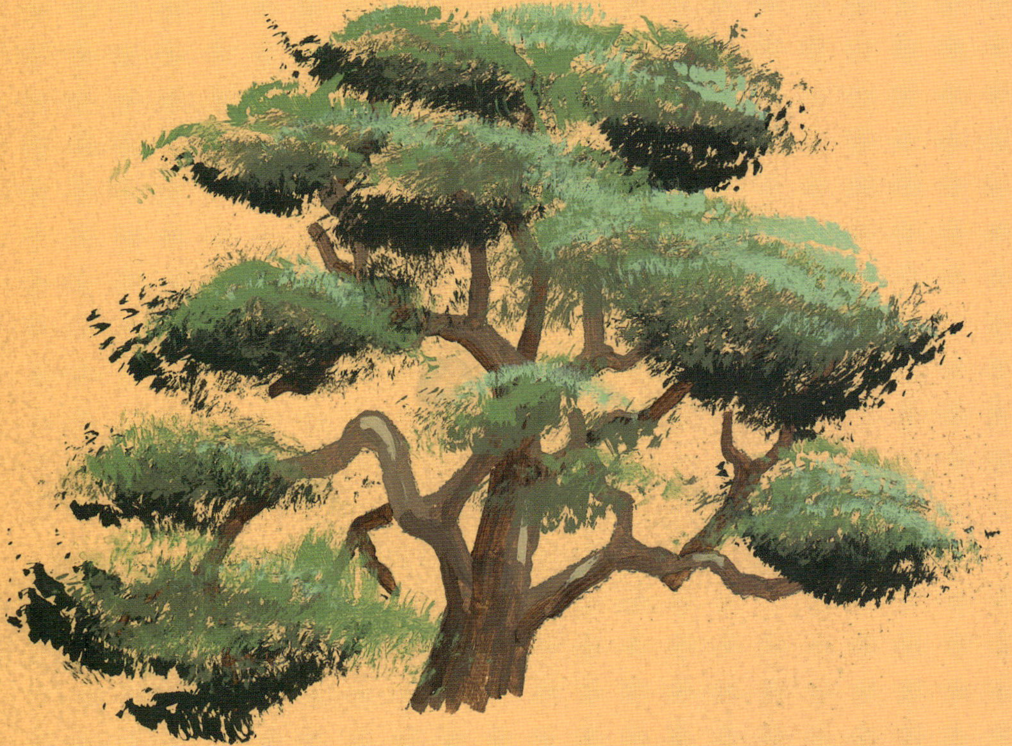

4. For brightest highlights, tap in the very light value sparingly, fan brush pointing up.

Lavender Fields

Step-by-Step

- Paint rows one at a time, beginning with the farthest and completing each row before moving to the next.
- Refer often to the value sketch.
- Dab mounds of lavender plants with a smaller scumbler brush for distant rows, larger scumbler for nearer rows.

Mix greens G1 - G5 for foliage. (Second Stage)

Add flowers in Final Stage.

- Mix lavenders P5, P7, and P9.
- Mix a lighter version of each lavender - P4, P6, and P8.
- Use lighter, cooler colors in the background, and transition to warmer colors as you move toward the foreground.

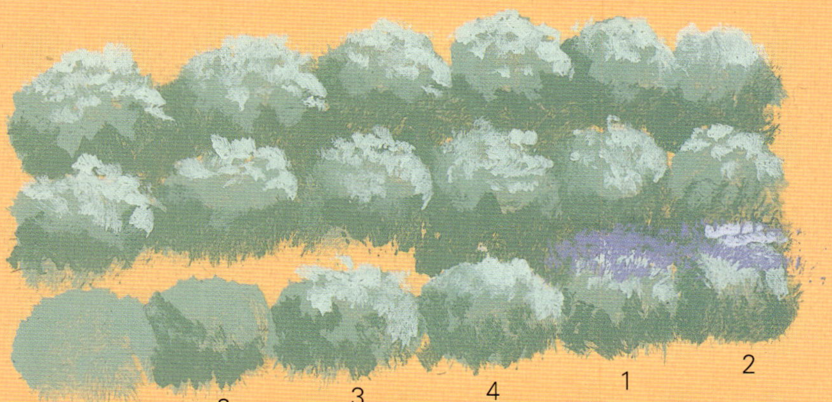

1 2 3 4 1 2

Paint foliage clumps in four steps. Complete Step 1 all across the row, then Step 2 all across the row, etc.

1. Dab in flattened, rounded forms, overlapping them slightly.
2. Shade bottom and between shapes.
3. Highlight top and brighter side.
4. Fill in between new row and previous row.

Add flowers in two steps, tapping with a fan brush.

1. Tap darker color.
2. Tap lighter color above and slightly overlapping darker color.

Row 1

Row 2

Row 3

Flowers on Row 1 are P4 and P5
Flowers on Row 2 are P6 and P7
Flowers on Row 3 are P8 and P9

Washed with W2 Washed with W1

NOTE: In the "Landscape Elements" section the lavender plant was painted with a fan brush. That is a good choice for a large "specimen" plant - perhaps in a decorative pot in a garden scene. Here scumbler brushes work well with a variety of plant sizes, as in the fields where larger foreground plants transition to small ones farther away.

The right side of the rows shows the effect of washes in the tree shadows in the foreground.

Use several light layers of washes. You can always add another wash to deepen color, but there is no way to lighten a wash once the paint has dried.

AUTUMN JEWEL

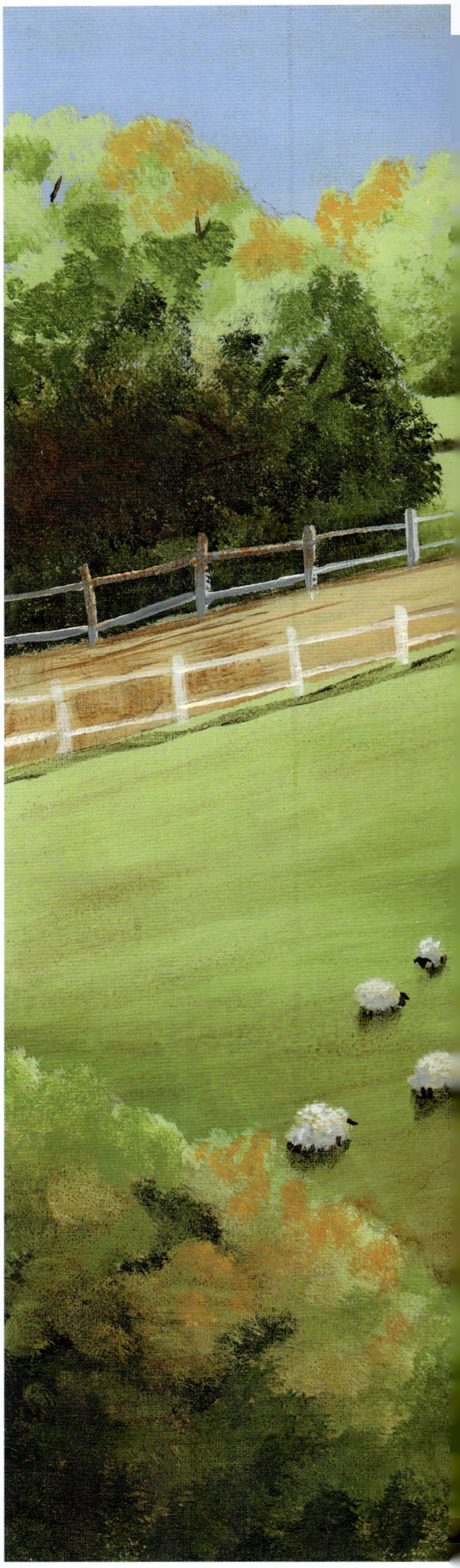

11" x 14"

I have a long acquaintance with beautiful, nostalgic covered bridges, but it wasn't until I was doing research for this book that I discovered their purpose. The bridges were covered not only to protect them from the weather, especially the weight of heavy snow, but also to keep horses from spooking at the sight of rushing water underfoot!

I placed the bridge close to the horizon line so the "X" made by the right-angle crossing of stream and road would not dominate the composition. I turned the bridge at an angle, so the viewer sees the road leading to it and a hint of the road on the other side. The stream is indicated by the darkness of the far bank, shaded as it drops to the water.

The entrance to the bridge is a strong focal point, supported by the value contrast of the light trim and dark interior, as well as the lines of the road and fences leading to it. Other elements in the landscape balance the bridge. The value contrasts between the far trees, the light far pasture, and the dark tree trunk serve this purpose. The darkness of the lower portion of the painting helps draw the eye down, and the sheep provide further interest.

Value Sketch

Refer to the value sketch to guide placement of darks and lights.

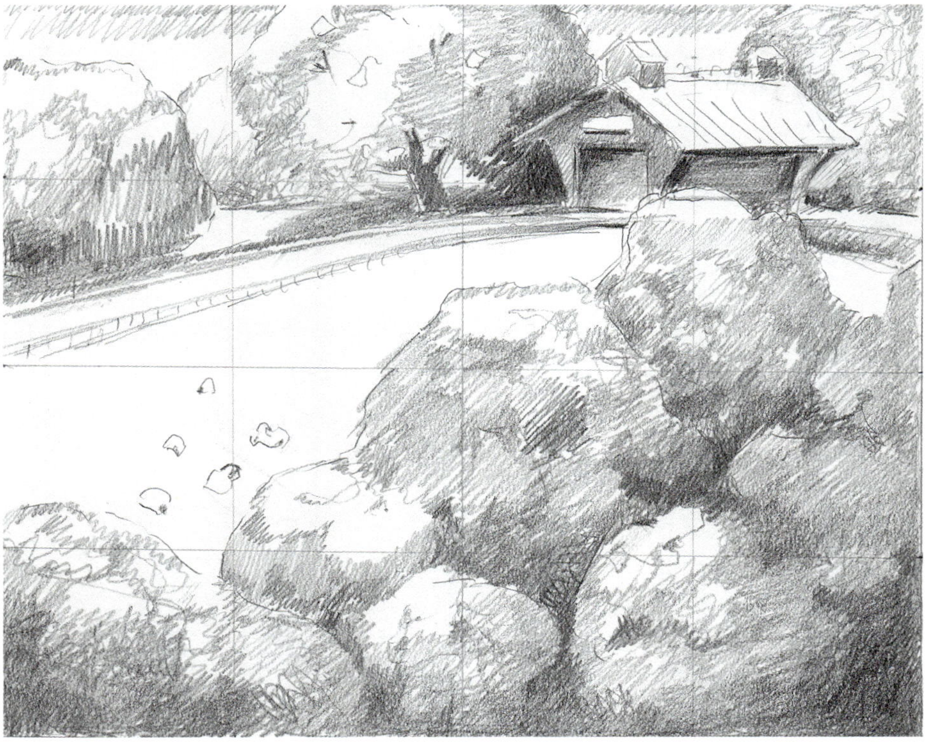

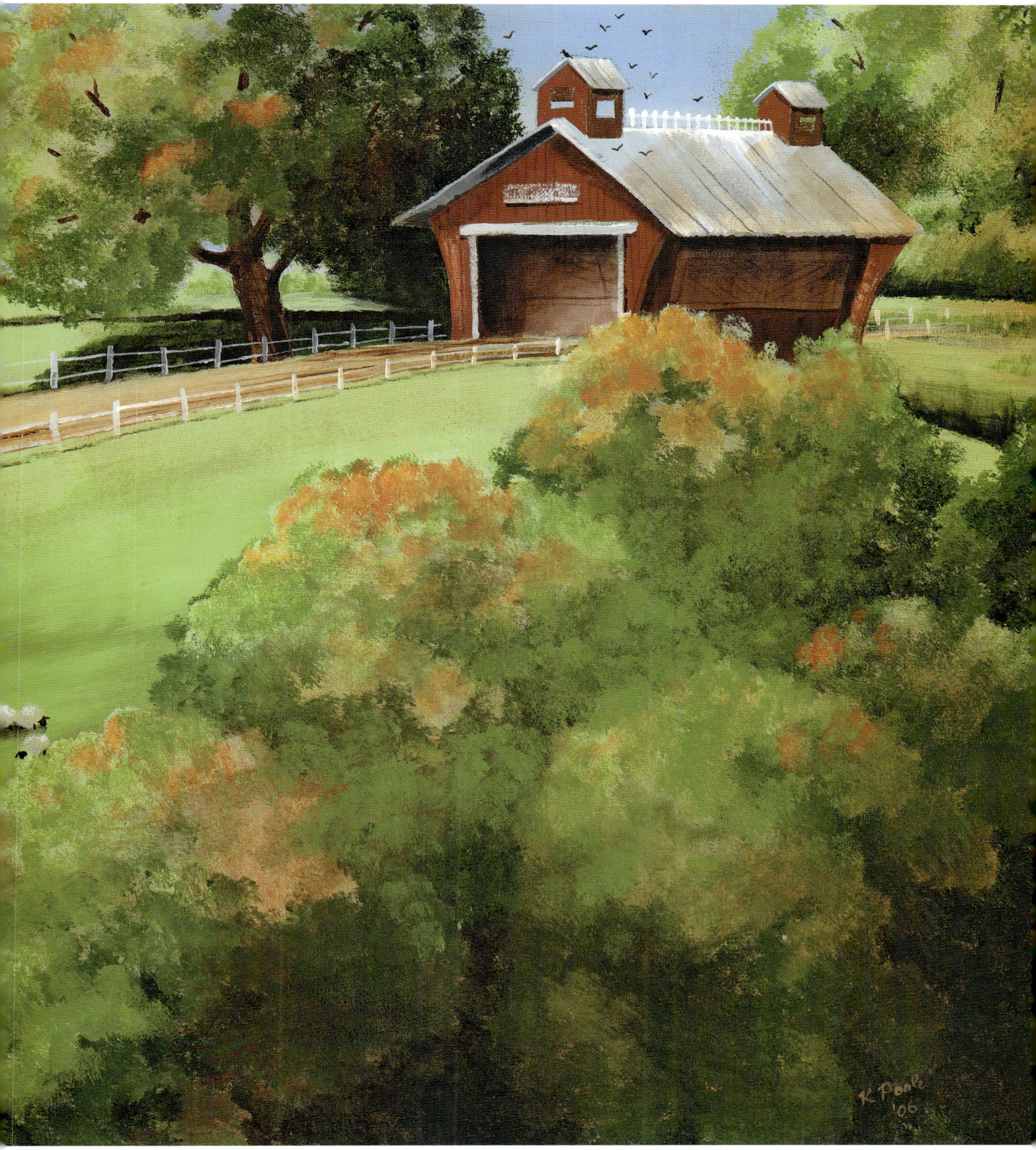
K Poole
'06

S1 Cerulean Blue + Titanium White + (Cobalt Blue)

Start here

S2 Titanium White + S1

Red Iron Oxide

B1 Burnt Umber + Red Iron Oxide

B2 Burnt Umber + Mars Black

B3 B1 + Titanium White

R1 Titanium White + R2

R2 Titanium White + Indanthrene Blue + Graphite Gray

R3 R2 + Graphite Gray

NOTE: Parentheses around a color name indicate that you should add just a touch of the color to the mix.

Sap Green Sequence

Refer to page 24 for mixing instructions.

very light | light | medium | dark | very dark

Used straight from the tube:

- Cadmium Red Medium
- Gold Ochre
- Cadmium Yellow Medium
- Yellow Ochre
- Burnt Sienna
- Burnt Umber

Toning color:

medium olive green acrylic paint for decorative painting

Color Scheme & Palette

The barn red reflects - and stands up to - the autumn colors in the foliage. It invites white trim, which provides value contrast to strengthen the barn as the focal point. A complementary color scheme using red and green is a good fit.

Used for mixing colors:
Buff Titanium
Cadmium Red Deep
Cadmium Yellow Deep
Cadmium Yellow Light
Cerulean Blue
Cobalt Blue
Graphite Gray
Indanthrene Blue
Mars Black
Red Iron Oxide
Sap Green
Titanium White

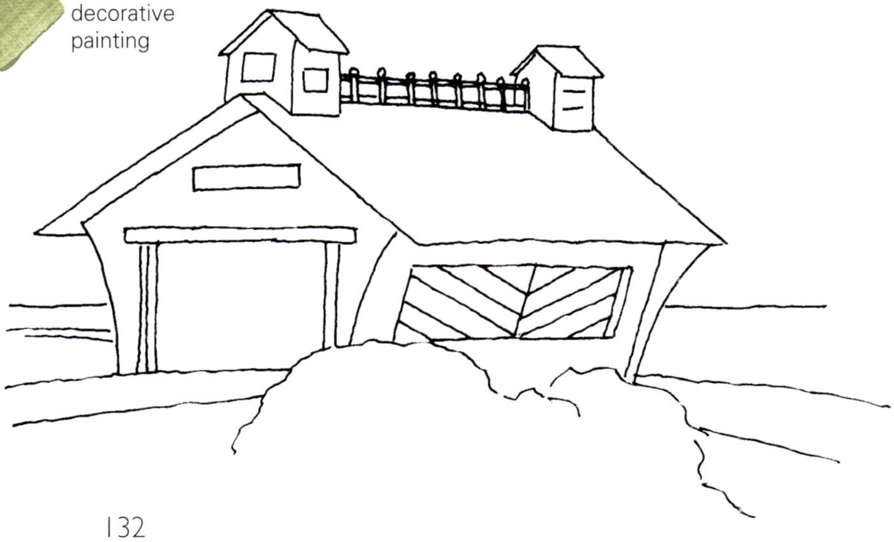

Pattern for Bridge

Enlarge @140% for actual size.

First Stage

1. Tone canvas with medium olive green. Let dry.
2. Lightly sketch horizon line. Transfer outline of bridge. Sketch road, edges of stream on both sides of bridge, and upper edges of foreground trees.
3. Using a #20 flat brush, start at top of sky with blue S1, transitioning smoothly to a narrow band of light blue S2 at horizon.
4. Paint background pasture Sap Green/very light. Paint shadows of trees with Sap Green/medium and Sap Green/dark.
5. Paint line indicating stream bank on left of bridge, using a #14 flat brush and Sap Green/dark.
6. Indicate stream bank on right with Sap Green/medium toward top of bank and Sap Green/dark toward stream.
7. Lay in foreground pasture with a #20 flat brush, Sap Green/light, and Sap Green/very light. With a large fan brush, blend roughly while paint is wet.
8. Paint road Buff Titanium. While paint is wet, brush in a little Gold Ochre and Burnt Umber.

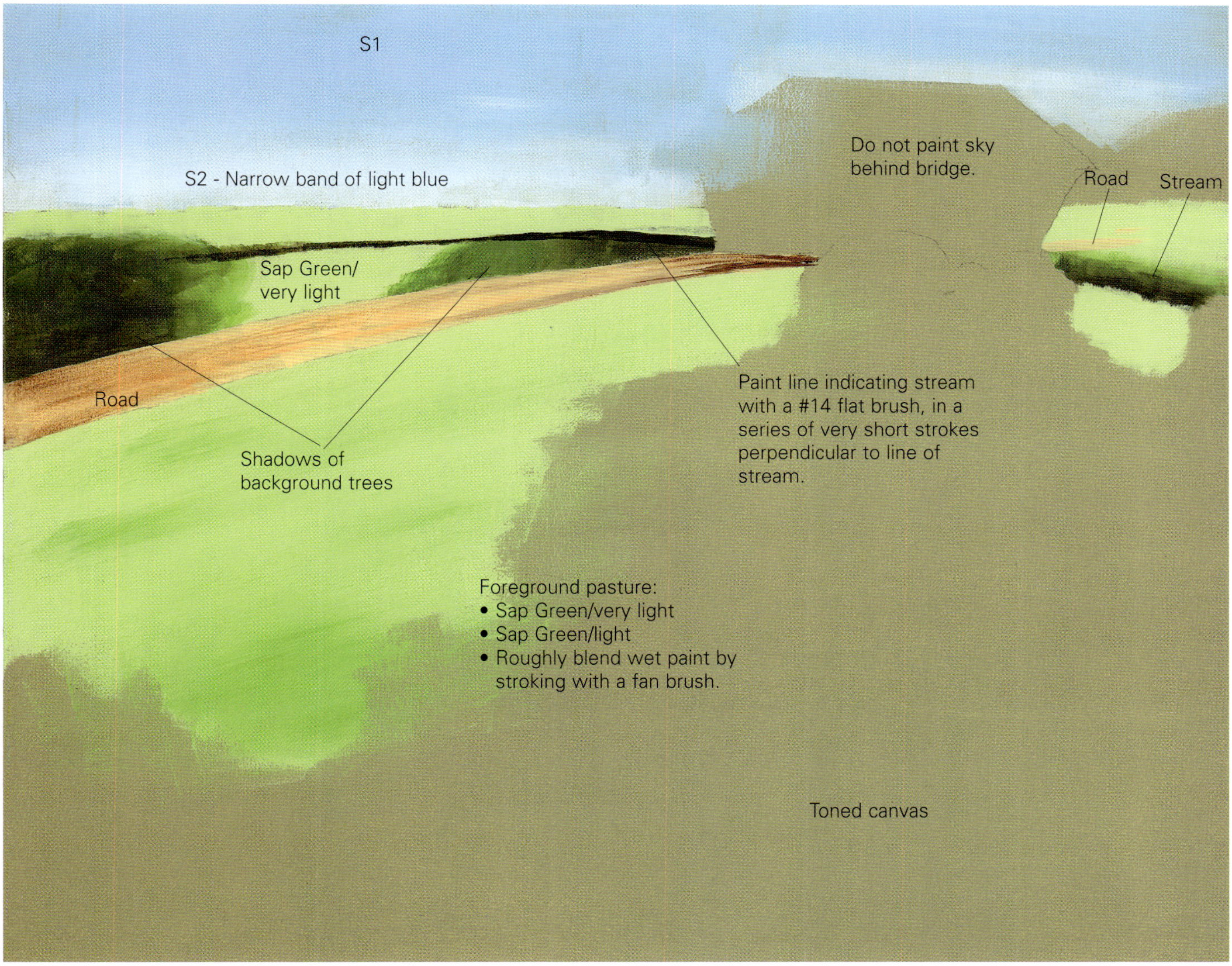

Second Stage

1. Paint tree trunk and branches with Burnt Umber. Shade with patches of Mars Black on right side of trunk and underside of branches.
2. Using a #6 scumbler brush, paint background trees with the greens of the Sap Green sequence. Follow the value sketch to place the various values of green. With a #1 liner, add a few sections of branches showing through the greenery.
3. Transfer bridge pattern. Block in walls of bridge and cupolas. Paint the end with the opening Red Iron Oxide, and side walls with reds B1 and B3.
4. Paint roofs of bridge and cupolas with light gray R1. While paint is wet, dab a little Titanium White along upper and lower edges and streak it toward center of roof with a fan brush. Keep strokes at same angle as edge of roof.
5. Paint undersides of roof overhangs dark gray R2, blending into Graphite Gray toward peak.
6. Paint inside of bridge dark at entrance, transitioning to a light color at lower right. Blend wet-in-wet, B2 to Red Iron Oxide, then to B3 lightened with additional Titanium White.

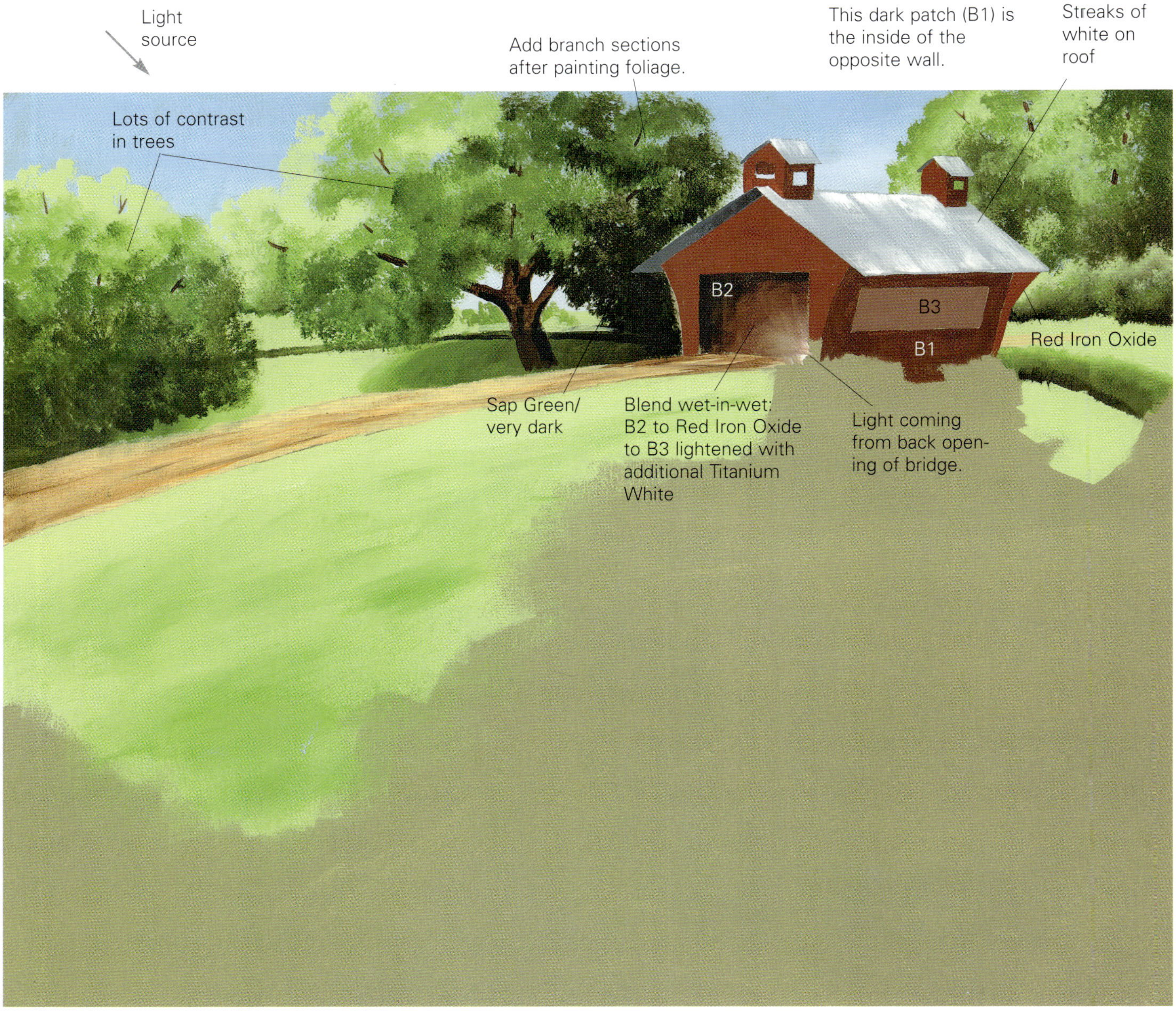

Third Stage

1. Refer to *Bridge Details* to complete the bridge.
2. Add a broken line of Sap Green/medium shadow under fence on near side of road.
3. With Titanium White, paint fence posts with a #1 liner and rails with a #0 liner. Paint posts taller, with wider spacing, nearer viewer. Go back over posts and rails that are in shadow with medium gray R2.
4. Scumble foliage on foreground trees with the greens in the Sap Green sequence, using the value sketch as a guide.

Final Stage

See finished painting.

1. Wash Burnt Sienna over trees, and a little over foreground pasture.
2. With a scumbler brush, dab in early autumn color, using Cadmium Red Medium, Cadmium Yellow Medium, Gold Ochre, and Yellow Ochre. Move freely among colors without washing brush to mix colors on the canvas.
3. Dab in sheep with Buff Titanium, then dab shadows of medium gray R2, and highlights of light gray R1 and light blue S2. Wash shadows under sheep with Payne's Gray. Paint faces, ears, and legs dark brown B2.
4. Deepen darkest areas of foliage with washes of Payne's Gray. ❑

Bridge Details

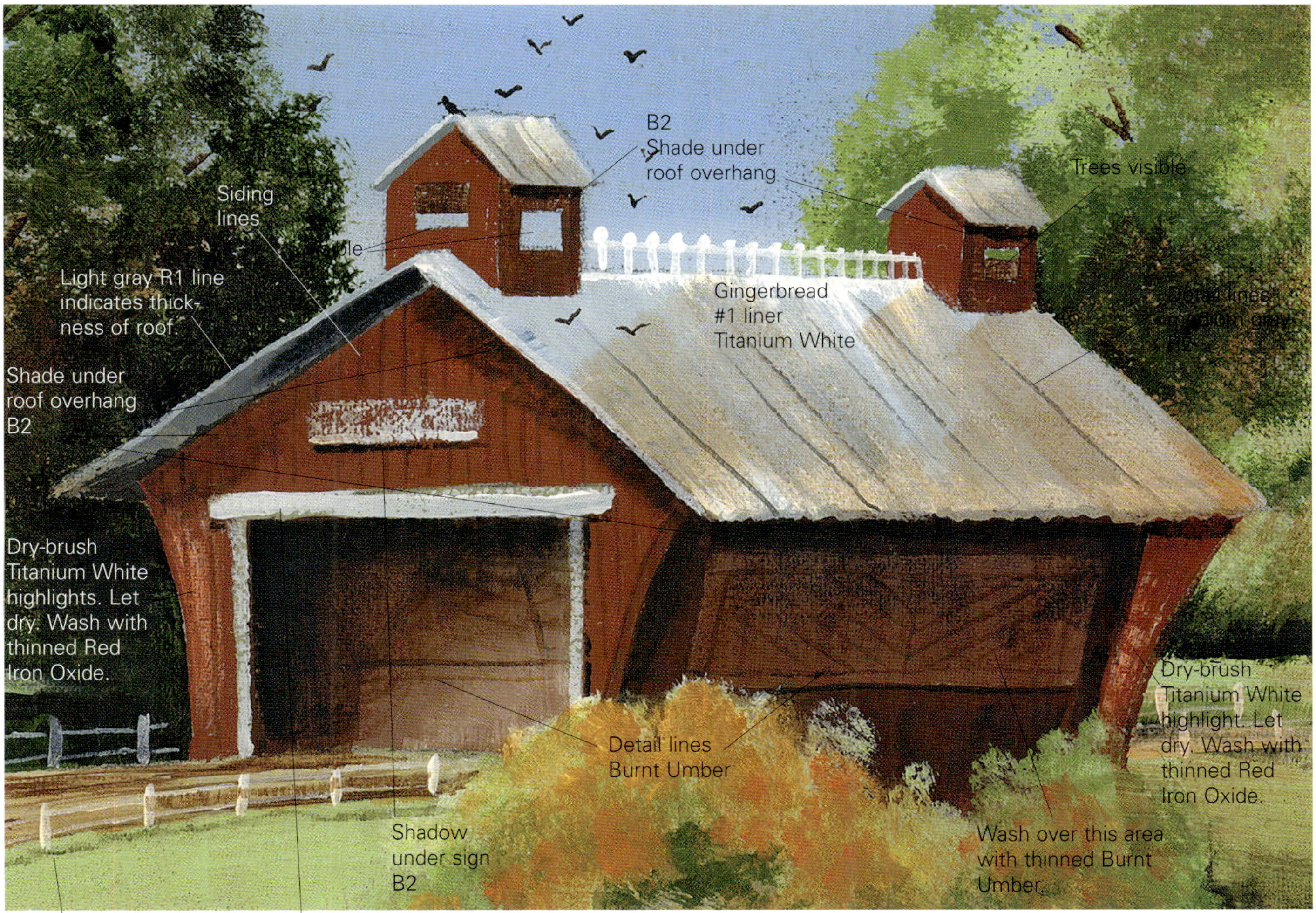

MY LOVELY POND

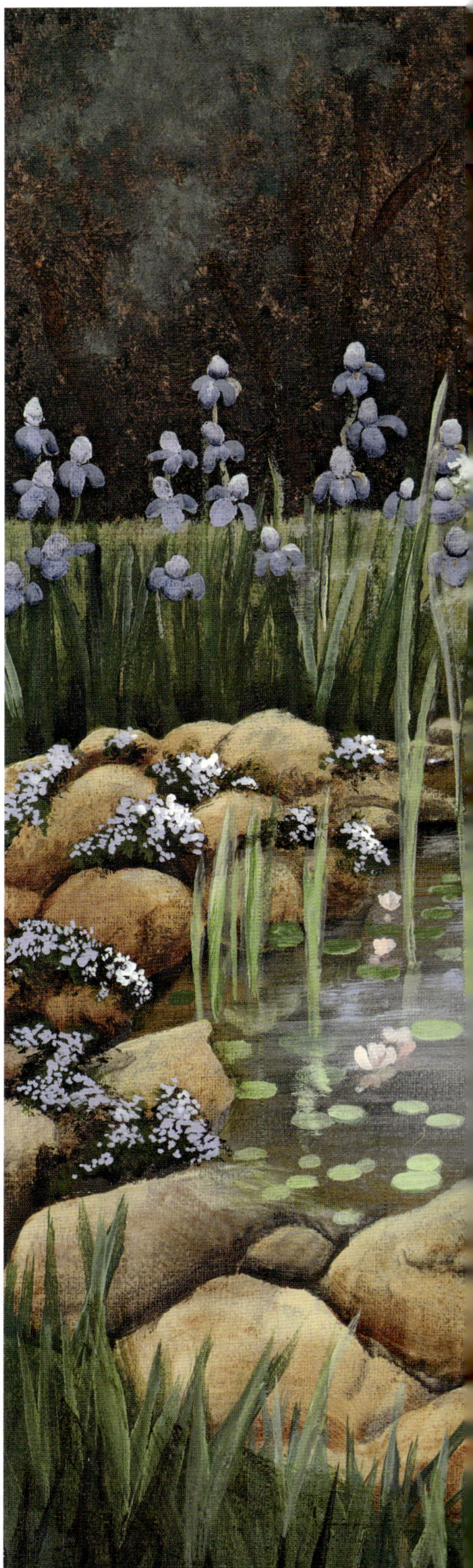

11" x 14"

This painting is based on a photograph of the pond in front of my house, but I changed many elements to make a more effective composition - some were eliminated, some were added, and some were moved.

The birdhouse is the focal point, but the eye wanders freely through the painting, following the curve of the rocks along the pond's edge, the clumps of the lily pads, and the succession of reflections on the water leading to the small inlet at the upper right. Mounded shapes are repeated throughout the painting.

Value Sketch

Refer to the value sketch to guide placement of darks and lights.

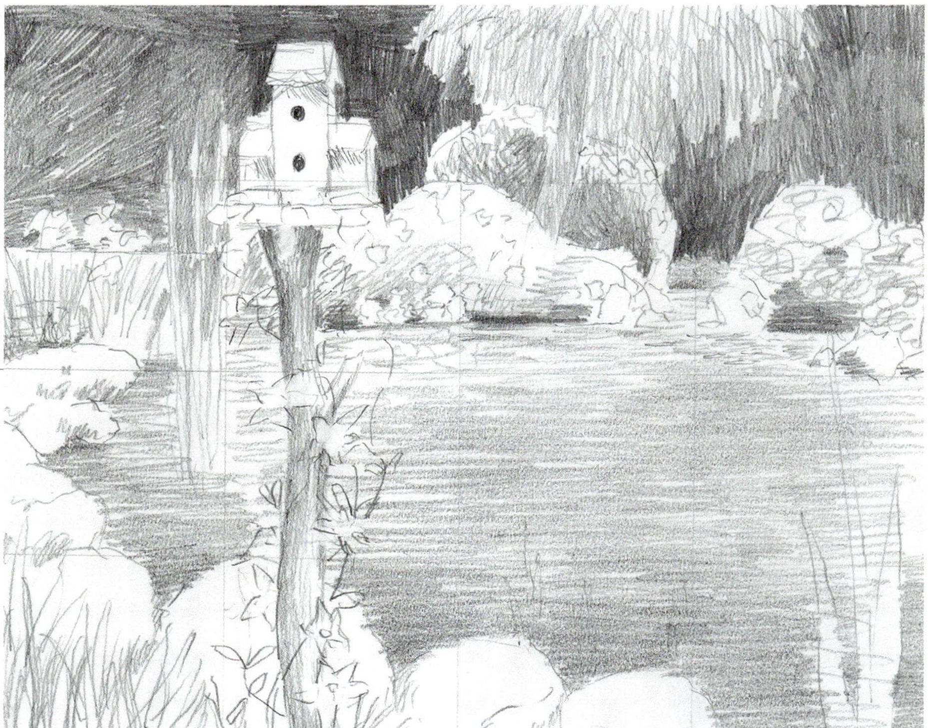

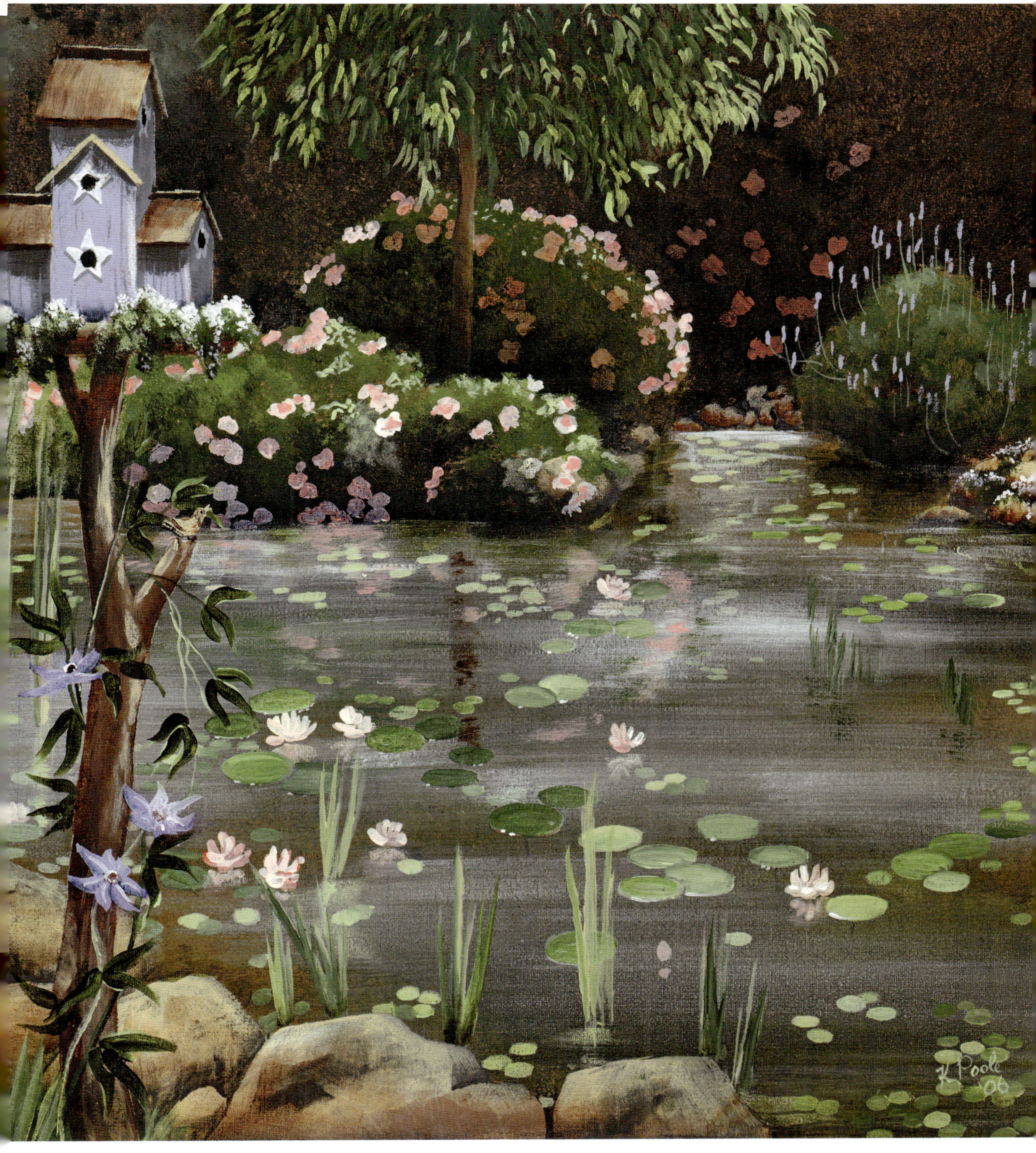
K Poole
'06

Color Scheme & Palette

This pink, green, and blue color scheme is not derived from the color wheel, which illustrates color theory as it relates to pigments, but from the primary colors of light - red, green, and blue. These three colors of light mixed together produce white light.

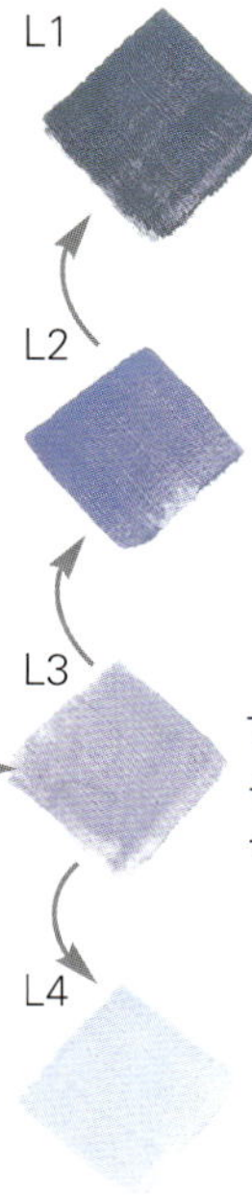

L1
L2
+ Graphite Gray

L2
L3
+ Ultramarine Blue

L3
Titanium White
+ Dioxazine Purple
+ Graphite Gray

Start here

L4
Titanium White
+ L3

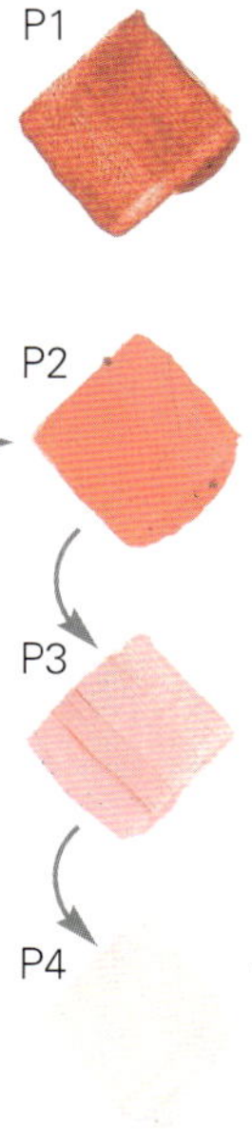

P1
Cadmium Red Deep
+ Buff Titanium
+ Titanium White

P2
Titanium White
+ Cadmium Red Medium

Start here

P3
Titanium White
+ P2

P4
Titanium White
+ P3

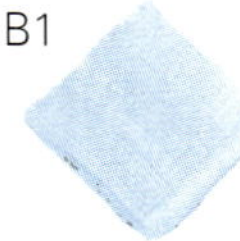

B1
Titanium White
+ Ultramarine Blue

Sap Green Sequence

Refer to Page 24 for mixing instructions.

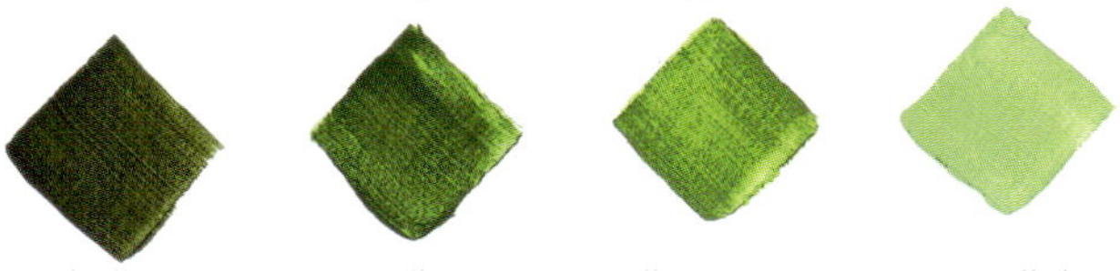

dark | medium | light | very light

Cool Green Sequence

Refer to Page 25 for mixing instructions.

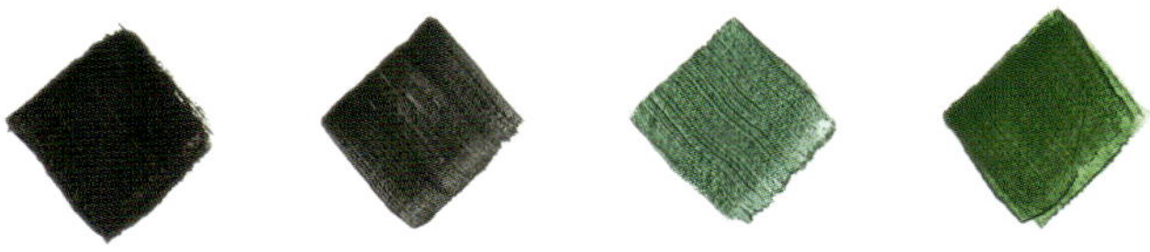

very dark | dark | medium | light

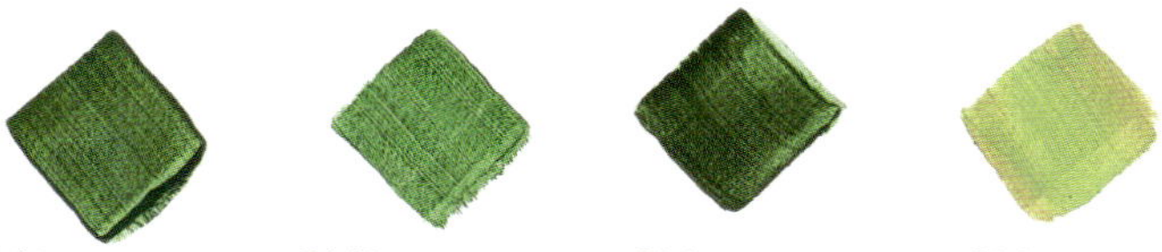

GM1
Sap Green medium mix
+
Cool Green medium mix

GM2
Sap Green light mix
+
Cool Green light mix

GM3
Sap Green medium mix
+
Cool Green dark mix

GM4
Sap Green very light mix
+
Buff Titanium

Used straight from the tube:

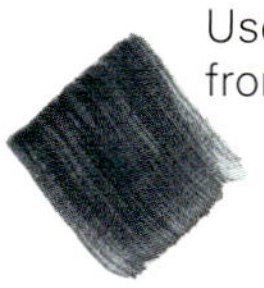

Payne's Gray

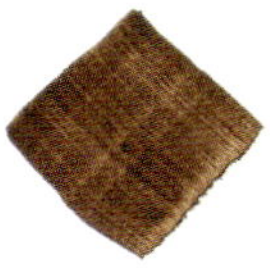

Burnt Umber

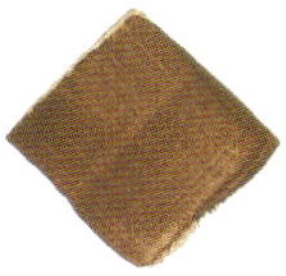

Toning color: golden brown acrylic paint for decorative painting

Used for mixing colors:

Buff Titanium
Cadmium Red Deep
Cadmium Red Medium
Cadmium Yellow Deep
Cadmium Yellow Light
Cobalt Green Deep
Cobalt Green Light
Dioxazine Purple
Graphite Gray
Mars Black
Sap Green
Titanium White
Ultramarine Blue

How to Paint from a Photo

- **Use as reference material for elements you arrange into your own composition.** For example, you may use photographs of clouds to guide you as you paint the clouds in your landscape.
- **Use as the beginning point for your painting and a reference for details.** What the camera sees is not always an effective composition. Unless you are striving for an exact likeness of a landscape, you can add, move, rearrange, and remove elements as you wish.

Photographs are protected by copyright, even if the photographer has not explicitly applied for that protection. They are works of art just like drawings and paintings, and are the valued intellectual property of their creators. So use your own photographs or books of photographic reference material for artists. You may wish to compile your own photo reference files.

First Stage

1. Tone canvas with golden brown, a good base color for the pond water. Let dry.
2. Sketch outlines of rose bushes, lavender plant, pond, patch of grass, and approximate outline of birdhouse. Mix generous quantities of the greens.
3. Using a 3/4" wash brush, wash thinned Sap Green/dark over entire pond.
4. Tap in dark forest background with a #4 scumbler, Cool Green/dark, and Cool Green/very dark.
5. Paint tree trunks in left background with Burnt Umber. With the scumbler, tap in a little Cool Green/medium and Cool Green/light to suggest large clumps of foliage. While paint is wet, tap in a very little GM4. Continue tapping to blend colors on the canvas.
6. Paint grassy area with a fan brush and GM4. Let dry. Tone down with a wash of thinned Sap Green/dark.
7. Use the #4 scumbler to dab in the three clumps of rose bush foliage, beginning with the one in back. Place the different values of the Sap Green sequence to give rounded forms. Tap in Cool Green/very dark in darkest areas.
8. Dab in lavender bush at right with a #4 scumbler and the Cool Green sequence colors. Dab/blend a very tiny bit of GM4.
9. Block in rocks with dry-brushed Buff Titanium. Use brush size to fit size of rocks. *(See Page 72, "Rocks with Flowers," for step-by-step procedures.)*

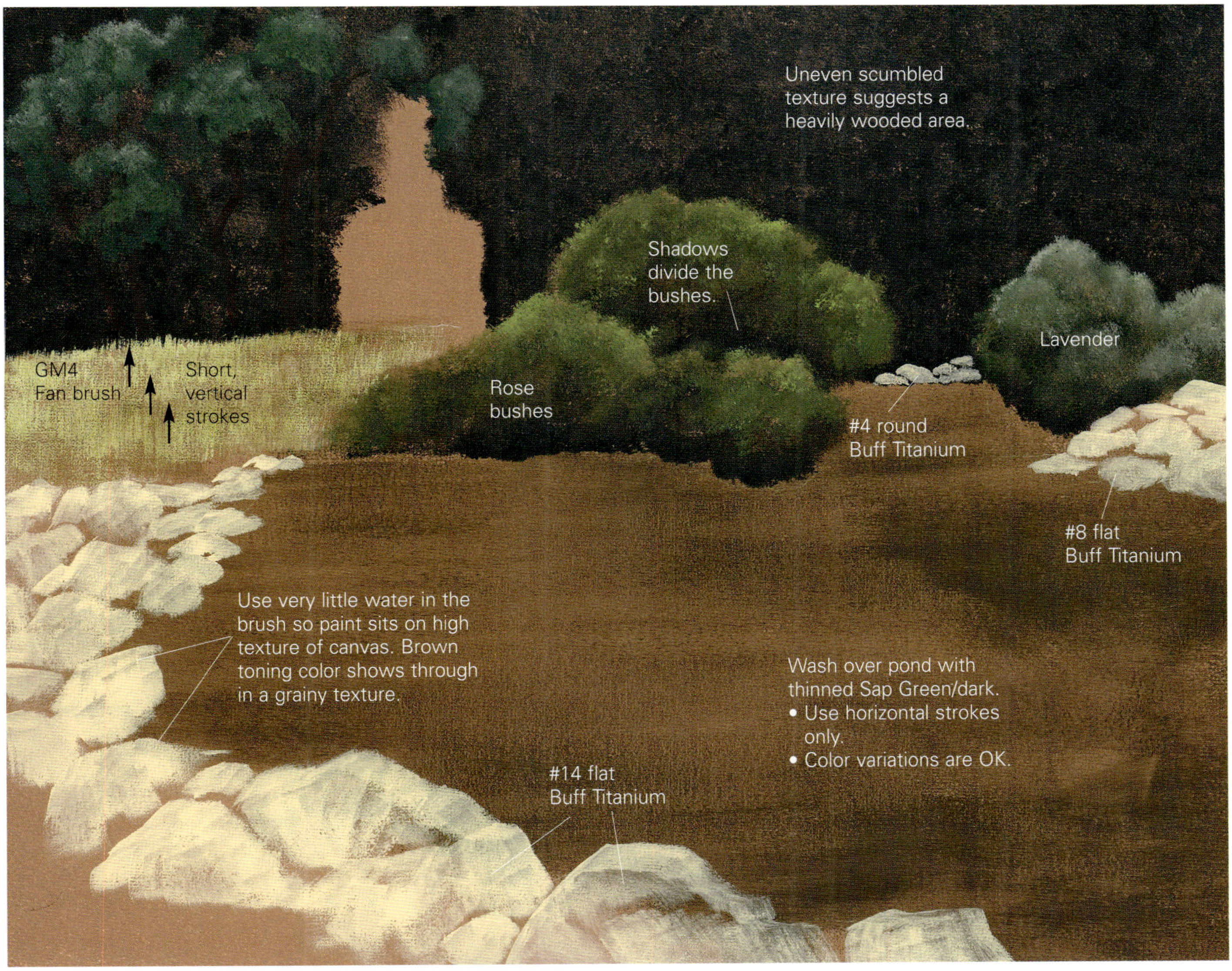

Second Stage

1. Paint background roses with a #3 round brush and dark pink P1. Let dry.
2. Shade bottom edges of tiny rocks with Graphite Gray. Let dry. Wash over all but the tops with thinned Burnt Umber.
3. Wash over background roses and rocks with thinned Cool Green/very dark.
4. Paint roses on the bushes with a #3 round brush and pinks P2, P3, and P4. Let dry.
5. Wash over front side of rear rose bush with thinned Sap Green/dark. Wash over front sides of front bushes with thinned Payne's Gray. This pushes them into the shade and enhances their round forms.
6. Paint weeping cherry trunk Burnt Umber. While paint is wet, brush on a little Buff Titanium and blend on the canvas. Shade with Payne's Gray toward bottom to tuck it behind the front rose bush.
7. Paint cherry tree leaves with Cool Green/medium, Cool Green/light, Sap Green/very light, and greens GM1, GM2, and GM3. Paint as overlapping individual leaves.
8. Paint thin lavender stems with a #00 liner and a mixture of Cool Green/light and GM4. Dot blossoms in short lines with the tip of a #1 liner and lavenders L2 and L3.
9. Stroke iris leaves with the chisel edge of a #12 flat brush. Start at base and pull upward while twisting brush slightly to get a point. Move randomly among greens GM1 through GM4 to get a range of color. Paint iris stems with a #1 liner and the same greens. Shade base of plants with thinned Cool Green/very dark.
10. Paint each iris flower in four strokes. Use a #3 round brush and L4 for the upward egg shape, and a #1 liner and L2 for the three downward drooping petals. Shade lightly with thinned Payne's Gray.
11. Paint sky reflections on water with light blue B1 and a large flat brush in smooth, random, horizontal streaks. Be sure to place a streak at top edge of inlet and in front of rose bushes.

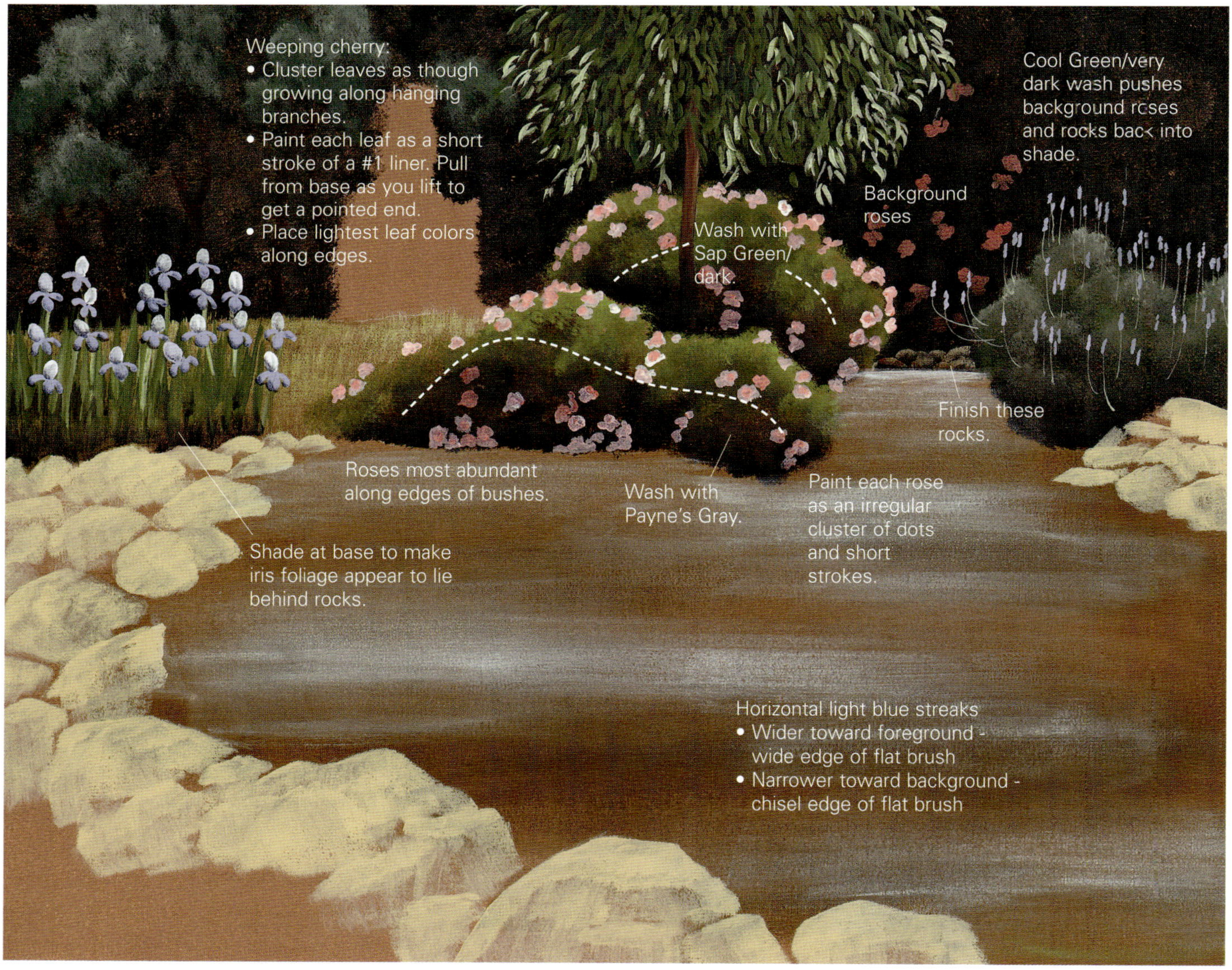

Third Stage

1. Wash over cherry tree with thinned Sap Green/medium.
2. Check value sketch. If necessary, darken bases of bushes with washes to ground them.
3. Shade rocks around pond. *(See Page 72, "Rocks with Flowers," for step-by-step procedures.)*
4. Follow shapes of rocks to tap in clumps of alyssum foliage with a #2 scumbler and Cool Green/very dark. Tap GM3 to lighten tops of clumps.
5. Dot alyssum flowers in clusters with the tip of a #1 liner - L2 at bottom of clusters, moving upward to L3, then L4. On clusters that drape toward the water, add a few highlight dots of Titanium White.
6. Paint slightly broken, mirror-image reflections of lavender, rose bushes, cherry tree, and rocks facing viewer. Use a flat brush, stroking back and forth horizontally on the chisel edge.
7. Paint foliage at lower left same as iris foliage, using a larger brush to get larger leaves. Wash over lower edge and corner of foliage clump with thinned Cool Green/dark to darken the base.
8. Transfer birdhouse pattern. Sketch post.
9. Paint post Burnt Umber. While paint is wet, work in a Buff Titanium highlight on right side. Shade left side with Payne's Gray. Let dry. Dry-brush strong Buff Titanium highlights on right side.
10. Establish birdhouse shape with lavenders L1 and L2.
11. Paint large roof areas Burnt Umber. While paint is wet, stroke in a little Buff Titanium down from top, and up from bottom of roof sections. Work strokes parallel to angled edge of each roof section.
12. Paint edge of peaked roof facing viewer with Buff Titanium.
13. Paint peak trim and forward edges of remaining roof sections Burnt Umber. Add a thin line of Buff Titanium highlight along top edges.

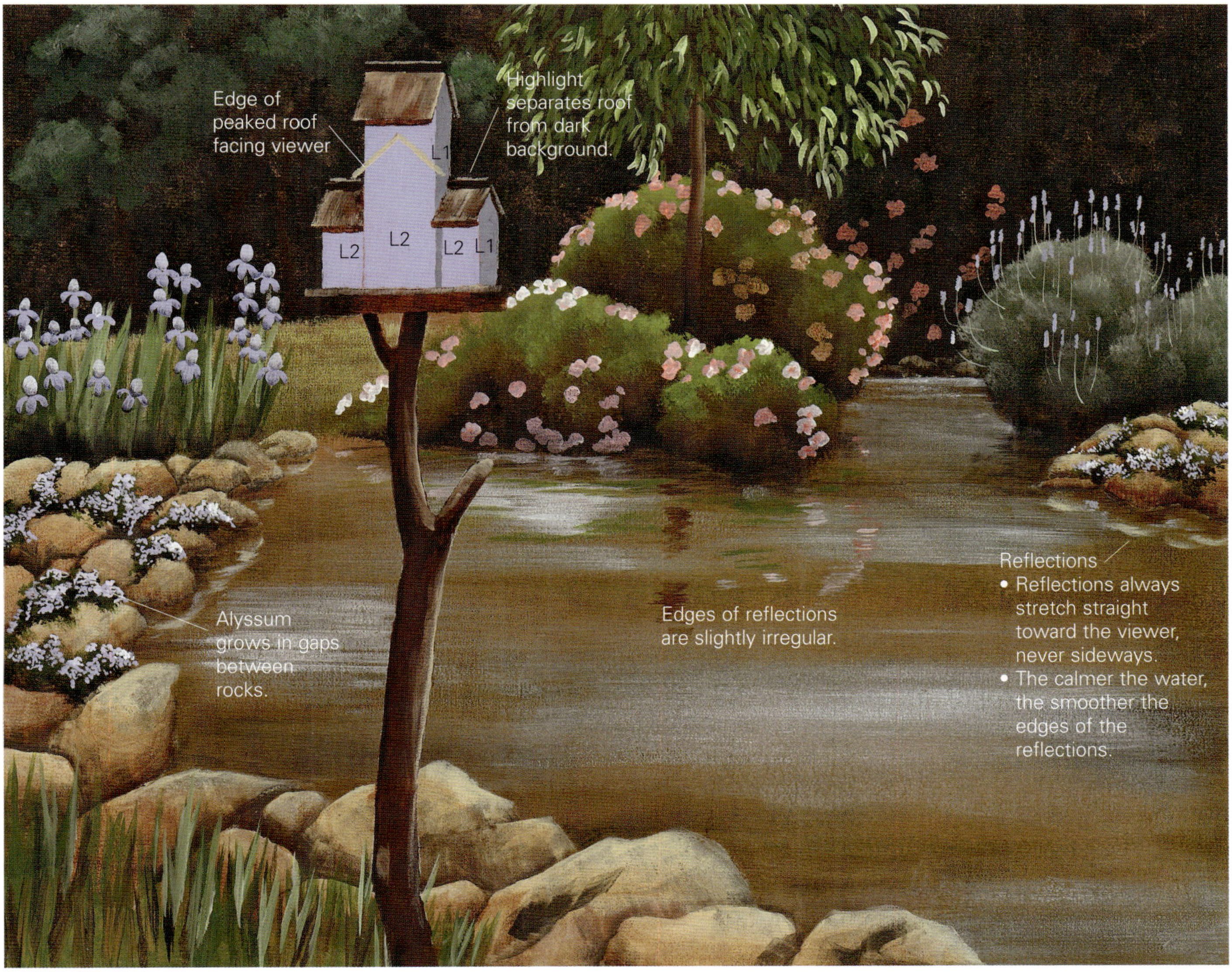

Final Stage

See finished painting and Birdhouse Details.

1. Paint water lily blossoms with pinks P1 - P4 and a #3 round brush, stroking each petal from tip to base.
2. Paint broken pink reflections with a #6 flat brush and back-and-forth horizontal strokes.
3. Paint round leaves with a #4 round brush. Move randomly among the greens (except Cool Green/dark and Cool Green/very dark) without washing brush between colors. Paint most of the smaller leaves lighter colors. Do not cover pond evenly; instead, place groups of leaves to lead the eye across and around pond. At top of pond (farthest from viewer) leaf ovals are very flat. At bottom edge (closest to viewer) leaf ovals are closer to round. Transition smoothly between these two extremes. Round leaves lie flat on pond surface, so they do not have reflections.
4. Paint cattails with the chisel edge of a #20 flat brush, using greens GM1 - GM4. Paint reflections as broken areas of color matching the cattails.
5. On birdhouse walls that face the viewer, paint a few texture lines with dark lavender L1.
6. Paint holes Mars Black. Paint stars surrounding holes lavender L4 on front, and medium lavender L2 on sides. Line shadows under front stars with Graphite Gray.
7. Dry-brush a little lavender L4 for highlights on the right vertical edge of center and right "apartments." Soften by running your fingertip over it.
8. Paint shadows under roof with Graphite Gray.
9. Add Payne's Gray shadow at base of wall.
10. Paint alyssum in birdhouse planter box. Tap in foliage with a #2 scumbler and Cool Green/very dark. Tap GM3 to lighten tops of clumps. Dot flowers in clusters with the tip of a #1 liner - L2 at bottom of clusters, moving upward to L3, then L4. Add a few highlight dots of Titanium White.
11. Paint clematis vines twining round the post with a #0 liner and some very dark and very light greens.
12. Moving among the greens, paint clematis leaves in clusters of three. With a #3 round brush, pull one stroke for each leaf, beginning at vine and lifting to create a point at the end.
13. Paint clematis flower petals in the same manner, with lavenders L2 and L3, stroking outward from blossom center.
14. Place a large dot of Burnt Umber at clematis flower center, surrounded by a ring of smaller dots of light lavender L4.
15. Paint center veins on some petals with lavender L4.
16. Wash blossoms unevenly with a little very thin Dioxazine Purple. ❑

Birdhouse Details

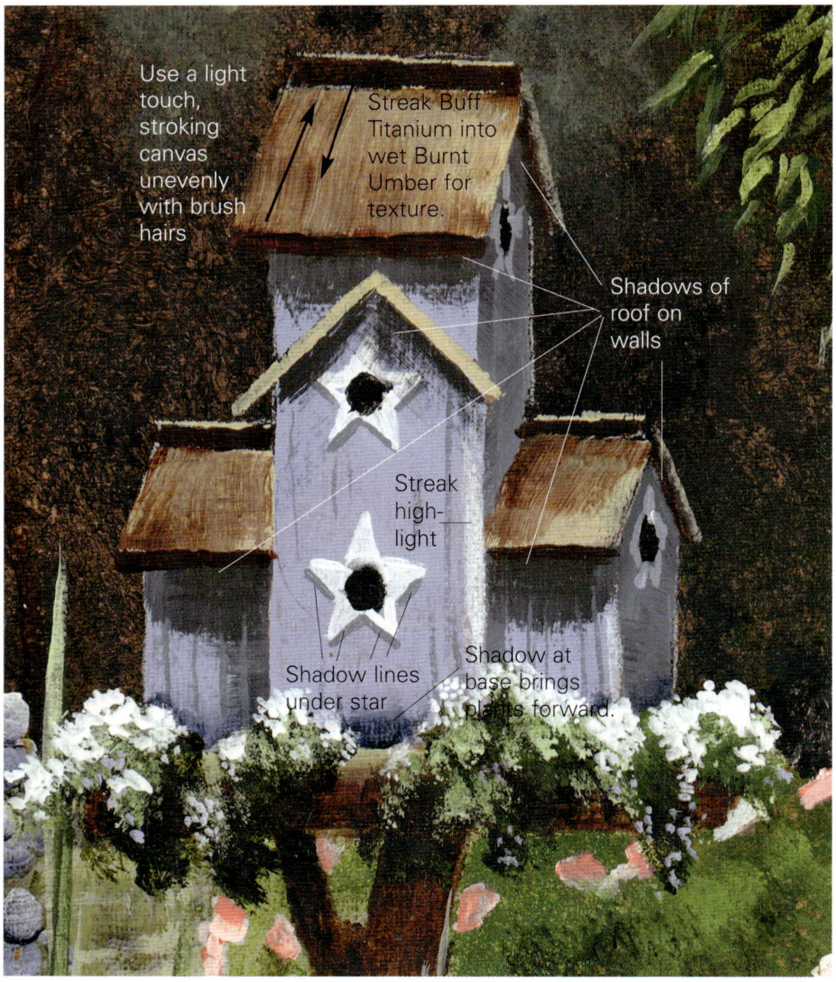

Birdhouse pattern (actual size)

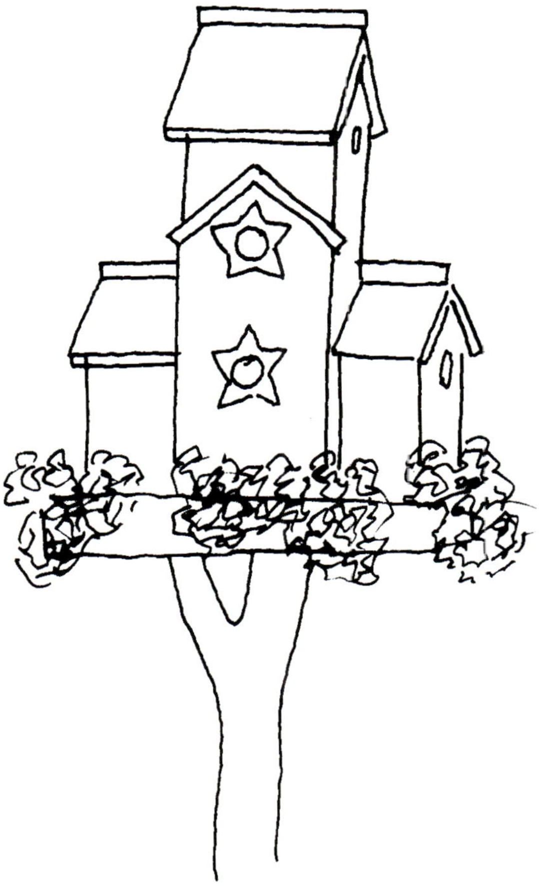

Metric Conversion Chart

Inches to Millimeters and Centimeters

Inches	MM	CM	Inches	MM	CM
1/8	3	.3	2	51	5.1
1/4	6	.6	3	76	7.6
3/8	10	1.0	4	102	10.2
1/2	13	1.3	5	127	12.7
5/8	16	1.6	6	152	15.2
3/4	19	1.9	7	178	17.8
7/8	22	2.2	8	203	20.3
1	25	2.5	9	229	22.9
1-1/4	32	3.2	10	254	25.4
1-1/2	38	3.8	11	279	27.9
1-3/4	44	4.4	12	305	30.5

Yards to Meters

Yards	Meters	Yards	Meters
1/8	.11	3	2.74
1/4	.23	4	3.66
3/8	.34	5	4.57
1/2	.46	6	5.49
5/8	.57	7	6.40
3/4	.69	8	7.32
7/8	.80	9	8.23
1	.91	10	9.14
2	1.83		

Index

Continued on next page

Index